T0211840

Lecture Notes in Computer Science   8419

Commenced Publication in 1973
Founding and Former Series Editors:
Gerhard Goos, Juris Hartmanis, and Jan van Leeuwen

For further volumes:
http://www.springer.com/series/7410

Aurélien Francillon · Pankaj Rohatgi (Eds.)

Smart Card Research and Advanced Applications

12th International Conference, CARDIS 2013
Berlin, Germany, November 27–29, 2013
Revised Selected Papers

 Springer

Editors
Aurélien Francillon
EURECOM
Biot
France

Pankaj Rohatgi
Cryptography Research Inc.
San Francisco, CA
USA

ISSN 0302-9743   ISSN 1611-3349 (electronic)
ISBN 978-3-319-08301-8   ISBN 978-3-319-08302-5   (eBook)
DOI 10.1007/978-3-319-08302-5
Springer Cham Heidelberg New York Dordrecht London

Library of Congress Control Number: 2014941234

LNCS Sublibrary: SL4 – Security and Cryptology

Printed on acid-free paper

Springer is part of Springer Science+Business Media (www.springer.com)

Preface

These proceedings contain the revised versions of the papers selected for presentation at CARDIS 2013, the 12th Smart Card Research and Advanced Application Conference, organized by the Chair for Security in Telecommunications (SecT), Technical University of Berlin, and held at the Moevenpick Hotel, Berlin, Germany.

The CARDIS conference, first held in Lille, France, in 1994, will turn 20 next year. Over these years, as smart cards became a pervasive, foundational technology for bootstrapping security and trust, CARDIS became the foremost international conference dedicated to research on all aspects of smart cards and their applications, including hardware design, operating systems, application software, security protocols, as well as physical and system security.

The conference provides an unparalleled forum for researchers from academia, industry, testing labs, and government organizations to present and discuss exploratory research and novel advances in this area. Its unique format allows authors to incorporate these discussions and feedback into the final papers that are published here.

This year, the CARDIS Program Committee reviewed 47 submissions and selected 17 papers for presentation at the conference. Each paper received at least three reviews and all submissions by the Program Committee members received at least five reviews. This task was performed by the 38 members of the Program Committee members with the help of 70 external reviewers. The technical program also featured three invited talks. The first invited speaker, Prof. Srdjan Capkun, from ETH, Zurich, presented "Selected Topics in Wireless Physical Layer Security". The second invited speaker, Dr. Mathias Wagner, Fellow and Chief Security Technologist at NXP Semiconductors, spoke about "Security in Industry — When is Good, Good Enough?". The third invited speaker, Mr. Olivier Thomas from Texplained, SARL, spoke on the topic of "Adequate Security".

CARDIS 2013 owes its success to the hard work and dedication of a number of people, and we would like to use this opportunity to thank them for their service. First and foremost, we would like to thank the members of the Program Committee and the external reviewers for conducting the task of evaluating and discussing the submissions with professionalism and within a short and abbreviated timeline. We are very grateful to Jean-Pierre Seifert, the general chair of CARDIS 2013, and his excellent team including Kevin Redon, Claudia Petzsch, and Juliane Kraemer for their flawless conference management. We are especially grateful to Kevin Redon for managing the conference website and making our task easier. We thank the CARDIS Steering Committee for giving us the privilege of serving as program chairs of this premier conference, and we especially thank Prof. Jean-Jacques Quisquater for organizing and publicizing this event and for his help and guidance throughout the process. Last, not least, we thank all the authors who submitted papers and all the attendees who contributed to the discussions and made the conference a memorable event.

November 2013

Aurélien Francillon
Pankaj Rohatgi

Organization

CARDIS 2013 was organized by the Chair for Security in Telecommunications (SecT), Technical University of Berlin.

Executive Committee

Conference General Chair

Jean-Pierre Seifert   TU Berlin and Deutsche Telekom Laboratories, TU Berlin

Conference Program Co-chairs

Aurélien Francillon   EURECOM, France
Pankaj Rohatgi   Cryptography Research, USA

Conference Publicity Chair

Jean-Jacques Quisquater   Université Catholique de Louvain, Belgium

Program Committee

Onur Aciicmez   Samsung, USA
N. Asokan   University of Helsinki, Finland
Gildas Avoine   UCL, Belgium
Guillaume Barbu   Oberthur, France
Christophe Clavier   University of Limoges, France
Elke De Mulder   Cryptography Research, USA
Hermann Drexler   Giesecke & Devrient, Germany
Martin Feldhofer   NXP, Austria
Nathalie Feyt   Thales, France
Berndt Gammel   Infineon, Germany
Michael Hauspie   LIFL, France
Michael Hutter   TU Graz, Austria
Kari Kostiainen   ETHZ, Switzerland
Jean-Louis Lanet   University of Limoges, France
Cédric Lauradoux   Inria, France
Stefan Mangard   Infineon Technologies, Germany
David Naccache   ENS, France
Svetla Nikova   K.U. Leuven, Belgium
Karsten Nohl   Security Research Labs, Germany

David Oswald	Ruhr University Bochum, Germany
Elisabeth Oswald	University of Bristol, UK
Eric Peeters	Texas Instruments, USA
Erik Poll	Radboud Universiteit Nijmegen, The Netherlands
Axel Poschmann	Nanyang Technological University, Singapore
Bart Preneel	K.U. Leuven, Belgium
Emmanuel Prouff	ANSSI, France
Matthieu Rivain	CryptoExperts, France
Jean-Marc Robert	ETS Montreal, Canada
Thomas Roche	ANSSI, France
Ahmad-Reza Sadeghi	TU Darmstadt, Germany
Jörn-Marc Schmidt	TU Graz, Austria
Lex Schoonen	Brightsight, The Netherlands
Sergei Skorobogatov	Cambridge University, UK
François-Xavier Standaert	UCL, Belgium
Frederic Stumpf	Escrypt GmbH, Germany
Marc Witteman	Riscure, The Netherlands

Additional Reviewers

Josep Balasch	Vincent Grosso	Roel Peeters
Lejla Batina	Mike Hamburg	Thomas Plos
Georg Becker	Christian Hanser	François Poucheret
Sonia Belaid	Annelie Heuser	Mathieu Renauld
Begül Bilgin	Johann Heyszl	Oscar Reparaz
Rafael Boix Carpi	Lars Hoffmann	Gokay Saldamli
Guillaume Bouffard	Dirmanto Jap	Falk Schellenberg
Cees Bart Breunesse	Eliane Jaulmes	Peter Schwabe
Xavier Carpent	Timo Kasper	Nicolas Sendrier
J.-C. Courrege	Thomas Korak	Dave Singelée
Rémy Daudigny	Pascal Lafourcade	Raphael Spreitzer
Fabrizio De Santis	Andy Leiserson	Pawel Swierczynski
Cécile Delerablée	Victor Lomne	Hien Thi Thu Truong
François Durvaux	Damien Marion	Sébastien Valette
Jan-Erik Ekberg	Mark Marson	Vincent Verneuil
Matthieu Finiasz	Marcel Medwed	Christian Wachsmann
Wieland Fischer	Bernd Meyer	Carolyn Whitnall
Laurie Genelle	Amir Moradi	Antoine Wurcker
Hannes Gross	Michael Muehlberghuber	

Sponsoring Institutions

NXP
Infineon
Cryptography Research
Oberthur Technologies
Brightsight
Gemalto

Event Support

1a Event Services Gmbh
Telekom Innovation Laboratories

Contents

Side Channel Countermeasures - Session Chair: Svetla Nikova

Side Channel and Fault Attacks - Session Chair: Berndt Gammel

Security Technologies - Session Chair: Benedikt Gierlichs

Evaluation of ASIC Implementation of Physical Random Number Generators Using RS Latches

Hirotaka Kokubo$^{(\boxtimes)}$, Dai Yamamoto, Masahiko Takenaka,
Kouichi Itoh, and Naoya Torii

Secure Computing Lab, Fujitsu Laboratories Ltd., 4-1-1 Kamikodanaka,
Nakahara-ku, Kawasaki, Kanagawa 211-8588, Japan
{kokubo.hirotaka,yamamoto.dai,ma,ito.kouichi,torii.naoya}@jp.fujitsu.com

Abstract. Embedded devices such as smart cards and smart phones are used for secure systems, for example automated banking machines and electronic money. The security of an embedded device depends strongly on secret information; cryptographic keys, nonces for authentication or seeds for a pseudo random number generator, which is generated by a Physical True Random Number Generator (PTRNG). If a PTRNG generates random numbers with a low entropy, the security of the embedded device has a vulnerability because secret information may be predictable by attackers due to the low entropy. Hence PTRNGs are required to provide high-quality physical random numbers even in an undesirable environment, that is, low/high temperature or supply voltage. PTRNGs also must be small-scale and consume low power due to the limited hardware resources in embedded devices.

In this paper, we fabricate and evaluate 39 PTRNGs using RS Latches on $0.18\,\mu$m ASICs. Physical random numbers were generated from the exclusive-OR of 256 RS latches' outputs. Our PTRNGs passed the SP800-90B Health Tests and the AIS31 Tests while changing both temperature (from $-20\,°$C to $60\,°$C) and voltage (1.80V $\pm10\%$), and thus, we were able to confirm that our PTRNGs have high-robustness against environmental stress. The power consumption and circuit scale of our PTRNG are 0.27mW and 984.5 gates, respectively. Our PTRNG using RS latches is small enough to be implemented on embedded devices.

Keywords: Random number generator · RS Latch · Metastability · AIS31 · SP800-90B

1 Introduction

Embedded devices such as smart cards and smart phones have become widespread in applications where high security is necessary, such as employee ID cards, electronic money and online banking. These embedded devices have cryptographic hardware for secure communications and identification/authentication. Cryptographic hardware achieves high-level security by using cryptographic

A. Francillon and P. Rohatgi (Eds.): CARDIS 2013, LNCS 8419, pp. 3–15, 2014.
DOI: 10.1007/978-3-319-08302-5_1, © Springer International Publishing Switzerland 2014

technologies such as symmetric-key cryptography and a pseudo random number generator. One of the security aspects for these cryptographic technologies depends on random numbers. This is because the random numbers are used for key generations for symmetric-key/public-key ciphers and seed generations for pseudo random number generators amongst other things. Random numbers with a low randomness cause the risk of prediction of the secret key and seed, which enables attackers to eavesdrop on communication contents and forge signatures. Hence, the quality of random numbers affects the security of embedded devices. Generally, random numbers are generated with physical random number generators (PTRNGs). Embedded devices with high-level security require PTRNGs which can generate high-quality random numbers. Additionally, embedded devices such as smart card and smart phone are often exposed to environmental changes, so attackers could intentionally lower the quality of the random numbers by freezing embedded devices. Therefore, PTRNGs should be able to generate high-quality random numbers regardless of the environmental changes. Moreover, PTRNGs should be able to integrate as an Large Scale Integration (LSI) for resource-limited embedded devices.

Some of the PTRNGs that can be integrated as digital LSI have been previously proposed, but there are many problems in terms of noise, power consumption, circuit scale and design cost. A PTRNG using RS latches has been proposed as a method to solve these problems. This PTRNG has been implemented only on FPGAs. Application specific integrated circuit (ASIC) implementation is necessary for the mass production of the PTRNGs because ASIC has the advantage of lower chip cost, lower power consumption and faster processing than FPGA. It is unknown whether or not a PTRNG on ASIC is able to generate high-quality random numbers. It is necessary to implement and evaluate the PTRNG on ASIC because random numbers are affected by the characteristics of the semiconductor, but as yet no evaluation has been made of such a PTRNG on ASIC and PTRNGs [1] have only been evaluated with the NIST SP800-22 randomness statistical tests [2]. It has not been evaluated by the tests dedicated to physical random numbers, namely AIS31 [3] and SP800-90B [4]. PTRNGs should be evaluated by these tests because the importance of PTRNGs has recently been gathering attention, and these tests for physical random numbers will be widely used in the future. Moreover, the robustness of PTRNG against temperature and voltage fluctuations must be evaluated.

Our Contributions. In this paper, we implement a PTRNG using RS latches on an ASIC based on the PTRNG on an FPGA [1]. The reason why we focus on this latch-based PTRNG is that its design cost is small and high-quality random numbers are expected to be generated in any environment. This paper makes four contributions; (1) We fabricated the PTRNG on a $0.18\,\mu m$ CMOS ASIC. We evaluated whether or not the PTRNG is able to generate random numbers on this ASIC. (2) We measured the power consumption and the circuit scale of the PTRNGs, and examined whether it can be installed in embedded devices. (3) We evaluated the quality of random numbers generated by our PTRNGs according to the AIS31 and SP800-90B randomness statistical tests for physical random numbers. (4) We examined whether our PTRNGs have the robustness against temperature and voltage fluctuations. As a result, our PTRNGs on an ASIC were found to be small and low-power enough to be implemented on embedded devices, and able to generate high-quality random numbers even if the environment changes, thus our PTRNGs can improve the security of embedded devices.

Organization of This Paper. This paper is organized as follows: Sect. 2 briefly introduces some work related to our research. Section 3 gives an outline of a PTRNG using RS Latches. Section 4 describes an ASIC implementation of the PTRNG. In addition, we measured the power consumption of the PTRNG on an ASIC. Section 5 evaluates the quality of the physical random numbers from the PTRNG by using the AIS31 and SP800-90B Health Tests. Finally, Sect. 6 gives a summary of this research.

2   Related Work

Figure 1 shows various PTRNGs on LSIs which have been proposed until now. The PTRNGs are classified into two types; analog-based one and digital-based one. Analog-based PTRNGs are based on random noise signals such as thermal noise, and they are known to be high-quality random number generators. However, the weak point of these PTRNGs is that they are difficult to integrate in high-density in an LSI due to the large-scale thermal sensors. Digital-based PTRNGs are categorized by entropy sources. One is to use the jitter of oscillators as an entropy source, for example ring oscillators-based PTRNGs [5]. A ring oscillator has a feedback structure composed of an odd number of NOT gates. Random numbers are obtained from the exclusive-OR of multiple ring oscillator outputs, and they have the robustness against temperature change. However, the PTRNGs in this category would be not suitable for embedded devices with limited resources because the ring oscillator has large power consumption, noise, and circuit scale. The other is to use the metastability of digital circuits. This type of PTRNG is suitable for embedded devices because of the small scale and low-power consumption. The prototypes of this PTRNG can generate high-quality random numbers [6–8]. However they need an additional dynamic adjustment for the voltage or of internal elements. This adjustment needs a dedicated full-custom circuit, which causes the large design cost at the transistor level. Moreover, it is necessary to re-design them when implementing on different CMOS technology because the PTRNGs often do not work as expected under a different CMOS technology.

Hata et al. have proposed a PTRNG using the metastability of RS latches and implemented it on an FPGA [1]. The design cost of this PTRNG is quite small because it uses only digital synchronous circuits. In addition, the PTNRG can save power consumption by stopping the clock signal inputted to the RS latches when the random numbers generation is not required. The random numbers from the PTRNG passes the NIST SP800-22 statistical tests [2]. For the above-mentioned reasons, the PTRNG proposed by Hata et.al. has better properties for embedded devices than other PTRNGs.

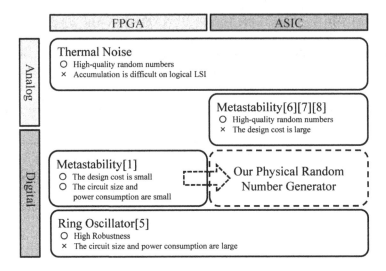

Fig. 1. Variety of physical random number generators.

3   Random Number Generator Using RS Latches

This section explains the method for generating physical random numbers that was proposed by Hata et al. in [1]. The PTRNGs that are using this method generates physical random numbers based on the metastability of RS latches.

Figure 2 shows an RS latch. An RS latch consists of 2 NAND gates, and is commonly used to store one bit information. When $input = 0$, the RS latch is stable with $output = 1$. When $input$ changes from 0 to 1, the RS latch temporarily enters a metastable state, and then, it is stable with $output = 0$ or 1. Physical random numbers can be obtained from $output$ by giving $input$ clock signals using this behavior. Ideally, the probability of outputting 0 and 1 is equal, but this probability is actually biased. This is because of the difference in wiring delay between gates, or the difference of drive capability between two NAND gates. In many cases, this RS latch generates only '0's or only '1's, so it is difficult to generate high-quality random numbers using only one RS latch. A PTRNG consisting of multiple RS latches and an exclusive-OR gate is proposed in [1]. This PTRNG generates random numbers from the exclusive-OR of multiple RS latches' outputs. This enables the PTRNG to exclude the biases and to generate high-quality random numbers.

Problems. There are two problems in [1]. (1) This PTRNG has implemented only on FPGAs. (2) This PTRNG has not been evaluated in various environments. It is difficult to implement an FPGA in mass-produced embedded devices such as smart cards due to a large power consumption and chip cost, so ASIC implementation is necessary for mass production. The PTRNGs for embedded devices must be able to generate high-quality physical random numbers in any environments. If the PTRNG generates random numbers with low

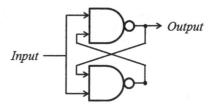

Fig. 2. RS latch

entropy due to environmental changes, the security of the embedded device is compromised because secret information may be predictable by attackers due to the low entropy. In general, the characteristics of a semiconductor, for example drive capability and wire delay, are influenced by both temperature and voltage changes. Therefore, the quality of random numbers from PTRNGs is affected by the both changes. Hence, the robustness against to the changes should be evaluated, but as yet it has not. In addition, the PTRNGs should be evaluated based on the SP800-90B Health Tests published in 2012, which is introduced for the tests of physical random number generators.

4   ASIC Implementation

We fabricate PTRNGs using RS latches on a $0.18\,\mu\mathrm{m}$ CMOS ASIC (Fujitsu CS86 series [9]). This PTRNG generates random numbers from the exclusive-OR of 256 RS latches' outputs. The RS latch was custom-designed on the circuit layout so that the wire lengths between the two NAND gates are the same, and was implemented as hard macro. Thus, the probability of the RS latch generating random numbers is expected to improve. 256 RS latches are implemented automatically by using circuit design tools. Hence, the design cost is quite small. The PTRNGs are assembled as DIP28 packages. Two types of the PTRNG were fabricated, namely 20 standard PTRNGs (using CS86MN, called MN-PTRNG) and 19 low-power-consuming PTRNGs (using CS86ML, called ML-PTRNG).

4.1   Measurement of Power Consumption and Circuit Scale

Embedded devices require low-power-consuming PTRNGs. We measured the power and current consumption of the PTRNGs with a direct current ammeter. According to our experimental measurements, the average power/current consumption of both MN-PTRNG and ML-PTRNG ASICs is $0.27\,m\,\mathrm{W}/0.15\,m\,\mathrm{A}$ and $0.252\,m\,\mathrm{W}/0.14\,m\,\mathrm{A}$ respectively. The current consumption of common ASICs used for contactless smart cards is approximately $1\,m\,\mathrm{A}$ [10]. The current consumption of our PTRNG was much smaller than this value, so is practical and useful. Additionally, we measured the circuit scale of our PTRNG. In the following discussion, one gate is equivalent to a 2-1 NAND gate (2-bit input and 1-bit output). The PTRNG consists of 256 RS latches, a 256-1 exclusive-OR gate, and a 1-bit flip-flop to store a random number temporarily. Our PTRNG was synthesized with the Design Compiler 2003.03, and the circuit scale was 984.3 gates. This circuit scale was smaller than the implementation of the PRESENT cipher which is one of the most famous ultra-lightweight ciphers [11]. In addition, this circuit size is smaller than the circuit size of Triple DES which is one of the most widely used in smart cards (e.g. MIFARE DESFire MF31CD40). We achieved PTRNGs with the very small circuit scale on an ASIC.

5   Evaluation

As mentioned in Sect. 3, PTRNGs may be influenced by both temperature and voltage fluctuations. This section evaluates whether our PTRNGs fabricated on ASICs generate high-quality random numbers regardless of environmental changes.

5.1   Evaluation System

Figure 3 shows our experimental system for the acquisition of random numbers. This figure is omitted excluding important parts. It consists of two boards: a custom-made board for the ASICs of the PTRNGs and a Spartan-3E starter kit board with a Xilinx FPGA for controlling the PTRNGs [12]. The core voltage to the PTRNGs was supplied by using a stabilizing power supply, which was able to adjust the supply voltage at intervals of 0.01V. The clock signals were input to the PTRNGs through the FPGA board. Random numbers generated by the PTRNGs were written to a micro SD card via a block RAM of the FPGA. We acquired not only the random numbers but also the output of each latch for our further evaluation.

In this environment, we evaluated the random numbers generated by all of the 39 PTRNGs while changing the temperature and voltage. The core voltage is changed to 1.65 V (1.80 V–10 %), 1.80V (standard) and 1.95V (1.80V+10 %) by the stabilizing power supply. The temperature was maintained at $-20\,°C$, $27\,°C$, and $60\,°C$ by using a constant temperature oven. Only the custom-made board for the PTRNGs was put in the constant temperature oven. The FPGA board was always operated at the rated voltage and room temperature. These two boards were connected through a low/high temperature resistant cable.

5.2   Evaluation of Randomness

We acquired approximately 5.5 M bits of random numbers from each PTRNG while changing the temperature and voltage. 351 cases of random numbers (3 temperatures × 3 voltages × 39 PTRNGs, 180 cases for MN-PTRNGs and 171 cases for ML-PTRNGs) was exhaustively evaluated according to both the SP800-90B Health Tests and the AIS31 Tests.

The NIST SP800-22 statistical tests [2], which are well known as tests for *pseudo* random numbers, had been used for physical random numbers. However,

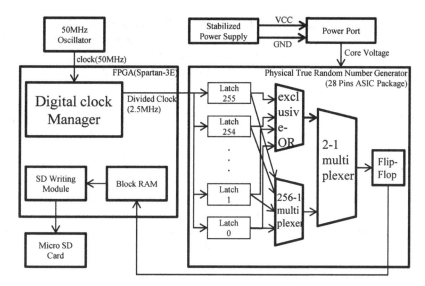

Fig. 3. Experimental system for the acquisition of random numbers

there is SP800-90B and AIS31 which are tests dedicated to *physical* random numbers now. We evaluated our PTRNGs according not to SP800-22 but to these tests in this paper.

NIST SP800-90B Health Tests. We evaluated whether our PTRNGs could generate high-entropy random numbers according to the repetition count test and the adaptive proportion test defined in SP800-90B [4]. The random numbers at various temperatures and voltages were tested as follows. A *"false positive rate"*, which is the probability of ideal true random numbers failing these tests, is set to 2^{-30} as recommended in SP800-90B.

[*Repetition Count Test*]
If the same value (0 or 1) appears consecutively c times or more in the sequence of random numbers, the random numbers are a failure, where $c = ceiling(1 + 30/min - entropy)$. In this paper, c is 32. *min-entropy* will be mentioned in Sect. 5.3.

[*Adaptive Proportion Test*]
Firstly, we obtained a 1-bit value from the beginning of the random numbers as a reference value. Secondly, we obtained one *block* from the succeeding random numbers. The bit length of a block is represented by *window size*, and if the reference value appears greater than *cutoff* times in a block, the random numbers are failure. The size of the *cutoff* is defined by the *false positive rate*, *min-entropy* and *window size*. This procedure was repeated until the end of the random numbers. In our evaluations, the *window size* and *cutoff* were 64, 51 in Test Settings I and are 4096, 2240 in Test Settings II, respectively. That is, about

84,700 blocks are evaluated in "Test Settings I" and about 1,350 blocks are evaluated in "Test Settings II", in each case of random numbers. We consider the PTRNGs pass the SP800-90B Health Tests if all blocks pass in both test settings. This means that the PTRNGs continuously generate random numbers with high-entropy.

Figures 4 and 5 show the rate of the PTRNGs that passed the SP800-90B Health Tests. The horizontal axis shows the environment at various temperatures and voltages. The vertical axis shows the rate of the PTRNGs that passed the tests. In the MN-PTRNGs, all cases pass this test as shown in Fig. 4. In the ML-PTRNGs, six cases failed the test in Fig. 5, and four cases out of the six happened when the temperature was $-20\,°C$. This may be because the ML-PTRNGs have a small number of RS latches outputting random numbers at a low temperature (details are discussed in Sect. 5.4). In contrast, the MN-PTRNGs can generate high-entropy random numbers even when the temperature and voltage change. Hence an MN-PTRNG is more suitable for generating physical random numbers than an ML-PTRNG.

AIS31 Tests. We evaluated the random numbers in various temperatures and voltages according to AIS31 Tests [3]. AIS31 is an evaluation criterion for the physical random number generators defined by BSI (i.e. the German Federal Office for Information Security). Tests in AIS31 include various statistical tests such as the Poker Test, the Long Run Test and the Uniform Distribution Test. AIS31 classifies PTRNGs into two classes; P1 Class and P2 Class. PTRNGs in P1 Class pass P1 Tests, and PTRNG in P2 Class pass P2 Tests. The PTRNGs in the P1 Class can be used for random number generation for challenge and response authentication. The PTRNGs in the P2 Class can be used for key and seed generations for pseudo random number generators, which provide higher security than PTRNGs in the P1 Class. It is desirable for PTRNGs to pass both of the tests because PTRNGs for embedded devices are used for various applications.

Figures 6 and 7 show the rate of PTNRGs that passed the AIS31 Tests. The horizontal and the vertical axises are the same as Figs. 4 and 5. If the PTRNG fails either of the P1 or P2 Tests, we regarded it as *failed* PTRNG. The MN-PTRNGs pass the tests in all cases as shown in Fig. 6, so our MN-PTRNGs have the robustness against temperature and voltage fluctuations, and can thus be used for secure embedded systems including key generation. The ML-PTRNGs, however, failed tests only in two cases out of 171, one of which was the same PTRNG as the failed PTRNG in the SP800-90B Health Tests. The next section discusses whether ML-PTRNGs are able to generate high-quality random numbers.

Further Evaluation by Increasing the Number of Latches. We expected that the quality of random numbers would be improved by increasing the number of implemented RS latches. This is because our PTRNGs generated random numbers as the exclusive-OR of 256 RS latch outputs. To verify this, we regarded

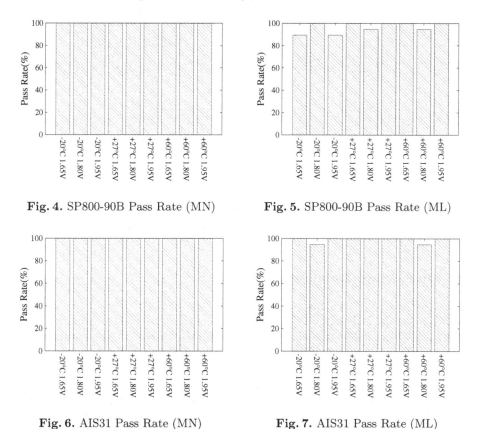

Fig. 4. SP800-90B Pass Rate (MN)   **Fig. 5.** SP800-90B Pass Rate (ML)

Fig. 6. AIS31 Pass Rate (MN)   **Fig. 7.** AIS31 Pass Rate (ML)

the exclusive-OR of 2 actual PTRNGs outputs as random numbers obtained from a virtual PTRNG with built-in 512 RS latches, and evaluated whether or not the quality of the random numbers was improved. The virtual PTRNGs were generated as follows. We focused on the PTRNGs failing at least one test. If there were even numbers of PTRNGs that failed the same test in the same environment, the exclusive-OR of each pair was regarded as the virtual PTRNG. Otherwise, the exclusive-OR of outputs from the failing PTRNG and the PTRNG with the lowest min-entropy in the same test/environment was regarded as the virtual PTRNG.

We evaluated the virtual PTRNGs according to the NIST SP800-90B Health Tests and AIS31 Tests. As a result, all the virtual PTRNGs passed both tests. Through this evaluation, we verify that the 256 latches are not sufficient for the ML-PTRNGs, while the quality of random numbers could be improved by increasing the number of RS latches. Hence we should carefully decide the number of implemented RS latches in consideration of both the quality of random numbers and the circuit space.

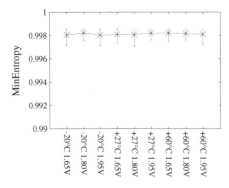
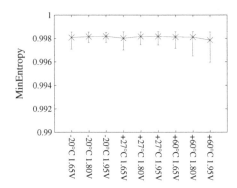

Fig. 8. MinEntropy of physical random number generator (MN)

Fig. 9. MinEntropy of physical random number generator (ML)

5.3   Min-Entropy Estimation

We use *minimum entropy* (i.e. min-entropy) as the objective criterion of randomness. Min-entropy is defined as the lower bound of the amount of information of a random variable [4]. The min-entropy per bit of the ideal true random numbers is 1 because the proportion of '0's and '1's is ideally 0.5. The method of estimating the min-entropy differs depending on whether the PTRNG is IID (Independent and Identically Distributed). Therefore, first, we implemented a software for IID verification tests [4], and evaluated our PTRNGs using this tests. As a result, the MN-PTRNGs passed all 180 cases, so we performed min-entropy estimation for IID sources (see Sect. 9.2 in [4]). In contrast, the ML-PTRNGs passed 166 out of 171 cases. We, however, we regarded the ML-PTRNGs as IID sources because they passed at least all tests under the normal conditions (i.e. 27 °C and 1.80 V). Min-entropy estimation as a non-IID sources will be part of our future work.

Figures 8 and 9 show the results of min-entropy estimation. The middle line, the upper line and the lower line show the average, maximum and minimum of the min-entropy per bits in all test cases, respectively. The min-entropy is very close to '1' (i.e. ideal min-entropy) in both types of PTRNGs. Hence our PTRNGs have a very high min-entropy regardless of the temperature or voltage.

5.4   Evaluation of Output from Each RS Latch

As mentioned previously, our PTRNGs, especially MN-PTRNGs, have the robustness against temperature and voltage fluctuations. This section evaluates the behavior of each RS latch in order to clarify the reason for the robustness. We defined a "random latch" as the RS latch whose output sequence includes at least one transition between 0 and 1, and defined a "constant latch" as the RS latch that generates only '0's or only '1's. We focus on two evaluation axes: the number of random latches and the quality of random numbers from each random latch.

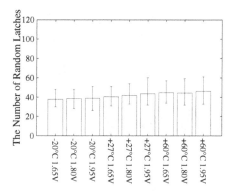

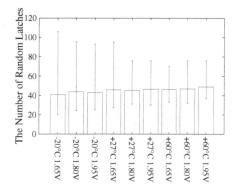

Fig. 10. Number of random latches (MN)

Fig. 11. Number of random latches (ML)

The Number of Random Latches. We acquired 21 K bits of output sequence from each RS latch while changing the temperature and voltage, and evaluated the number of random latches. In Figs. 10 and 11, the bar graphs, the upper and lower of lines show the average, maximum and minimum of the number of random latches in the test cases respectively. The higher temperature and voltage, the larger average number of random latches in both types of PTRNGs, except in some cases. At −20 °C and 1.65 V, the number of random latches reaches a minimum of 20 in ML-PTRNG. In addition, there are some transitions from constant latch to random latch whenever the environment changes. The number of random latches in an MN-PTRNGs, whose average is approximately 40, is more stable than in an ML-PTRNG.

The Quality of Random Numbers from Each Random Latch. The quality of each random latch is one of the most important metrics for the quality of a random number as well as the number of random latches. Thus, we evaluated the quality of the output sequence from each random latch. We acquired approximately 21 K bits of output from each RS latch and examined the proportion of '1's in the output sequence. For the ideal random latch, the proportion of '1' is 50 %.

Figures 12 and 13 show the rate of the number of random latches by the proportion of '1's. Here, [a,b] and (a,b) represent closed and open intervals respectively. For example, [30 %, 40 %) and (60 %, 70 %] represents 30 % ≤ x < 40 % and 60 % < x ≤ 70 %, where x is the proportion of '1's in the output. The lowest part of bar graph indicating [40 %, 60 %] represents random latches outputting high-quality random numbers (i.e. "high-quality random latch"). There are approximately 5 % high-quality random latches in any environment. Additionally, most random latches generate biased output.

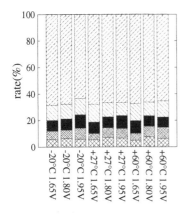

Fig. 12. The characteristics of random latches (MN)

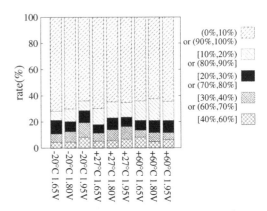

Fig. 13. The characteristics of random latches (ML)

5.5 Discussion

We consider the results of Sect. 5.4. In any environment, there are approximately 40 random latches, and approximately 5 % of all random latches are the high-quality random latch. Hence, there is expected to be about 2 high-quality random latches in any environment. Moreover, a number of random latches including biased ones are expected to contribute to improve the quality of random numbers.

As mentioned in Sect. 5.2, our PTRNGs can generate high-quality random numbers that pass the tests for physical random number generators in any environment. The min-entropy is stable at high level, and they can be used effective entropy source. We validate our PTRNGs using RS latches work stably and effectively on an ASIC. Circuit scale and power consumption of our PTRNGs are quite small. Our PTRNG generates high-quality random numbers in even worse conditions. Hence, our PTRNG is very suitable for embedded devices.

6 Conclusion and Future Work

In this paper, we fabricated 2 types of the PTRNGs using RS latches on ASICs, and evaluated the robustness of the PTRNGs against temperature and voltage fluctuations. We validated that the PTRNG can generate random numbers at a standard voltage and room temperature. Furthermore, we evaluated the random numbers generated in various conditions, where the temperature was between $-20\,^{\circ}\mathrm{C}$ and $60\,^{\circ}\mathrm{C}$ and the voltage was between $1.65\,\mathrm{V}$ and $1.95\,\mathrm{V}$, in line with the AIS31 Tests [3], SP800-90B Health Tests [4], IID Verification Tests [4] and Min-Entropy Estimation [4]. As a result, we found that all MN-PTRNGs (the PTRNG on CS86MN with a standard power consumption) generates high-quality random numbers which pass all of the above-mentioned tests in various environments. Our PTRNGs also generated high-quality random numbers continually because the min-entropy is stable at high values. Some of the ML-PTRNGs (the PTRNG on CS86MLwith low power consumption) failed some tests, but the quality of random numbers, however, is expected to be improved by increasing the number of RS latches implemented. For these reasons, our PTRNGs that use RS latches on an ASIC have the robustness against temperature and voltage fluctuations. The circuit scale and the power consumption of the PTRNGs were 984.3 gates and $0.27\,m$ W respectively. Hence our PTRNGs were small-size and had a low power consumption, which is suitable for embedded devices. Our PTRNGs are high-quality entropy sources and can be used for various purposes such as cryptographic keys, nonces for authentication and seeds for pseudo random number generators. Future work will include discussion on the experiment in larger fluctuations of temperature, voltage and clock-frequency and countermeasure against side-channel attacks.

References

1. Hata, H., Ichikawa, S.: FPGA implementation of metastability-based true random number generator. IEICE Trans. Inf. Syst. **E95–D**(2), 426–436 (2012)
2. NIST, Special Publication 800-22, A Statistical Test Suite for Random and Pseudorandom Number Generators for Cryptographic Applications (2010)
3. BSI, AIS31, Functionality classes and evaluation methodology for true (physical) random number generators (2001)
4. NIST, Special Publication 800–90B, Recommendation for the Entropy Sources Used for Random Bit Generation (2012)
5. Sunar, B., Martin, W.J., Stinson, D.R.: A provably secure ture random number generator with built-in tolerance to active attacks. IEEE Trans. Comput. **56**(1), 109–119 (2007)
6. Bellido, M., Acosta, A., Valencia, M., Barriga, A., Huertas, J.: Simple binary random number generator. Electron. Lett. **28**(7), 617–618 (1992)
7. Kinniment, D., Chester, E.: Design of an on-chip random number generator using metastability. In: Proceedings of the ESSCIRC 2002, vol. 4(6), pp. 595–598 (2002)
8. Tokunaga, C., Blaauw, D., Mudge, T.: True random number generator with a metastability-based quality control. IEEE J. Solid-State Circuits **43**(1), 78–84 (2008)
9. Fujitsu Semiconductor, Semicustom CMOS Standard Cell CS86 Series (2011). http://www.fujitsu.com/downloads/MICRO/fma/pdf/e620209_CS86_ASIC.pdf
10. Finkenzeller, K.: RFID Handbook: Fundamentals and Applications in Contactless Smart Cards and Identification, 2nd. Wiley, Chichester (2003)
11. Bogdanov, A., Knudsen, L.R., Leander, G., Paar, C., Poschmann, A., Robshaw, M.J.B., Seurin, Y., Vikkelsoe, C.: PRESENT: an ultra-lightweight block cipher. In: Paillier, P., Verbauwhede, I. (eds.) CHES 2007. LNCS, vol. 4727, pp. 450–466. Springer, Heidelberg (2007)
12. Xilinx: Spartan-3E starter kit board. http://www.xilinx.com/products/boards-and-kits/HW-SPAR3E-SK-US-G.htm

From New Technologies to New Solutions
Exploiting FRAM Memories to Enhance Physical Security

Stéphanie Kerckhof[1]([✉]), François-Xavier Standaert[1], and Eric Peeters[2]

[1] ICTEAM/ELEN/Crypto Group, Université Catholique de Louvain,
Charleroi, Belgium
[2] Texas Instruments, Dallas, TX, USA
{stephanie.kerckhof,fstandae}@uclouvain.be, e-peeters@ti.com

Abstract. Ferroelectric RAM (FRAM) is a promising non-volatile memory technology that is now available in low-end microcontrollers. Its main advantages over Flash memories are faster write performances and much larger tolerated number of write/erase cycles. These properties are profitable for the efficient implementation of side-channel countermeasures exploiting pre-computations. In this paper, we illustrate the interest of FRAM-based microcontrollers for physically secure cryptographic hardware with two case studies. First we consider a recent shuffling scheme for the AES algorithm, exploiting randomized program memories. We exhibit significant performance gains over previous results in an Atmel microcontroller, thanks to the fine-grained programmability of FRAM. Next and most importantly, we propose the first working implementation of the "masking with randomized look-up table" countermeasure, applied to reduced versions of the block cipher LED. This implementation provides unconditional security against side-channel attacks (*of all orders!*) under the assumption that pre-computations can be performed without leakage. It also provides high security levels in cases where this assumption is relaxed (e.g. for context or performance reasons).

1 Introduction

Providing (physical) security against side-channel attacks is a challenging task for cryptographic designers [10]. This is especially true for low-cost embedded devices, with strongly constrained resources. Typical examples of countermeasures in this context include masking [3] and shuffling [9]. But in both cases, the concrete security levels attained by the protected implementations highly depend on hardware assumptions, in particular the amount of noise in the measurements which may not be sufficient, e.g. in 8-bit devices [19,20]. The performance overhead they imply can also be significant [7,15]. As a result, such countermeasures are usually combined in a somewhat heuristic manner, in order to ensure "practical" security against a wide enough category of adversaries [16].

In parallel to these advances, some more recent works have tried to formalize the problem of physical security, in order to extend the guarantees of provable security from algorithms and protocols to implementations. The main challenge

A. Francillon and P. Rohatgi (Eds.): CARDIS 2013, LNCS 8419, pp. 16–29, 2014.
DOI: 10.1007/978-3-319-08302-5_2, © Springer International Publishing Switzerland 2014

in this case is to find relevant restrictions of the adversaries. A typical example is the one of leakage-resilient cryptography, where the assumption is that the information leakage of a single algorithm run is bounded (see, e.g. [5] for an early reference, [17] for a recent one, and many other proposals in between). Alternatively, another line of work is based on the assumption of secure pre-computations, e.g. in order to prevent "continual memory attacks", as formalized by Brakerski et al. [2] and by Dodis et al. [4]. The one-time programs introduced at Crypto 2008 are another (extreme) way to exploit such secure pre-computations [6]: they essentially correspond to a program that can be executed on a single input, whose value can be specified at run time. Nevertheless, the practical relevance of these solutions is still limited by sometimes unrealistic hardware assumptions and (mainly), by large performance overheads.

In this paper, we start from the observation that both for practice-oriented and theory-oriented countermeasures against side-channel analysis, the exploitation of secure pre-computations is highly related to the problem of fast and efficient non-volatile storage. In this context, a significant drawback of the mainstream Flash memories is that write operations are slow and energy-consuming. Furthermore, their number of tolerated write/erase cycles is also limited (from 10 k to 100 k, typically), which may prevent their frequent use for cryptographic operations. Interestingly, the recently available Ferroelectric RAM (FRAM) provides a solution to these issues[1]. As a result, we investigate whether it can be used as a technology enabler to improve the performances and security of protected implementations. For this purpose, we first consider the shuffling countermeasure, and its instantiation for the AES algorithm based on randomized program memories proposed in [20]. We show that FRAM allows significantly improved performances in terms of pre-computation time. Next, we discuss the application of these new memories to the Randomized Look-Up Table (RLUT) countermeasure [18]. It can be viewed as a type of one-time program specialized to side-channel analysis, or as a generic masking scheme that provides unconditional security against side-channel attacks of all orders (i.e. independent of the statistical moment estimated by the adversary). We provide the first working implementation of this solution applied to reduced versions of the block cipher LED [8], and analyze its performances in various settings. In particular, we investigate the contexts of complete and secure pre-computations, and the tradeoffs corresponding to partial (and partially leaking) ones. We reach performances that are close to higher-order masking in the latter case [15], while complete and secure pre-computations also ensures much higher security levels at practically reachable cost. Therefore, our results suggest that FRAM is a promising solution for improving the security of low-cost tokens such as smart cards, especially when some pre-computations can be performed in a safe environment.

---

[1] Strictly speaking, FRAM is not a new technology as it was introduced as a high-security alternative to Flash memories back in the early 2000s by Fujitsu. However, FRAM-based smart cards did not make it to mass market at that time, due to excessive manufacturing costs and limited ability to reduce cell transistor size.

The rest of the paper is structured as follows. Section 2 provides the necessary background on FRAM and discusses our security model. Section 3 contains the implementation results of the shuffling with randomized program memory countermeasure, and their comparison with the previous work from Asiacrypt 2012. Section 4 describes the RLUT countermeasures, our proposed implementation and the various tradeoffs it provides. Finally, conclusions are in Sect. 5.

2 Background

2.1 FRAM Microcontrollers

Standard solutions for non-volatile storage such as Flash and EEPROM usually suffer from long programming times, as well as a high voltage required to program bit cells with hot carrier injection or Fowler-Nordheim tunneling effect. In addition, the charge pump overhead as well as the high current supply they require make these technologies not ideal for applications where frequent data logging or ultra-low-power write operations are needed (e.g. all RF applications such as e-passport, RF Banking Card, . . .). FRAM is a promising alternative that combines the advantages of non-volatile memories with much faster write speed (e.g. 125 ns per 64-bit word for the 130-nm TI FRAM technology exploited in MSP430FR devices), less power (82 uA/MHz active power in the same technology) and infinite (10^{15}) write-erase cycle performances.

FRAM stores information through the use of a stable electric dipole found in ferroelectric crystals (insensitive to the magnetic field). The polarization-voltage hysteresis loops for such materials are very similar to the B-H curve of magnetic materials. Exploiting this fact, a FRAM bit cell structure consists of a ferroelectric capacitor containing the crystal. The capacitor is connected to a plate line, bit lines, and a transistor switch to access it. This is also referred to as a 1T-1C memory cell mode (Fig. 1, left). By contrast, 2T-2C memory cell modes (Fig. 1, right) would store the data as 2 opposite values in each 1T-1C cell of its

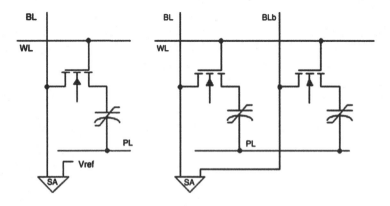

Fig. 1. FRAM bit cell modes: left: 1T-1C structure, right: 2T-2C structure.

structure (similar to what is found in EEPROM for instance). Reading the data from FRAM occurs by placing a voltage on the plate line. The idea is that for every read operation, one tries to set the cell to a 0 state. If the voltage causes the dipoles inside the capacitor to flip its orientation, then a large charge Q is generated on the bit line. On the contrary, if the orientation of the dipole is already negative prior to applying the voltage to the plate line in a read cycle, then the dipole direction does not flip, and only a small charge Q is induced on the bit line. The difference can be measured by a sense amplifier. An important consequence of this description is that FRAM reads are destructive, and therefore require a refresh process. Nevertheless, this process is automatically completed by the controller and therefore transparent to the user.

In this paper, we used a microcontroller of the MSP430FRxxxx family from Texas Instruments. This type of microcontrollers provides an ultra-low-power 16-bit RISC CPU, and a set of instructions performing operations on either 8 or 16 bits of data. The available non-volatile FRAM memory can have a size of up to 64 kb (microcontrollers with 128- and 256-kilobyte capabilities are already announced). All the developed code was made for a MSP430FR5739 microcontroller, containing 16 kb of FRAM, and was tested using the MSP-EXP430FR5739 experimenter's board and Code Composer Studio 5.3.

2.2 Security Model

The following sections mainly aim at demonstrating the efficiency of FRAM-based cryptographic computations. Yet, since we consider implementations protected against side-channel attacks, it is important to say a few words about the security model we rely on. Both for the shuffling in Sect. 3 and for the RLUT countermeasure in Sect. 4, we can consider two alternatives:

1. *Secure pre-computations.* That is, the permutations used in shuffling and the randomized program used in RLUT are pre-computed without leakage, prior to the execution of the cryptographic algorithm. As a result, the security of the shuffling is exactly the one analyzed at Asiacrypt 2012 [20]. And the security of the RLUT countermeasure is unconditional: even an adversary accessing the (identity) leakage of all the intermediate computations in the target implementation would not recover any information about its key.
2. *Leaking pre-computations.* That is, the permutations used in shuffling and the randomized program used in RLUT are computed online, and leaking information. In this case, the security of both countermeasures is less investigated, and essentially depends on how much information is leaked during precomputation (in fact, the same observation holds for most countermeasures exploiting randomness, e.g. masking). Note however that the randomness used to protect these implementations is generated on-chip, and is never output. Hence, adversaries can only mount SPA attacks against it. As a result, we can informally state that our implementations will remain secure in this context, as long as one can guarantee SPA security for this part of the computation (a similar informal separation between SPA and DPA was used to argue about the security of fresh re-keying schemes, e.g. in [12]).

Note that in terms of security, the main advantage of FRAM is to make the first model more realistic. Indeed, one could (at least theoretically) imagine to implement a randomized program with SRAM memories. But in addition to performances that would most likely be poor in this case, such a solution should anyway be implemented online (hence leaking), since SRAM is volatile.

3   Improving Past Results: The Shuffling Case

Shuffling the execution order of independent operations is a possible solution to improve security of cryptographic implementations against side-channel attacks. The goal of shuffling is to distribute the intermediate cipher values over a given period of time, so that an attacker will only be able to observe a chosen intermediate value at a particular moment in time with a certain probability. A typical example of independent operations that can be shuffled is the SubBytes layer in the AES. Indeed, whatever the order in which each of the 16 S-Box's outputs is generated, the result of the SubBytes layer will not be affected.

A previous work on shuffling, proposed 3 implementations of the AES on an Atmel ATMega644p microcontroller [20]: a basic one with double indexing, an optimized one with randomized execution path, and a variant with randomized program memory. In this paper, we focus on this third proposal, for which FRAM technology provides significant improvements (the two first ones lead to essentially similar performances, independent of the non-volatile memory used). Randomizing the program memory corresponds to rewriting the code in a randomized way before each algorithm run. In other words, a pre-computation phase modifies (inside the code) which registers and memory addresses will be used during the execution, which then remains essentially the same as an unshuffled one. While promising in principle, such an instantiation of the shuffling idea faces some limitations when implemented in Flash-based Atmel microcontrollers. First, even when only a few bytes need to be modified, a complete memory page must be erased and rewritten, which takes a lot of time (more or less 4.5 ms each time a page is written or erased). Next, the memory can only be rewritten a limited number of times (namely 10 000). Hence, FRAM-based microcontrollers are natural candidates to relax these limitations as we now detail.

Implementing the AES algorithm with randomized program memory requires three main functions. First, a permutation generator must be defined - we used exactly the same implementation as proposed in [20]. Next, it is necessary to have an AES description with well defined sets of 16 independent operations, on which the shuffling can be applied. Although such operations are easily found for SubBytes and AddRoundKey, their specification is more difficult for ShiftRows and MixColumns, for which the 16 bytes are not manipulated independently. This implies that their output cannot be stored at the same location as their input, resulting in the need of 16 additional bytes of temporary storage. Furthermore, the FRAM microcontroller we use has only 12 CPU registers, which is not enough to store a complete AES state. Therefore, each independent operation needs to access the FRAM with absolute addressing, which is more time

Table 1. AES program size (in bytes) and cycle counts in the MPS430FR5739.

Unprotected AES		Code size	Data size	Cycle count
		1076	52	5800
Shuffled AES	Perm. generation	194	18	2240
	Code shuffling	418	0	2751
	AES execution	2404	146	8479
	Total	3016	164	13470

consuming than working on registers. As for the implementations of Asiacrypt 2012, dummy key-schedule operations have also been added to the "on-the-fly" key-schedule, in order to obtain enough independent operations for this part of the implementation as well [20]. Eventually, the last function needed is the one randomizing the code before execution. This randomization was achieved by modifying the bytes of instructions referring to the cipher state's or round key's memory addresses. Interestingly, since the code and the data are both stored in the same FRAM memory, modifying some bytes of the code or some bytes of cipher state and round key takes exactly the same amount of time.

Our implementation results are available in Table 1 (and are given for encryption only). For reference, we first implemented an unshuffled version of the AES in the MSP430FR5739 microcontroller. Even if performance comparisons obtained with different technologies always have to be considered with care, it is worth noticing that it is slightly more time-consuming than Atmel ones (e.g. the open source AES Furious requires 3546 cycles to execute [13]). This is mainly a consequence of the limited number of registers available in FRAM microcontrollers, leading to more frequent memory accesses. By contrast and as expected, the pre-computation time required to shuffle the code is strongly reduced, from 18 ms in Atmel devices to 0.19 ms (running the chip at 16 MHz), which corresponds to a ratio of approximately 100. This is the main advantage of our implementation. Note finally the increased data size and cycle count for executing the AES in its shuffled version, which is essentially due to the previously mentioned execution of dummy key-schedules. We conclude that the overhead required to shuffle the AES algorithm based on a randomized program memory is now in line with practical applications constraints.

4 Making New Results Possible: The RLUT Case

The previous section described how FRAM memories allow significant speedups for shuffled implementations exploiting randomized program memories. In this section, we show how similar ideas can be used to enable the efficient implementation of the RLUT countermeasure. For this purpose, we first recall the intuition behind this countermeasure, then describe its application to reduced versions of the block cipher LED, and finally discuss implementation results.

4.1   Description of the Countermeasure

We will focus on the protection of a single S-box that is the most challenging part of the countermeasure. Intuitively, it is convenient to start from the first-order Boolean masking depicted in Fig. 2. In this scheme, a random mask m is first added to the sensitive value x which is then sent trough the combination of a bitwise key addition $\oplus$ and S-box S. A correction function C is used (taking both $x \oplus m \oplus k$ and m as input) in order to produce the output mask q such that $\mathsf{S}(x \oplus m \oplus k) = \mathsf{S}(x \oplus k) \oplus q$. Such an implementation typically gives rise to 4 leakage points denoted as L_1, L_2, L_3 and L_4 on the figure (L_2 being the combination of two parts). It ideally guarantees that statistical moments of order 2 will have to be estimated by an adversary in order to recover secret information. The word "ideally" here refers to the fact that physical defaults such as glitches can lead to exploitable information in lower-order statistical moments [11]. For example, the leakage point L_2 on the figure corresponds to the manipulation of $x \oplus m \oplus k$ leading to $\mathsf{L}_2^a(x \oplus m \oplus k)$, and m leading to $\mathsf{L}_2^b(m)$, in parallel. It implies first-order exploitable information if these two parts of the leakage function are not independent[2]. Boolean masking can be naturally generalized to d shares ($d = 2$ in the example of Fig. 2), leading to an (ideal as well) data complexity increase proportional to $(\sigma_n^2)^d$, with σ_n^2 the variance of the noise in the leakage samples, as demonstrated by Chari et al. [3].

From this description, a first step towards the RLUT countermeasure is the observation that if the master key is fixed and for n-bit S-boxes, one can replace the computation of $\mathsf{S}(x \oplus k)$ by a pre-computed table of size $2^n \times n$ (the correction function can be implemented similarly as a table of size $2^{2n} \times n$). It directly leads to the implementation of Fig. 3, which is functionally equivalent to the previous one, but where the key addition has been "included" in a key-dependent permutations $\mathsf{P}_k(x)$. From the side-channel security point-of-view, it still corresponds to a first-order secure implementation. Next, and in order to provide unconditional security against side-channel attacks of all orders, the main idea is to replace the Boolean masking operation $x \oplus m$ by an extension to three shares denoted as $\mathsf{G}_i(x, m) = x \oplus m \oplus a_i$, where a_i is a n-bit random mask that is pre-computed in a leakage-free environment. These operations, illustrated in Fig. 4, can also be implemented as tables of size $2^{2n} \times n$, so that the shares a_i will never be manipulated during the "online" execution of the algorithm. If the G_1 (resp. G_2) function is refreshed before each run of the protected implementation, it guarantees that no information can be extracted from the leakage points $(\mathsf{L}_1, \mathsf{L}_2)$ (resp. $(\mathsf{L}_3, \mathsf{L}_4)$). We additionally need G_1 and G_2 (i.e. their hidden a_i shares) to be independent, in order to avoid fourth-order leakages taking advantage of the correlation between the tables' inputs and outputs. Eventually, it remains to randomize the permutation $\mathsf{P}_k(x)$ (and the correction function C) in order to completely hide the key, even from identity leakage functions, as represented in Fig. 5. This way, a non-linear S-box can be computed securely. This leads to an implementation in which the operations G_1, G_2, R and RC are

---

[2] As a typical example, $\mathsf{L}_2 = \mathsf{L}_2^a + \mathsf{L}_2^b$ would correspond to an ideal implementation, while $\mathsf{L}_2 = \mathsf{L}_2^a \cdot \mathsf{L}_2^b$ would leak first-order information, as discussed in [19].

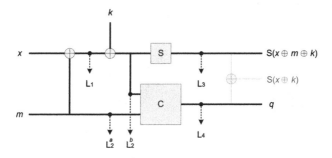

Fig. 2. Boolean masking.

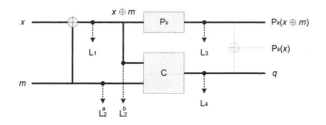

Fig. 3. Boolean masking with LUTs.

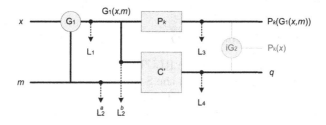

Fig. 4. Randomized Boolean masking with LUTs.

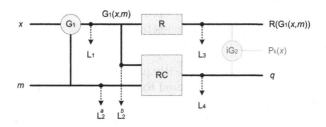

Fig. 5. Randomized Boolean masking with randomized LUTs.

Algorithm 1. Table refreshing.

- **input:** P_k.
1. Pick $a_1 \xleftarrow{R} \{0,1\}^n$;
2. Pick $a_2 \xleftarrow{R} \{0,1\}^n$
3. Pick $a_3 \xleftarrow{R} \{0,1\}^n$;
4. Pre-compute $\mathsf{G}_1(I, J) = I \oplus J \oplus a_1$;
5. Pre-compute $\mathsf{R}(I) = \mathsf{P}_k(I) \oplus a_2$;
6. Pre-compute $\mathsf{G}_2(I, J) = I \oplus J \oplus a_3$;
7. Pre-compute $\mathsf{RC}(I, J) = \mathsf{r}(I) \oplus \mathsf{p}_k(I \oplus J \oplus a_1) \oplus a_3$;
- **output:** $\mathsf{G}_1, \mathsf{R}, \mathsf{G}_2, \mathsf{RC}$.

Algorithm 2. S-box evaluation on input x.

- **input:** $\mathsf{G}_1, \mathsf{R}, \mathsf{RC}$.
1. Pick $m \xleftarrow{R} \{0,1\}^n$;
2. Compute $\mathsf{G}_1(x, m)$;
3. Compute $\mathsf{R}(\mathsf{G}_1(x, m))$;
4. Compute $\mathsf{RC}(\mathsf{G}_1(x, m), m)$;
- **output:** $\mathsf{R}(\mathsf{G}_1(x, m))$, $\mathsf{RC}(\mathsf{G}_1(x, m), m)$.

pre-computed according to Algorithm 1, and executed according to Algorithm 2. Extending this S-box computation to a complete cipher is straightforward: we just need independent tables for all the S-boxes. As for the linear operations, they have to be applied independently on the two shares that are explicitly manipulated by the leaking device, just as in standard Boolean masking.

4.2   Application to Reduced LED

The previous section suggests that the RLUT countermeasure has high memory requirements, that strongly depend on the S-box size used in the block cipher to protect. In particular, given a N_r-round cipher with N_s S-boxes per round, the implementation of the RLUT countermeasure essentially requires storing:

- A *table map* that corresponds to all the a_i shares generated during precomputation, with memory cost estimated as $(N_s \cdot N_r) \cdot 2 + N_s$ n-bit words (where the factor 2 corresponds to the fact that excepted for the first round, the share a_1 in Algorithm 1 is always provided by the previous round).
- A *randomized program* that corresponds to the tables R and RC, with memory cost estimated as $N_r \cdot N_s$ tables of size $2^n \times n$ and $2^{2n} \times n$, respectively.

Note that operations G_i are never explicitly used during the cipher execution, but for the first round to mask, and last round to unmask after a secure computation is completed. Following these estimations, and as discussed in [18], it is natural to consider a cipher with 4-bit S-boxes for this purpose. In the following, we will consider reduced (16-bit) versions of the LED cipher illustrated in Fig. 6.

While such a cipher is naturally too small for being deployed in actual applications, we use it to refine our model for RLUT performance estimates. As will be discussed in the next sections, scaling to larger number of rounds and block

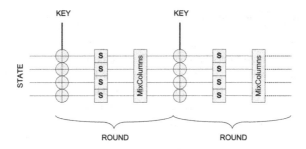

Fig. 6. Reduced version of the block cipher LED.

size (e.g. the full 64-bit LED cipher) will be possible in soon available 128- and 256-kilobyte versions of our FRAM microcontroller. In the figure, the 4-bit S-boxes of LED are denoted as S, and its linear diffusion layer as MixColumns.

4.3 Implementation in FRAM Microcontrollers

We now describe how to implement reduced (with up to 4 rounds) LED ciphers within the 16 kb of FRAM available in our MSP430FR microcontroller.

The first building block required in a RLUT-masked implementation is a randomness generator (needed to produce the a_i values of Algorithm 1). For illustration, we used a LFSR with CRC-32 polynomial for this purpose (alternative ways of generating randomness could of be considered, e.g. using a leakage-resilient PRG if leaking pre-computations are considered [5,17]).

Next, the part computing the randomized program can be implemented quite straightforwardly, following the description in Sect. 4.1. The trickiest bit was to efficiently arrange 4-bit outputs into memory bytes, without giving any unnecessary information on the RLUT input values[3]. Using one byte to store two consecutive RLUT outputs was rejected, since accessing one or the other value in the byte would have led to different code behaviors, depending on the LSB bit of the RLUT's input. Instead, we stored the outputs coming from two different RLUTs for the same input value in a single byte. This time, the LSB (resp. MSB) part of one byte will be accessed when an odd (resp. even) word of the state needs to be computed, giving no information on the word's value itself. Based on this strategy, the RLUTs R and RC can be generated efficiently from the cipher key, the S-Box and the table map, that are all stored in memory.

Eventually, the last piece of code concerns the execution of the block cipher itself. Again, the fact that the operations are performed on 4-bit words had to be taken into account while accessing the variables or tables stored in memory. One round of the reduced algorithm is executed by first reading the R and RC tables' outputs, corresponding to the cipher state and mask intermediate values. Then, the MixColumn layer is executed on each of the shares. It is implemented using an Xtime table, as suggested in the specifications of LED [8].

---

[3] This has no impact on the security in case of secure pre-computation, but may increase the information leakage in case of online randomization of the tables.

4.4   Results and Discussion

As described in Sect. 4.2, an estimation of the memory size required to store the table map and randomized program of the RLUT countermeasure can be derived from the number of rounds N_r, the number of S-Boxes per round N_s and the S-Box bit-size n. This estimation is illustrated by the dashed line of Fig. 7, in the case where $N_s = 4$, $n = 4$ and N_r varies from 1 to 4. A plain line representing the actual results we obtained for our implementation is also plotted. The two curves follow the same trend, with the offset separating them corresponding to the code size needed to implement the cipher itself (i.e. excluding the tables for which the memory requirements are growing with N_r - see the detailed results in Appendix A, Table 2). Interestingly, these results suggest that for any parameters N_r, N_s and n, the memory requirements needed to implement a block cipher protected with the RLUT countermeasure can be quite accurately predicted. For example, such an implementation for a full (64-bit) version of the block cipher LED (corresponding to $N_r = 32$, $N_s = 16$ and $n = 4$) would roughly require a memory size of 70 kb, and could therefore be implemented in the soon available 128-kilobyte FRAM microcontrollers.

The question of accurate predictions can also be asked for pre-computation time: estimates for this metric were similarly provided in [18]. Namely, the time needed to generate the RLUTs can be approximated with $((N_s.N_r).2 + N_s) + (N_s.N_r).2^n + (N_s.N_r).2^{2n}$ "elementary operations" (where the first term corresponds to randomness generation, and the later ones correspond to the refreshing of the R and RC tables). Our actual implementation results directly allow translating these "elementary operations" into a concrete number of clock cycles. The results in Fig. 8 (also reported in Appendix A, Table 3) again confirm a nice correlation with predictions. Namely, the main difference between both curves is a factor 40, which presumably corresponds to the number of cycles needed to perform each elementary operations. Extrapolating these results to the full (64-bit) version of the LED block cipher suggests pre-computation time complexities

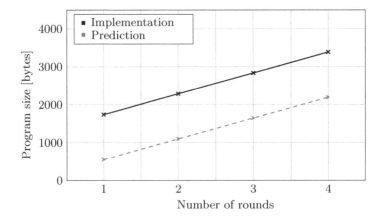

Fig. 7. Program size of the LED cipher protected with RLUTs.

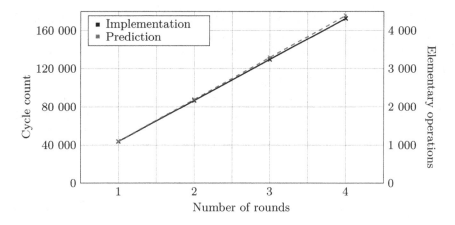

Fig. 8. Pre-computation time of the LED cipher protected with RLUTs.

around 140 000 elementary operations, corresponding to 5 600 000 cycles (i.e. an execution time of 35 ms at 16 MHz), which would be acceptable for some applications (and is likely to be improved with technology scaling).

Eventually, it is worth noticing that time and memory complexities could be reduced by exploiting some performance vs. security tradeoffs. A first solution would be an implementation for which only some rounds are masked with RLUTs, while the others use standard masking schemes. For example, one could protect only the first and last 4 rounds of (full, 64-bit) LED, i.e. 8 out of 32, resulting in an approximate reduction of the time and memory complexities down to 25 % of their original values. However, this solution may be risky in front of advanced attacks such as algebraic ones, that can exploit the leakage of the middle rounds [14]. Another approach to reduce the pre-computation time consists in refreshing only a fraction of the table map (and randomized program) after each cipher execution, and to perform this refreshing randomly. Interestingly, such a tradeoff would also take advantage of the non-volatile capacities of FRAM memories, since the complete randomized program could be pre-computed offline, while only a part of it would be modified online. It is flexible since the fraction of RLUTs modified per cipher executions could be adapted to the application requirements. As an illustration, modifying 10 % of the RLUTs in (full, 64-bit) LED would reduce the pre-computation time to approximately 560 000 cycles, which is getting close to the performances of a third-order masked AES (470 000 cycles in [15]). Combining the two approaches would of course be possible as well, e.g. by randomizing the first- and last-round tables in priority.

5   Conclusion

Our results put forward that FRAM is a promising technology in the context of side-channel resistant cryptographic hardware, since it enables the efficient implementation of various countermeasures taking advantage of pre-computations. The case of RLUTs is particularly relevant to illustrate this observation.

Indeed, they have never been implemented so far, they will soon be applicable to complete block ciphers, and may lead to high security levels for small embedded devices, independent of hardware assumptions that may be hard to fulfill. Important scopes for further investigations include the evaluation of the security levels obtained in the context of partially leaking pre-computations. In particular, analyzing the online refreshing of partially randomized programs mentioned in Sect. 4.4 would be very useful. Besides, the design of block ciphers that are well suited to implementations with RLUTs (e.g. with light(er) non-linear layers and strong(er) linear ones) is another interesting research avenue.

Acknowledgements. Stéphanie Kerckhof is a PhD student funded by a FRIA grant, Belgium. François-Xavier Standaert is a research associate of the Belgian Fund for Scientific Research (FNRS-F.R.S.). This work has been funded in parts by the Walloon region WIST program project MIPSs, by the European Commission through the ERC project 280141 (acronym CRASH) and by the European ISEC action grant HOME/2010/ISEC/AG/INT-011 B-CCENTRE.

A   RLUT Implementation Results

See Tables 2 and 3.

Table 2. Program size of the LED cipher protected with RLUTs (in bytes).

	Code size	Data size	Total
1 Round	1180	562	1742
2 Rounds	1180	1112	2292
3 Rounds	1180	1662	2842
4 Rounds	1180	2212	3392

Table 3. Cycle counts of the LED cipher protected with RLUTs.

	Randomness generation	RLUTs generation	LED execution	Total
1 Round	1422	41 910	404	43 736
2 Rounds	2208	83 807	642	86 657
3 Rounds	2991	125 716	883	129 590
4 Rounds	3770	167 617	1118	172 505

References

1. 51th Annual IEEE Symposium on Foundations of Computer Science FOCS 2010, Las Vegas, Nevada, USA, pp. 23–26. IEEE Computer Society, 23–26 October 2010
2. Brakerski, Z., Kalai, Y.T., Katz, J., Vaikuntanathan, V.: Overcoming the hole in the bucket: public-key cryptography resilient to continual memory leakage. In: FOCS [1], pp. 501–510

3. Chari, S., Jutla, C.S., Rao, J.R., Rohatgi, P.: Towards sound approaches to counteract power-analysis attacks. In: Wiener, M. (ed.) CRYPTO 1999. LNCS, vol. 1666, pp. 398–412. Springer, Heidelberg (1999)
4. Dodis, Y., Haralambiev, K., López-Alt, A., Wichs, D.: Cryptography against continuous memory attacks. In: FOCS [1], pp. 511–520
5. Dziembowski, S., Pietrzak, K.: Leakage-resilient cryptography. In: FOCS, pp. 293–302. IEEE Computer Society (2008)
6. Goldwasser, S., Kalai, Y.T., Rothblum, G.N.: One-time programs. In: Wagner, D. (ed.) CRYPTO 2008. LNCS, vol. 5157, pp. 39–56. Springer, Heidelberg (2008)
7. Grosso, V., Standaert, F.-X., Faust, S.: Masking vs. multiparty computation: how large is the gap for AES? In: Bertoni, G., Coron, J.-S. (eds.) CHES 2013. LNCS, vol. 8086, pp. 400–416. Springer, Heidelberg (2013)
8. Guo, J., Peyrin, T., Poschmann, A., Robshaw, M.: The LED block cipher. In: Preneel, B., Takagi, T. (eds.) CHES 2011. LNCS, vol. 6917, pp. 326–341. Springer, Heidelberg (2011)
9. Herbst, C., Oswald, E., Mangard, S.: An AES smart card implementation resistant to power analysis attacks. In: Zhou, J., Yung, M., Bao, F. (eds.) ACNS 2006. LNCS, vol. 3989, pp. 239–252. Springer, Heidelberg (2006)
10. Mangard, S., Oswald, E., Popp, T.: Power Analysis Attacks - Revealing the Secrets of Smart Cards. Springer, New York (2007)
11. Mangard, S., Popp, T., Gammel, B.M.: Side-channel leakage of masked CMOS gates. In: Menezes, A. (ed.) CT-RSA 2005. LNCS, vol. 3376, pp. 351–365. Springer, Heidelberg (2005)
12. Medwed, M., Standaert, F.-X., Großschädl, J., Regazzoni, F.: Fresh re-keying: security against side-channel and fault attacks for low-cost devices. In: Bernstein, D.J., Lange, T. (eds.) AFRICACRYPT 2010. LNCS, vol. 6055, pp. 279–296. Springer, Heidelberg (2010)
13. Poettering, B., Furious, R.: http://point-at-infinity.org/avraes/
14. Renauld, M., Standaert, F.-X.: Algebraic side-channel attacks. In: Bao, F., Yung, M., Lin, D., Jing, J. (eds.) Inscrypt 2009. LNCS, vol. 6151, pp. 393–410. Springer, Heidelberg (2010)
15. Rivain, M., Prouff, E.: Provably secure higher-order masking of AES. In: Mangard, S., Standaert, F.-X. (eds.) CHES 2010. LNCS, vol. 6225, pp. 413–427. Springer, Heidelberg (2010)
16. Rivain, M., Prouff, E., Doget, J.: Higher-order masking and shuffling for software implementations of block ciphers. In: Clavier, C., Gaj, K. (eds.) CHES 2009. LNCS, vol. 5747, pp. 171–188. Springer, Heidelberg (2009)
17. Standaert, F.-X., Pereira, O., Yu, Y.: Leakage-resilient symmetric cryptography under empirically verifiable assumptions. In: Canetti, R., Garay, J.A. (eds.) CRYPTO 2013, Part I. LNCS, vol. 8042, pp. 335–352. Springer, Heidelberg (2013)
18. Standaert, F.-X., Petit, C., Veyrat-Charvillon, N.: Masking with randomized look up tables. In: Naccache, D. (ed.) Cryphtography and Security: From Theory to Applications. LNCS, vol. 6805, pp. 283–299. Springer, Heidelberg (2012)
19. Standaert, F.-X., Veyrat-Charvillon, N., Oswald, E., Gierlichs, B., Medwed, M., Kasper, M., Mangard, S.: The world is not enough: another look on second-order DPA. In: Abe, M. (ed.) ASIACRYPT 2010. LNCS, vol. 6477, pp. 112–129. Springer, Heidelberg (2010)
20. Veyrat-Charvillon, N., Medwed, M., Kerckhof, S., Standaert, F.-X.: Shuffling against side-channel attacks: a comprehensive study with cautionary note. In: Wang, X., Sako, K. (eds.) ASIACRYPT 2012. LNCS, vol. 7658, pp. 740–757. Springer, Heidelberg (2012)

Attacks on Masking - Session Chair: Michael Hutter

Low Entropy Masking Schemes, Revisited

Vincent Grosso[1]([✉]), François-Xavier Standaert[1], and Emmanuel Prouff[2]

[1] ICTEAM/ELEN/Crypto Group, Université catholique de Louvain,
Louvain-la-Neuve, Belgium
vincent.Grosso@uclouvain.be
[2] ANSSI, 51 Bd de la Tour-Maubourg, 75700 Paris 07 SP, France

Abstract. Low Entropy Masking Schemes (LEMS) are a recent countermeasure against side-channel attacks. They aim at reducing the randomness requirements of masking schemes under certain (adversarial and
implementation) conditions. Previous works have put forward the interest of this approach when such conditions are met. We complement these
investigations by analyzing LEMS against adversaries and implementations that deviate from their expected behavior, in a realistic manner.
Our conclusions are contrasted: they confirm the theoretical interest of
the countermeasure, while suggesting that its exploitation in actual products may be risky, because of hard(er) to control hardware assumptions.

1 Introduction

Masking is a frequently considered countermeasure against side-channel attacks.
In a masked implementation, any sensitive data is split into several shares, and
all the computations are performed on the shared values only. For this purpose,
the algorithm must be written in a way that is consistent with this representation of the sensitive data. The resulting process, usually called d-sharing scheme
when the data is split in d shares, is expected to provide improved physical
security since: (i) more "points of interest" (i.e. more dimensions in the leakage distribution) may have to be identified and exploited concurrently by the
adversary, and (ii) if the masking scheme is carefully implemented (i.e. if the
leakages of all the shares are independent), higher-order moments of the leakage
distribution have to be estimated to reveal key-dependent information. The latter property is known as the "d-1th-order SCA security" [4]. It has been shown
that the data complexity of a successful attack against such an implementation
increases exponentially with the number of shares (first in the restricted context of single-bit DPA[3], then experimentally in more general contexts [13], and
more recently using the mutual information put forward in [12] as evaluation
metric [9]).

Quite naturally, a central condition for this SCA security guarantees to hold
is that all the shares are uniformly distributed, which implies strong randomness requirements in masked implementations [5]. Starting from this observation, a recent line of works - denoted as Low Entropy Masking Schemes (LEMS)
in the following- has investigated possibilities to maintain the security order

A. Francillon and P. Rohatgi (Eds.): CARDIS 2013, LNCS 8419, pp. 33–43, 2014.
DOI: 10.1007/978-3-319-08302-5_3, © Springer International Publishing Switzerland 2014

of masked implementations with reduced randomness requirements [1,2,7,8]. LEMS can be seen as 2-sharing schemes, with the particularity that any n-bit sensitive value x is randomized with a mask variable M chosen within a subset (aka code) of the 2^n possible masks. In this setting, preserved security orders can be obtained with reduced randomness requirements under two important conditions:

1. *Adversarial condition.* The attacks performed are only univariate, i.e. they exploit exclusively the leakage of the masked value $x \oplus M$.
2. *Implementation condition.* The leakage function's deterministic part is linear in the bits of $x \oplus M$ (such as, e.g. for the Hamming weight function).

These results directly raise the question whether such conditions are realistic - i.e. whether LEMS can give rise to actual security improvements in practical scenarios. In order to answer this question, this paper provides a systematic evaluation of these assumptions, leading to two main results.

1. *On the adversarial condition.* In general, it is of course natural to consider multivariate attacks, since the shares used in any masked implementation have to be generated on chip, which possibly leaks information. We analyze such bivariate attacks and show that despite the reduced number of masks, LEMS still provide first-order security in this case (with a slight security degradation). We further confirm that if an adversary is limited (for some reasons) to univariate attacks, LEMS allow ensuring security orders of 2 or 3, as previously demonstrated by Carlet et al. [2] and Nassar et al. [8].
2. *On the implementation condition.* We show that as soon as the leakage function's deterministic part deviates from a purely linear one, the security guarantees provided by LEMS vanish, even in the univariate attack context. We further illustrate that the security order of the countermeasure is reduced according to the degree of the leakage function, e.g. that a quadratic leakage function is less damaging than a cubic one, quartic one, ... and additionally provide an explanation of this phenomenon (see Sect. 3.2).

Summarizing, the first (adversarial) condition may not be a too big issue in practice. Given that maximum 2-share implementations are considered[1], LEMS are a theoretically relevant solution to mask under the assumption of linear leakage functions, since it maintains the security order of univariate (resp. bivariate) attacks to two or three (resp. one). By contrast the second (implementation) condition seems more difficult to fulfill, since the shape of a leakage function is typically hard to control by cryptographic designers. We conclude that despite its theoretical interest, the deployment of LEMS in actual embedded devices should be considered with care, and standard masking schemes are generally safer to implement because of easier-to-verify hardware assumptions.

---

[1] Current results in LEMS do not provide generalizations to more shares.

2   Background

2.1   Univariate vs. Multivariate / 1st-Order vs. Higher-Order Attacks

Let X be a sensitive variable and $\mathbf{L} = [L_1, L_2, \ldots, L_d]$ be a leakage trace. A side-channel attack typically exploits the conditional distributions $\Pr[X|\mathbf{L}]$ in order to recover information about X. We say that the attack is univariate if it exploits unidimensional leakage vectors $\mathbf{L} = [L_1]$. We say that the attack is bivariate if it exploits bidimensional leakage vectors $\mathbf{L} = [L_1, L_2]$. More generally, the attack is said to be d-variate if it exploits multidimensional leakage vectors with d samples $\mathbf{L} = [L_1, L_2, \ldots, L_d]$. Note that finding the samples of interest in a leakage trace is usually challenging, which may be a reason for some adversaries to restrict themselves to univariate attacks when it is possible. Of course, leaving leakage samples aside may only result in a loss of information, hence a suboptimal attack.

Independent of the dimensionality of the leakage distribution, the order of a side-channel attack relates to the smallest (mixed) statistical moment that leaks sensitive information. For this purpose, we use the following definitions:

Definition 1 (Central moment of order d). *Let X be a random variable, then the central moment of order d of X is defined by:*

$$\mathsf{E}((X - \mathsf{E}(X))^d),$$

Definition 2 (Central mixed moment of orders $d_1, \ldots, d_r$). *Let $\{X_i\}_{i=1}^r$ be a set of r random variables, then the central mixed moment of orders $d_1, \ldots, d_r$ of $\{X_i\}_{i=1}^r$ is defined by:*

$$\mathsf{E}((X_1 - \mathsf{E}(X_1))^{d_1} \times \cdots \times (X_r - \mathsf{E}(X_r))^{d_r}).$$

In both definitions, $\mathsf{E}(.)$ denotes the expectation operator. For simplicity, we will sometimes denote the integer value $d = \sum_i d_i$ as the order of the central mixed moment of a tuple $(X_i)_{i=1..r}$. Central moments are typically used in univariate attacks (e.g against hardware implementations, where the different shares of a masked implementation are manipulated in parallel). Central *mixed* moments are typically used in multivariate attacks (e.g. against software implementations, where the different shares of a masked implementation are processed sequentially). Intuitively, the dimensionality of an attack has a direct impact on its time complexity (since it determines the number of samples on which the distinguisher has to be applied). By contrast the order of an attack mainly relate to its data complexity (since the number of measurements required to estimate a statistical moment increases with the order of this moment) [3,9].

2.2   Low Entropy Masking Schemes

As detailed in the introduction, the main goal of LEMS is to guarantee high security orders for masked implementations, with less randomness requirements than traditional masking schemes. For this purpose, the mask M (which is bit-wise added to the sensitive datum s) is chosen as part of a sub-set of the definition set of s. Different solutions have been published in the literature. In the rest of the paper, we will use the code proposed in [1], next referred to as C_{16}, and to the one proposed in [8], next referred to as C_{12}. Both subsets are designed for 8-bit sensitive values (i.e. are typically applicable to protect the registers of 8-bit devices). Following previous analyzes, LEMS with C_{12} is expected to provide security against first- and second-order attacks, while LEMS with C_{16} is expected to provide security against first-, second- and third-order attacks (under the adversarial and implementation conditions stated in introduction). Codes are specified as: $C_{12} = \{0x03, 0x18, 0x3f, 0x55, 0x60, 0x6e, 0x8c, 0xa5, 0xb2, 0xcb, 0xd6, 0xf9\}$, $C_{16} = \{0x10, 0x1f, 0x26, 0x29, 0x43, 0x4c, 0x75, 0x7a, 0x85, 0x8a, 0xb3, 0xbc,$ $0xd6, 0xd9, 0xe0, 0xef\}$. Both were selected amongst the lowest size set that provides the required security order, while the first one minimizes the mutual information metric defined in the next subsection as additional criteria.

2.3   Evaluation Framework

We will analyze the LEMS countermeasure based on the evaluation framework introduced in [12], which holds in two main steps. First, an Information Theoretic (IT) analysis is performed, in order to analyze the leakages independent of the adversary exploiting them. It is aimed to capture the quality of a countermeasure in a worst-case scenario. Next, a security analysis is performed, in order to evaluate the actual data complexity required by an adversary to exploit the available leakage (e.g. in order to turn it into a key recovery). For this purpose, we will consider the following simulated leakages. Let s be a sensitive value (i.e. the target of the attack), M a variable representing a word of the code used to protect the sensitive value, and N_1, N_2 two normally distributed noise variables, with mean 0 and variance σ^2. We define our leakages as:

$$L_1 = \mathsf{L}(s \oplus M) + N_1,$$
$$L_2 = \mathsf{L}(M) + N_2,$$

where $\mathsf{L}(.)$ is a polynomial in the bits of the input. In the following, we will assume this polynomial to be the Hamming weight function (excepted in Subsect. 3.2, where we will consider higher-degree polynomials). Furthermore, we will consider both univariate attacks exploiting only the leakage sample L_1, and bivariate attacks exploiting L_1 and L_2 jointly[2]. This implies computing the following information theoretic metric in the univariate case:

$$\mathrm{PI}(S; L_1) = \mathrm{H}[S] - \sum_{s \in \mathcal{S}} \Pr[s] \sum_{l_1 \in \mathcal{L}} \Pr_{\text{chip}}[l_1|s] \cdot \log_2 \Pr_{\text{model}}[s|l_1],$$

---

[2] Note that the univariate attacks considered in LEMS are different than the classical univariate higher-order DPAs, where a combination of the two leakage samples (e.g. their normalized product) is exploited by the adversary [10]. Any such combination would provide leakages and successful attacks similar to the ones of a bivariate attack, with an information loss similar to the one investigated in [13].

and its extension to two dimensions in the bivariate case:

$$\text{PI}(S; L_1, L_2) = \text{H}[S] - \sum_{s \in \mathcal{S}} \Pr[s] \sum_{l_1, l_2 \in \mathcal{L}} \Pr_{\text{chip}}[l_1, l_2 | s] \cdot \log_2 \Pr_{\text{model}}[s | l_1, l_2].$$

Let us denote the probability density function of a Gaussian distribution taken on input x, with mean μ (resp. mean vector $\boldsymbol{\mu}$) and variance σ^2 (resp. covariance matrix Σ) as $\mathcal{N}(x | \mu, \sigma^2)$ (resp. $\mathcal{N}(x | \boldsymbol{\mu}, \Sigma)$). We will generally compute the probabilities in these equations as follows (e.g. in the bivariate case):

$$\Pr_{\text{model}}[s | l_1, l_2] = \frac{\mathcal{N}(l_1, l_2 | \boldsymbol{\mu}_s, \Sigma_s)}{\sum_{s^* \in \mathcal{S}} \mathcal{N}(l_1, l_2 | \boldsymbol{\mu}_{s^*}, \Sigma_{s^*})}, \tag{1}$$

for unprotected implementations, and:

$$\Pr_{\text{model}}[s | l_1, l_2] = \frac{\sum_{m^* \in C} \mathcal{N}(l_1, l_2 | \boldsymbol{\mu}_{s, m^*}, \Sigma_{s, m^*})}{\sum_{s^* \in \mathcal{S}} \sum_{m^* \in C} \mathcal{N}(l_1, l_2 | \boldsymbol{\mu}_{s^*, m^*}, \Sigma_{s^*, m^*})}, \tag{2}$$

for masked implementations (and similarly for LEMS), with all the secrets and masks distributed uniformly over their specified set. That is, the leakage distributions conditioned on the sensitive values will be modeled as Gaussian mixtures, where each mode corresponds to a mask value. Following the discussion in [11] and since we are considering simulated experiments, the probability distributions $\Pr_{\text{chip}}$ and $\Pr_{\text{model}}$ will be identical in most of our evaluations. This implies that the Perceived Information (PI) will be identical to the (classical) Mutual Information (MI) in most cases. As only exception, we will also evaluate the information leakage of a suboptimal bivariate adversary, who models leakage distributions conditioned on the sensitive values as single (bivariate) Gaussians, i.e. who simplifies Eq. 2 into Eq. 1, even in the masked case. This boils down to summarizing the second-order information in the covariance between the leakage samples l_1 and l_2. By plotting the MI/PI metrics in function of the noise variance, we can directly obtain intuition about the order of the masking, which simply corresponds to the slope of these curves [13].

Following the information theoretic analysis, we will apply a security analysis and compute the success rate (as defined in [12]) of template attacks against the target s, using $\Pr_{\text{model}}[s | l_1]$ and $\Pr_{\text{model}}[s | l_1, l_2]$ as leakage models. This will allow us to evaluate the data complexities of these worst-case attacks in Sect. 4.

3   Information Theoretic Analysis of LEMS

3.1   Hamming Weight Leakages

Our IT analysis of LEMS and its comparison with other masking schemes are in Fig. 1, from which the following observations can be extracted.

Starting with the univariate case (in the left part of the figure), we first observe that information leakage is only available if a strict subset of the 2^n possible masks is available (e.g. the curves —×— and —▪— are stuck to zero in

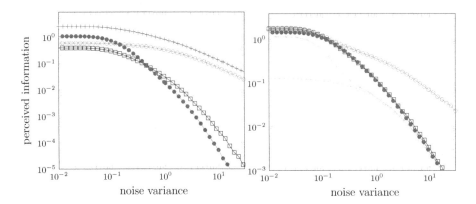

Fig. 1. Information theoretic analysis of different masking schemes. Left: univariate attacks. Right: bivariate attacks. The curve ⊹⊹ is for the unprotected case. The curves ⊟ ● ⊝ are for LEMS with C_{12}, C_{16} and a badly chosen code, respectively. The curve ‑‑‑ is for masking with the full set (only non-zero in the bivariate case). The curve is for the bivariate attack using approximated Gaussian templates (in place of Gaussian mixtures) for masking with the full set.

this case, hence not represented in this part of the figure). We also note that a badly chosen code (e.g. $C = \{0x00, 0x01, 0x02, \ldots, 0x0B\}$) leads to first-order univariate weaknesses for the LEMS countermeasure, as witnessed by the slope of the curve ⊝ that is parallel to the one of the unprotected implementation ⊹. This confirms the requirement to use uniform randomness in the security proofs of standard masking schemes, e.g. [6,9]. By contrast and as expected, the LEMS countermeasure with codes C_{12} and C_{16} enforces second- and third-order security against univariate side-channel attacks (i.e. curve ⊟ has slope 3 and curve ● has slope 4). Interestingly, we also see that C_{12} leads to a slightly smaller information leakage than C_{16} for low noise values - which is also expected since minimizing the information leakages was considered as an additional optimization criteria in the selection of C_{12} only.

Next in the bivariate case, we first observe that most attacks (i.e. using all masks with Gaussian or Gaussian mixture modeling, and using C_{12} or C_{16}) converge towards the same slope as the noise increases. The slope of these curves is 2 implying first-order security in all these cases The curve ⊝ is again a counter-example, because of a badly chosen code. So an important conclusion is that the first (adversarial) condition mentioned in introduction for LEMS to provide improved security against univariate attacks does not imply a penalty in the security order when considering bivariate attacks. By contrast, we observe a small security degradation for small noise values, i.e. a constant information leakage loss between curves ⊟ ● and ‑‑‑, similar to the difference between C_{12} and C_{16} in univariate attacks. Interestingly, we also observe the impact of incorrect modeling for these small noise values. That is, when considering Gaussian mixture leakage models - as for curve ‑ - we see a "wave" in the information theoretic curve that is not found when simplifying the mixtures into a simpler Gaussian model - as for curve ─○─ . This wave can be explained by the fact that characterizing the full distribution with a Gaussian mixture allows exploiting higher-order moments that are easy to estimate for low noise values (and hard to estimate with more noise). By contrast, the Gaussian modeling only exploits two statistical moments (i.e. mean vector, covariance matrix), leading to less (and more regular) information leakage. A similar reason makes the Gaussian modeling impossible to apply to univariate attacks against LEMS with C_{12} and C_{16}: since such attacks only leak in the third- and fourth-order moments of the conditional leakage distributions, a Gaussian model with only two statistical moments will not be able to characterize this information.

3.2   Polynomial Leakages

The previous subsection provided IT curves under the assumption that the implementation constraint mentioned in introduction is fulfilled. Since such a constraint may be difficult to verify in practice, we now investigate the consequences of a leakage function deviating from purely linear. For this purpose, we replace the previously used Hamming weight leakage function by a polynomial of higher degree. Such a polynomial is of the form $\mathsf{L}(s) := \sum_i a_i s_i + \sum_i \sum_j b_{i,j} s_i \times s_j + \sum_i \sum_j \sum_k c_{i,j,k} s_i \times s_j \times s_k$, where s_i denotes the ith bit of the sensitive value s, and a_i, $b_{i,j}$ and $c_{i,j,k}$ are some constants. For simplicity, we will consider the case where $\forall i \; a_i = a \in \{0,1\}$, $\forall i,j \; b_{i,j} = b \in \{0,1\}$ and $\forall i,j,k \; c_{i,j,k} = c \in \{0,1\}$.

The results of our investigations in this advanced context are plotted in Fig. 2. The main conclusion is that the security guarantee claimed by LEMS does not hold in this case. Interestingly, we can even observe a relation between the degree

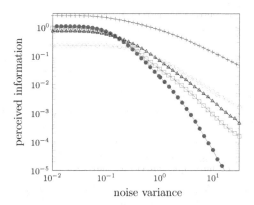

Fig. 2. IT analysis for polynomial leakage functions and LEMS with C_{16}. The curve ─●─ is for the Hamming weight leakage function. The curve ─□─ is for the leakage function with a = 0, b = 1 and c = 0. The curve ─○─ is for the leakage function with a = 0, b = 0 and c = 1. The curve ─▲─ is for the leakage function with a = 1, b = 1 and c = 1. The curve ─+─ is for the unprotected case in the previous subsection.

of the leakage function polynomial and the security order. Namely, the higher the degree, the lower the order - see, e.g. curves —□— —◇— —▲—. This relation can be explained as follows. Say the leakage corresponding to $s \oplus M$ in the LEMS countermeasure only contains information in its fourth-order moment (as for C_{16}). Since M is not uniform, we know that raising this leakage to the fourth power, i.e. computing $(\mathsf{L}_{\mathrm{lin}}(s \oplus M) + N_1)^4$ will lead to first-order information, while raising the noise to the fourth power as well. Say now the leakage function is not linear anymore, but quartic. Then the same first-order information will be found in samples of the form $\mathsf{L}_{\mathrm{quart}}(s \oplus M) + N_1$, i.e. without amplifying the noise. More generally, if the leakage function only contains terms of a single degree, the security order of LEMS will be divided accordingly. For example, the curve —◇— for which L has degree 3 has slope $4/3$, the curve —□— for which L has degree 2 has slope $4/2{=}2$, ... As for leakage functions with terms of various degrees, the situation is intermediate, e.g. the curve —▲— for which L has degree 3 but contains terms of degree 1 and 2, has slope between the previous ones.

4   Security Analysis of LEMS

We now confirm the previous IT evaluations with security analyses. For this purpose, we compute 1st-order success rates (as defined in [12]) estimated over 10000 independent experiments, in various scenarios. These results aim to translate information leakages into a number of measurements to recover the key. Note that higher-order success rates could be considered as well (to express the trade-off between time and data complexities in side-channel attacks). However, they do not reveal more intuition regarding the security of LEMS vs. masking.

4.1   Univariate Attacks

Our first experiments correspond to univariate template attacks with different noise levels, and are given in Fig. 3. A preliminary observation is that, as in the previous section, Gaussian templates are not able to exploit information in this case (i.e. only Gaussian mixture models lead to successful key recoveries). Next and more importantly, the two parts of the figure clearly illustrate that the impact of estimating higher-order statistical moments in masking and LEMS mostly reveals itself as noise increases (as already highlighted in [13]). That is, the difference between the success rates attacking an unprotected implementation vs. LEMS with C_{12} or C_{16} is more significant in the right part of the figure. This confirms the information theoretic evaluations in the previous section, where the slope of the different curves also becomes stable as noise increases.

As additional experiment, we also wanted to test the usual intuition that the success rate of a template attack is highly correlated with the information leakage measured with the PI estimated thanks to the same (here Gaussian mixture) leakage model. For this purpose, it is interesting to observe that the IT curves corresponding to LEMS with C_{12} and C_{16} intersect in the left part of Fig. 1. Therefore, we launched template attacks against these two countermeasures,

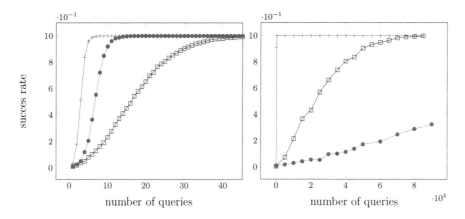

Fig. 3. Univariate template attacks with Gaussian mixture leakage model. Left: $\sigma^2 = 10^{-4}$. Right $\sigma^2 = 10$. The curves —□— are for LEMS with C_{12}. The curves —•— are for LEMS with C_{16}. The curves —+— are for the unprotected implementation.

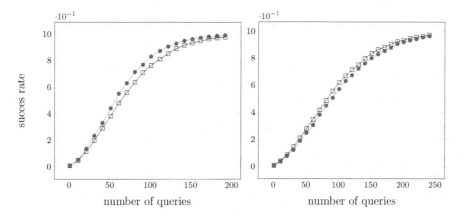

Fig. 4. Univariate template attacks with Gaussian mixture leakage model. Left: $\sigma^2 = 0.4$. Right $\sigma^2 = 0.5$. The curves —□— and —•— are for LEMS with C_{12} and C_{16}.

with noise variance just left ($\sigma^2 = 0.4$) and right ($\sigma^2 = 0.5$) of this intersection. The results of these attacks are plotted in Fig. 4, were we indeed observe that the success rate is slightly higher (resp. lower) when using codes C_{12} and C_{16}, depending on the noise. That is, LEMS with C_{16} delivers more information at low noise levels, but has higher security order, and consequently becomes less informative when enough noise is present in the measurements.

4.2   Bivariate Attacks

To conclude this work, we also paid attention to the efficiency of bivariate template attacks with Gaussian mixture modeling, as reported in Fig. 5. Here,

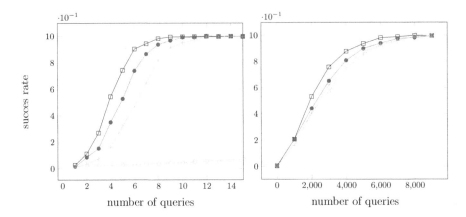

Fig. 5. Bivariate template attacks with Gaussian mixture leakage model. Left: $\sigma^2 = 10^{-4}$. Right $\sigma^2 = 10$. The curves —□— are for LEMS with C_{12}. The curves —●— are for LEMS with C_{16}. The curves —— and —— are for masking with the full set, using Gaussian and Gaussian mixture leakage modeling, respectively.

the most revealing feature is that, as already indicated by the information theoretic analysis in the right part of Fig. 1, both LEMS and masking with the full set have the same security order. As a result, the impact of noise on the separation between the success rate curves is the opposite of the one in the previous subsection. Namely, as noise increases, these curves get closer. This effect is particularly significant in attacks using Gaussian modeling, i.e. curves —— - because it implies a significant loss of information for low noise values (see Fig. 1). Besides, and as they all correspond to the estimation of a second-order moment in the leakage probability distribution, the data complexity of these attacks is naturally lower than the one when considering univariate attacks against LEMS with C_{12} and C_{16} in Fig. 3. This eventually confirms that while LEMS indeed provides interesting security guarantees against univariate attacks, their worst-case security level is only obtained by analyzing bivariate ones.

5   Wrapping Up

The consequences of our analysis for LEMS are contrasted. First, while its adversarial condition may not always be practically relevant, the investigations in Sects. 3.1 and 4.2 suggest that the countermeasure remains an interesting alternative to mask with reduced randomness requirements, even if adversaries exploit bivariate leakages (as there is no penalty for the security order in this case). By contrast, the observations in Sect. 3.2 suggest that the security of LEMS is highly dependent on the (hard to control) leakage function. In particular, the apparition of higher-degree terms in this function directly implies an exploitable penalty in the security order of the countermeasure.

Acknowledgments. Work funded in parts by the European Commission through the ERC project 280141 (acronym CRASH) and the European ISEC action grant HOME/2010/ISEC/AG/INT-011 B-CCENTRE project. F.-X. Standaert is an associate researcher of the Belgian Fund for Scientific Research (FNRS-F.R.S.).

References

1. Bhasin, F., Carlet, C., Guilley, S.: Theory of masking with codewords in hardware: low-weight dth-order correlation-immune boolean functions. Cryptology ePrint Archive, Report 2013/303 (2013). http://eprint.iacr.org/
2. Carlet, C., Danger, J.-L., Guilley, S., Maghrebi, H.: Leakage squeezing of order two. In: Galbraith, S., Nandi, M. (eds.) INDOCRYPT 2012. LNCS, vol. 7668, pp. 120–139. Springer, Heidelberg (2012)
3. Chari, S., Jutla, ChS, Rao, J.R., Rohatgi, P.: Towards sound approaches to counteract power-analysis attacks. In: Wiener, M. (ed.) CRYPTO 1999. LNCS, vol. 1666, p. 398. Springer, Heidelberg (1999)
4. Coron, J.-S., Prouff, E., Rivain, M.: Side channel cryptanalysis of a higher order masking scheme. In: Paillier, P., Verbauwhede, I. (eds.) CHES 2007. LNCS, vol. 4727, pp. 28–44. Springer, Heidelberg (2007)
5. Grosso, V., Standaert, F.-X., Faust, S.: Masking vs. multiparty computation: how large is the gap for AES? In: Bertoni, G., Coron, J.-S. (eds.) CHES 2013. LNCS, vol. 8086, pp. 400–416. Springer, Heidelberg (2013)
6. Ishai, Y., Sahai, A., Wagner, D.: Private circuits: securing hardware against probing attacks. In: Boneh, D. (ed.) CRYPTO 2003. LNCS, vol. 2729, pp. 463–481. Springer, Heidelberg (2003)
7. Maghrebi, H., Guilley, S., Danger, J.-L.: Leakage squeezing countermeasure against high-order attacks. In: Ardagna, C.A., Zhou, J. (eds.) WISTP 2011. LNCS, vol. 6633, pp. 208–223. Springer, Heidelberg (2011)
8. Nassar, M., Guilley, S., Danger, J.-L.: Formal analysis of the entropy / security trade-off in first-order masking countermeasures against side-channel attacks. In: Bernstein, D.J., Chatterjee, S. (eds.) INDOCRYPT 2011. LNCS, vol. 7107, pp. 22–39. Springer, Heidelberg (2011)
9. Prouff, E., Rivain, M.: Masking against side-channel attacks: a formal security proof. In: Johansson, T., Nguyen, P.Q. (eds.) EUROCRYPT 2013. LNCS, vol. 7881, pp. 142–159. Springer, Heidelberg (2013)
10. Prouff, E., Rivain, M., Bevan, R.: Statistical analysis of second order differential power analysis. IEEE Trans. Comput. **58**(6), 799–811 (2009)
11. Renauld, M., Standaert, F.-X., Veyrat-Charvillon, N., Kamel, D., Flandre, D.: A formal study of power variability issues and side-channel attacks for nanoscale devices. In: Paterson, K.G. (ed.) EUROCRYPT 2011. LNCS, vol. 6632, pp. 109–128. Springer, Heidelberg (2011)
12. Standaert, F.-X., Malkin, T.G., Yung, M.: A unified framework for the analysis of side-channel key recovery attacks. In: Joux, A. (ed.) EUROCRYPT 2009. LNCS, vol. 5479, pp. 443–461. Springer, Heidelberg (2009)
13. Standaert, F.-X., Veyrat-Charvillon, N., Oswald, E., Gierlichs, B., Medwed, M., Kasper, M., Mangard, S.: The world is not enough: another look on second-order DPA. In: Abe, M. (ed.) ASIACRYPT 2010. LNCS, vol. 6477, pp. 112–129. Springer, Heidelberg (2010)

On the Vulnerability
of Low Entropy Masking Schemes

Xin Ye[(✉)] and Thomas Eisenbarth

Worcester Polytechnic Institute, Worcester, MA, USA
{xye,teisenbarth}@wpi.edu

Abstract. Low Entropy Masking Schemes (LEMS) have been proposed
to offer a reasonable tradeoff between the good protection against side-
channel attacks offered by masking countermeasures and the high overhead that results from their implementation. Besides the limited analysis
done in the original proposals of LEMS, their specific leakage characteristics have not yet been analyzed. This work explores the leakage behavior
of these countermeasures and shows two different methods how the leakage can be exploited, even by generic univariate attacks. In particular,
an attack that exploits specific properties of RSM for AES as well as a
more generic attack making very little assumptions about the underlying LEMS are introduced. All attacks are practically verified by applying
them to publicly available leakage samples of the RSM countermeasure.

1   Motivation

Side channel attacks such as Power and EM analysis are still a major concern
for embedded cryptographic solutions, in particular for cryptographic
smart cards. One of the earliest and most studied countermeasure techniques
is *masking* [4,7,20]. Masking, if done correctly, significantly increases the complexity of a successful attack. Results go as far as proving the impossibility
of first-order attacks for appropriately masked implementations and leakages
covered in the corresponding assumptions. This means that the simplest and
probably most popular attacks such as classical DPA [8], CPA [3] and MIA [6]
become impractical or in many cases even infeasible.

One major drawback of masking schemes is the significant overhead needed
for their realization, especially for popular ciphers such as the AES. Computational overheads are usually significant and are due to mask processing and
other adjusted computation such as just-in-time recomputation of look-up tables,
or their redundant storage. In addition, masking schemes usually assume uniformly distributed random masks, i.e. a sufficiently good randomness generator
has to be implemented and queried in addition to the protected cryptographic
scheme. Hence, masking usually adds significant time and space overhead to
cryptographic implementations in both hardware and software. Motivated by
this overhead is the idea of reducing the entropy of the mask. Using fewer mask
values can reduce the number of special cases that have to be handled by the

A. Francillon and P. Rohatgi (Eds.): CARDIS 2013, LNCS 8419, pp. 44–60, 2014.
DOI: 10.1007/978-3-319-08302-5_4, © Springer International Publishing Switzerland 2014

implementation, allowing for a possible tradeoff between side channel resistance and performance. While one could argue that this is a common approach in protecting logic styles [15], only limited work has been proposed to apply low-entropy masking at the architecture level [2, 12, 13]. These works claim that first-order attacks are still prevented. However, while analysis of masking logic styles suggests remaining leakage [17], no deeper analysis of possible weaknesses has been performed. This work takes a first systematic step in that direction.

Contribution. In this paper we formalize low entropy masking schemes and reveal the vulnerability of their limited protection. We propose two leakage composition based attacks to show how to exploit the weakened leakage even by univariate adversaries. Experiments are performed on a software implementation of Rotating Sboxes Masking (RSM) to verify the validity of the proposed attacks.

The rest of the paper is organized as follows: Sect. 2 reviews the low entropy masking schemes and gives the adversarial model for these schemes; Sect. 3 introduces the leakage distribution decomposition attack (LDDA); Sect. 4 proposes the leaking set collision attack (LSCA); experiments are carried out in Sect. 5 to verify LDDA and LSCA using measurements from DPA contest V4; and finally conclusions are made in Sect. 6.

2   Background

In the following we give a detailed definition of low-entropy masking schemes and the assumed adversarial model and show why low-entropy masking schemes can thwart standard attacks like DPA and CPA.

2.1   Low Entropy Masking Schemes

Low entropy masking schemes (LEMS) are a countermeasure against side channel attacks (SCA). Like other masking schemes, they try to randomize the observed leakage by applying random values to intermediate states. However, the size of the mask alphabet is reduced, resulting in a limited extend of randomization of leaking states. For example, for a LEMS protected implementation of AES, the mask set $\mathcal{M}$ is a strict subset of $\{0, 1\}^8$ such that the number of applicable mask values is much smaller than 256. The Rotating SBoxes Masking (RSM) scheme proposed in [13] is a realization of LEMS. It is a Boolean masking scheme that uses 16 mask values uniformly at random to protect AES internal states. In general, we denote the set of masks $\mathcal{M} = \{m_1, m_2, ..., m_s\} \subset \mathbb{F}_2^n$. We say a LEMS has masking entropy of $\log s$ if mask values are chosen uniformly at random from this set. The RSM is therefore said to have 4 bits of mask entropy. Furthermore, authors in [12] proposed a selection criterion of optimal mask values for LEMS. According to this guideline the following 16 byte values (written in hex format) are used as the mask set in the DPA contest V4.

$$\mathcal{M} = \{00, 0F, 36, 39, 53, 5C, 65, 6A, 95, 9A, A3, AC, C6, C9, F0, FF\}$$

The 16 chosen values form an $[8, 4, 4]$ linear code. It is therefore not surprising that they satisfies the *self-complementary* property: $\overline{\mathcal{M}} = \mathcal{M}$. Namely, $m \in \mathcal{M}$ if and only if $\bar{m} \in \mathcal{M}$, where $\bar{m}$ is the bitwise inversion of m.

The benefit of applying LEMS lies in the fact that it saves lots of computation when compared to a full entropy masking scheme (FEMS) where $s = 2^n$. The latter usually suffers from the huge amount of additional computation as a consequence of repeated masking/de-masking for the non-linear operation of a block cipher (e.g. Sbox in AES). One example is the Generalized Look-Up Table countermeasure proposed in [16]. It increases the size of a single Sbox sufficiently to make parallelized implementation of AES on FPGAs infeasible. However, with fewer masks, the total number of necessary extra-computations can be kept at an acceptable level or even completed from pre-computations (e.g. defining masked sbox as look up tables). In short, LEMS enables more efficient implementation of a masking countermeasure. Unavoidably, applying LEMS causes some loss of protection when compared to FEMS. The natural question is how much security has been sacrificed and whether an attacker can construct an efficient attack to break the LEMS. Experiments in [13] show that RSM can resist univariate attacks including first and second-order DPA and CPA. The work uses MIA as the metric to get a quantification of 0.015 bit of information leakage in the described experimental setup, motivating a claim that such a low amount should be hard to exploit.

2.2 Adversarial Model

We assume an adversarial model with the following notations. Let X be the partial input/output (i.e. knowntext) of the algorithm known to the adversary (e.g. one byte of plaintext of encryption), k be the partial key in use, $Y = f_k(X)$ be the sensitive algorithmic state value to be protected. Here f is the target function which is usually a part of the algorithm. Let $\mathcal{M} = \{m_1, ..., m_s\}$ be the set of masks. When $M \in \mathcal{M}$ is applied in a first-order masking scheme $\mathrm{MASK}(\cdot, \cdot)$, $Y_M = \mathrm{MASK}(Y, M)$ is generated internally to protect the sensitive Y. The masked output Y_M is also called the leaking value (or masked state). The observed univariate leakage Λ is considered as the functional evaluation of the leaking value Y_M in the leakage function $L(\cdot)$ as expressed in Eq. (1).

$$\Lambda = L(Y_M) = L(\mathrm{MASK}(f_k(X), M)) \tag{1}$$

The set of all leaking values for Y is denoted as $Y_{\mathcal{M}} = \{Y_{m_1}, ..., Y_{m_s}\}$. A sensitive internal state y is protected by leaking values y_{m_i} with equal probability because the mask is chosen uniformly at random from $\mathcal{M}$.

In sum, the knowledge of the adversary includes the input X, target function f, and the univariate leakage Λ for processing leaking values Y_M. Our first attack in Sect. 3 also assumes the adversary to know the mask set $\mathcal{M}$, while in our second attack in Sect. 4 we only assume the mask set to satisfy the self-complementary property; the attacker does not necessarily need to know the mask values.

3   Leakage Distribution Decomposition Attack

LEMS are designed to resist low statistical order DPA/CPA attacks while maintaining small computational overhead. The low level of leakage indicated by the mutual information $I(HW(Y_M); Y)$, as quantified in [12,13], however, does not exclude the possibility of a univariate attack. In this section we analyze the composition of the leakage distribution under the protection of LEMS. We propose a univariate attack that can correctly decompose the observed one-dimensional distribution of leakage into several sub-distributions.

3.1   Leakage Distribution Composition

With the masking countermeasure, one algorithmic internal state Y can produce side channel leakage Λ through multiple leaking values $Y_{m_1}, ..., Y_{m_s}$. Consequently, the conditional entropy of leakage $H(\Lambda \mid Y)$ increases, making the classical attacks harder to succeed. According to Eq. (1) the leakage Λ depends on the knowntext X and the mask M, which are the main sources of entropy. If the knowntext is fixed to one value $X = x$ at a time, the leakage entropy is lowered because only mask values are changed and LEMS only contains a small number of masks.

We use $\mathcal{D}_{M \in \mathcal{M}}^{X=x}[\Lambda]$ (or simply $\mathcal{D}_{\mathcal{M}}^{x}[\Lambda]$) to denote the leakage distribution under the condition that the knowntext X is fixed to x and the mask M is chosen uniformly at random from the mask set $\mathcal{M}$. In this situation, $X = x$ implies only one sensitive value $y = f_k(x)$ is to be protected by the masks, which results in the leaking set $(y)_{\mathcal{M}}$. Processing each leaking value y_{m_i} produces leakage $L(y_{m_i})$. The respective leakage observations form a leakage sub-distribution denoted by $\mathcal{D}_{M=m_i}^{X=x}[\Lambda]$ (or simply $\mathcal{D}_{m_i}^{x}[\Lambda]$)[1]. Since the leaking set $(y)_{\mathcal{M}}$ contains s leaking values, the observed leakage distribution $\mathcal{D}_{\mathcal{M}}^{x}[\Lambda]$ is a composition of s sub-distributions, namely,

$$\mathcal{D}_{\mathcal{M}}^{x}[\Lambda] = \frac{1}{s}\sum_{i=1}^{s}\mathcal{D}_{m_i}^{x}[\Lambda] = \frac{1}{s}\sum_{i=1}^{s}\mathcal{D}[L(y_{m_i})] \qquad (2)$$

This equality actually comes from the law of total probability, i.e.

$$p[\Lambda = \lambda \mid X = x] = \sum_{i=1}^{s} p[\Lambda = \lambda \mid M = m_i, X = x] \cdot Pr[M = m_i]$$

$$= \frac{1}{s}\sum_{i=1}^{s} p[\Lambda = \lambda \mid M = m_i]$$

simply because $\mathcal{D}_{\mathcal{M}}^{x}[\Lambda]$ has the same meaning as the pmf/pdf $p[\Lambda = \lambda \mid X = x]$ and $\mathcal{D}_{m_i}^{x}[\Lambda]$ the same as $p[\Lambda = \lambda \mid M = m_i, X = x]$.

---

[1] The notation $\mathcal{D}_{M=m_i}^{X=x}[\Lambda]$ is of the same meaning of leakage distribution as $\mathcal{D}[L(y_{m_i})]$. Both describe the leakage for processing y_{m_i}. The former emphasizes leakage decomposition and the latter focuses on connecting with estimated sub-distributions.

It is important to see that in LEMS the distribution $\mathcal{D}_{\mathcal{M}}^x[\Lambda]$ with fixed input x is different from the overall leakage distribution $\mathcal{D}[\Lambda]$ where the knowntext is not fixed. The former is a mixture of only s sub-distributions, while the latter is composed of all 2^n sub-distributions caused by all 2^n leaking values. In fact, the proposed leakage distribution decomposition attack (LDDA) makes use of this difference to explore the weakness of LEMS. It also indicates that the univariate LDDA cannot be extended to attack FEMS where both $\mathcal{D}_{\mathcal{M}}^x[\Lambda]$ and $\mathcal{D}[\Lambda]$ are composed of 2^n sub-distributions and hence not distinguishable from each other.

3.2 Procedure of Leakage Distribution Decomposition Attack

Prior to the attack, the adversary needs to estimate the sub-distributions $\mathcal{D}[L(v)]$ of leakage for each leaking value v. We discuss this issue in more detail in Sects. 3.3 and 3.4. Here the attacker is assumed to have already obtained a precise estimation of sub-distributions. We show how this idea of decomposition in leakage distribution converts to a side channel attack. For each subkey hypothesis g and each prefixed knowntext $X = x$, the adversary follows a three-step procedure.

1. Find the hypothetical leaking set $(\hat{y})_{\mathcal{M}}$;
2. Compute the hypothetical mixture $\hat{\mathcal{D}}_{\mathcal{M}}^x[\hat{\Lambda}]$;
3. Evaluate the distance $\texttt{Dist}(\hat{\mathcal{D}}_{\mathcal{M}}^x[\hat{\Lambda}] \| \mathcal{D}_{\mathcal{M}}^x[\Lambda])$ between the mixture and the observed distribution.

More specifically, with the subkey hypothesis g for a subkey k, the adversary computes $\hat{y} = f_g(x)$ and its respective masked states $\hat{y}_{m_i} = \text{MASK}(\hat{y}, m_i)$ for all $m_i \in \mathcal{M}$. Since each hypothetical leaking value y_{m_i} contributes as one component $\hat{\mathcal{D}}[L(\hat{y}_{m_i})]$ of the leakage distribution, the adversary rebuilds the hypothetical mixture of all the s sub-distributions as

$$\hat{\mathcal{D}}_{\mathcal{M}}^x[\hat{\Lambda}] = \frac{1}{s}\sum_{i=1}^{s}\hat{\mathcal{D}}[L(\hat{y}_{m_i})] \tag{3}$$

Next, the adversary measures the similarity of the hypothetical mixture $\hat{\mathcal{D}}_{\mathcal{M}}^x[\hat{\Lambda}]$ and the observed distribution $\mathcal{D}_{\mathcal{M}}^x[\Lambda]$. A distance metric $\texttt{Dist}(\hat{\mathcal{D}}_{\mathcal{M}}^x[\hat{\Lambda}] \| \mathcal{D}_{\mathcal{M}}^x[\Lambda])$ is evaluated for this purpose. In general, a small value of the computed distance metric indicates the two distributions are close to each other. A typical instantiation of the distance metric is the Kolmogorov-Smirnov distance suggested by [22,23], which is later used in our experiments.

The adversary repeats the three-step procedure for all subkey hypotheses and all prefixed x. Her final decision for the correct subkey k is the hypothesis k^* that results in the lowest averaged distance as in Eq. (4). The attack is successful if $k^* = k$.

$$k^* = \underset{g}{\text{argmin}}\left\{\frac{1}{|\mathcal{X}|}\sum_{x \in \mathcal{X}}\texttt{Dist}(\hat{\mathcal{D}}_{\mathcal{M}}^x[\hat{\Lambda}] \| \mathcal{D}_{\mathcal{M}}^x[\Lambda])\right\} \tag{4}$$

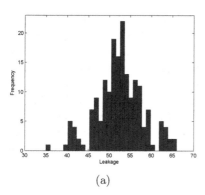
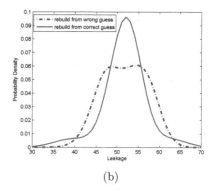

(a)   (b)

Fig. 1. The observed leakage distribution (a) VS the hypothetical mixtures (b). The rebuilt mixture from the correct guess has a similar shape to the observed distribution while the mixture from the wrong guess is quite different from the observed distribution.

Please note that the LDDA does not predict each individual *leaking state*. Instead, it analyzes the entire predicted *leaking set*. Figure 1a, b give an intuitive idea of how the decomposition of the observed distribution works for correct and incorrect subkey guesses.

Validity. If the subkey guess g is correct, i.e. $g = k$, then $\hat{y} = f_g(x) = f_k(x) = y$ and the prediction of leaking set is correct $(\hat{y})_{\mathcal{M}} = (y)_{\mathcal{M}}$. Given precise estimations of sub-distributions, the rebuilt mixture $\hat{\mathcal{D}}_{\mathcal{M}}^x[\hat{\Lambda}]$ from Eq. (3) will be close to the observed distribution $\mathcal{D}_{\mathcal{M}}^x[\Lambda]$ because

$$\hat{\mathcal{D}}_{\mathcal{M}}^x[\hat{\Lambda}] = \frac{1}{s}\sum_{i=1}^{s}\hat{\mathcal{D}}[L(\hat{y}_{m_i})] = \frac{1}{s}\sum_{i=1}^{s}\mathcal{D}[L(y_{m_i})] = \mathcal{D}_{\mathcal{M}}^x[\Lambda]$$

However if the hypothesis is wrong, i.e. $g \neq k$, then $\hat{y} = f_g(x) \neq f_k(x) = y$ for most of the inputs x, hence the hypothetical leaking set $(\hat{y})_{\mathcal{M}}$ has a low probability[2] to be the same as the actual leaking set $(y)_{\mathcal{M}}$. It follows that with high probability the rebuilt mixture $\hat{\mathcal{D}}_{\mathcal{M}}^x[\hat{\Lambda}]$ differs significantly from the observed $\mathcal{D}_{\mathcal{M}}^x[\Lambda]$ and hence their distance metric output should be large.

3.3 LDDA With Profiling

We have mentioned that the adversary should estimate the sub-distributions before mounting the LDDA attack. This has a straightforward solution by combining a profiling phase. More specifically, the profiling adversary is also assumed to have full control of the masks during the profiling stage – she knows each mask

---

[2] An exception is when $(\hat{y})_{\mathcal{M}}$ is a permutation of $(y)_{\mathcal{M}}$ for some particular g and x. Such exception occurs with small probability because the predicted leaking states take the range of entire $\{0,1\}^n$ rather than $\mathcal{M}$.

that is applied in each invocation. This assumption is frequently used in previous work [9,14,18]. The described attacks require at least bi-variate leakages consisting of the sample for processing the mask and the sample for the masked state. Hence, these approaches are not applicable for univariate attacks. Nevertheless, the profiling capability allows the adversary to build univariate leakage templates for each leaking value $v = \text{MASK}(f_{k'}(x), m)$ on another device that runs the same crypto algorithm with a different but known key k'. In other words, although the low entropy masking protection mingles different sub-distributions $\mathcal{D}[L(v)]$ together to achieve confusion, the assumed profiling adversary can still isolate each from the mixture. The isolated $\mathcal{D}[L(v)]$ can then serve as a sub-distribution look up table, enabling the adversary to rebuild the hypothetical mixture (the second step of LDDA) easily.

3.4 LDDA Without Profiling

Allowing the adversary having profiling capability is sometimes demanding. We show that sub-distribution estimation is also feasible for adversaries who are not granted with such privilege. This is achieved by assuming a leakage model and estimating the expression of leakage function explicitly. For a clear illustration, we assume the commonly accepted Hamming weight leakage model for a LEMS protected AES. It should be mentioned that advanced techniques of non-profiling leakage modeling such as linear regression model [5] may play a similar role if adjusted properly. With the Hamming weight model, the leakage Λ is expressed as a linear function of the Hamming weight of the leaking states with additive white Gaussian noise ϵ. I.e.

$$\Lambda = aHW(Y_M) + b + \epsilon$$

where the coefficients a, b are unknown constants, and the noise $\epsilon \sim \mathcal{N}(0, \sigma^2)$ is mean zero and the noise level σ is also unknown. Since the sub-distributions $\mathcal{D}[L(v)]$ for processing leaking value v can now be represented as $\mathcal{N}(\Lambda; aHW(v) + b, \sigma^2)$, estimating sub-distributions is simplified to estimating the unknown parameters a, b, σ. Meanwhile, it is easy to see that the overall leakage distribution $\mathcal{D}[\Lambda]$ is a weighted composition of nine Gaussian curves. I.e.

$$\mathcal{D}[\Lambda] \approx \sum_{h=0}^{8} w_h \mathcal{N}(\Lambda; ah + b, \sigma^2) \tag{5}$$

where $0 \leq w_h \leq 1$ is the proportion of the normal curve $\mathcal{N}(\Lambda; ah + b, \sigma^2)$ and $\sum_{h=0}^{8} w_h = 1$. It follows that the Hamming weight h of leaking values Y_M forms a Binomial distribution and the weight parameters $w_h = \binom{8}{h}/2^8$, provided that the knowntext X is uniformly distributed. It is because xoring and SBoxing are one-to-one mappings. They deliver the uniform distribution from X to the sensitive Y and its masked output Y_M.

Finally, we solve the parameter estimation as an optimization problem. Optimal choices of a, b, σ should minimize the difference between the two sides of

Eq. (5), namely, the observed overall leakage distribution and the composition of the parameterized sub-distributions. We set it as the objective function in Eq. (6). Furthermore, the optimization should be associated with the restriction that the statistical characteristics of the two sides should be approximately equal as in (7). Examples of the restriction functions are the statistical moments including $\text{Mean}(\mathcal{D}[\varLambda]) \approx 4a + b$, $\text{Var}(\mathcal{D}[\varLambda]) \approx \sigma^2 + 2a^2$ (derived from analysis of variance) and etc. The optimally parameterized $\mathcal{N}(\varLambda; aHW(v) + b, \sigma^2)$ can then serve as a sub-distribution look up table, enabling the adversary to carry out the LDDA.

$$\texttt{Minimize } \texttt{Dist}(\mathcal{D}[\varLambda] \| \sum_{h=0}^{8} w_h \mathcal{N}(\varLambda; ah + b, \sigma^2)) \tag{6}$$

$$\texttt{StatChar}(\mathcal{D}[\varLambda]) \approx \texttt{StatChar}(\sum_{h=0}^{8} w_h \mathcal{N}(\varLambda; ah + b, \sigma^2)) \tag{7}$$

It should be mentioned that the non-profiling LDDA is heavily influenced by the accuracy of leakage modeling. Large bias results in the derived sub-distributions being significantly different from the actual leakage function and hence reduces the efficiency or even disables the LDDA.

4   Leaking Set Collision Attack

The previously discussed LDDA follows a 'decompose'-then-'rebuild' approach to compare the distributions of leakage. We now propose a second attack named leaking set collision attack (LSCA). It circumvents the 'rebuild' step and allows adversary directly comparing related distributions and therefore gains the benefit of avoiding the sub-distribution estimation.

4.1   Existence of Leaking Set Collisions

The approach extends side channel collision attacks [11,19] by defining collisions between two leaking sets. Two distinct knowntexts $x \neq x'$ are said to induce a *leaking set collision* if the respective leaking sets are the same, i.e.

$$(y)_\mathcal{M} = \{y_{m_1}, ..., y_{m_s}\} = \{y'_{m_1}, ..., y'_{m_s}\} = (y')_\mathcal{M}$$

For Boolean masking schemes, the existence of leaking set collisions is a consequence of the *self-complementary property* for the choice of the mask values suggested in [12,13]. It indicates that if m is chosen as a possible mask value, so should its bitwise inverse $\bar{m} = m \oplus 1^n$ as explained in Sect. 2.1 (1^n denotes the all-1 bit string, e.g. 0xff for a byte). One simple choice is $y' = \bar{y}$. Because for any $m \in \mathcal{M}$,

$$(\bar{y})_m = \bar{y} \oplus m = y \oplus 1^n \oplus m$$
$$= y \oplus \bar{m} = y_{\bar{m}} \in (y)_\mathcal{M}$$

This proves $(\bar{y})_{\mathcal{M}} \subset (y)_{\mathcal{M}}$. Similarly the other direction $(\bar{y})_{\mathcal{M}} \supset (y)_{\mathcal{M}}$ also holds and hence $(y)_{\mathcal{M}} = (\bar{y})_{\mathcal{M}}$. On the other hand, this choice $y' = \bar{y}$ identifies a relation between the respective knowntexts x, x' by setting $f_k(x') = \overline{f_k(x)}$. It is equivalent to

$$x' = f_k^{-1}(1^n \oplus f_k(x)) \tag{8}$$

It implies that the knowntext pair $\langle x, x' \rangle$ derived from Eq. (8) results in a leaking set collision between $(y)_{\mathcal{M}}$ and $(y')_{\mathcal{M}}$.

4.2 Building a Leaking Set Collision Attack

An importance consequence of the leaking set collision is that the respective underlying leakage distributions are identical. In fact, the set collision $(y)_{\mathcal{M}} = (y')_{\mathcal{M}}$ implies the both $\mathcal{D}_{\mathcal{M}}^x[\Lambda]$ and $\mathcal{D}_{\mathcal{M}}^{x'}[\Lambda]$ have the same composition of sub-distributions.

$$\mathcal{D}_{\mathcal{M}}^x[\Lambda] = \frac{1}{s}\sum_{i=1}^{s} \mathcal{D}[L(y_{m_i})] = \frac{1}{s}\sum_{i=1}^{s} \mathcal{D}[L(y'_{m_i})] = \mathcal{D}_{\mathcal{M}}^{x'}[\Lambda]$$

Therefore, the empirically observed leakage distributions $\mathcal{D}_{\mathcal{M}}^x[\Lambda]$ and $\mathcal{D}_{\mathcal{M}}^{x'}[\Lambda]$ should be very close to each other. We now show how to convert this into a side channel attack against LEMS protected AES. The Sbox of the first round is chosen as the target function. Hence, the sensitive states y, y' are the s-box outputs and the knowntexts x, x' are the corresponding plaintext byte values[3]. The paired relation in Eq. (8) is then instantiated as in the following pairing equality in (9).

$$x' = \texttt{Pairing}(x, k) = k \oplus S^{-1}(\texttt{0xff} \oplus S(x \oplus k)) \tag{9}$$

It indicates that the plaintext pair $\langle x, x' \rangle$ which satisfies the paring equality forms a leaking set collision at their respective masked outputs.

The adversary, however, does not know the subkey k and cannot directly plug in the pairing equality to derive a collision. Nevertheless, she can make subkey hypothesis g and check for collisions just like a standard side channel attacker. A detailed attacking procedures is shown in Algorithm 1. It firstly sorts all leakages according to their respective plaintext x so that the empirical distributions $\mathcal{D}_{\mathcal{M}}^x[\Lambda]$ are obtained for all possible x. The adversary then starts testing subkey hypotheses. With each hypothesis g, she computes the hypothetical pairing $x' = \texttt{Pairing}(x, g)$ defined in Eq. (9). The two sets of related leakage distributions $\mathcal{D}_{\mathcal{M}}^x[\Lambda]$ and $\mathcal{D}_{\mathcal{M}}^{x'}[\Lambda]$ are fetched and their similarity is measured using the distance metric $\texttt{Dist}()$. In practice, the adversary can add up the computed distances derived from all possible collisions (line 8 of the algorithm). The decision

---

[3] The same approach can be applied to arbitrary intermediate states, as long as they are a non-linear function of x and k: For states y that are linear functions of x and k, e.g. the s-box input, the key cancels out so that the knowntext pair become independent from the key, making the conversion into an attack infeasible.

Algorithm 1. Leaking Set Collision Attack on RSM-AES

Input: Number of traces q; Knowntexts $x_1, ..., x_q$; leakages $\lambda_1, ..., \lambda_q$
Output: Subkey Decision k^*
    Precomputation:
1: **for** $x = 0$ **to** 255 **do**
2:    $\mathcal{D}_{\mathcal{M}}^x[\Lambda] = \{\lambda_i \mid x_i = x\}$ ▷ collect leakage whose knowntext is x
3: **end for**
    Key recovery:
4: **for** $g = 0$ **to** 255 **do**
5:    $\delta_g = 0$
6:    **for** $x = 0$ **to** 255 **do**
7:       $x' = \texttt{Pairing}(x, g)$ ▷ compute hypothetical pairing x'
8:       $\delta_g = \delta_g + \texttt{Dist}(\mathcal{D}_{\mathcal{M}}^x[\Lambda] \| \mathcal{D}_{\mathcal{M}}^{x'}[\Lambda])$ ▷ sums the distances from all pairings
9:    **end for**
10: **end for**
11: $k^* = \text{argmin}_g \{\delta_g\}$
12: **return** k^*

strategy is similar to LDDA: the adversary determines as the correct subkey the hypothesis k^* that results in the smallest overall distance. The attack is successful if $k^* = k$.

Validity. If the key hypothesis is correct, i.e. $g = k$, then the derived pairing $x' = \texttt{Pairing}(x, g) = \texttt{Pairing}(x, k)$ is exactly the same as the true pairing equality in Eq. (9). It follows that a leaking set collision $(y)_{\mathcal{M}} = (y')_{\mathcal{M}}$ is generated. Hence the compared distributions should feature a low distance metric quantity $\texttt{Dist}(\mathcal{D}_{\mathcal{M}}^x[\Lambda] \| \mathcal{D}_{\mathcal{M}}^{x'}[\Lambda])$. However if the subkey hypothesis is wrong, the computation yields

$$y' = S(x' \oplus k) = S(g \oplus S^{-1}(\text{0xff} \oplus S(x \oplus g)) \oplus k)$$

It is different from $\bar{y} = \text{0xff} \oplus S(x \oplus k)$ for most x. Hence the resulting leaking set $(y)_{\mathcal{M}}$ has low probability to completely overlap $(y')_{\mathcal{M}}$ and the two distributions have high probability to differ significantly.

Complexity. It should be mentioned that the roles of x and x' of a hypothetical pairing are symmetric for any hypothesis. That is, if x' is a hypothetical pairing of x satisfying $x' = \texttt{Pairing}(x, g)$, then reversely x is also a pairing of x' satisfying $x = \texttt{Pairing}(x', g)$. Here is a simple proof.

$$\begin{aligned} x'' = \texttt{Pairing}(x', g) &= g \oplus S^{-1}(\text{0xff} \oplus S(x' \oplus g)) \\ &= g \oplus S^{-1}(\text{0xff} \oplus S(S^{-1}(\text{0xff} \oplus S(x \oplus g)))) \\ &= g \oplus (x \oplus g) = x \end{aligned}$$

This symmetry implies there are a total of 128 possible leaking set collisions for all 256 knowntexts x. It suffices to make only 128 distance comparisons for testing one hypothesis. Therefore the total complexity is 256×128 distance computations to recover one key byte.

Comparing LSCA with LDDA. One common feature of LDDA and LSCA is that both attacks are achieved by comparing leakage distributions. More precisely, the compared leakage distributions refer to the leakages $\mathcal{D}_{\mathcal{M}}^x[\Lambda]$ with some prefixed knowntext x. It results in a lowered leakage entropy which become exploitable by the two attacks.

There are also many differences between the two attacks. Firstly, the LDDA compares empirically observed leakage distribution with the rebuilt hypothetical mixtures, while the LSCA compares two sets of distributions that are both obtained empirically. Therefore, the correct subkey hypothesis in the LDDA measures the closeness of the empirical distribution to its underlying distribution. In the LSCA it measures the closeness between two empirical distributions that are sampled from the same underlying distribution. Secondly, the LDDA requires sub-distribution estimations to complete the "rebuild" step, while the LSCA avoid this. We have seen that estimating sub-distributions not only adds some complexity or even requires profiling privilege, but is also influenced by the accuracy of leakage modeling. Thus the LSCA does not suffer from the modeling bias. Last but not the least, the LDDA requires the mask set $\mathcal{M}$ to be known but the LSCA only requires the self-complementary property for the masking set $\mathcal{M}$. To sum up, the LDDA shows the explicit composition of leakages and the LSCA makes use of leakage composition implicitly and is more efficient in practice.

5   Experiments

In this section, we carry out the LDDA and LSCA described in Sects. 3 and 4. Our experiments are performed on the measurements from DPA contest V4 [1]. It is a software implementation of AES-256 protected by the RSM countermeasure (cf. Sect. 2.1) and a total of 100,000 leakage measurements are provided. All attacks are performed on a univariate leakage sample representing the leakage of the first round AES output of SBox. Before showing our result we want to mention as reference that [13] shows 0 success rate for DPA, CPA and VPA based on 150,000 observations of a hardware implementation of RSM. It also reports 0.001 to 0.012 bit of information being leaked from mutual information analysis.

5.1   LDDA with Profiling

We firstly implemented LDDA using the template attack approach and we assume full knowledge of the mask application during the profiling stage as detailed in Sect. 3.3. A total of 50,000 measurements are used to build the templates, i.e. the 256 sub-distributions $\mathcal{D}[L(v)]$ of leakages for processing each possible leaking state v. The obtained sub-distributions are represented as 256

Gaussian curves $\mathcal{N}(\Lambda; \mu_v, \sigma_v^2)$. Upon the completion of sub-distribution estimation, another 2,000 to 16,000 measurements are used to test all 256 subkey hypotheses using the 3-step LDDA. In particular, the rebuilt distribution from each hypothesis is now instantiated as a Gaussian mixture,

$$\hat{\mathcal{D}}_{\mathcal{M}}^x[\hat{\Lambda}] = \frac{1}{s} \sum_{v \in (\hat{y})_{\mathcal{M}}} \mathcal{N}(\hat{\Lambda}; \mu_v, \sigma_v^2)$$

resulting in a model similar to [10]. The Gaussian mixture is compared with the observed distribution $\mathcal{D}_{\mathcal{M}}^x[\Lambda]$ using Kolmogorov-Smirnov (KS) distance metric.

Figure 2 shows the profiling LDDA hypothesis testing for the first subkey byte. We can see that LDDA succeed – the correct subkey $k = 108$ always gives the smallest KS distance among the 256 subkey hypotheses–whenever more than 2000 traces are used for testing. It verifies the correctness of the LDDA that only the correct hypothesis yields a correct decomposition of the leakage distribution. The four plots also show that the KS-distance drops when increasing the number of testing traces. In particular, the averaged KS distance for the correct subkey

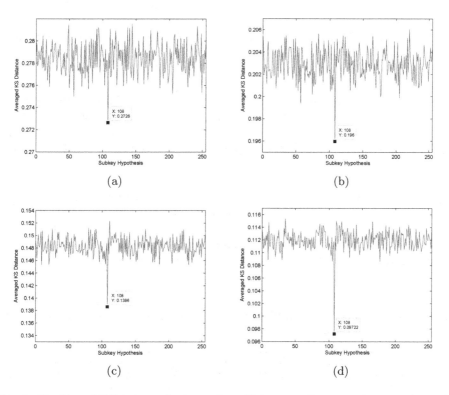

Fig. 2. Profiling LDDA hypothesis testing: Kolmogrov-Smirnov distance (y-axis) between observed leakage distribution and rebuilt Gaussian mixture from all subkey hypotheses (x-axis) with the profiled sub-distributions. Experiments use 2,000 traces (a); 4,000 traces (b); 8,000 traces (c); and 16,000 traces (d).

hypothesis drops from 0.273 all the way to 0.097. While for the wrong hypotheses, the average drops from 0.279 to around 0.112. The reason is that the computed distance depends on two main factors: *(1)* the correctness of the prediction of the leaking set $Y_\mathcal{M}$ (the effect exploited by LDDA); and *(2)* the sampling errors: viewing the observed leakage (the empirical one) as the samples from its underlying distribution (the true one approximated during the profiling). The law of large numbers implies that the empirical distribution of the leakage converges to its underlying distribution when increasing the number of leakages. Therefore, using more testing traces reduces the influence of the sampling error and hence decreases the overall KS distance metric. As a consequence, the correct hypothesis becomes better distinguishable from the wrong guesses.

5.2   LDDA Without Profiling

Our second group of experiments carries out the LDDA without a profiling stage as described in Sect. 3.4. Each experiments estimate different combinations of the required parameters in the presented optimization problem in Eqs. (6) and (7). The guessing entropy from [21] is used for the evaluation of the attack. That is, the subkey k is said to have guessing entropy t if the KS distance for k is on average the t-th smallest value among all KS distances for all hypotheses. Results are summarized in Table 1.

It can be seen from the table that the correct subkey k has very low guessing entropy of 1 or 2 if more than 40,000 traces are used in the optimal estimation cases. Even for the worst estimation case shown in the table, the guessing entropy is still 33. The average estimation cases indicate that the non-profiling LDDA enables a reasonable attack – the guessing entropy is kept at an acceptable level–whenever more than 60,000 measurements are used.

It can be seen that the non-profiling LDDA needs much more traces to succeed comparing to the profiling LDDA. Notice that the latter serves as the closest approximation to the real leakage function and the non-profiling LDDA here is merely derived from a coarse modeling of the leakage function – a noised linear transformation of the Hamming weight. The performance difference between the two methods indicates that a more precise estimation of sub-distributions yields better attacking performance for the non-profiling LDDA.

Table 1. Performance evaluation using Guessing Entropy (GE) for the non-profiling LDDA. Best case is evaluated with optimal estimation of parameters; Worst case is with non-optimal estimation.

Number of traces	20,000	40,000	60,000	80,000	100,000
GE (average case)	19.74	16.65	4.02	2.93	1.31
GE (worst case)	30	33	11	9	5
GE (best case)	9	2	2	1	1

5.3   Experiments for Leaking Set Collision Attack

The third group of experiments mounts the LSCA described in Sect. 4. Figure 3 shows the hypothesis testing of one LSCA attack using 10,000 to 40,000 traces. The correct subkey hypothesis $k = 108$ gives clear lowest KS distance metric when more than 15,000 traces are used. The distinguishability of the correct subkey increases with the number of traces that are used. Similar to the situation of profiling LDDA, we can observe a drop in the magnitude of the KS distance for the same hypothesis when the number of traces increases. The reason is still the reduction of sampling errors by using more traces.

In addition, we use the provided 100,000 traces to run as many independent experiments as possible for evaluating the LSCA attack. Table 2 summarizes the attacking performance using guessing entropy and t-th order success rate. It can be seen that the LSCA starts a stable success (GE $= 1$ and 1st order success rate is 100 %) with more than 12288 traces, namely, 48 traces per plaintext byte. It is interesting to see that even with a total of 8192 traces (32

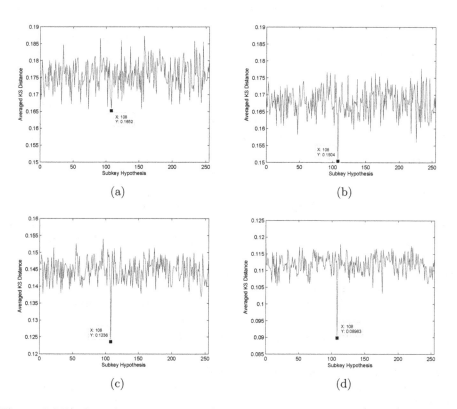

(a)   (b)

(c)   (d)

Fig. 3. LSCA hypothesis testing: Kolmogrov-Smirnov distance (y-axis) between observed leakage distributions for the pairings induced from subkey hypothesis (x-axis). Experiments use 10,000 traces (a); 15,000 traces (b); 20,000 traces (c); and 40,000 traces (d).

Table 2. LSCA performance evaluation

Number of traces	4096	8192	12288	16384
Guessing entropy	34.17	5.33	1.00	1.00
1st order success rate	0	33.3 %	100.0 %	100.0 %
4th order success rate	33.3 %	66.7 %	100.0 %	100.0 %

traces per plaintext), making 4 guesses still ensures 2/3 success rate. The overall performance is much better than the non-profiling LDDA. However, the comparison with the profiling LDDA shows that the LSCA loses some success rate and requires more traces. The possible reason is that LSCA expands the sampling error. Since the two observed distributions $\mathcal{D}_{\mathcal{M}}^x[\Lambda]$ and $\mathcal{D}_{\mathcal{M}}^{x'}[\Lambda]$ are two sampling distributions from the same underlying distribution because of the set collision, the distance $\mathtt{Dist}(\mathcal{D}_{\mathcal{M}}^x[\Lambda]\|\mathcal{D}_{\mathcal{M}}^{x'}[\Lambda])$ is composed of two components: the distance from $\mathcal{D}_{\mathcal{M}}^x[\Lambda]$ to the underlying distribution and the distance from the underlying distribution to $\mathcal{D}_{\mathcal{M}}^{x'}[\Lambda]$. Although the compositional effect is not necessarily as strong as doubling the distance, it is very likely that the sampling error is expanded in the LSCA. While the profiling LDDA only measures one sampling error: the difference between the observed $\mathcal{D}_{\mathcal{M}}^x[\Lambda]$ and its underlying distribution. No expansion of sampling error is occurred in the profiling LDDA. Nevertheless, with the slight sacrifice of success rate, the LSCA makes the full use of leakage similarity from the generated the leaking set collisions and therefore does not need assuming profiling capability nor the full control of masks.

6   Conclusion

This work proposes two univariate attacks to overcome the limited protection achieved with the low entropy masking schemes. The first attack—Leakage Distribution Decomposition Attack (LDDA)—reveals the composition of the observed leakage distribution. The second attack—Leaking Set Collision Attack (LSCA)—extends the concept of side channel collision attacks and does not rely on detailed knowledge of the leakage model or function. Both of the two attacks compare leakage distributions and therefore they have a relatively high requirement on the number of traces. The attacks show that studying a countermeasure with resistance of the first, second or even higher order CPA/DPA is not sufficient to guarantee the resistance to other univariate attacks.

Acknowledgments. We would like to thank the reviewers for the helpful comments. This material is based upon work supported by the National Science Foundation under Grant No. 1261399.

References

1. The dpa contest v4. http://www.dpacontest.org/v4/
2. Bhasin, S., He, W., Guilley, S., Danger, J.-L.: Exploiting fpga block memories for protected cryptographic implementations. In: 2013 8th International Workshop on Reconfigurable and Communication-Centric Systems-on-Chip (ReCoSoC) (2013)
3. Brier, E., Clavier, C., Olivier, F.: Correlation power analysis with a leakage model. In: Joye, M., Quisquater, J.-J. (eds.) CHES 2004. LNCS, vol. 3156, pp. 16–29. Springer, Heidelberg (2004)
4. Coron, J.-S., Goubin, L.: On boolean and arithmetic masking against differential power analysis. In: Paar, C., Koç, Ç.K. (eds.) CHES 2000. LNCS, vol. 1965, pp. 231–237. Springer, Heidelberg (2000)
5. Doget, J., Prouff, E., Rivain, M., Standaert, F.-X.: Univariate side channel attacks and leakage modeling. J. Crypt. Eng. 1, 123–144 (2011)
6. Gierlichs, B., Batina, L., Tuyls, P., Preneel, B.: Mutual information analysis. In: Oswald, E., Rohatgi, P. (eds.) CHES 2008. LNCS, vol. 5154, pp. 426–442. Springer, Heidelberg (2008)
7. Golic, J., Tymen, C.: Multiplicative masking and power analysis of AES. In: Kaliski, B.S., Koç, Ç.K., Paar, C. (eds.) CHES 2002. LNCS, vol. 2523. Springer, Heidelberg (2003)
8. Kocher, P.C., Jaffe, J., Jun, B.: Differential power analysis. In: Wiener, M. (ed.) CRYPTO 1999. LNCS, vol. 1666, pp. 388–397. Springer, Heidelberg (1999)
9. Lemke-Rust, K., Paar, C.: Analyzing side channel leakage of masked implementations with stochastic methods. In: Biskup, J., López, J. (eds.) ESORICS 2007. LNCS, vol. 4734, pp. 454–468. Springer, Heidelberg (2007)
10. Lemke-Rust, K., Paar, C.: Gaussian mixture models for higher-order side channel analysis. In: Paillier, P., Verbauwhede, I. (eds.) CHES 2007. LNCS, vol. 4727, pp. 14–27. Springer, Heidelberg (2007)
11. Moradi, A., Mischke, O., Eisenbarth, T.: Correlation-enhanced power analysis collision attack. In: Mangard, S., Standaert, F.-X. (eds.) CHES 2010. LNCS, vol. 6225, pp. 125–139. Springer, Heidelberg (2010)
12. Nassar, M., Guilley, S., Danger, J.-L.: Formal analysis of the entropy/security trade-off in first-order masking countermeasures against side-channel attacks. In: Bernstein, D.J., Chatterjee, S. (eds.) INDOCRYPT 2011. LNCS, vol. 7107, pp. 22–39. Springer, Heidelberg (2011)
13. Nassar, M., Souissi, Y., Guilley, S., Danger, J.-L.: RSM: a small and fast countermeasure for AES, secure against 1st and 2nd-order zero-offset scas. In: Design, Automation Test in Europe Conference Exhibition (DATE) (2012)
14. Oswald, E., Mangard, S.: Template attacks on masking—resistance is futile. In: Abe, M. (ed.) CT-RSA 2007. LNCS, vol. 4377, pp. 243–256. Springer, Heidelberg (2006)
15. Popp, T., Mangard, S.: Masked dual-rail pre-charge logic: DPA-resistance without routing constraints. In: Rao, J.R., Sunar, B. (eds.) CHES 2005. LNCS, vol. 3659, pp. 172–186. Springer, Heidelberg (2005)
16. Prouff, E., Rivain, M.: A generic method for secure SBox implementation. In: Kim, S., Yung, M., Lee, H.-W. (eds.) WISA 2007. LNCS, vol. 4867, pp. 227–244. Springer, Heidelberg (2008)
17. Schaumont, P., Tiri, K.: Masking and dual-rail logic don't add up. In: Paillier, P., Verbauwhede, I. (eds.) CHES 2007. LNCS, vol. 4727, pp. 95–106. Springer, Heidelberg (2007)

18. Schindler, W., Lemke, K., Paar, C.: A stochastic model for differential side channel cryptanalysis. In: Rao, J.R., Sunar, B. (eds.) CHES 2005. LNCS, vol. 3659, pp. 30–46. Springer, Heidelberg (2005)

19. Schramm, K., Leander, G., Felke, P., Paar, C.: A collision-attack on AES. In: Joye, M., Quisquater, J.-J. (eds.) CHES 2004. LNCS, vol. 3156, pp. 163–175. Springer, Heidelberg (2004)

20. Schramm, K., Paar, C.: Higher order masking of the AES. In: Pointcheval, D. (ed.) CT-RSA 2006. LNCS, vol. 3860, pp. 208–225. Springer, Heidelberg (2006)

21. Standaert, F.-X., Malkin, T.G., Yung, M.: A unified framework for the analysis of side-channel key recovery attacks. In: Joux, A. (ed.) EUROCRYPT 2009. LNCS, vol. 5479, pp. 443–461. Springer, Heidelberg (2009)

22. Veyrat-Charvillon, N., Standaert, F.-X.: Mutual information analysis: how, when and why? In: Clavier, C., Gaj, K. (eds.) CHES 2009. LNCS, vol. 5747, pp. 429–443. Springer, Heidelberg (2009)

23. Whitnall, C., Oswald, E., Mather, L.: An exploration of the Kolmogorov-Smirnov test as a competitor to mutual information analysis. In: Prouff, E. (ed.) CARDIS 2011. LNCS, vol. 7079, pp. 234–251. Springer, Heidelberg (2011)

A Machine Learning Approach
Against a Masked AES

Liran Lerman[1,2]([✉]), Stephane Fernandes Medeiros[1],
Gianluca Bontempi[2], and Olivier Markowitch[1]

[1] Quality and Security of Information Systems, Département d'informatique,
Université Libre de Bruxelles, Brussel, Belgium
llerman@ulb.ac.be
[2] Machine Learning Group, Département d'informatique,
Université Libre de Bruxelles, Brussel, Belgium

Abstract. Side-channel attacks challenge the security of cryptographic devices. One of the widespread countermeasures against these attacks is the masking approach. In 2012, Nassar *et al.* [21] presented a new lightweight (low-cost) Boolean masking countermeasure to protect the implementation of the AES block-cipher. This masking scheme represents the target algorithm of the DPAContest V4 [30]. In this article, we present the first machine learning attack against a masking countermeasure, using the dataset of the DPAContest V4. We succeeded to extract each targeted byte of the key of the masked AES with 26 traces during the attacking phase. This number of traces represents roughly twice the number of traces needed compared to an unmasked AES on the same cryptographic device. Finally, we compared our proposal to a stochastic attack and to a strategy based on template attack. We showed that an attack based on a machine learning model reduces the number of traces required during the attacking step with a factor two and four compared respectively to template attack and to stochastic attack when analyzing the same leakage information. A new strategy based on stochastic attack reduces this number to 27.8 traces (in average) during the attack but requires a larger execution time in our setting than a learning model.

Keywords: Side-channel attack · Masking · Profiled attack · Machine learning · Stochastic attack · Template attack

1 Introduction

Embedded devices such as smart cards, mobile phones, and RFID tags are widely used in our everyday lives. These devices implement cryptographic operations allowing to secure, for example, bank transfers, buildings and cars. For this, several cryptographic primitives can be used such as an encryption function. During the execution of an encryption algorithm, the device processes secret information. These secret information could be retrieved with physical attacks

A. Francillon and P. Rohatgi (Eds.): CARDIS 2013, LNCS 8419, pp. 61–75, 2014.
DOI: 10.1007/978-3-319-08302-5_5, © Springer International Publishing Switzerland 2014

against the physical device by analyzing unintentional leakages such as the power consumption [14], the processing time [13], the electromagnetic emanation [7] or a combination of them [28].

In recent years the cryptographic community explored new attacks based on machine learning models. These methods demonstrate that template attacks (that can be considered as the strongest leakage analysis in an information theoretic sense [4]) overestimate the security of embedded devices in several scenarios. Lerman et al. [15,16] compared a template attack with a binary machine learning approach, based on non-parametric methods, against cryptographic hardware devices implementing a symmetric and an asymmetric cryptographic algorithm. Hospodar et al. [10,11] analyzed a software implementation of a portion of a block cipher. Their experiments support the idea that non-parametric techniques can be competitive and sometimes better (i.e. less traces in the attacking phase) than template attack. Heuser et al. [9] generalized this idea by analyzing multi-class classification models in several contexts. In the same year Bartkewitz [1] applied a multi-class machine learning model allowing to improve the attack success with respect to the binary approach. Recently, Lerman et al. [17] proposed a machine learning approach that takes into account the temporal dependencies between power values. This method improves the success rate of an attack in a low signal-to-noise ratio with respect to classification methods. In the same year, Martinasek et al. [20] applied a neural network in order to extract one byte of the key of AES. Their method retrieves the secret value with probability around 0.9 using only one measured power leakage.

In parallel with attacks, the embedded systems industry implements countermeasures. They counteract side-channel attacks by inducing a leakage independent of the secret target value. It is worth to mention that so far all the attacks based on machine learning were applied on unprotected cryptographic devices. It was still unclear whether the results of the previous works are still the same in a protected environment. During the attacking phase, for a specific countermeasure and for a specific device, open questions are: (1) How many traces are required against a protected device with a machine learning model compared to a strategy based on template attack or based on stochastic attack? (2) How many traces are required by a machine learning model attacking a protected device compared to an unprotected device? (3) What is the impact of the number of traces used in the profiling step by a machine learning model attacking a protected device? We aim to answer these questions by proposing an original efficient combination between a machine learning model and a non-profiled attack. Our requirements are fast-execution, low-memory usage and high success rate of the attack (i.e. realistic attack scenarios).

We made a detailed assessment of the proposed approach by considering four public datasets with different number of traces during the profiling phase and ten public datasets during the attacking phase. These traces were collected on a smart card that implements the block-cipher AES protected by a masking scheme. All our datasets were extracted from the public dataset of the

DPAContest V4 [30], *"an initiative towards an international benchmarking reference"* [30], thus allowing reproducing all our experiments.

This paper is organized as follows. Section 2 discusses non-profiled attacks, profiled attacks and masking countermeasures. Section 3 introduces our original attack based on a machine learning approach against a masking scheme. Section 4 illustrates the power of our proposal with several datasets. Section 5 concludes this paper with several future works.

2   Preliminaries

2.1   Side-Channel Attack

During the execution of an encryption algorithm, the cryptographic device processes a function f

$$f \colon \mathcal{M} \times \mathcal{O} \to \mathcal{F} \tag{1}$$

$$s = f_O(m) \tag{2}$$

called a sensitive variable [25] where $O \in \mathcal{O} = \{O_0, O_1, ..., O_{K-1}\}$ is a key-related information where $\mathcal{O} = \{0, 1\}^{l_1}$ and l_1 is the size of the secret value used in f (e.g. one byte of the secret key), $m \in \mathcal{M} = \{0, 1\}^{l_2}$ represents a public information where l_2 is the size of the public value used in f (e.g. one byte of the plaintext) and $\mathcal{F} = \{0, 1\}^{l_3}$ is the codomain of f where l_3 is the size of the output of f. The adversary targets this function during the attack.

Let

$$^j T_i = \left\{ ^j_t T_i \in \mathbb{R} \mid t \in [1; n] \right\} \tag{3}$$

be the j-th leakage information (called trace) associated to the i-th target value. We consider the leakage information $^j_t T_i$ of the device at time t depending on the output of $f_{O_i}(m)$ such that

$$^j_t T_i = L(f_{O_i}(m)) + \epsilon \tag{4}$$

where $\epsilon \in \mathbb{R}$ is the noise following a Gaussian distribution with zero mean and L is the leakage model

$$L \colon \mathcal{F} \to \mathcal{Q} \tag{5}$$

$$Q = L(f_O(m)) \tag{6}$$

where $\mathcal{Q} \subset \mathbb{R}$. Examples of models L are the Hamming weight (HW) and the Hamming distance [19].

Non-profiled Attack

The non-profiled attack represents a common approach in order to attack a cryptographic device. This attack estimates the output value of $f_O(m)$ for each possible target value O. Then, the estimated leakage model $\hat{L}$ transforms this output value to allow, *in fine*, to compare the real and the predicted leakage information with a distinguisher D. This paper focuses on univariate Correlation Power Analysis (CPA) where the distinguisher represents the Pearson correlation estimator.

Profiled Attack

Let $\Pr[A]$ be the probability of A and let $\Pr[A \mid B]$ be the probability of A given B. The profiled attack strategy represents a more efficient attack by a deeper leakage estimation. It estimates (with a set of traces called learning set) a template $\Pr\left[{}^{j}T_i \mid L(f_{O_i}(m)); \theta_i\right]$ (where θ_i is the parameter of the probability density function) for each target value during the profiling step. The learning set is measured on a controlled device similar to the target chip. Once a template is estimated for each target value, the adversary classifies a new trace T (measured on the target device) during the attacking step with a profiled model $A(T)$ that computes the value $\hat{O}$ which maximizes the *a posteriori* probability

$$\hat{O} = A(T) = \arg\max_{O \in \mathcal{O}} \Pr\left[L\left(f_O\left(m\right)\right) \mid T\right] \tag{7}$$

$$= \arg\max_{O \in \mathcal{O}} \frac{\Pr\left[T \mid L\left(f_O\left(m\right)\right)\right] \times \Pr\left[L\left(f_O\left(m\right)\right)\right]}{\Pr\left[T\right]} \tag{8}$$

$$= \arg\max_{O \in \mathcal{O}} \hat{\Pr}\left[T \mid \hat{L}\left(f_O\left(m\right)\right)\right] \times \hat{\Pr}\left[\hat{L}\left(f_O\left(m\right)\right)\right] \tag{9}$$

where the *apriori* probabilities $\hat{\Pr}\left[\hat{L}\left(f_O\left(m\right)\right)\right]$ are estimated by the user.

Several approaches exist in order to estimate $\Pr\left[T \mid L\left(f_O\left(m\right)\right)\right]$ such as the parametric template attack [4], the stochastic attack [27] and the non-parametric machine learning models [10,15]. The former assumes that this probability follows a Gaussian distribution for each target value.

The stochastic attack modelizes the leakage model L at time t with a regression model ${}_t h$, i.e.

$$\overset{j}{_t}T_i = L\left(f_{O_i}\left(m\right)\right) + \epsilon \tag{10}$$

$$= {}_t h\left(f_{O_i}\left(m\right)\right) + {}_t R \tag{11}$$

$$= {}_t c + \sum_{u=1}^{U} {}_t\alpha_u\, g_u\left(f_{O_i}\left(m\right)\right) + {}_t R \tag{12}$$

where ${}_t R$ is a residual Gaussian noise at time t, $\{{}_t c, {}_t\alpha_1, {}_t\alpha_2, ..., {}_t\alpha_U\}$ is the parameter of the regression model ${}_t h$ and $\{g_1, g_2, ..., g_U\}$ is the basis used in the regression. Usually each function g_j equals to

$$g_j\left(f_{O_i}\left(m\right)\right) = \mathrm{Bit}_j\left(f_{O_i}\left(m\right)\right) \tag{13}$$

where $\mathrm{Bit}_j\left(x\right)$ returns the j-th bit of x. Then, the attacker assumes that $\Pr\left[T \mid L\left(f_{O_i}\left(m\right)\right)\right]$ follows the Gaussian distribution $\mathcal{N}\left(h\left(f_{O_i}\left(m\right)\right), \Sigma\right)$ where $h(x)$ equals to $\{{}_1 h(x), {}_2 h(x), ..., {}_n h(x)\}$ and $\Sigma \in \mathbb{R}^{n \times n}$ is the covariance matrix of the residual term.

The non-parametric machine learning models make no assumption on the density distribution functions. For example Random Forest model (RF) [2] builds a set of decision trees that classifies a trace based on a voting system. Support Vector Machine (SVM) [5] discriminates traces associated to different target values with hyperplanes. We refer to [1, 9–11, 15–17] for deeper explanations on the parametric template attack and on the non-parametric machine learning models.

2.2 Masking Countermeasure

Based on secret sharing, the masking countermeasure aims to reduce the unintentional leakage information of a cryptographic device [3]. For this, the method masks a public information m with d uniformly distributed random values $v = \{v_0, v_1, ..., v_{d-1}\} \in \mathcal{V}^d$ changing at each execution where $\mathcal{V} = \{0, 1\}^{l_4}$ and l_4 is the size of each random value. This approach is called a masking scheme of order d. In a theoretical point of view, the security level of a masked implementation against side-channel attacks increases exponentially with d [3] when the amount of noise in the traces is sufficient [29].

Potentially, an adversary can retrieve the secret information by using an attack of order $d + 1$ (where the attacker considers $d + 1$ targets: the set of d random mask values and a key-related information). More precisely, the $(d+1)$-order non-profiled attack combines $d + 1$ points in each trace associated to the mask values (e.g. points correlated to HW $(f_O (m \oplus v))$ and to HW (v_i)). Then, after this combination, a classical non-profiled attack is performed. However, it turns out that the mask values still influence the result of this combination (in a CPA context) and, as a result, an attack against a masked implementation needs more traces than against an unmasked implementation [22].

3 Machine Learning Approach Against Masking Countermeasure

In a secure implementation context, it is necessary that the mask values remain secret. It is quite natural to wonder whether an adversary can retrieve information on these secret values by analyzing the leakage information. Indeed, once the mask values is revealed or removed, the attacker is able to execute an efficient non-profiled or profiled attack.

In 2008, Werner Schindler [26] extended the stochastic attack to a masking context by taking into account the mask value v in the deterministic part. The main advantage of this approach is that we need a smaller set of measurements during the profiling step compared to TA applied to masking [26].

Oswald et al. [22] evaluated several approaches to attack a masked implementation with a combination between TA and CPA. In the same year, Gierlichs et al. [8] extended these practical proposals with a theoretical analysis. The first approach (called Templates Before Preprocessing) uses template attack to extract the values of the estimated leakage information of the $d + 1$ masked information (e.g. $HW((f_O(m \oplus v))$ and $HW(v_i)$) before combining them and to apply a CPA. The second approach (called Templates During Preprocessing) forces a bias into the mask values by removing traces associated to certain mask values. For this, the template attack extracts mask-related information and keeps a subset of traces associated to a subset of mask values. Then a CPA on the selected traces reveals the key. The third approach (called Templates After Preprocessing) uses template attack to extract the unmasked sensitive value (e.g. $HW(f_O(m))$) and performs a CPA on the extracted unmasked sensitive value. The last approach (called Template based DPA) performs a template attack against the masking implementation by replacing $Pr[T \mid L(f_O(m))]$ in Eq. 9 with

$$\hat{Pr}[T \mid L(f_O(m))] = \sum_{v \in \mathcal{V}^d} \hat{Pr}[T \mid L(f_O(m \oplus v)) \wedge v] \times \hat{Pr}[v] \qquad (14)$$

As a result, we need $card(\mathcal{Q}) \times card(\mathcal{V}^d)$ templates (where $card(x)$ represents the cardinality of the set x), one for each possible combination of $L(f_O(m \oplus v))$ and v.

We propose a new approach that uses a machine learning approach in order: (1) to bypass the problem of combining masks-related information that still keeps a dependence to mask values (unlike the d-order non-profiled attack, the Templates Before Preprocessing and the Templates After Preprocessing); (2) to keep all traces in the attacking step (unlike the Templates During Preprocessing); (3) to reduce the number of templates from $|\mathcal{Q}| \times |\mathcal{V}^d|$ to $|\mathcal{V}^d|$ (compared to the Template based DPA) leading to several advantages. In a theoretical point of view: (i) the number of required data increases with the number of templates (c.f. we need one learning set per template that leads to a gigantic workload in the profiling step [26]) and (ii) the imbalanced class problem [12] arises in the Template based DPA according to the density distribution of $L(f_O(m))$ (unlike our proposal). In a practical point of view, in the case of the DPAContest V4, the adversary has no control on the attacked device and, as a result, we (empirically) estimated that template based DPA needs a large number of measurements in the profiling step - at least 40,000 traces each of 435,002 samples, representing more than 2^{34} bytes of information - in order to have at least one trace per template with probability 0.99 when the Hamming weight leakage model is chosen. For the same problem, our proposal needs at least 200 traces (i.e. a realistic attack scenario). In practice, we need at least 48,698 traces for template based DPA and at least 35 for our proposal when considering the dataset of the DPAContest V4.

We suggest to apply a profiled attack to extract the mask values before a non-profiled attack that retrieves the secret key. Note that this approach is generalizable to the case where a profiled attack is used to extract the secret key. Furthermore, we assume to be in the worst case scenario where the adversary knows the mask values used during the profiling phase. Our requirements are fast-execution, low-memory usage and high success rate (i.e. realistic attack scenarios). Efficient methods to perform profiled attacks have been proposed recently [1, 9–11, 15, 16]. These methods use a machine learning model that returns the target value after a learning (profiling) step. Concerning the non-profiled attack, several approaches exist. One of the most efficient methods represents the CPA that does not require any estimation probability density function. Note that our method can be extended to other (nonlinear) distinguishers.

4   Experiments and Discussion

4.1   Target Implementation

The experiments were carried out on electromagnetic emission leakages that are freely available on the DPAContest V4 website [30] in order to easily reproduce the results. The target cryptographic device (an Atmel ATMega-163 smart card) implements in software the masked block-cipher AES-256 in encryption mode without any mode of operation. Each trace has $435,002$ samples associated to the same secret key and measured during the first round. The masking scheme is a variant of the *"Rotating Sbox Masking"* [21]; an additive Boolean masked scheme with masked SBox. According to its authors, it has a low-cost design and keeps performances and complexity close to the unprotected scheme (in a hardware context) while being resistant against several side-channel attacks. The purpose of the DPAContest is to retrieve the first 128 key bits. As we target the first 128 key bits and since the first round of AES-128 and AES-256 are the same, in the following we focus on AES-128.

Briefly, the masking scheme generates several mask values based on one 4-bit random value (called offset value) for each encryption. We refer to [21, 30] for additional information on the masking scheme and on the acquisitions setup.

4.2   Experimental Results

For the sake of fairness, we compared different attacks based on the same target value and the same dataset: each attack extracts first the offset value before applying a CPA to find the key value. Note that an adversary targeting the offset or the mask value leads to the same result in our case: the (Pearson) correlation between them equals one. We suggest to target the mask value when the setting differs.

Finding the Offset Value on Traces
Before proceeding with the quantitative analysis, we reports here a preliminary visualization phase that allowed us to find the points that are the highest correlated with the secret offset. For the sake of time and memory, we computed the Pearson correlation between each instant of 1500 traces and the offset values (see Fig. 1). It is worth emphasizing that several instants are (significantly) correlated with the target value. Except in the middle of traces, the visualization suggests that there is a high amount of information on the offset value available in each trace. As a consequence, we should expect that the profiled model would output the right offset value with a high probability.

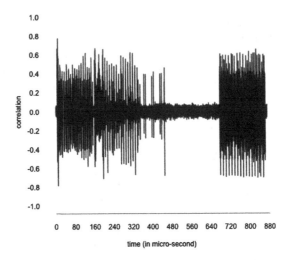

Fig. 1. Correlation between offset and power values at each time in the first round of the masked AES.

Model Selection

This section assesses and compares several classifiers that extract the secret offset value. We considered four different types of multiclass classification models: Support Vector Machine (SVM), Random Forest (RF), Template Attack (TA) and Stochastic Attack (SA). We used two disjoint sets: a learning set of 1500 traces to estimate the parameters of each model and a validation set of 1500 traces to measure their success rate in predicting the right offset value. During the feature selection step, in each trace, we selected 50 instants that are the highest linearly correlated with the offset value[1]. We did not considered other feature selection methods (such as *"Principal Component Analysis"* [23] or *"minimum Redundancy Maximum Relevance"* [24]) due to their massive memory requirements or time consuming while our dataset contained $1500 \times 435,002$ bytes $> 2^{29}$ bytes[2]. In spite of the low feature selection complexity, we observed a high success rate of the models.

Figures 2, 3, 4 and 5 report the success rate to predict the right offset value as a function of the number of points (that were selected from the sorted 50 instants) used in each trace for respectively SVM, RF, TA and SA. We can extract the following observations. First, as expected, the higher the number of traces in the learning set (from 25 % to 100 % of 1500 traces), the higher the accuracy. Secondly, the number of selected points in each trace influences the success rate: the higher the number of features, the higher the success rates for

---

[1] The 50 instants are sorted in descending order with respect to their correlation coefficient in absolute value.

[2] Each sample of the trace is an 8-bit value. The limit of R - the used program language - is 2^{31} bytes for a matrix.

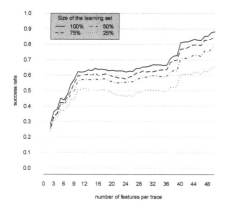

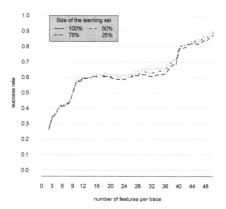

Fig. 2. Support Vector Machine.   **Fig. 3.** Random Forest.

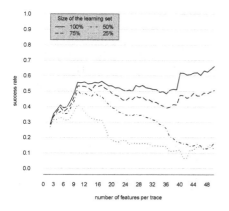

Fig. 4. Template Attack.   **Fig. 5.** Stochastic Attack.

SVM, RF and SA. It is interesting to remark that in a small learning set context (i.e. less than 75 % of the entire learning set) the TA reduces its success rate when the number of features goes beyond a certain size. This is presumably due to the ill-conditioning of the covariance matrix when the number of features is too large. In the other hand, the success rate of the new proposal based on SA varies only slightly in function of the size of the learning set.

Figure 6 combines the three previous plots by choosing the best size for the learning set (i.e. 100 % of 1500 traces). The success rates of SVM, RF and SA are similar and greater than the success rate of TA. Note that we did not select the best meta-parameter values for SVM and RF (such as the number of trees in the RF) but only the best number of features (from 2 to 50) to predict the target value. The default values of the implementation of SVM [6] and RF [18]

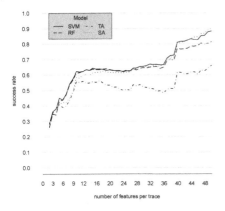

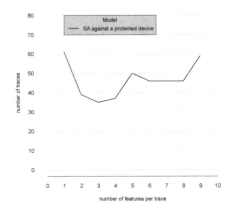

Fig. 6. SVM vs RF vs TA vs SA.

Fig. 7. Number of traces during the attacking phase in function of the number of features.

were used[3]. As a consequence, we do not claim that the SVM configurations and the RF configurations are necessarily the best one for profiled attack neither for our experiments. However, our experiments show that a profiled attack based on a machine learning model extracts more information on the offset value than a strategy based on TA for the presented task.

Based on the above considerations, and in order to choose the best learning model, we looked at the learning time and the prediction time of the offset, based on one trace, as a function of the number of selected points (see Figs. 8 and 9)[4]. TA has the lowest learning time while its prediction time increases exponentially in the number of selected features. SVM has a lower learning time and a reasonable prediction time compared to RF. As a result, in the attacking step, we use only SVM as the machine learning model. We do not report the results for SA as we used an unoptimized and nonpublic implementation. According to the previous results, we selected 50 features for SVM, TA and SA leading to a success rate of respectively 0.88, 0.66 and 0.90.

Attacking Step

During the attacking step we considered four settings targeting the Hamming weight of the MaskedSubBytes. In the first setting, CPA extracts the secret key on an unmasked implementation (i.e. the non-profiled attack always receives the correct offset value). The second setting targets the masked implementation where a SVM extracts the mask value and where a CPA searches the secret key. In the third and fourth experiments, the SVM is changed by respectively the

---

[3] SVM had a radial kernel with a gamma equals to the inverse of the data dimension and a cost of 1. RF had 500 trees.

[4] The experiments were executed on a MacBook Pro with 2.66 GHz Intel Core 2 Duo, 8 GB 1067 MHz DDR3.

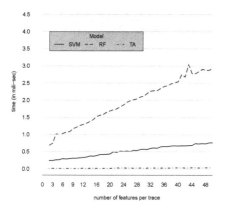 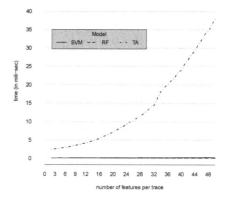

Fig. 8. Time to process a trace in the learning step (in milli-sec) per number of feature selected.

Fig. 9. Time to process a trace in the attacking step (in milli-sec) per number of feature selected.

TA and the SA. We repeated ten times each setting with a different set of traces during the attacking phase while the learning set remains the same.

Figure 10 summarizes the number of key bytes found as a function of the number of traces used (in average) during the non-profiling phase for each setting. We found the key with 16.3 traces (with less than 5 s of execution time) for the unmasked implementation. For the masked implementation, we extracted the key with 26 traces (with less than 20 s of execution time) by using the SVM, with 27.8 traces (with less than 80 s of execution time) by using the SA and with 56.4 traces (with less than 45 s of execution time) by using the TA. Figure 11 shows the minimum, the maximum and the average number of traces used to find the key. Compared to each strategy applied on the protected device, the SVM (combined with the CPA) leads to the closest results to an unprotected configuration.

For the sake of completeness, we also implemented the state-of-the-art stochastic attack on the masking scheme without a non-profiling step as proposed by Werner Schindler [26]. Figure 7 shows the number of traces needed on a validation set in function of the number of features used. The stochastic attack needs more than 40 traces to find the key when the model considers more than 5 features and it reaches the minimum with 3 features. According to Fig. 10, SA needs 107 traces in average in order to extract the 16 key bytes on a testing set (with less than 180 s of execution time).

4.3 Discussions

The experimental results of the previous sections suggest some considerations. First, the masking scheme proposed by the DPAContest V4 can be practically attacked with a combination between profiled and non-profiled attacks. Our strategy represents a combination between a SVM and a CPA that required 26 traces during the attacking step to extract the key of the implementation of a

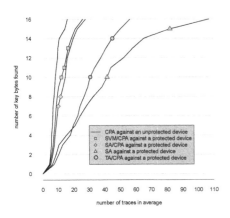

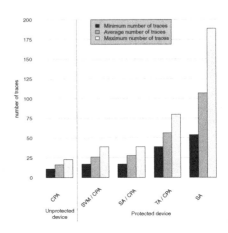

Fig. 10. Comparison of attacks against unprotected and protected AES.

Fig. 11. Min., max. and average number of traces used by each attack to find the key.

masked AES-128. In comparison, in the same device, a CPA against an unmasked implementation required in average 16.3 traces. SVM succeeds to extract information on the offset because the cryptographic device chooses different operations in function of this value (e.g. the choice of the masked SBox). Furthermore, the success of the attack is related to the implementation: the device manipulates the sixteen State bytes sequentially while they can be manipulated in parallel on a FPGA. Moreover, the cryptographic device selects randomly only one offset during whole of the encryption. As a result, many points in a trace relate to the chosen offset.

The attack should be improved by increasing the number of points selected in each trace. Indeed, Fig. 2 shows that the maximum value of the success rate is still not reached. However, Fig. 8 shows that the learning step time increases linearly with the number of points selected in each trace. As a result, there is a trade off to be made between the accuracy of the model and its learning speed.

The major consideration concerns accuracy since the experimental results show that in several settings, machine learning improves the success of attacks with respect to a strategy based on TA or to the state-of-the-art SA. More precisely, a machine learning model needs four times less traces than the state-of-the-art SA on masking scheme and two times less traces than a strategy based on TA. However, a new strategy based on SA becomes very competitive (in term of data complexity during the attacking phase) as the machine learning model but with a longer execution time than the machine learning model.

We submitted our best attack to the DPAContest V4 in order to have a validation of our results by a third party. According to this contest, the combination of SVM with CPA needs 22 traces with 0.528 s to retrieve a new AES-128 key with their computational power.

5   Conclusion and Perspectives

In this paper we have introduced an efficient machine learning approach in order to evaluate the security level of a masked implementation of AES. Specifically, we have extended the results of previous related works to protected devices [1, 9–11, 15–17]. The machine learning approach against a masked cryptographic algorithm consists in attacking first the mask with a machine learning model (i.e. a profiled attack) before targeting the secret key with for example a non-profiled attack.

We showed that stochastic attack or a strategy based on template attack overestimates the security level of protected device while the machine learning approach improves significantly this estimation. The main reason of the superiority of machine learning arises with the result of the multivariate Gaussianity tests that we carried out and that reject the hypothesis that the traces follow a Gaussian distribution in a high number of configurations. Therefore, a machine learning model extracts more information on the secret information (than template attack) by analyzing the same leakage information.

The complexity of the non-profiling step mainly depends on the quality of the profiled model. The higher the success to retrieve the mask, the lower the number of traces during the attacking phase. As a result, compared to a template attack, a learning model improves the probability to find the true mask value from 0.66 to 0.88 that implies a reduction of the number of traces in average during the attacking phase from 56.4 to 26. Regarding the state-of-the-art stochastic attack, the learning model divides the number of traces during the attacking phase by four. However, a new strategy based on stochastic attack reduces this number to 27.8 traces (in average) during the attack. In our context, the main advantage of a machine learning approach represents its speed: 80 s of execution time for a strategy based on SA while the machine learning model requires four times less. In comparison, a non-profiled attack against an unmasked implementation needs 17 traces with 5 s of execution time on the same cryptographic device. Therefore, the masked implementation increases the data complexity of the attack by two and the time complexity by four.

The quality of the profiled attacks mainly depends on the number of points selected on the traces. A robust feature selection method allowed to reach a high success rate to find the mask value by the profiled model. Interesting and as expected, the number of traces in the learning set of the machine learning model influences the result in a masking context (the higher the better). This is due to a reduction of the variance of the model.

We believe that our work opens up new avenues for interesting further research works. Among them, experiments must be performed on different public datasets of masking or hiding implementations which should be available in the DPAContest V4. If such experiments confirm the above results, then there are important implications. Strategies based on template attack or stochastic attack against countermeasures scheme may be shown to be less suitable for security level estimation in the worst case scenario compared to a machine learning approach.

References

1. Bartkewitz, T., Lemke-Rust, K.: Efficient template attacks based on probabilistic multi-class support vector machines. In: Mangard, S. (ed.) CARDIS 2012. LNCS, vol. 7771, pp. 263–276. Springer, Heidelberg (2013)
2. Breiman, L.: Random forests. Mach. Learn. **45**, 5–32 (2001)
3. Chari, S., Jutla, C.S., Rao, J.R., Rohatgi, P.: Towards sound approaches to counteract power-analysis attacks. In: Wiener, M. (ed.) CRYPTO 1999. LNCS, vol. 1666, p. 398. Springer, Heidelberg (1999)
4. Chari, S., Rao, J.R., Rohatgi, P.: Template attacks. In: Kaliski Jr, B.S., Koç, C.K., Paar, C. (eds.) CHES. LNCS, vol. 2523, pp. 13–28. Springer, Heidelberg (2002)
5. Cortes, C., Vapnik, V.: Support-vector networks. Mach. Learn. **20**(3), 273–297 (1995)
6. Dimitriadou, E., Hornik, K., Leisch, F., Meyer, D., Weingessel, A.: e1071: misc functions of the department of statistics (e1071), TU Wien, R package version 1.6 (2011)
7. Gandolfi, K., Mourtel, Ch., Olivier, F.: Electromagnetic analysis: Concrete results. In: Koç, Ç.K., Naccache, D., Paar, C. (eds.) CHES 2001. LNCS, vol. 2162, p. 251. Springer, Heidelberg (2001)
8. Gierlichs, B., Janussen, K.: Template attacks on masking: an interpretation. In: Lucks, S., Sadeghi, A.-R., Wolf, C., (eds.) WEWoRC (2007)
9. Heuser, A., Zohner, M.: Intelligent machine homicide. In: Schindler, W., Huss, S.A. (eds.) COSADE 2012. LNCS, vol. 7275, pp. 249–264. Springer, Heidelberg (2012)
10. Hospodar, G., Gierlichs, B., Mulder, E.D., Verbauwhede, I., Vandewalle, J.: Machine learning in side-channel analysis: a first study. J. Crypt. Eng. **1**(4), 293–302 (2011)
11. Hospodar, G., Mulder, E.D., Gierlichs, B., Vandewalle, J., Verbauwhede, I.: Least squares support vector machines for side-channel analysis. In: Second International Workshop on Constructive SideChannel Analysis and Secure, pp. 99–104. Design Center for Advanced Security Research Darmstadt (2011)
12. Japkowicz, N., Stephen, S.: The class imbalance problem: a systematic study. Int. Data Anal. J. **6**(5), 429–449 (2002)
13. Kocher, P.C.: Timing attacks on implementations of Diffie-Hellman, RSA, DSS, and other systems. In: Koblitz, N. (ed.) CRYPTO 1996. LNCS, vol. 1109, pp. 104–113. Springer, Heidelberg (1996)
14. Kocher, P.C., Jaffe, J., Jun, B.: Differential power analysis. In: Wiener, M. (ed.) CRYPTO 1999. LNCS, vol. 1666, p. 388. Springer, Heidelberg (1999)
15. Lerman, L., Bontempi, G., Markowitch, O.: Side channel attack: an approach based on machine learning. In: Second International Workshop on Constructive Side Channel Analysis and Secure Design, pp. 29–41. Center for Advanced Security Research Darmstadt (2011)
16. Lerman, L., Bontempi, G., Markowitch, O.: Power analysis attack: an approach based on machine learning. Int. J. Appl. Crypt. **3**(2), 97–115 (2014)
17. Lerman, L., Bontempi, G., Ben Taieb, S., Markowitch, O.: A time series approach for profiling attack. In: Gierlichs, B., Guilley, S., Mukhopadhyay, D. (eds.) SPACE 2013. LNCS, vol. 8204, pp. 75–94. Springer, Heidelberg (2013)
18. Liaw, A., Wiener, M.: Classification and regression by randomforest. R News **2**(3), 18–22 (2002)
19. Mangard, S., Oswald, E., Popp, T.: Power Analysis Attacks- Revealing the Secrets of Smart Cards. Springer, Heidelberg (2007)

20. Martinasek, Z., Zeman, V.: Innovative method of the power analysis. Radio Eng. **22**(2), 586–594 (2013)
21. Nassar, M., Souissi, Y., Guilley, S., Danger, J-L.: RSM: a small and fast counter-measure for AES, secure against 1st and 2nd-order zero-offset SCAs. In: Rosenstiel W.,Thiele, L. (eds.) DATE, pp. 1173–1178. IEEE (2012)
22. Oswald, E., Mangard, S.: Template attacks on masking—resistance is futile. In: Abe, M. (ed.) CT-RSA 2007. LNCS, vol. 4377, pp. 243–256. Springer, Heidelberg (2006)
23. Pearson, K.: On lines and planes of closest fit to systems of points in space. Philos. Mag. **2**(6), 559–572 (1901)
24. Peng, H., Long, F., Ding, C.: Feature selection based on mutual information criteria of max-dependency, max-relevance, and min-redundancy. IEEE Trans. Pattern Anal. Mach. Intell. **27**(8), 1226–1238 (2005)
25. Rivain, M., Dottax, E., Prouff, E.: Block ciphers implementations provably secure against second order side channel analysis. In: Nyberg, K. (ed.) FSE 2008. LNCS, vol. 5086, pp. 127–143. Springer, Heidelberg (2008)
26. Schindler, W.: Advanced stochastic methods in side channel analysis on block ciphers in the presence of masking. J. Math. Crypt. **2**(3), 291–310 (2008)
27. Schindler, W., Lemke, K., Paar, Ch.: A stochastic model for differential side channel cryptanalysis. In: Rao, J.R., Sunar, B. (eds.) CHES 2005. LNCS, vol. 3659, pp. 30–46. Springer, Heidelberg (2005)
28. Standaert, F.-X., Archambeau, C.: Using subspace-based template attacks to compare and combine power and electromagnetic information leakages. In: Oswald, E., Rohatgi, P. (eds.) CHES 2008. LNCS, vol. 5154, pp. 411–425. Springer, Heidelberg (2008)
29. Standaert, F.-X., Veyrat-Charvillon, N., Oswald, E., Gierlichs, B., Medwed, M., Kasper, M., Mangard, S.: The world is not enough: another look on second-order DPA. In: Abe, M. (ed.) ASIACRYPT 2010. LNCS, vol. 6477, pp. 112–129. Springer, Heidelberg (2010)
30. DPAContest V4 (2013). http://www.dpacontest.org/home/

Side Channel Attacks - Session Chair: François-Xavier Standaert

Clustering Algorithms for Non-profiled Single-Execution Attacks on Exponentiations

Johann Heyszl[1]([✉]), Andreas Ibing[2], Stefan Mangard[3], Fabrizio De Santis[2,4], and Georg Sigl[2]

[1] Fraunhofer Institute AISEC, Munich, Germany
johann.heyszl@aisec.fraunhofer.de
[2] Technische Universität München, Munich, Germany
andreas.ibing@in.tum.de,
{desantis,sigl}@tum.de
[3] Graz University of Technology, Graz, Austria
stefan.mangard@iaik.tugraz.at
[4] Infineon Technologies AG, Munich, Germany

Abstract. Most implementations of public key cryptography employ exponentiation algorithms. Side-channel attacks on secret exponents are typically bound to the leakage of single executions due to cryptographic protocols or side-channel countermeasures such as blinding. We propose for the first time, to use a well-established class of algorithms, i.e. unsupervised cluster classification algorithms such as the k-means algorithm to attack cryptographic exponentiations and recover secret exponents *without any prior profiling, manual tuning or leakage models*. Not requiring profiling is of significant advantage to attackers, as are well-established algorithms. The proposed non-profiled single-execution attack is able to exploit any available single-execution leakage and provides a straight-forward option to combine simultaneous measurements to increase the available leakage. We present empirical results from attacking an FPGA-based elliptic curve scalar multiplication using the k-means clustering algorithm and successfully exploit location-based leakage from high-resolution electromagnetic field measurements to achieve a low remaining brute-force complexity of the secret exponent. A simulated multi-channel measurement even enables an error-free recovery of the exponent.

Keywords: Exponentiation · Side-channel attack · Non-profiled · Single-execution · Unsupervised clustering · Simultaneous measurements · EM

1 Introduction

The main computations in public key cryptosystems are modular exponentiations with secret exponents or elliptic curve scalar multiplications with secret scalars.

Stefan Mangard – This research has been conducted while working for Infineon Technologies AG, Munich, Germany.

A. Francillon and P. Rohatgi (Eds.): CARDIS 2013, LNCS 8419, pp. 79–93, 2014.
DOI: 10.1007/978-3-319-08302-5_6, © Springer International Publishing Switzerland 2014

In both cases, the same exponentiation algorithms are employed to serially process exponents. In DSA or ECDSA, the exponents are different for every execution, e.g., chosen randomly as ephemeral secrets. RSA employs the same exponent multiple times, but exponent blinding [15] is often used as a counter-measure against side-channel analysis to use different exponents in every execution. Hence, side-channel attackers may only exploit *single executions* to recover a secret exponent. To prevent conventional SPA and timing attacks [15] the operation sequences during the serial processing of the exponents are rendered as homogeneous as possible. Algorithms like the square-and-multiply(-always), double-and-add(-always) or the Montgomery ladder algorithm are examples with constant operation sequences. However, a certain amount of side-channel leakage during single executions, i.e., single-execution leakage, about serially and independently processed bits or digits during the exponentiation cannot be prevented in many cases [5,14,21,24]. This may for instance be location-based leakage [12], address bit leakage [14], or operation-dependent leakage, e.g., when square and multiply operations can be distinguished [5].

We propose to specifically take advantage of well-established cluster classification algorithms [9] in general and the k-means algorithm for example to exploit any of such single-execution leakage and to recover secret exponents *without any prior profiling, manual tuning or heuristic leakage models. It is of significant advantage for an attacker if no profiling is required* because profiling can easily be prevented by using e.g., exponent blinding in the implementation or by executing the accessible exponentiation with public inputs on a different cryptographic engine as the private operation. Segments of the exponentiation which correspond to different exponent bits or digits are classified to find similar segments in an unsupervised way and by using algorithms from the *well-researched field of pattern classification*. This is contrary to previous attempts which use individual algorithms. An unsupervised classification equals the recovery of a secret exponent. Unsupervised clustering is generally useful in side-channel analysis when profiling information is not available and an exhaustive partitioning is computationally infeasible. The success of a correct classification of the exponent bits depends on the amount of available leakage signal in a certain measurement. Clustering algorithms further allow to determine posterior probabilities for classified bits. Hence, if only a part of the secret exponent is classified correctly, an attacker may brute-force bits with low posterior probabilities first. This enables a *straight-forward approach to cope with erroneous bits and allows to significantly reduce the secret's entropy*, thus, brute-force complexity, even if a complete recovery is impossible. The only way for an attacker to gather more leakage is to perform simultaneous measurements in multiple channels because attackers are *not* able to collect measurements from repeated executions since exponents change in every execution. Clustering algorithms allow for a straight-forward approach to *combine such simultaneous side-channel measurements*.

In an empirical study, we demonstrate the proposed attack and exploit the location-based single-execution leakage [12] of an FPGA-based implementation of an elliptic curve scalar multiplication using the k-means clustering algorithm.

We employ high-resolution measurements of the electromagnetic field and select measurement positions without prior profiling. The main result from our practical experiments is that the proposed method successfully reduces the remaining brute-force complexity of the secret scalar to a well-acceptable level in two out of nine cases. Additionally, we show how a combination of simultaneous measurements leads to a complete recovery of the scalar in a simulated setting.

Related work is discussed in Sect. 2. We present the non-profiled clustering attack on exponentiation algorithms in Sect. 3. In Sect. 4, we describe our practical evaluation of the attack and discuss countermeasures. Conclusions are provided in Sect. 5.

2   Related Work

In the following, we present related work in three aspects of this contribution: other attacks on exponentiation algorithms, previous applications of cluster analysis, and combination of measurements.

On Side-Channel Attacks on Exponentiations. Schindler and Itoh [21] present an attack against *multiple blinded* executions of exponentiation algorithms assuming that a single execution does not provide enough leakage. Our contribution presents a complement rather than an alternative to Schindler and Itoh's attack since we propose cluster classification algorithms as a *single execution attack* and means to improve the exploitation of any single-execution leakage. Walter [24] describes a single-execution side-channel attack on m-ary ($m > 2$) sliding window exponentiation algorithms. He recognizes pre-computed multiplier values in segments of the digit-wise exponentiation and uses his own algorithm to scan through the segments in one single pass and partition them into buckets according to their pair-wise similarity. While the main idea of our contribution is similar to the one described by Walter, we propose to employ unsupervised cluster classification algorithms which have been thoroughly researched in other statistical applications instead of using an individual algorithm which has not been investigated by the respective scientific community. In this way, our approach can be extended to a wide range of exponentiation algorithms and exploit any available kind of single-execution leakage of independent exponent bits or digits.

There are many published side-channel attacks on exponentiations based on the correlation coefficient. Messerges et al. [19] first mention cross-correlation of measurement segments to compare them and then perform a classification based on manually tuned thresholds. Witteman et al. [25] present an SPA attack on the square-and-multiply-always algorithm by cross-correlating measurements of consecutive operations sharing the From our view, using a correlation coefficient as a measure of similarity only incorporates linear relations while disregarding absolute values, thus, contained information. Hence, it is only meaningful in cases when absolute values are of different scales such as when comparing heuristic models of power consumption to actual measurements or when comparing measurements from different setups. Amiel et al. [2] and Clavier et al. [7] correlate heuristic leakage models from fixed multiplier values with the measurement to recover the exponent. Perin et al. [20] exploit bit-dependent differences in exponentiation algorithms using measurements of electromagnetic fields. However, they require averaging of multiple measurements in their practical results, which is infeasible in realistic circumstances. Algorithmically they simply subtract exponentiation segments from each other and use manually tuned thresholds to recover information. Hence, and contrary to us, all those approaches require a manual tuning of thresholds and, in part, heuristic leakage models as well as ad-hoc algorithms. Our approach using well-established algorithms provides an algorithmic advantage compared to them. Furthermore, we use the Euclidean distance instead of the correlation coefficient as a similarity metric to incorporate the maximum amount of contained information when comparing segments of the same measurement.

On Previous Applications of Cluster Analysis in SCA. There are previous contributions which mention cluster analysis in the context of side-channel analysis. Batina et al. [3] propose Differential Cluster Analysis (DCA) as an extension to DPA. Instead of a difference-of-means test as in classic DPA, a cluster criterion is used as statistical distinguisher. However, they do *not use unsupervised cluster classification algorithms*. In [4,18], this work is extended by considering PCA. Lemke-Rust and Paar [16] propose a *profiled* multi-execution attack against masked implementations of symmetric algorithms using the expectation-maximization clustering algorithm and a training set for the estimation of the clusters. In a profiled setting, they estimate mixture densities of clusters for known key values and unknown mask values using multiple executions. Contrarily, our approach is a *non-profiled* attack.

On the Combination of Measurements. A combination of simultaneous measurements can generally improve the success of side-channel attacks. Agrawal et al. [1] combine simultaneous measurements of the power consumption and electromagnetic field for profiled template attacks. Standaert and Archambeau [23] extend this and apply Principal Component Analysis (PCA) and Fisher's Linear Discriminant Analysis (LDA) to reduce the data dimensionality for template attacks. They also present a simple approach to combine simultaneous measurements for classic Differential Power Analysis (DPA) by treating measurements from different channels jointly. Souissi et al. [22] and Elaabid et al. [10] extend Correlation-based differential Power Analysis (CPA) [6] to combine simultaneous measurements by using products [10] or sums [22] of correlation coefficients. Contrary to previous contributions, our approach presents a way of combining measurements for a non-profiled single-execution attack.

3   Non-profiled Clustering to Attack Exponentiations

When attacking exponentiation algorithms used in public key cryptography, only a single execution is available to an attacker to recover a secret exponent because of cryptographic protocols or protection against side-channel analysis.

In the following subsections we first describe the term single-execution leakage and how measurement traces are segmented into samples for classification.

As a main part, we describe how to apply unsupervised clustering algorithms for a non-profiled and non manually-tuned attack. For the case that the attack is not entirely successful due to insufficient single-execution leakage, we describe an approach to cope with classification errors to achieve low remaining brute-force complexities nonetheless. Finally, we describe how to use multiple simultaneous measurements to gather more leakage.

3.1   Single-Execution Side-Channel Leakage of Exponentiations

The common property of all popular exponentiation algorithms, e.g., binary, m-ary, or sliding window exponentiations is that the computation is segmented and performed in a loop. In every segment, the same operations are repeated to process independent bits or digits of the exponent. (If the operations would be different and depending on exponent bits, the implementation would be prone to conventional SPA and timing attacks [15].) We use the case of binary exponentiations which process the exponent bit-wise for our explanations. The square-and-multiply-always algorithm for instance repeatedly either performs a square-and-multiply, or a square-and-dummy-multiply operation, depending on each processed bit. Such repeated operations share similarities for equal bits. Depending on the implementation and included countermeasures, different side-channels can be exploited to detect such similarities. We refer to the side-channel information about different bits which is leaked in single executions of exponentiations as *single-execution side-channel leakage*. Our approach is able to exploit any kind of such single-execution leakage.

Figure 1 abstractly depicts a side-channel measurement of a timing-safe binary exponentiation algorithm in the upper part. The observed computation consists of a loop with multiple iterations of constant timing which correspond to single exponent bits. The algorithm could e.g. be a square-and-multiply-always, double-and-add-always, or Montgomery ladder algorithm. Such a side-channel measurement trace vector $t = (t_1, ..., t_l)$ of an exponentiation contains l measurement values t_x and covers the entire execution. Binary algorithms process n bits during this time in total. To exploit the single-execution leakage of n independent bits, the trace is cut into n multivariate samples $t_i = (t_{(1+(i-1)\frac{l}{n})}, ..., t_{(i\frac{l}{n})})$, $1 \leq i \leq n$ of equal length $\frac{l}{n}$ where each sample then corresponds to one bit. Figure 1 also depicts an abstract example for how a side-channel measurement

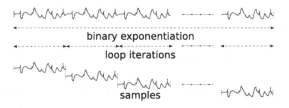

Fig. 1. Segmenting a side-channel measurement of an exponentiation into samples

is cut into samples. The segmentation borders can e.g. be derived from visual inspection or comparison of shifted trace parts.

3.2 Clustering of Samples Reveals the Secret without Profiling

The multivariate samples t_i contain the leakage of independent, secret exponent bits. Hence, the samples belong to *one of two* classes, i.e., ω_A and ω_B. (When attacking m-ary, or sliding window exponentiation algorithms, m classes are expected.) All side-channel measurements are affected by normally distributed measurement- and switching noise. Therefore, samples within classes ω_j, $j \in \{A, B\}$ are normally distributed around means $\boldsymbol{\mu}_j$. The distance between these means $\boldsymbol{\mu}_j$ is caused by the exploited single-execution leakage. Hence, the distribution of samples t_i in two classes ω_A and ω_B can be described as $p(t_i|\omega_A) \sim \mathcal{N}(\boldsymbol{\mu}_A, \boldsymbol{\Sigma}_A)$ and $p(t_i|\omega_B) \sim \mathcal{N}(\boldsymbol{\mu}_B, \boldsymbol{\Sigma}_B)$.

The correct partition of samples t_i into classes ω_A and ω_B is unknown to the attacker. The number of possible partitions equals 2^n for binary exponentiations with n bit exponents. Testing all possible partitions equals brute-forcing a secret and is computationally infeasible for realistic exponent sizes. Template attacks find these classifications through matching against *templates which are found in a profiling phase*. Other related work use cross-correlation and *manually tuned thresholds* as well as individual and ad-hoc algorithms.

However, we found that *well-researched unsupervised cluster classification algorithms* such as *k-means clustering* [9] can be used to find partitions effectively and *without any manual methods or prior profiling. Hence, we propose to use such algorithms for single-execution side-channel attacks on exponentiation algorithms. Finding a correct partition, or classification, equals the recovery of the secret exponent.* If the correct partition is found, there are only two possibilities to assign the bit values 0 and 1 to two classes ω_A and ω_B, hence, to recover the secret exponent.

The choice of a clustering algorithm depends on the shape of the clusters, hence the distribution of samples within clusters. We decided to start with a simple model of cluster distributions and assume that *all variables (dimensions) within the multivariate samples t_i are independent* and exhibit equal variances σ^2 within the two classes. Hence, the distribution of both classes ω_A and ω_B can be described as $p(t_i|\omega_j) \sim \mathcal{N}(\boldsymbol{\mu}_j, \sigma^2 \boldsymbol{I})$, $j \in \{A, B\}$. The *optimal* classification algorithm *under these assumptions* is the *k-means clustering algorithm* which is depicted in Algorithm 1. It uses the *Euclidean distance* as a similarity metric and estimates k cluster means $\boldsymbol{\mu}_j$, $j \in \{1, k\}$. In the case of binary algorithms, k equals 2 and two classes ω_A and ω_B are expected.

Initially, k random samples t_i are randomly selected as means and the remaining samples are classified according to shortest Euclidean distance. Then, in iterations, new means are computed within each class, and the classification according to shortest Euclidean distance is repeated until the classification is stable in subsequent iterations. The k-means algorithm is usually executed multiple times and the best result in terms of a *sum-of-squared-error* criterion is finally selected in order to prevent the algorithm from getting stuck in local maxima.

Algorithm 1. Unsupervised k-means clustering algorithm [9]

input: samples t_i, $1 \leq i \leq n$, number of clusters k
output: cluster means μ_j, $1 \leq j \leq k$ and classification $c_i \in [1..k]$, $1 \leq i \leq n$
1: initialize by picking k random samples t_i as start values for μ_j, $1 \leq j \leq k$
2: **repeat**
3:     assign samples t_i to classes $c_i \in [1..k]$ from shortest distance to μ_j, $1 \leq j \leq k$
4:     compute new μ'_j as mean of all samples t_i with $c_i = j$
5: **until** $\mu'_j = \mu_j \; \forall \, j$, assign μ_j new values μ'_j and repeat

---

Clustering algorithms essentially estimate cluster parameters to perform classifications. This estimation of clusters could be improved by using more samples from multiple executions in a first step, even though the secret would then be different in every execution. The actual attack would then be performed in a second step and certainly only target a single execution.

Decorrelation and Reduction of Dimensions. If the samples derived from measurements do not comply with the model which is required for the application of k-means (described above), the results will be worse than theoretically possible. The k-means algorithm assumes statistical independence of dimensions (variables) in the samples, thus, uncorrelated noise influences. However, subsequent measurement values of the power consumption possibly contain the same switching noise influence. One way to handle this is to employ the *expectation-maximization clustering algorithm* which provides more degrees of freedom in such cases (because it also models the covariance between variables). However, it requires a significant overhead in computation. Alternatively, if necessary, this can be coped with by employing Principal Component Analysis (PCA) [9]. PCA performs a projection into a lower dimensional, *orthogonal* space by maximizing the variance in the samples. Hence, the remaining dimensions are uncorrelated. (As a drawback, this is performed without regard of cluster distributions or cluster discriminants which could possibly lead to inferior results.) PCA can certainly also be used to reduce the amount of dimensions in the samples t_i for computational reasons.

3.3   Brute-Force Complexity to Handle Classification Errors

If a recovered exponent cannot be verified as being entirely correct, at least one sample (bit) is misclassified by the algorithm. We propose a way to cope with such situations. Clustering algorithms allow to derive posterior class-membership probabilities [9] for all samples t_i along with their classification. For instance when employing the *k-means* clustering algorithm, samples which are classified into class ω_A and are close to the separating plane between ω_A and ω_B have a low posterior probability of belonging to class ω_A. An attacker may approach misclassifications by brute-forcing samples with low posterior probabilities first. A straight-forward approach is to iteratively consider an increasing range of samples i with the lowest posterior probabilities and brute-force their classification until all erroneous samples are included in this range, thus, a correct classification is achieved. Given that m equals the final number, which the attacker certainly does not know from the beginning, he would proceed iteratively and increase the number of included bits i starting from 1 until m is reached. The required brute-force complexity to handle classification errors can, thus, be given as an upper bound by using the sum formula of a geometric series. Including the mandatory step of brute-forcing the classes-to-bit-values assignment (A and B to 0 and 1), this required brute-force complexity equals $2 \times \sum_{i=1}^{m} 2^i = 2^{m+1+1} - 2$ for $m > 0$ and can be defined as 2 for $m = 0$ (classification entirely correct; one out of two trial for correct class-to-bit-value assignment). *This means that even if the exponent is not recovered entirely, the entropy can be significantly reduced which is a significant advantage over previous methods which do not provide such a mechanism to cope with errors during an attack.*

3.4 Combining Side-Channel Measurements

The success of single-execution attacks on exponentiation algorithms generally suffers from insufficient leakage [5,21]. Countermeasures introduce superficial noise to decrease the signal-to-noise ratio of the leakage or aim at reducing the leakage signal directly. Averaging repeated measurements with equal input values is a simple example for an approach to decrease such noise. But this is not feasible if the secret changes in every execution which is the case for most cryptographic exponentiations. Hence, simultaneous measurements are the only way for an attacker to increase the gathered side-channel leakage. Clustering algorithms allow to combine simultaneous side-channel measurements in a straight-forward way. This is achieved by generating multivariate samples using values from all measurements. As an example, samples $\mathbf{t}_i^1$ from measurement 1 are combined with samples $\mathbf{t}_i^2$ from measurement 2 leading to combined samples $\mathbf{t}_i^{\text{combined}} = (\mathbf{t}_i^1, \mathbf{t}_i^2)$. This improves the classification, if the new measurements contain additional leakage information. *Hence, we propose to improve clustering-based single-execution attacks through combining the contained information from multiple, simultaneous side-channel measurements.*

4   Practical Evaluation

In this section, we practically demonstrate our proposed attack against an FPGA-based ECC implementation. As a single-execution side-channel leakage, we exploit location-based leakage [12] revealed by high-resolution measurements of the electromagnetic field [13]. Following the principle that our attack is non-profiled, we do not use any prior knowledge to find measurement positions with high leakage.

4.1   Design-Under-Test and Measurement Setup

Our target is an implementation of an elliptic curve scalar multiplication configured into a *Xilinx Spartan-3 (XC3S200)* FPGA. It gets affine x- and y-coordinates of a base point P and a scalar d as input and returns affine x- and y-coordinates of the resulting point $d \cdot P$. The result is computed using the Montgomery ladder algorithm presented by López and Dahab [17] which is a binary exponentiation algorithm processing a 163 bit scalar bitwise in a uniform operation sequence. This prevents timing-based single-execution leakage. The projective coordinates of the input point are randomized [8] as a countermeasure against differential power analysis. However, the design exhibits location-based information leakage [12] because it uses working registers depending on the value of the processed scalar bit and no protection mechanism against this is included. For these reasons, the design is eligible for our attack and we exploit this single-execution leakage using high-resolution electromagnetic field measurements.

Backside access to integrated circuit dies generally requires less practical effort in case of plastic or smartcard packages. The plastic package on the backside of the FPGA was removed mechanically to enable measurements close to the die surface. We use an inductive near-field probe with a 100 μm resolution, built-in 30 dB amplifier, and external 30 dB amplifier (both with a noise figure of 4.5 dB). The detected location-based leakage depends on the measurement position on the surface of the die [12]. Since our attack is non-profiled, we are unable to find a position with high leakage through prior profiling. Instead, we choose measurement positions by geometrical means. Figure 2 shows those 9 positions marked with circles and annotated with numbers. They are organized in an 3 by 3 array with 1.5 mm distance in x- and y-direction. These geometries seem feasible for an actual array of electromagnetic probes [22]. The dashed rectangle depicts the surface of the FPGA die which measures $\approx 5000 * 4000$ μm. We performed the attack on those measurements.

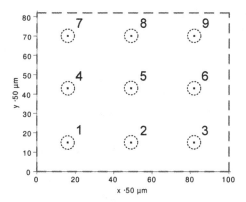

Fig. 2. FPGA die area as dashed rectangle with array of marked measurement positions

Furthermore, we demonstrate a combination of simultaneous measurements to increase the leakage in a simulated setting. Since we did not have an array probe or multiple probes at hand, we simulated this by moving one probe to the marked positions and repeated the measurement with exactly equal processed values. Hence, we prevent the device from changing the exponent and random numbers during repeated executions. While this simplification is not exactly the same as simultaneously using multiple probes, we are convinced that the results are still conclusive.

All measurements were recorded at a sampling rate of $5\,\mathrm{GS/s}$ and compressed by using the sum of squared values in every clock cycle ($\mathrm{V^2s}$) to reduce the amount of data and computation complexity during clustering. Through synchronization of the oscilloscope and the function generator, we prevent frequency jitter and drift in the measurements.

4.2   Clustering Individual Measurements

We performed our clustering-based attack on individual measurements. Hence, we segmented every measurement into multivariate samples t_i. Each sample contains 551 compressed values of 551 clock cycles during which one exponent bit is processed. Figure 3 depicts a cut-out of four consecutive samples (14 to 17) from the measurement at position 3 for illustrative purposes. The borders of the samples are depicted as vertical dashed lines after every 551 cycles. The exponent bit values which are processed in the segments are annotated, however, the corresponding single-execution leakage is not clearly visible.

We attacked the individual measurements by employing the unsupervised *k-means* clustering algorithm Algorithm 1 to classify the samples in two clusters as described in Sect. 3.2. The runtime on a regular PC was neglegible and in the range of seconds. We assess the quality of the result by computing the remaining brute-force complexity required to recover the entirely correct scalar after clustering as described in Sect. 3.3. Figure 4 depicts the resulting brute-force complexity for every individual measurement position according to Fig. 2 and Table 1 displays them in tabular form (columns marked with '1' to '9').

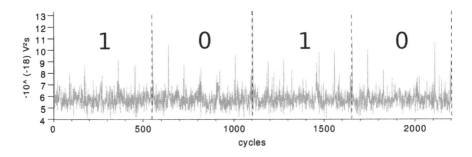

Fig. 3. Four samples (14 to 17) from the compressed measurement at position 3

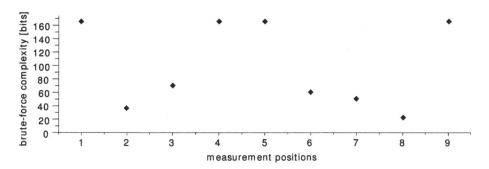

Fig. 4. Remaining brute-force complexity after clustering *individual measurements*

Table 1. Brute-force complexity after clustering single and combined measurements

Measurement positions	1	2	3	4	5	6	7	8	9	all
Brute-force complexity [bits]	165	37	70	165	165	60	51	22	165	**0**

As a main result of our practical study, we are able to report that in two out of nine cases, for the measurements at position 8 and 2, the remaining brute-force complexity (22 and 37 bits) is clearly within a practical reach. An attacker could, thus, repeat a measurement at different positions, perform the attack including the incremental brute-force and eventually be successful with a high probability. *This clearly demonstrates the capabilities of unsupervised cluster classification as a non-profiled single-execution attack on exponentiation algorithms to exploit single-execution leakage.*

Positions 1, 4, 5 and 9 lead to a brute-force complexity of 165 bits which is the maximum value $(163 + 1 + 1$ bits) indicating that the clustering algorithm led to largely incorrect results. Possible reasons for this are insufficient signal-to-noise ratios of the exploited leakage, outlier samples, or that the k-means algorithm is insufficient since the assumed model of cluster distributions does not fit. (An influence of one bit of some internal ALU operation for the separation of two clusters is impossible since each sample contains many ALU operations with different data.)

4.3   Clustering Combined Measurements

The results from clustering individual measurements lead to remaining brute-force complexities greater than zero and in seven out of nine cases beyond limits for practical brute-force. As a second step, we demonstrate how simultaneous side-channel measurements can be combined to reduce the remaining brute-force complexity, hence, improve the attack. We combined the measurements as described in Sect. 3.4 and repeated the k-*means* clustering. *As an important result we report, that the classification then leads to a remaining brute-force*

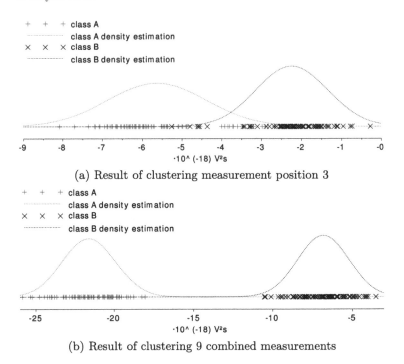

(a) Result of clustering measurement position 3

(b) Result of clustering 9 combined measurements

Fig. 5. Visual representation of clustering results to show gain of combination

complexity of zero, denoted as 'all' in Table 1. This clearly demonstrates the advantage of combining measurements for attacking exponentiation algorithms using unsupervised clustering algorithms.

Figure 5(a), (b) *demonstrate the advantage of combining measurements* in an more illustrative way. Figure 5(a) visually represents the **result after clustering** the *single measurement at position number* 1. The clustering algorithm output two cluster means μ_A and μ_B and samples which are classified according to a separation plane in the middle between those means (equals classification according to shortest Euclidean distance). For the illustration of this clustering result, we projected all multivariate samples t_i (multi-dimensional) onto a line (one-dimensional) which extends through both cluster means. As such, the resulting single values per sample are linear combinations of all vector dimensions according to the weighting factors determined by the clustering result. After this projection, the two cluster distributions become clearly observable. For the illustration, we use the correct scalar to mark the samples according to their proper class membership. Additionally, we estimate the two assumed Gaussian distributions and depict two curves, denoted as *class A/B density estimation*. It is obvious that the two distributions overlap in Fig. 5(a) which means that there have been misclassifications. Many samples are across the wrong side of the half distance between the two distributions which corresponds to the separation plane. This leads to the high brute-force complexity reported in Table 1.

Figure 5(b) depicts a similar linear projection of the **result after clustering** of 9 combined measurements. *It can be observed clearly, that the separation of the two classes is significantly improved by the combination of measurements which also complies with the brute-force complexity of 0 reported in Table 1.*

4.4 Countermeasures

Generally, all methods which reduce the signal-to-noise ratio of arbitrary single-execution leakage, either by reducing the single-execution leakage signal, or increasing the noise level, make our attack more difficult since the attacker is limited in the number of measurements he can record simultaneously. There is no dedicated other countermeasure except for such general ones.

Location-based single-execution leakage as it is exploited in this practical attack can specifically be prevented by randomizing variable locations [12], by balancing registers and their signal paths, or by locating them in an interleaved way that they cannot be distinguished [11].

5   Conclusion

We demonstrate that unsupervised clustering algorithms are powerful for attacking a wide range of exponentiation algorithms in single-execution settings and *without any prior profiling or manually tuned thresholds, which is of significant advantage for attackers.* Instead of individual ad-hoc algorithms we propose to use well-research cluster classification algorithms. Any available single-execution side-channel leakage can be exploited.

In a practical evaluation we successfully recover the secret scalar from an FPGA-based ECC implementation. Individual measurements of the electromagnetic field partly lead to sufficiently low remaining brute-force complexities. By performing the attack including the incremental brute-force at several positions, the attacker might get successful with a realistic effort. Additionally, we provide evidence for the advantage of combining simultaneous measurements. This means that instead of finding specifically good measurement positions, an attacker might simply combine leakage information from multiple simultaneous measurements.

Acknowledgments. This work was partly funded by the German Federal Ministry of Education and Research in the project SIBASE through grant number 01IS13020.

References

1. Agrawal, D., Rao, J.R., Rohatgi, P.: Multi-channel attacks. In: Walter, C.D., Koç, Ç.K., Paar, C. (eds.) CHES 2003. LNCS, vol. 2779, pp. 2–16. Springer, Heidelberg (2003)

2. Amiel, F., Feix, B., Villegas, K.: Power analysis for secret recovering and reverse engineering of public key algorithms. In: Adams, C., Miri, A., Wiener, M. (eds.) SAC 2007. LNCS, vol. 4876, pp. 110–125. Springer, Heidelberg (2007)

3. Batina, L., Gierlichs, B., Lemke-Rust, K.: Differential cluster analysis. In: Clavier, C., Gaj, K. (eds.) CHES 2009. LNCS, vol. 5747, pp. 112–127. Springer, Heidelberg (2009)

4. Batina, L., Hogenboom, J., van Woudenberg, J.G.J.: Getting more from PCA: first results of using principal component analysis for extensive power analysis. In: Dunkelman, O. (ed.) CT-RSA 2012. LNCS, vol. 7178, pp. 383–397. Springer, Heidelberg (2012)

5. Bauer, S.: Attacking exponent blinding in RSA without CRT. In: Schindler, W., Huss, S.A. (eds.) COSADE 2012. LNCS, vol. 7275, pp. 82–88. Springer, Heidelberg (2012)

6. Brier, E., Clavier, C., Olivier, F.: Correlation power analysis with a leakage model. In: Joye, M., Quisquater, J.-J. (eds.) CHES 2004. LNCS, vol. 3156, pp. 16–29. Springer, Heidelberg (2004)

7. Clavier, C., Feix, B., Gagnerot, G., Roussellet, M., Verneuil, V.: Horizontal correlation analysis on exponentiation. In: Soriano, M., Qing, S., López, J. (eds.) ICICS 2010. LNCS, vol. 6476, pp. 46–61. Springer, Heidelberg (2010)

8. Coron, J.-S.: Resistance against differential power analysis for elliptic curve cryptosystems. In: Koç, Ç.K., Paar, C. (eds.) CHES 1999. LNCS, vol. 1717, pp. 292–302. Springer, Heidelberg (1999)

9. Duda, R.O., Hart, P.E., Stork, D.G.: Pattern Classification, 2nd edn. Wiley-Interscience, Hoboken (2001)

10. Elaabid, M.A., Meynard, O., Guilley, S., Danger, J.-L.: Combined side-channel attacks. In: Chung, Y., Yung, M. (eds.) WISA 2010. LNCS, vol. 6513, pp. 175–190. Springer, Heidelberg (2011)

11. He, W., de la Torre, E., Riesgo, T.: An interleaved EPE-Immune PA-DPL structure for resisting concentrated EM side channel attacks on FPGA implementation. In: Schindler, W., Huss, S.A. (eds.) COSADE 2012. LNCS, vol. 7275, pp. 39–53. Springer, Heidelberg (2012)

12. Heyszl, J., Mangard, S., Heinz, B., Stumpf, F., Sigl, G.: Localized electromagnetic analysis of cryptographic implementations. In: Dunkelman, O. (ed.) CT-RSA 2012. LNCS, vol. 7178, pp. 231–244. Springer, Heidelberg (2012)

13. Heyszl, J., Merli, D., Heinz, B., De Santis, F., Sigl, G.: Strengths and limitations of high-resolution electromagnetic field measurements for side-channel analysis. In: Mangard, S. (ed.) CARDIS 2012. LNCS, vol. 7771, pp. 248–262. Springer, Heidelberg (2013)

14. Itoh, K., Izu, T., Takenaka, M.: Address-bit differential power analysis of cryptographic schemes OK-ECDH and OK-ECDSA. In: Kaliski, B.S., Koç, Ç.K., Paar, C. (eds.) CHES 2002. LNCS, vol. 2523, pp. 129–143. Springer, Heidelberg (2003)

15. Kocher, P.C.: Timing attacks on implementations of Diffie-Hellman, RSA, DSS, and other systems. In: Koblitz, N. (ed.) CRYPTO 1996. LNCS, vol. 1109, pp. 104–113. Springer, Heidelberg (1996)

16. Lemke-Rust, K., Paar, C.: Gaussian mixture models for higher-order side channel analysis. In: Paillier, P., Verbauwhede, I. (eds.) CHES 2007. LNCS, vol. 4727, pp. 14–27. Springer, Heidelberg (2007)

17. López, J., Dahab, R.: Fast multiplication on elliptic curves over $GF(2^m)$ without precomputation. In: Koç, Ç.K., Paar, C. (eds.) CHES'99. LNCS, vol. 1717, pp. 316–327. Springer, Heidelberg (1999)

18. Mavroeidis, D., Batina, L., van Laarhoven, T., Marchiori, E.: PCA, eigenvector localization and clustering for side-channel attacks on cryptographic hardware devices. In: Flach, P.A., De Bie, T., Cristianini, N. (eds.) ECML PKDD 2012, Part I. LNCS, vol. 7523, pp. 253–268. Springer, Heidelberg (2012)
19. Messerges, T.S., Dabbish, E.A., Sloan, R.H.: Power analysis attacks of modular exponentiation in smartcards. In: Koç, Ç.K., Paar, C. (eds.) CHES 1999. LNCS, vol. 1717, pp. 144–157. Springer, Heidelberg (1999)
20. Perin, G., Torres, L., Benoit, P., Maurine, P.: Amplitude demodulation-based EM analysis of different RSA implementations. In: Design, Automation Test in Europe Conference Exhibition (DATE), 2012, pp. 1167–1172, Mar 2012
21. Schindler, W., Itoh, K.: Exponent blinding does not always lift (partial) SPA resistance to higher-level security. In: Lopez, J., Tsudik, G. (eds.) ACNS 2011. LNCS, vol. 6715, pp. 73–90. Springer, Heidelberg (2011)
22. Souissi, Y., Bhasin, S., Guilley, S., Nassar, M., Danger, J.-L.: Towards different flavors of combined side channel attacks. In: Dunkelman, O. (ed.) CT-RSA 2012. LNCS, vol. 7178, pp. 245–259. Springer, Heidelberg (2012)
23. Standaert, F.-X., Archambeau, C.: Using subspace-based template attacks to compare and combine power and electromagnetic information leakages. In: Oswald, E., Rohatgi, P. (eds.) CHES 2008. LNCS, vol. 5154, pp. 411–425. Springer, Heidelberg (2008)
24. Walter, C.D.: Sliding windows succumbs to big MAC attack. In: Koç, Ç.K., Naccache, D., Paar, C. (eds.) CHES 2001. LNCS, vol. 2162, pp. 286–299. Springer, Heidelberg (2001)
25. Witteman, M.F., van Woudenberg, J.G.J., Menarini, F.: Defeating RSA multiply-always and message blinding countermeasures. In: Kiayias, A. (ed.) CT-RSA 2011. LNCS, vol. 6558, pp. 77–88. Springer, Heidelberg (2011)

Optimization of Power Analysis
Using Neural Network

Zdenek Martinasek[✉], Jan Hajny, and Lukas Malina

Department of Telecommunications, Brno University of Technology,
Technicka 12, 612 00 Brno, Czech Republic
martinasek@feec.vutbr.cz

Abstract. In power analysis, many different statistical methods and power consumption models are used to obtain the value of a secret key from the power traces measured. An interesting method of power analysis based on multi-layer perceptron was presented in [1] claiming a 90 % success rate. The theoretical and empirical success rates were determined to be 80 % and 85 %, respectively, which is not sufficient enough. In the paper, we propose and realize an optimization of this power analysis method which improves the success rate to almost 100 %. The optimization is based on preprocessing the measured power traces using the calculation of the average trace and the subsequent calculation of the difference power traces. In this way, the prepared power patterns were used for neural network training and of course during the attack. This optimization is computationally undemanding compared to other methods of preprocessing usually applied in power analysis, and has a great impact on classification results. In the paper, we compare the results of the optimized method with the original implementation. We highlight positive and also some negative impacts of the optimization on classification results.

Keywords: Power analysis · Neural network · Optimization · Preprocessing

1 Introduction

Power analysis (PA) measures and analyzes the power consumption of cryptographic devices depending on their activity. It was introduced by Kocher in [2]. The goal of PA is to determine the sensitive information of cryptographic devices from the measured power consumption and to apply the obtained information in order to abuse the cryptographic device. There are two basic methods of power analysis: simple PA and differential PA. The attacker tries to determine the secret key directly from the traces measured in the simple power analysis (SPA). In the most extreme case, this means that the attacker attempts to reveal the key based on one single power trace. The goal of the differential power analysis (DPA) attacks is to reveal the secret key of the cryptographic module by using

A. Francillon and P. Rohatgi (Eds.): CARDIS 2013, LNCS 8419, pp. 94–107, 2014.
DOI: 10.1007/978-3-319-08302-5_7, © Springer International Publishing Switzerland 2014

a large number of power traces that have been recorded while the device was encrypting or decrypting various input data. Power analysis is widely discussed and belongs to the most popular types of side channel analysis methods because the attacker does not need any expensive special equipment. A detailed description of power analysis including side-channel sources, testbed, statistical tests and countermeasures is summarized in the book [3].

1.1   Related Work

Simple power analysis attacks were described by Kocher in [2]. A typical example of SPA is the attack on the implementation of the RSA (Rivest Shamir Adleman) asymmetric cryptographic algorithm, where the difference in power consumption between the operations of multiplication and squaring can be observed [4]. Template based attacks are another type of SPA attack, which were introduced in [5]. Practical aspects of template attacks have been discussed in [6,7].

The concept of the DPA attack was first described also in [2] and the basic principle was introduced on a DES algorithm using the statistical method based on the Difference of Means. Subsequently, applicable statistical tests were discussed in [8]. An important question of the impact of preprocessing the measured data on the effectiveness of DPA was presented in [9,10]. The application of the correlation coefficient as a statistical method in DPA was described in [11] and nowadays, this method is one of the most widely used. A detailed description of the general schema on which all power analyses are based and the best known statistical tests including the basic power simulation models are given in [3,12].

One of the first examples of digital signal processing applied to side channel analysis can be found in [13]. Digital filtering is used to facilitate attacks based on side channel analysis for devices such as Xilinx Field Programmable Gate Arrays (FPGAs) [14], Radio Frequency Identification (RFID) devices [15–17] and Cortex-M3 SoC [18].

Neural networks (NN) are used mostly in the cryptography branch to realize key distribution [19], hash functions [20], random number generators [21], in public-key cryptography [22], and in the exchange protocols [23] (similar to the Diffie-Hellman protocol). The publications [24,25] dealing with the use of NN in the side channel cryptanalysis are mostly focused on acoustic side channels, where NN are used for the classification of captured records of buttons pressed on a keyboard.

In the field of power analysis, the possibility of using neural networks was first published in [26]. Naturally, this work was followed by other authors, e.g. [27–29], who dealt with the classification of individual power prints. These works are mostly oriented towards reverse engineering based on power print classification. The usage of neural networks for the classification of a secret key value has been sparsely published and tested yet. Works [30–33] dealing with this issue are based on machine learning algorithm such as support vector machines (SVM).

An interesting method based on typical multi-layer perceptron (MLP) was demonstrated in [1]. In this work, a neural network was used for the classification of the AES secret key. This power analysis method uses a typical two-layer perceptron (three-layer neural network if we take into consideration the input layer) to determine the secret key value only from one power trace measured. First classification results were really promising and this method achieved a successful classification of 90 % for the first byte of the secret key. The method was thoroughly tested using 2560 power traces and an empirical success rate of around 85 % was determined. The theoretical success rate determined from the results was only about 80 %. Other negative characteristics were revealed during the subsequent testing, e.g. the distribution of the maximum probability values or the low probability value of selected key estimation.

1.2   Our Contribution

Our contribution lies in the optimization of the power analysis method described in [1]. We minimize the above-mentioned negative characteristics of the method implementation to increase the success rate of classification. The optimization is based on preprocessing the power traces measured, using the calculation of the average trace and the subsequent calculation of the difference power traces. Preprocessed power patterns are used for the neural network training and, naturally, during the attack phase, in the same way as described in [1]. This optimization is computationally undemanding compared to other methods of preprocessing usually applied in power analysis (e.g. filtering [34]) and has a great impact on the classification results. In the paper, we compare the results of the optimized method with the original implementation. We highlight the positive and also some small negative impacts of the optimization on the classification results. Both methods were verified using 2, 560 power traces corresponding to all the values of the secret key to analyze the repeatability and feasibility of the method. In the original paper, the cross-validation was not used to verify the neural network, we decided to compare the original method implementation with the optimized method, using the typical 10-fold cross-validation. In data mining and machine learning, the 10-fold cross-validation is the most common way to verify the model. Our contribution can be summarized in the following main points:

- optimization proposal,
- implementation of optimization,
- comparison of results,
- cross-validation of both implementations.

2   Method and Testbed Description

The following text summarizes the most important facts about the original implementation of the power analysis method and the experimental setup. The fundamental goal of the method is to obtain from the power trace measured the secret key value, which is stored in the cryptographic module. In the following text, we denote the secret key stored in the attacked cryptographic module as K_{sec}, and the estimated value of secret key, which was determined using a neural network, as K_{est}. Naturally, if the method works correctly, the values K_{est} and K_{sec} are equal at the end of the classification process. Assume that the secret key can be expressed in bytes as $K_{sec} = \{k_1, k_2, \ldots, k_N\}$ for $0 \le k_i \le 255$, where N represents the secret key length and i each step of the method. The method assumes sequential classification as most DPA attacks do, which means that the classification is realized byte by byte. This power analysis determines the first byte k_1 of the secret key in the first step and the second byte k_2 in the second step, and so on. The difference between individual steps is in the division of the power traces measured into parts corresponding to the time intervals in which the cryptographic device works with the respective bytes of the secret key. The method is divided into three phases:

– The first phase is the preparation of power consumption patterns, where the attacker has to prepare the training set to train the neural network. The attacker must know the type of the cryptographic module on which he wants to realize the attack.
– The second phase is the preparation and training of the neural network using the power patterns measured in the first phase.
– The third phase is the attack. The attacker measures the power consumption of the device under attack and inserts the measured power trace to the input of the trained neural network. The neural network assigns the probability vector to the power consumption that contains probabilities for all key estimates. The estimate key with the highest probability should be equal to the secret key stored in the device under attack.

It is clear that it is not suitable to measure and classify the power trace corresponding to the whole cryptographic algorithm but it is better to locate some important operations where the cryptographic module works with intermediate result and the secret key. The AddRoundKey and SubBytes operations represent a suitable place in the power trace of the AES algorithm.

A complete AES algorithm with a key length of 128 bits was implemented into the cryptographic module and the synchronization was performed only for the AddRoudnKey and SubBytes operations in the initialization phase of the algorithm. The program allowed incrementing and decrementing the first byte of the secret key (k_1) and indicated this operation by sending the respective value via a serial port to a computer. In [1] and in our experiment, the measurements were focused on the first byte of the secret key but we claim that this power analysis method is able to classify the whole AES secret key from only one measured power trace. Therefore, the term secret key denotes the first byte of the secret key in the following text. The synchronization signal and the communication with the computer did not affect the power consumption of the cryptographic module. The cryptographic module was represented by the PIC 8-bit microcontroller, and for the power consumption measurement we used the CT-6 current probe and the Tektronix DPO-4032 digital oscilloscope. We used standard operating conditions with 5 V power supply.

A well known fact is that noise always poses the problem during the power consumption measurement. We performed the experimental measurements of a

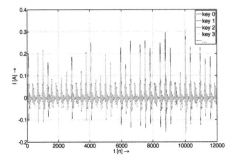

Fig. 1. Original power patterns.

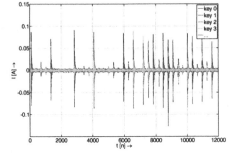

Fig. 2. Preprocessed power patterns.

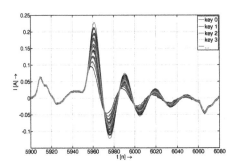

Fig. 3. Detail of original patterns.

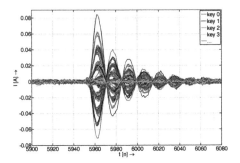

Fig. 4. Detail of preprocessed patterns.

test bed made according to the information provided in [3] and we established that the noise level was distributed according to the normal distribution with the parameters $\mu = 0\,\text{mA}$ and $\sigma = 5\,\text{mA}$. Every stored power trace was calculated as an average power trace from ten power traces measured using the digital oscilloscope to reduce electronic noise. More information about the testbed is given in [12,35]. Our other experiments with power analysis and implementation, for example power consumption measurement of smart phone encrypted data, are reported in [36,37].

3   Proposed Optimization

The optimization is based on the preprocessing of power traces measured during the first phase of the method, where the training patterns are prepared. During this phase, the attacker tries to obtain the training patterns of power consumption for the AddRoundKey and SubBytes operations for all variants of the secret key byte k_1 (256 possible variants). Figure 1 shows the power patterns for all values of the secret key cut out from the whole power trace for the first byte, and Fig. 3 shows a detail of the power peak at time $t[n] = 6,000$. From these figures, it is clear that the measured power traces are greatly synchronized and divided into several groups. These power patterns were stored and used for the neural network training in the original method proposal and implementation [1] (it was used three times 256 power traces for neural network training). We magnified the differences in the power traces measured to improve the classification results. Increased differences were achieved by employing a preprocessing process based on the calculation of average power traces corresponding to every key value. The main principle of preprocessing is described in the following text.

The measured power traces are functions with discrete time. We denote the measured power traces corresponding to every secret key value as $P[i, n]$, where n represents the discrete time $n = \{0, \ldots, 12000\}$, and i represents all possible secret key byte values from 0 to 255. Subsequently, we can calculate an average trace $\bar{A}$ using the following equation:

$$\bar{A}[n] = \frac{1}{256} \sum_{i=0}^{255} P[i, n].\tag{1}$$

The training patterns for the optimized implementation are calculated as a subtraction of measured traces from the average trace and are denoted as P_D:

$$P_D[i, n] = \bar{A}[n] - P[i, n] = \frac{1}{256} \sum_{i=0}^{255} P[i, n] - P[i, n].\tag{2}$$

Figure 2 shows the resulting power patterns after preprocessing and Fig. 4 shows the corresponding power peak detail at time $t[n] = 6,000$. The resulting patterns were stored and used for the neural network training in the optimized implementation. If we compare these two sets of patterns, it is clear that after preprocessing the patterns show the places where the power traces are different.

4   Comparison of Classification Results

The neural network was implemented and trained in Matlab using the Netlab neural network toolbox in the same way as described in [1]. The implementation differs only in the preprocessing of power pattern according to the optimization proposal described in Sect. 3. To compare the suitability of optimization, we measured once again the whole set of power traces corresponding to all the secret key values and this set was subsequently analyzed using the created and trained neural network. The measured traces were stored in the matrix and all matrix rows (all power traces) were classified using the neural network. In this manner, we obtained classification results for all possible key values and the first notion of how successful the optimized method is when compared to the original implementation.

The classification of all power traces gave the matrices $\mathbf{R_D}$ of dimension 255×255. The row index corresponds to the value of a secret key K_{sec} and the column index corresponds to the value of a key estimate K_{est}. In other words,

Table 1. Part of the resulting matrices.

	Original implementation **R**					Optimized implementation **R_D**				
$\vdots$	...	...	...	...	... ...	...	...	...	...
2	0.00%	0.00%	6.46%	0.00%	... 0.00%	0.00%	92.86%	0.00%	...
1	0.00%	66.42%	0.00%	0.00%	... 0.00%	99.87%	0.00%	0.00%	...
0	36.77%	0.00%	0.00%	0.00%	... 98.23%	0.00%	0.00%	0.00%	...
K_{sec}/K_{est}	0	1	2	3	... 0	1	2	3	...

the neural network assigned to every measured power trace a probability vector for individual key estimates. Table 1 shows a really small part of the resulting matrix R_D together with the original results matrix R. From Table 1 it can be seen that the neural network classified the power trace corresponding to $K_{sec} = 0$ with a probability of 98.23 % for the key estimate $K_{est} = 0$ and other estimates with zero probability in the optimized implementation (we do not take into consideration the whole output vector in this demonstration). The neural networks classified the power trace corresponding to $K_{sec} = 0$ with a probability of 36.77 % for the key estimate $K_{est} = 0$ in the original implementation. From this small comparison of the results obtained, we can confirm the increase in the probability of correct key estimates. For example, probability estimates for correct key 0 and 1 increased from 36.77 % and 66.42 % to 98.23 % and 99.87 % respectively.

The whole matrix R of classification is shown graphically in Fig. 5 and matrix R_D is shown in Fig. 6. Each row of the matrix corresponds to the output probability vector, which is the result of power trace classification. Each column contains the probability of an individual key estimate. The main goal of the method is to have the estimate key value equal to the secret key value after classification. In other words, the function $K_{est} = K_{sec}$ is true. The function $K_{est} = K_{sec}$ is visible in both matrices but in R_D it is much more distinguishable because the correct classified probabilities consist of values between 90 % and 100 % and thus the line is darker. The graphs also show the reduction of alternative variants of classification and thus the absence of parallel lines with the function $K_{est} = K_{sec}$ in Fig. 6. The graphs displayed in Figs. 7 and 8 confirm this desired property. These graphs show the classification results (output probability vectors) for five chosen secret keys for both implementations. Appropriate probability vectors for the chosen $K_{sec} = 5, 41, 81, 129, 248$ values are distinguished by color and the optimized implementation is shown in Fig. 8 and original implementation in Fig. 7. If we compare the results, for example, for the power trace $K_{sec} = 5$ of the optimized implementation, the increase in the correct key estimate from 35 % to 96 % is clearly visible while other possible key estimates were fully suppressed. This desired property, i.e. suppressing potential key estimates was confirmed for the other three chosen secret keys (41, 81, 248). For the last chosen power trace corresponding to the secret key 129, alternative key estimates were also suppressed, except one, but the probability of correct key estimate increased

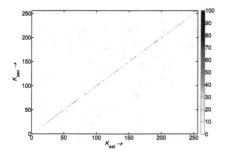

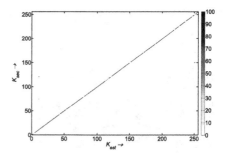

Fig. 5. Graphically depicted matrix **R**.

Fig. 6. Graphically depicted matrix $\mathbf{R_D}$.

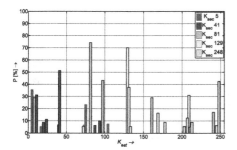

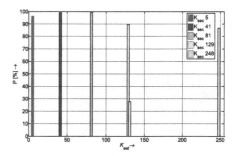

Fig. 7. Probability vector for five secret keys of the original method.

Fig. 8. Probability vector for five secret keys of the optimized method.

from 70 % to 90 %. From these results, we conclude that proposed optimization allows a significant increase in the classification results because the probability of correct key estimates is increased and the other possible key estimates are suppressed.

On the other hand, a complete suppression of alternative probabilities can be negative, because the probability of a correct key estimate was always the second highest probability for all erroneously classified keys in the original implementation. The attacker would use this feature if it happened that the key was badly classified at the end of the attack. If the optimization suppressed all alternative possibilities of key estimates, similarly like in Fig. 8, the attacker would not be able to try a second key estimate.

However, it is necessary to investigate all selected key estimates from the tested set because during this investigation, the theoretical success rate about 80 % was calculated in the original implementation. The main problem of wrongly classified key estimations was the low value of the selected highest probability. Figure 9 shows these selected highest probabilities of power traces corresponding to all the values of the secret key for the original implementation. In other words, it shows which key estimate was classified with the highest probability for a specific power trace. The graph is displayed with two Y-axes for better clarity.

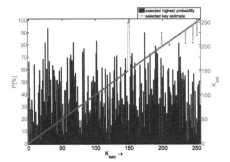

Fig. 9. The highest selected probabilities of original implementation.

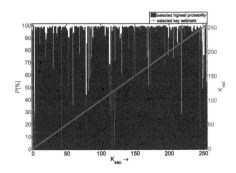

Fig. 10. The highest selected probabilities of optimized implementation.

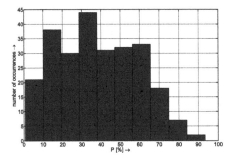

Fig. 11. Histogram of highest probabilities of original implementation.

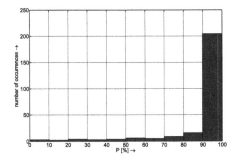

Fig. 12. Histogram of highest probabilities of optimized implementation.

The X-axis represents the secret key values and the blue Y-axis shows the probability of the highest selected probability while the red Y-axis corresponds to the chosen key estimate. The shape of the function $K_{est} = K_{sec}$ is again clearly visible and only a few points interrupt the linear progression. From the whole proofing set (256 power traces measured), the neural network classified a wrong key estimate sixteen times in the original implementation. Classification errors occurred for key estimates with low values of the highest probability. The average value of the highest probability which led to the wrong classification was 17 %. From these results, the theoretical border of correct classification was established as 20 %. For key estimates with a selected highest probability lower than 20 %, the probability of wrong classification is higher. Figure 9 shows that the occurrence of 14 %, 18 % and 20 % probabilities is no exception. Figure 11 displays a histogram of selected highest probabilities for the original implementation. From the histogram, it can be seen that probabilities of up to 10 % occurred twenty-one times while the probabilities of 10–20 % occurred thirty-eight times, which makes a total of 59 occurrences of all 256 values. The total number of keys potentially predisposed to incorrect classification is about 23 %, which means that the original method theoretically works with a success rate of about 80 %.

These results obtained from the first implementation were promising but the success rate was not sufficient. This was the main reason why we tried an optimized implementation to increase the selected highest probabilities and thus reduce the wrongly classified keys. Figure 10 shows the selected highest probabilities for the optimized implementation with the course of the function $K_{est} = K_{sec}$ is almost smooth and containing only nine wrongly classified keys. If we compare these results with the first implementation results, we achieve a decrease in wrong classification from 16 to 9, which corresponds to an improvement of 43 %. These results clearly demonstrate the functionality and suitability of preprocessing the power traces measured for classification using a neural network. Nine wrongly classified key estimates correspond to 3.5 % of the power traces measured. Therefore, we can declare that the optimized method identified the correct value of the secret key in 96.5 % of cases. During repeated tests (another training of the neural network with the identical training set), the optimized method achieved a correct classification of 95–98 %.

Figure 12 displays a histogram of the selected highest probabilities for the optimized implementation. From the histogram, it can be seen that probabilities of 10 % to 70 % occurred only five times on average. Probabilities of 70 % and 80 % occurred ten times and fifteen times, respectively. The largest representation in the selected maximum probability is that of the 90 % to 100 % probabilities, which occurred two hundred and five times. The histogram confirmed the increase of the maximum probabilities, thus increasing the occurrence of the 90 % probability. The total number of keys potentially predisposed to wrong classification is reduced from 20 % to 5 % after optimization.

5   Cross Validation

A ten-times larger set of power consumptions was measured and used for a detailed comparison of the original and optimized method in the same manner as described in [1]. Ten power traces were independently stored for each value of the secret key. The set composed of 2, 560 power traces was classified using neural networks in the same manner as described in the previous sections. The number of wrongly classified key estimates and the overall success rate are given in Table 2. The original method achieved a correct secret key classification in 85 % and the optimized method achieved a correct secret key classification in 94 %. These results confirm the previous results including the correct calculation of the theoretical success rate and the necessity of optimization. We can state that the optimized method achieved results that were better by 10 %.

Table 2. Classification results for 2560 power traces.

Method	Number of errors [−]	Success rate [%]
Original implementation	378	**85.23**
Optimized implementation	139	**94.57**

In the original paper, the cross-validation was not used for the verification of the neural network. We decided to compare the original method with the optimized method using the typical 10-fold cross-validation. In data mining and machine learning, the 10-fold cross-validation is the most common method of model verification. Cross validation is a statistical method of evaluating and comparing learning algorithms by dividing data into two segments: one is used to learn or train a model and the other is used to validate the model. In typical cross validation, the training and validation sets must cross-over in successive rounds such that each data point has a chance of being validated against. Our set of 2560 measured power traces consisted of 10 power traces corresponding to every secret key value, therefore we used 9 power traces for neural network training and one for testing in every step of validation. The results of 10-fold cross-validation are summarized in Table 3, where err denotes the number of wrongly classified key estimates and $\overline{err}$ denotes the average value of wrong estimates calculated from every step of the cross-validation.

Table 3. Number of errors for 10-fold cross-validation.

Step of cross-validation	1	2	3	4	5	6	7	8	9	10	$\overline{err}$	Success rate [%]
Original implementation $err[-]$	10	5	12	17	8	17	13	14	7	12	11.5	95.71
Optimized implementation $err[-]$	0	0	0	0	1	0	1	0	0	0	0.2	**99.92**

The results obtained reveal that the original implementation is able to classify the secret key with a success rate of around 95 %. It is better than the assumption stated above. This difference is caused by the size of the training set. In the original implementation, 3 power traces for every secret key value for neural network training and one for testing were used. In comparison with the cross-validation, 9 power traces for neural network training and one for testing were used. The results of cross-validation confirm the positive impact of optimization on classification results. The optimized method is able to classify the secret key value with almost 100 % success rate.

6   Conclusion

In the paper, we presented and realized an optimization method of the power analysis based on multi-layer perceptron. The optimization was based on pre-processing the measured power traces using the calculation of the average trace and the subsequent calculation of the difference power traces. These power patterns were used for neural network training and, naturally, during the attack phase. We compared the classification results of the optimized method with the original implementation and evaluated the positive and negative impact of optimization on classification results.

The proposed optimization allowed a significant improvement in the classification results because the probability of correct key estimates was increased and the other possible key estimates were suppressed. On the other hand, a complete suppression of alternative probabilities can be negative because the attacker is not able to try a second key estimate if the key estimate with the highest probability is wrong.

In the original paper, cross-validation was not used to verify the neural network and thus we compare the original method with the optimized method, using the typical 10-fold cross-validation. The result of cross-validation confirm the positive impact of optimization on classification result. The optimized method is able to classify the secret key value with almost a 100 % success rate.

The features of the optimized method can be summarized in the following points:

- optimization is computationally undemanding,
- places where power traces differ can be highlighted,
- probability corresponding to correct key estimations is increased,
- probability corresponding to incorrect key estimations is suppressed,
- number of keys potentially predisposed to wrong classification is reduced,
- negative impact consists in a complete suppression of alternative probabilities.

Acknowledgments. This research work is funded by the Ministry of Industry and Trade of the Czech Republic, project FR-TI4/647. Measurements were run on computational facilities of the SIX Research Center, registration number CZ.1.05/2.1.00/03.0072.

References

1. Martinasek, Z., Zeman, V.: Innovative method of the power analysis. Radioengineering **22**(2), 586–594 (2013)
2. Kocher, P.C., Jaffe, J., Jun, B.: Differential power analysis. In: Wiener, M. (ed.) CRYPTO 1999. LNCS, vol. 1666, pp. 388–397. Springer, Heidelberg (1999)
3. Mangard, S., Oswald, E., Popp, T.: Power Analysis Attacks: Revealing the Secrets of Smart Cards (Advances in Information Security). Springer-Verlag New York Inc., Secaucus (2007)
4. Joye, M., Olivier, F.: Side-channel analysis. In: van Tilborg, H.C.A., Jajodia, S. (eds.) Encyclopedia of Cryptography and Security, pp. 1198–1204. Springer, New York (2011)
5. Chari, S., Rao, J.R., Rohatgi, P.: Template attacks. In: Kaliski, B.S., Koç, Ç.K., Paar, C. (eds.) CHES 2002. LNCS, vol. 2523, pp. 13–28. Springer, Heidelberg (2003)
6. Rechberger, C., Oswald, E.: Practical template attacks. In: Lim, C.H., Yung, M. (eds.) WISA 2004. LNCS, vol. 3325, pp. 440–456. Springer, Heidelberg (2005)
7. Hanley, N., Tunstall, M., Marnane, W.P.: Using templates to distinguish multiplications from squaring operations. Int. J. Inf. Secur. **10**(4), 255–266 (2011)
8. Coron, J.S., Naccache, D., Kocher, P.: Statistics and secret leakage. ACM Trans. Embed. Comput. Syst. **3**(3), 492–508 (2004)
9. Joye, M., Paillier, P., Schoenmakers, B.: On second-order differential power analysis. In: Rao, J.R., Sunar, B. (eds.) CHES 2005. LNCS, vol. 3659, pp. 293–308. Springer, Heidelberg (2005)

10. Herbst, C., Oswald, E., Mangard, S.: An AES smart card implementation resistant to power analysis attacks. In: Zhou, J., Yung, M., Bao, F. (eds.) ACNS 2006. LNCS, vol. 3989, pp. 239–252. Springer, Heidelberg (2006)
11. Brier, E., Clavier, C., Olivier, F.: Correlation power analysis with a leakage model. In: Joye, M., Quisquater, J.-J. (eds.) CHES 2004. LNCS, vol. 3156, pp. 16–29. Springer, Heidelberg (2004)
12. Martinasek, Z., Clupek, V., Krisztina, T.: General scheme of differential power analysis. In: 2013 36th International Conference on Telecommunications and Signal Processing (TSP), pp. 358–362 (2013)
13. Messerges, T.S., Dabbish, E.A., Sloan, R.H., Messerges, T.S., Dabbish, E.A., Sloan, R.H.: Investigations of power analysis attacks on smartcards. In: USENIX Workshop on Smartcard Technology, pp. 151–162 (1999)
14. Moradi, A., Barenghi, A., Kasper, T., Paar, C.: On the vulnerability of FPGA bitstream encryption against power analysis attacks: extracting keys from xilinx Virtex-II FPGAs. In: Proceedings of the 18th ACM Conference on Computer and Communications Security, CCS '11, pp. 111–124. ACM, New York (2011)
15. Plos, T., Hutter, M., Feldhofer, M.: Evaluation of side-channel preprocessing techniques on cryptographic-enabled HF and UHF RFID-Tag prototypes. In: Dominikus, S. (ed.) Workshop on RFID Security 2008, Budapest, Hungary, pp. 114–127, 9–11 July 2008
16. Kasper, T., Oswald, D., Paar, C.: Side-channel analysis of cryptographic rfids with analog demodulation. In: Juels, A., Paar, C. (eds.) RFIDSec 2011. LNCS, vol. 7055, pp. 61–77. Springer, Heidelberg (2012)
17. Oswald, D., Paar, C.: Breaking Mifare DESFire MF3ICD40: power analysis and templates in the real world. In: Preneel, B., Takagi, T. (eds.) CHES 2011. LNCS, vol. 6917, pp. 207–222. Springer, Heidelberg (2011)
18. Barenghi, A., Pelosi, G., Teglia, Y.: Improving first order differential power attacks through digital signal processing. In: Proceedings of the 3rd international conference on Security of information and networks, SIN '10, pp. 124–133. ACM (2010)
19. Kim, H.M., Kang, D.J., Kim, T.H.: Flexible key distribution for scada network using multi-agent system. In: ECSIS Symposium on Bio-inspired, Learning, and Intelligent Systems for Security, pp. 29–34 (2007)
20. Lian, S., Sun, J., Wang, Z.: One-way hash function based on neural network. CoRR abs/0707.4032 (2007)
21. Wang, Y.H., Shen, Z.D., Zhang, H.G.: Pseudo random number generator based on hopfield neural network, pp. 2810–2813 (2006)
22. Liu, N., Guo, D.: Security analysis of public-key encryption scheme based on neural networks and its implementing. In: Wang, Y., Cheung, Y., Liu, H. (eds.) CIS 2006. LNCS (LNAI), vol. 4456, pp. 443–450. Springer, Heidelberg (2007)
23. Mislovaty, R., Perchenok, Y., Kanter, I., Kinzel, W.: Secure key-exchange protocol with an absence of injective functions. Phys. Rev. E **66**, 066102 (2002)
24. Fiona, A.H.Y.: ERG4920CM Thesis II Keyboard Acoustic Triangulation Attack. Ph.D. thesis, Department of Information Engineering, The Chinese University of Hong Kong (2006)
25. Zhuang, L., Zhou, F., Tygar, J.D.: Keyboard acoustic emanations revisited. In: Proceedings of the 12th ACM Conference on Computer and Communications Security, CCS '05, pp. 373–382. ACM, New York (2005)
26. Quisquater, J.J., Samyde, D.: Automatic code recognition for smart cards using a kohonen neural network. In: Proceedings of the 5th conference on Smart Card Research and Advanced Application Conference, CARDIS'02, Berkeley, CA, USA, vol. 5, p. 6–6 (2002)

27. Kur, J., Smolka, T., Svenda, P.: Improving resiliency of java card code against power analysis. In: Mikulaska kryptobesidka, Sbornik prispevku, pp. 29–39 (2009)
28. Martinasek, Z., Macha, T., Zeman, V.: Classifier of power side channel. In: Proceedings of NIMT2010 (September 2010)
29. Yang, S., Zhou, Y., Liu, J., Chen, D.: Back propagation neural network based leakage characterization for practical security analysis of cryptographic implementations. In: Kim, H. (ed.) ICISC 2011. LNCS, vol. 7259, pp. 169–185. Springer, Heidelberg (2012)
30. Heuser, A., Zohner, M.: Intelligent machine homicide - breaking cryptographic devices using support vector machines. In: Schindler, W., Huss, S.A. (eds.) COSADE 2012. LNCS, vol. 7275, pp. 249–264. Springer, Heidelberg (2012)
31. Bartkewitz, T., Lemke-Rust, K.: Efficient template attacks based on probabilistic multi-class support vector machines. In: Mangard, S. (ed.) CARDIS 2012. LNCS, vol. 7771, pp. 263–276. Springer, Heidelberg (2013)
32. Hospodar, G., Gierlichs, B., Mulder, E.D., Verbauwhede, I., Vandewalle, J.: Machine learning in side-channel analysis: a first study. J. Cryptogr. Eng. 1(4), 293–302 (2011)
33. Lerman, L., Bontempi, G., Markowitch, O.: Side channel attack: an approach based on machine learningn. In: COSADE 2011 - Second International Workshop on Constructive Side-Channel Analysis and Secure Design, pp. 29–41 (2011)
34. Oswald, D., Paar, C.: Improving side-channel analysis with optimal linear transforms. In: Mangard, S. (ed.) CARDIS 2012. LNCS, vol. 7771, pp. 219–233. Springer, Heidelberg (2013)
35. Martinasek, Z., Zeman, V., Sysel, P., Trasy, K.: Near electromagnetic field measurement of microprocessor. Przegl. Elektrotechniczny 89(2a), 203–207 (2013)
36. Malina, L., Clupek, V., Martinasek, Z., Hajny, J., Oguchi, K., Zeman, V.: Evaluation of software-oriented block ciphers on smartphones. In: Danger, J.-L., Debbabi, M., Marion, J.-Y., Garcia-Alfaro, J., Heywood, N.Z. (eds.) FPS 2013. LNCS, vol. 8352, pp. 353–368. Springer, Heidelberg (2014)
37. Hajny, J., Malina, L., Martinasek, Z., Tethal, O.: Performance evaluation of primitives for privacy-enhancing cryptography on current smart-cards and smartphones. In: Garcia-Alfaro, J., Lioudakis, G., Cuppens-Boulahia, N., Foley, S., Fitzgerald, W.M. (eds.) DPM 2013 and SETOP 2013. LNCS, vol. 8247, pp. 17–33. Springer, Heidelberg (2014)

Time-Frequency Analysis
for Second-Order Attacks

Pierre Belgarric[1,3], Shivam Bhasin[1], Nicolas Bruneau[1,4(✉)],
Jean-Luc Danger[1,5], Nicolas Debande[1,6], Sylvain Guilley[1,5], Annelie Heuser[1],
Zakaria Najm[1], and Olivier Rioul[2,7]

[1] TELECOM-ParisTech, Crypto Group, Paris, France
`nicolas.bruneau@telecom-paristech.fr`
[2] TELECOM-ParisTech, Digital Communications Group, Paris, France
[3] Orange Labs, Applied Cryptography Group, Issy-les-Moulineaux, France
[4] STMicroelectronics, AST Division, Rousset, France
[5] Secure-IC S.A.S., Rennes, France
[6] SERMA ITSEF, Pessac, France
[7] École Polytechnique, Palaiseau, France

Abstract. Second-order side-channel attacks are used to break first-order masking protections. A practical reason which often limits the efficiency of second-order attacks is the temporal localisation of the leaking samples. Several pairs of leakage samples must be combined which means high computational power. For second-order attacks, the computational complexity is quadratic. At CHES '04, Waddle and Wagner introduced attacks with complexity $\mathcal{O}(n \log_2 n)$ on traces collected from a *hardware* cryptographic implementation, where n is the window size, by working on traces auto-correlation. Nonetheless, the two samples must belong to the same window which is (normally) not the case for *software* implementations. In this article, we introduce preprocessing tools that improve the efficiency of bi-variate attacks (while keeping a complexity of $\mathcal{O}(n \log_2 n)$), even if the two samples that leak are far away one from the other (as in software). We put forward two main improvements. Firstly, we introduce a method to avoid losing the phase information. Next, we empirically notice that keeping the analysis in the frequency domain can be beneficial for the attack. We apply these attacks in practice on real measurements, publicly available under the DPA Contest v4, to evaluate the proposed techniques. An attack using a window as large as 4000 points is able to reveal the key in only 3000 traces.

Keywords: Bi-variate attacks · Zero-offset 2O-CPA · Discrete Hartley transform · Leakage in phase

This work is partially funded by ANR/JST project SPACES: https://spaces.enst.fr/.
Nicolas Debande – This work has been conducted while Nicolas Debande was with Morpho, Osny, France.
Annelie Heuser – Google European fellow in the field of privacy and is partially founded by this fellowship.

A. Francillon and P. Rohatgi (Eds.): CARDIS 2013, LNCS 8419, pp. 108–122, 2014.
DOI: 10.1007/978-3-319-08302-5_8, © Springer International Publishing Switzerland 2014

1   Introduction

Side-Channel Attacks (SCA [1]) and corresponding protection techniques have been a hot research topic for over a decade now. Data masking [6] is one of few popular side-channel countermeasures, which motivates thorough investigations of higher-order SCA as e.g., in [12,15]. The following study deals mainly with *second-order SCA* which is used to break a first-order masking countermeasure. A particular case of second-order SCA is when the two shares used by the masking scheme are processed or leak simultaneously. In this case, Waddle and Wagner introduced an attack at CHES '04 [15], which consists in raising the traces to the power two. Such an attack, a so-called *zero-offset SCA*, is commonly used against hardware or parallel implementations. However, for software implementations, the two shares naturally leak at different dates or time samples. The second-order attacks which combine two different time samples are termed *bi-variate SCA*. The two different leakage samples are referred to as $\mathcal{L}(t_0)$ and $\mathcal{L}(t_1)$ in the following. Despite bi-variate attacks may be powerful, a practical implementation might need a large amount of effort from the part of the attacker. The main problem of bi-variate attacks is to find the exact temporal localization (t_0, t_1) corresponding to leakages $\mathcal{L}(t_0)$ and $\mathcal{L}(t_1)$. Incidentally, depending on the implementation, there might exist several such pairs.

To avoid finding the pair (t_0, t_1) explicitly, Waddle and Wagner introduced a method called FFT-2DPA, which only requires to find a window in which both leakages are included. More precisely, the attacker computes the auto-correlation on this window, which combines the two leakages $\mathcal{L}(t_0)$ and $\mathcal{L}(t_1)$ multiplicatively. Thus, it is possible to utilize a regular zero-offset SCA on the auto-correlation trace. The authors of [15] suggest, to compute the auto-correlation as the inverse Fourier transform of the square modulus of the trace Fourier transform of the window of size n. This way, the preprocessing time has $\mathcal{O}(n \log_2 n)$ complexity, which is sub-quadratic.

Another category of second-order SCA are collision-based attacks. A particular case where *collision attacks* are efficient, is when the same mask is reused for each substitution box (S-box) of the crypto-algorithm. There exist two sub-categories of collision attacks: *correlation-collision* attacks and *collision-correlation* attacks. If the unmasked input of the S-box is biased, then correlation-collision attacks (see for instance [10]) can be applied. Otherwise, collision-correlation attacks [2] are more suitable. However, when the masking scheme does not reuse one mask to protect multiple unrelated sensitive variables, collisions attacks in general are not appropriate.

Summing up, apart from FFT-2DPA, bi-variate attacks usually require the knowledge of the samples $\mathcal{L}(t_0)$ and $\mathcal{L}(t_1)$. If the leakage models $\mathcal{M}_0$ and $\mathcal{M}_1$ corresponding to the leakages $\mathcal{L}(t_0)$ and $\mathcal{L}(t_1)$ are known, then the optimal strategy consists in combining them with a *centered product* [12]. We denote this attack as "2O-CPA". Note that, if the leakage can be approximated, then a *linear-regression* approach can mitigate the absence of accurate knowledge of the models $\mathcal{M}_0$ and $\mathcal{M}_1$ [4].

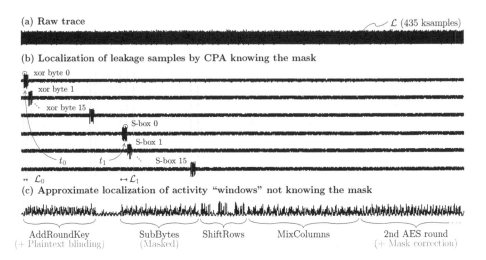

(a) Raw trace $\mathcal{L}$ (435 ksamples)

(b) Localization of leakage samples by CPA knowing the mask

xor byte 0

xor byte 1

xor byte 15

S-box 0

S-box 1

t_0 t_1 S-box 15

$\mathcal{L}_0$ $\mathcal{L}_1$

(c) Approximate localization of activity "windows" not knowing the mask

AddRoundKey   SubBytes   ShiftRows   MixColumns   2nd AES round
(+ Plaintext blinding)   (Masked)   (+ Mask correction)

Fig. 1. Analyses on traces collected from the first round of a masked AES in software

Figure 1(a) shows the trace $\mathcal{L}$ of the beginning of an AES encryption on a smartcard. We see about 3100 clock cycles (435000 time samples). It is not possible to distinguish individual operations by visual inspection of the trace.

One way to identify the precise timing of individual operations, consists in using a clone device, where the masks can be set to zero or are known. In this case, several monovariate CPAs [1] can be computed to disclose the exact sample(s) in which each operation leaks as illustrated in Fig. 1(b). Such an analysis seems impossible, without the access to a clone device. However, without any information on the masks, an attacker can compute the several moments or filter the traces. Figure 1(c) plots the variance of the average of the traces computed over each clock cycle. It clearly reveals the structure of one AES round: AddRound-Key (16 identical operations), followed by SubBytes (16 identical operations), ShiftRows (3 identical operations on rows — indeed, the first row is unchanged by ShiftRows), MixColumns (4 identical operations on columns), and AddRound-Key again (corresponding to the second round). The notations in Fig. 1 are as follows: $\mathcal{L}_0$ and $\mathcal{L}_1$ ($\mathcal{L}_0, \mathcal{L}_1 \subset \mathcal{L}$; $\mathcal{L}(t_0) \in \mathcal{L}_0$ and $\mathcal{L}(t_1) \in \mathcal{L}_1$) are the windows in which the shares #0 and #1 are expected to leak (they correspond to the so-called *educated guesses* coined by Oswald et al. [11]); n_0 and n_1 are the width of windows $\mathcal{L}_0$ and $\mathcal{L}_1$, in terms of sample count. For the sake of simplicity, we assume $n_0 = n_1 = n$. Typically, $\mathcal{L}$ has few hundreds of thousand samples (e.g., 435000 in Fig. 1), whereas n_0 and n_1 may vary from a few hundreds to a couple of thousands.

Our Contributions. In this paper, we propose five practical methods to make 2O-CPA attacks feasible on first-order masking schemes. All five proposed methods are generic in nature and need no knowledge of leaking time samples. The common feature of our attacks is to turn a bivariate leakage into a monovariate leakage (thanks to a combination that creates a sum of weighted products), that can be exploited by a classical zero-offset second-order attack. We base ourselves in the role of an attacker, who has a rough estimate of the zones in $\mathcal{L}$ where the leakages t_0 and t_1 are likely to be situated (that we call time intervals $\mathcal{L}_0$ and $\mathcal{L}_1$). In particular, our preprocessing methods convert two leakage windows of size n into a new window of size $2n$ or n, depending on the applied technique. Remarkably, these operations remain in complexity $\mathcal{O}(n \log_2 n)$, i.e., sub-quadratic. We show that our methods allow faster attacks (in terms of number of queries for the 2O-CPA to reach 80 % success rate) than the generalization of FFT-2DPA on two windows. This gain comes from two major factors:

1. The *phase information* is kept intact, and
2. The operation is performed in *frequency domain*.

As shown later, the leakage has a specific signature in terms of waveform shape, and in our implementation, there are multiple occurrences in time of the leakage. The representation in the frequency domain allows to regroup all these leakages, that combine constructively because they share the same waveform. Thus, the gain in terms of success rate is evident, since the signal is magnified at constant noise. Besides, from a computational point of view, the attack still stays on a linear number of points (n or $2n$).

Outline of the Paper. The rest of the paper is organized as follows. Preliminaries of tools related to time-frequency conversion are introduced in Sect. 2. Section 3 describes the five proposed preprocessing techniques, using time-frequency conversion tools. The attacks are then applied on a real masking implementation running on an 8-bit AVR smartcard (in Sect. 4). Section 5 provides further insights into the proposed attacks and their standing as compared to the state-of-the-art. Finally, conclusions and perspectives are drawn in Sect. 6.

2   Tools for Time-Frequency Analysis

This section provides a short background on common tools used in time-frequency analysis, which are then used in the proposed attacks in Sect. 3.

2.1   Discrete Fourier Transform

Definition 1 (DFT). *The discrete Fourier transform of a sequence $Y \in \mathbb{R}^n$ is another sequence $\mathsf{DFT}\,[Y] \in \mathbb{C}^n$ such as*

$$\mathsf{DFT}\,[Y]\,(f) = \frac{1}{\sqrt{n}} \sum_{t=0}^{n-1} Y(t) \cdot \exp\left(-2\pi \imath f t / n\right),$$

where $\imath$ is one of the (square) roots of 1 in $\mathbb{C}$ that is different from ± 1.

Property 1 (Inverse DFT). The DFT can be inversed with the inverse DFT such that $\mathsf{IDFT}\left[\mathsf{DFT}\left[Y\right]\right] = Y$, where $\mathsf{IDFT}\left[Z\right](t) = \frac{1}{\sqrt{n}}\sum_{f=0}^{n-1} Z(f) \cdot \exp\left(+2\pi \imath ft/n\right)$.

Definition 2 (Cross-correlation). *The* (circular) cross-correlation *of two discrete sequences X and Y of n samples is defined by*

$$(X \star Y)(t) = \sum_{t'=0}^{n-1} X(t') \cdot Y(t' + t \mod n).$$

Theorem 1 (Cross-correlation theorem). *Again let X and Y be two discrete sequences of n samples in time domain, then*

$$(X \star Y)(t) = \sqrt{n} \cdot \mathsf{IDFT}\left[\overline{\mathsf{DFT}\left[X\right]} \cdot \mathsf{DFT}\left[Y\right]\right],$$

where $\overline{\cdot}$ denotes complex conjugation.

2.2 Discrete Hartley Transform

The application of a DFT on a sequence of real numbers results in a sequence of complex numbers. The discrete Hartley transform [7] (DHT) was proposed as a real-valued alternative to the DFT as DHT multiplies each real input by $\cos + \sin$ instead of $\cos - \imath \sin$ as in DFT:

Definition 3 (DHT). *The* discrete Hartley transform *of a sequence $Y \in \mathbb{R}^n$ is another sequence $\mathsf{DHT}\left[Y\right] \in \mathbb{R}^n$ such as:*

$$\mathsf{DHT}\left[Y\right](f) = \frac{1}{\sqrt{n}}\sum_{t=0}^{n-1} Y(t) \cdot \left(\cos\left(2\pi \, ft/n\right) + \sin\left(2\pi \, ft/n\right)\right).$$

Property 2 (Link between Fourier and Hartley transforms). The DHT of the temporal signal Y can be obtained from the DFT by:

$$\mathsf{DHT}\left[Y\right](f) = \Re\,\mathsf{DFT}\left[Y\right](f) - \Im\,\mathsf{DFT}\left[Y\right](f).$$

Reciprocally, the DFT of the signal Y can be computed from the DHT with the formula:

$$\mathsf{DFT}\left[Y\right](f) =$$
$$\tfrac{1}{2}\left(\mathsf{DHT}\left[Y\right](f) + \mathsf{DHT}\left[Y\right](-f)\right) - \tfrac{1}{2}\left(\mathsf{DHT}\left[Y\right](f) - \mathsf{DHT}\left[Y\right](-f)\right).$$

Property 3 (DHT Involution). The DHT is its own inverse; $\forall Y \in \mathbb{R}^n, \mathsf{DHT}\left[\mathsf{DHT}\left[Y\right]\right] = Y$. The proof is given in [7].

As such, the DHT avoids two computationally undesirable characteristics of the DFT:

1. the inverse DHT is identical with the direct transform — it is not necessary to keep track of $+\imath$ and $-\imath$ versions;
2. more importantly, the DHT has real rather than complex values. As a consequence, in a 2O-CPA, the computation of the correlation coefficient can be done in the frequency spectrum without any loss of information.

2.3   Fast Fourier Transform

The DFT (resp. IDFT) is directly obtainable from the FFT (resp. IFFT), that runs in $\mathcal{O}(n \log_2 n)$ complexity [5]. The computational complexity of DHT is also $\mathcal{O}(n \log_2 n)$, as it is simply obtained as the difference between the real and imaginary parts of the FFT.

3   New Second-Order Attacks with Time-Frequency Preprocessing

3.1   Why Do We Need New Attacks?

In first-order masking implementations, it is expected that each mask is reused (at least twice). Unfortunately, as shown in Fig. 1, the distance between two leakages using the same mask can be about 100000 samples. Therefore, the attacker, in practice, needs *two distinct* windows where the mask is reused, assuming for the sake of simplicity both of size n. Since the exact temporal localization of t_0 and t_1 corresponding to the leakages $\mathcal{L}(t_0)$ and $\mathcal{L}(t_1)$ is unknown to the attacker, he would have to mount $\binom{n}{2}$ 2O-CPAs, resulting in $\mathcal{O}(n^2)$ complexity, which can become impractical for large n.

Another method would be to apply the approach of FFT-2DPA. However, one window in which $\mathcal{L}(t_0)$ and $\mathcal{L}(t_1)$ are included would be too large (e.g., 100000 time samples), therefore to overcome this problem we straightforwardly extend the idea of Waddle and Wagner to the case of two distinct windows $\mathcal{L}_0$ and $\mathcal{L}_1$. In particular, we consider two different approaches to treat $\mathcal{L}_0$ and $\mathcal{L}_1$. First, we use the concatenation:

Definition 4 (auto-corr). *Let us denote $\mathcal{L}_{01}$ as the concatenation in time of $\mathcal{L}_0$ and $\mathcal{L}_1$. Then* auto-corr $= (\mathcal{L}_{01} \star \mathcal{L}_{01}) = \mathsf{IDFT}\left[\left|\mathsf{DFT}\left[\mathcal{L}_{01}\right]\right|^2\right]$.

Second, if the size of the windows, $\mathcal{L}_0$ and $\mathcal{L}_1$ have equal width (i.e., $n_0 = n_1 = n$), the attacker can compute cross-correlation between $\mathcal{L}_0$ and $\mathcal{L}_1$, which we call x-corr.

Definition 5 (x-corr). x-corr $= (\mathcal{L}_0 \star \mathcal{L}_1) = \mathsf{IDFT}\left[\overline{\mathsf{DFT}\left[\mathcal{L}_0\right]} \cdot \mathsf{DFT}\left[\mathcal{L}_1\right]\right]$.

Interestingly, both auto-corr and x-corr can be computed in a complexity $\mathcal{O}(n \log_2 n)$, owing to the cross-correlation Theorem 1. Moreover, the *preprocessing* stage turns a *bi-variate* leakage into a *uni-variate* leakage. Indeed, the expressions auto-corr(t) and x-corr(t) contain the product $\mathcal{L}(t_0) \cdot \mathcal{L}(t_1)$, which is exploited by a 2O-CPA. So, the optimal prediction function is the same as in any bi-variate 2O-CPA. Thus, after the preprocessing with either auto-corr or x-corr, an attacker can simply perform a zero-offset SCA on the resultant trace to find the secret key.

However, we noticed two essential drawbacks when using the straightforward extension from Waddle and Wagner:

- First of all, as the DFT of the signals are processed via a *modulus* (See e.g., Definition 4), the *phase information is lost*.

– Second, returning in the timing domain is less efficient than staying in the frequency domain: indeed, as will be seen with on our practical examples (Sect. 4), the leaks in software usually feature *many peaks* in time domain, that nonetheless have a *common signature* in frequency domain.

3.2   New Attacks in Frequency Domain

Based on the previous definitions and observations, we introduce 5 new pre-processing methods, which intend to capture the leakage directly in frequency domain without transferring it back into time domain. Similar as for auto-corr and x-corr, we divide methods into two distinct classes. The first class consists of so-called *"one window"* methods, which utilizes the concatenated window $\mathcal{L}_{01}$ from two individual windows $\mathcal{L}_0$ and $\mathcal{L}_1$ resulting in an output of $2n$. The second class of methods (*"two windows"* methods) are capable to combine two windows of size n into a single window also of size n.

As analysis methods we use DFT and DHT (see Definition 3 in Sect. 2). The four resultant preprocessing techniques are summarized in Table 1.

Table 1. Variants of considered preprocessing attacks

Function \ ⟨name⟩	DFT [·]	DHT [·]
concat-⟨name⟩(f)	$|DFT[\mathcal{L}_{01}]|^2$	$DHT[\mathcal{L}_{01}]^2$
window-⟨name⟩(f)	$|DFT[\mathcal{L}_0] \cdot DFT[\mathcal{L}_1]|$	$DHT[\mathcal{L}_0] \cdot DHT[\mathcal{L}_1]$

In order to reveal the secret key an attacker applies a zero-offset CPA on the output of these preprocessing techniques and the optimal prediction function $\mathcal{M}_{01}$, which we specify in Sect. 4.

Additionally as a "heuristic" method, we consider the max-corr attack to cope with a complex 2O-CPA (i.e., $\rho(\,\cdot\,,\,\cdot\,) \in \mathbb{C}$). More precisely,

$$\text{max-corr} = \max(|\rho(\Re\mathrm{e}(DFT[\mathcal{L}_{01}]), \mathcal{M}_{01})|, |\rho(\Im\mathrm{m}(DFT[\mathcal{L}_{01}]), \mathcal{M}_{01})|).$$

Beware that the suffix "corr" in "max-corr" refers to the Pearson correlation coefficient "ρ" of the high-order CPA, and not to any auto- or cross-correlation.

Concluding, in total we proposed five new methods of the same complexity $\mathcal{O}(n \log_2 n)$ to mount second-order attacks on a first-order masking implementation. The described methods are applied on a real masked AES implementation running on a smartcard in the following section.

4   Experimental Validation

4.1   Software Implementation of the Protected AES

To test our methods, we use the publicly available traces of DPA contest v4 [14], which uses a low-cost masking protection applied on AES, called Rotating S-box Masking (RSM). RSM is a first-order countermeasure in which the S-boxes

$\mathbb{F}_{2^8} \rightarrow \mathbb{F}_{2^8}$ are (statically) precomputed. The same mask is XORed to one plaintext byte (T) and to some S-box output (corresponding to another plaintext byte T'). In this case, collision attacks might be applicable to the design. However, we considered an attack based on the combination of two "heterogeneous" leakage models. The applicable (*centered*) leakage models are given by: $\mathcal{M}_0 = w_H(T \oplus M) - 4$ and $\mathcal{M}_1 = w_H(\text{Sbox}[T' \oplus K] \oplus M) - 4$, where T, T', K are respectively two bytes of the plaintext and one byte of the key, and where $w_H(\cdot)$ is the Hamming weight function. Thus, the prediction function $\mathcal{M}_{01}$ for all our preprocessing methods is given by $\mathcal{M}_{01} = \mathbb{E}[(\mathcal{M}_0 \cdot \mathcal{M}_1)|T, T', K]$.

4.2 Leakage Detection

In the following we ensure that both leakage models $\mathcal{M}_0$ and $\mathcal{M}_1$ are suitable for our evaluation. We first perform a CPA on the traces, assuming the mask to be a known quantity in order to identify the most leaking points and to verify our assumed leakage models. The prediction functions knowing the mask are simply: $\mathcal{M}_0^m = \mathbb{E}[\mathcal{M}_0|T, M]$ and $\mathcal{M}_1^m = \mathbb{E}[\mathcal{M}_1|T', K, M]$.

Figure 2(a) shows the correlation between the leakage $\mathcal{L}_0$ and the model $\mathcal{M}_0^m$ using 10000 measurements. We additionally marked the time instants when the correct key takes the highest correlation (i.e., $k^* = \max_k \rho(\mathcal{L}_1, \mathcal{M}_1^m)$), which amounts in 433 time instants over the window of 6000 points. Figure 2(b) shows the correlations using $\mathcal{M}_1^m$, where in 94 time instants the correct key takes the highest correlation, moreover, these instants are less spread than for the XOR operation. Further, Fig. 3 shows the mean consumption of each class of the highest correlation peak around the time instant ≈ 3000. One can clearly detect that the classification according to $\mathcal{M}_0^m$ (resp. $\mathcal{M}_1^m$) is reasonable. We therefore maintain our models $\mathcal{M}_0$ and $\mathcal{M}_1$ capturing the XOR and the $\text{Sbox}[\cdot]$ operation. The average number of traces to break the key using $\mathcal{M}_1^m$ is about 15 (*very low!*) for a success rate $\geqslant 80\%$, as can be seen in Fig. 4(a).

4.3 Empirical Evaluation

First of all, we confirm that a direct application of a 1O-CPA (Brier et al. [1]) using model $\mathcal{M}_0$ or $\mathcal{M}_1$ on the whole trace $\mathcal{L}$ does not allow to retrieve any key byte using 100000 traces. No preprocessing was applied on the traces before the attack. Then, we applied a bi-variate 2O-CPA by multiplying the two most leaking samples for models $\mathcal{M}_0^m$ and $\mathcal{M}_1^m$. The success rate is given in Fig. 4(b). About 300 traces are sufficient to break the key with probability $\geqslant 80\%$.

For our empirical evaluation we choose 3 different sets of window sizes n: small $n = \{50, 200\}$, medium $n = \{500, 2000\}$, large $n = \{4000, 6000\}$. So, autocorr, concat-dft & concat-dht are calculated on a window of size $2n$, whereas x-corr, window-dft & window-dht utilize two windows each with size n. Since only a fixed number of measurement traces (100000) are provided by the DPA contest v4, we were restricted in the number of retries. More precisely, for small windows we computed the success rate using up to 2000 traces and we were therefore able

(a)   (b)

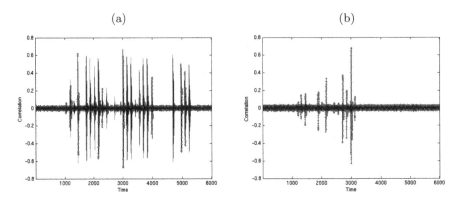

Fig. 2. Correlation $\rho(\mathcal{L}_0, \mathcal{M}_0^m)/\rho(\mathcal{L}_1, \mathcal{M}_1^m)$ knowing the mask M; correlation of k^* is displayed in black; time instants when $k^* = \max_k \rho(\mathcal{L}_0, \mathcal{M}_0^m)/k^* = \max_k \rho(\mathcal{L}_1, \mathcal{M}_1^m)$ are marked with a red diamond (Color figure online)

(a) $\mathbb{E}\left[\mathcal{L}_0 | \mathcal{M}_0^m\right]$ (b) $\mathbb{E}\left[\mathcal{L}_1 | \mathcal{M}_1^m\right]$

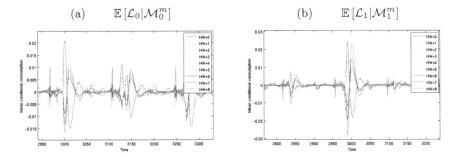

Fig. 3. Mean consumption conditioned by each leakage model class $\mathcal{M}_0^m$ and $\mathcal{M}_1^m$

(a)   Prediction function $= \mathcal{M}_1^m$ (b)   Prediction function $= \mathcal{M}_{01}$

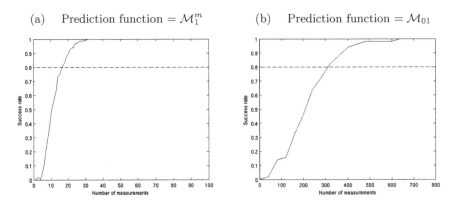

Fig. 4. Success rate of (a) univariate CPA attack on $\mathcal{L}(t_1)$ knowing the mask and (b) bi-variate 2O-CPA attack on $\mathcal{L}(t_0) \cdot \mathcal{L}(t_1)$ knowing (t_0, t_1) but ignoring the mask

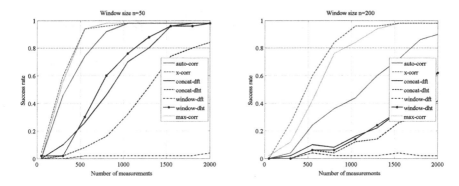

Fig. 5. Success rate when using a small window size

to compute $^{100000}/_{2000} = 50$ retries, accordingly, for medium windows 25 retries, and for large windows 10 retries were possible.

The success rate for a window of smaller size ($n = 50$ and $n = 200$) is shown in Fig. 5. In both cases, auto-corr and x-corr are the most efficient preprocessing methods, followed by the window-dht, concat-dft, and concat-dht, whereas window-dft is not able to retrieve the correct key. This confirms that the preprocessing of Waddle and Wagner is relevant when the time instants of the leakages are well known a priori. However, we also note that for such small windows, an exhaustive search of the interesting (t_0, t_1) is not deterrent (computationally speaking), and would yield better success rates (recall Fig. 4(b)).

The efficiency of the attacks is changed when using a window of medium size (see Fig. 6). The usage of x-corr seems only reasonable when the window size is sufficiently small, whereas the efficiency of window-dft and concat-dht increases when provided with more time instants. Interestingly, one can observe that window-dht is more efficient when using a window size of 500 as x-corr with smaller window size. This is an illustration that the attack manages to properly combine constructively the plurality of leakage instants in the trace (recall the multiple leakage peaks in Fig. 2(a) and (b)).

When increasing the window size up to $n = 4000$ and $n = 6000$ the difference between window-dht, concat-dht, and concat-dft becomes greater. Remarkably, even for large window sizes (two windows with each 6000 time instants), window-dht is still able to efficiently reveal the secret key. It is about equivalent in terms of efficiency with max-corr. Thus, this confirms that *attacks remain very practical, even though the attacker does not have a precise idea about the leakage location.*

From Table 2, we can deduce that when the attacker knows the leakage samples, i.e., a small window size, x-corr is the best attack. Moving from small to medium windows, window-dht proves to be the best attack. Finally, max-corr seems to be the best attack for large window size. This means that max-corr is well suited for practical cases because only a minimum assumption on the knowledge of leakage samples is required, thus, the attacker is able to choose a large window. As already underlined, another noteworthy observation from Table 2 is

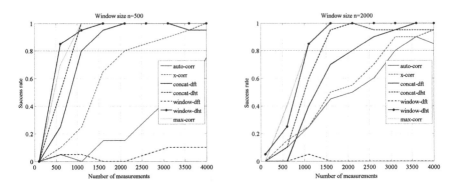

Fig. 6. Success rate when using a medium window size

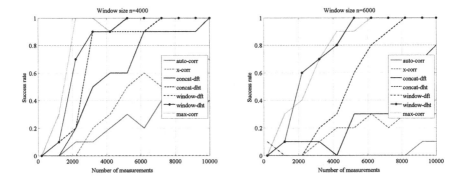

Fig. 7. Success rate when using a large window size

that, x-corr takes more traces to disclose the key for a window of 200 points as compared to window-dht for a window of 500 points.

5   Discussion

5.1   Benefits of the Proposed Attacks

Preprocessing Speed-up. Turning bi-variate into mono-variate leakage is actually a matter of trade-off:

- the computational power is lowered while exploiting the traces (because the research of (t_0, t_1) is skipped);
- at the expense of a greater noise in the estimation of the distinguisher (hence more traces to guess the key), due to the inaccurate location of the leakages in the window(s).

The use of our methods can be justified for software traces, that can be so long (millions of samples) that a complexity in $\mathcal{O}(n^2)$ is prohibitory. For instance,

Table 2. Comparison of performance of proposed methods against attack efficiency.

Window size	Best attack	Number of traces for SR $\geqslant 0.8$
50	x-corr	450
200	x-corr	750
500	window-dht	550
2000	window-dht max-corr	550
4000	max-corr	1950
6000	max-corr	3000

with window size $n = 6000$, the complexity of our preprocessing (in terms of "multiplications" count) is roughly $n \log_2 n \approx 75300$ or 0.0753×10^6, whereas an exhaustive search of pairs (t_0, t_1) requires $\frac{n(n-1)}{2} \approx 18 \times 10^6$ tries. So our attack method is very light in computation time. Now, in terms of number of traces to break the key, our method requires about 3000 traces instead of 300 knowing the most leaking samples, which remains reasonable.

Resilience to Traces Desynchronization. Our techniques can withstand a global desynchronization in the acquisition of the traces. It can happen that the traces are offset one w.r.t. the others, due to the lack of a reliable synchronization signal. It is already known that DFT based techniques (if the phase is ignored) can work even in this case [8]. (We do not consider here countermeasures like dummy cycles addition [3].) So concat-dft, window-dft and max-corr resist traces disalignment.

5.2 Explanation of the Results: Why are Attacks in Frequency Domain More Efficient when the Window Width is Large?

When the correlation is computed on auto-corr or x-corr signals, i.e., in the time domain, the leakage $\mathcal{L}(t_0) \cdot \mathcal{L}(t_1)$ is "dissimulated" into the numerous other terms $\mathcal{L}(t) \cdot \mathcal{L}(t')$, for $(t, t') \neq (t_0, t_1)$. Thus, when the window becomes too large, the signal-to-noise ratio at each point of the auto-corr/x-corr becomes very small. Of course, when the size of the window is small, it is possible to distinguish efficiently.

On the contrary, we see from Fig. 8 that the leakage is well localized in a few frequencies[1]. Those frequencies are around 20 MHz, which corresponds to the dynamic of the CMOS logic (see the duration of the *bounces* in Fig. 3: it is about 25 samples, i.e., 50 ns). The clock frequency is equal to 3.57 MHz, which is much smaller. Interestingly, the leakage *is not* modulated by the periodic clock signal.

---

[1] Three or four frequencies are especially leaky, which is much less than the tens of leakages dates in the time domain – cf. Fig. 2.

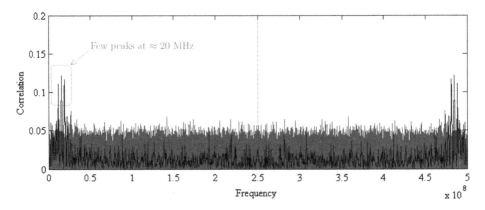

Fig. 8. Correlation coefficient on a 2O-CPA on concat-dft in frequency domain when using $n = 6000$ and 10000 traces (we recall that the sampling rate is $F_S = 500\,\text{Msample/s}$)

When the window size n is large, the frequency resolution of the DFT or the DHT is high, so it is more likely that the signal is decomposed close to the main leaking frequencies (i.e., the 20 MHz frequency value is well approximated in the domain of the DFT/DHT — recall that frequencies are *quantified*, i.e., discrete variables $f \in F_S/n \times [\![0, n-1]\!]$, where F_S is the sampling rate). Additionally, there are many leaking samples in the timing window (recall Fig. 2), but the Fourier transform manages to constructively sum them up.

5.3   Comparison with the State-of-the-Art

There are several existing methods to evaluate the resistance against second-order attacks in the state-of-the-art. Among the most recent published methods that can be applied to evaluate our masking scheme, we can consider a direct 2O-CPA with pointwise multiplication of $\mathcal{L}(t_0) \cdot \mathcal{L}(t_1)$ by using the detection method proposed in [13]. As explained in Sect. 4.1, two heterogeneous leakage variables that share information about the mask can be extracted from the power traces. In our case these two leakages depend respectively on $\{T, M\}$ and $\{T', K, M\}$. Formally, in a fixed chosen plaintext scenario it is possible to identify the leakage points by searching the couples of points that maximizes the quantity: $\hat{I}(\mathcal{L}(t); \mathcal{L}(t'))$, where $\hat{I}$ denotes the estimator of the mutual information.

This method, although more efficient than performing $\binom{n}{2}$ 2O-CPA, remains of quadratic, i.e., $\mathcal{O}(n^2)$, complexity. Besides, it cannot be applied directly to the context of known plaintexts (*random, not chosen*) scenario. In [13], an extension of this method is presented. It is possible to consider the couples of points that maximize: $\hat{I}(\mathcal{L}(t); \mathcal{L}(t'); \mathcal{M}_1)$, where $\mathcal{M}_1$ is a model of the leakage. This value is high when the variation of the leakage depends on $\{T, M\}$. In our case (DPA contest v4), the variation of the leakage also depends on another plaintext byte T', thus this method will be less practical. This method could be extended by using: $\hat{I}(\mathcal{L}(t);\mathcal{L}(t');\mathcal{M}_0;\mathcal{M}_1)$. In this case, we have to consider a quadrivariate mutual information analysis that is likely to be little efficient in the presence of noise, and would require more traces to identify the leakage points. Our methods (cf. Sect. 3.2) basically skip the detection step, and perform a direct 2O-CPA on larger windows than in [15].

Among the state-of-the-art methods, Moradi and Mischke reported at CHES '13 [9] a similar approach as [15], where the attack is performed in time basis after point combination. In the case they report, the two leaking time samples are close in time (a few tens of clock cycles), and the low-pass filtering of the acquisition system mixes the two signals. The scenario of the attack is thus the same. The difference is however that the "overlapping" of the two leaking signals is done for free in Moradi and Mischke's setup, whereas it is forced by a preprocessing in our case. Indeed, in our masking scheme, the two sensitive variables masked with the same mask M are not used consecutively.

6   Conclusions and Perspectives

We present five preprocessing techniques that turn a bi-variate attack into a second-order zero-offset attack. Our technique applies even if the two leakage samples to be combined are far from each other. Remarkably, the proposed methods need only a rough estimate of the location of two windows (around t_0 and t_1), where the two leaks can be found purportedly. The regularity of encryption algorithms, such as the AES, facilitates the identification of the elementary operations, like plaintext blinding and S-box calls.

In addition, we notice that our techniques have the potential to scale for higher-order attacks. For instance, imagine $d+1$ shares that are leaking at time samples $t_0, t_1, \ldots, t_d$. If the attacker is only able to know an approximate window $\mathcal{L}_i$ containing t_i ($i \in [\![0, d]\!]$), then window-dht becomes simply $\prod_{i=0}^{d} \mathsf{DHT}\,[\mathcal{L}_i]$. The working factor of this dth-order CPA attack method is that this product, once expanded, contains terms of the form $\prod_{i=0}^{d} \mathcal{L}(t_i)$, which indeed combines multiplicatively the leakage from *all* the shares.

References

1. Brier, E., Clavier, C., Olivier, F.: Correlation power analysis with a leakage model. In: Joye, M., Quisquater, J.-J. (eds.) CHES 2004. LNCS, vol. 3156, pp. 16–29. Springer, Heidelberg (2004)
2. Clavier, C., Feix, B., Gagnerot, G., Roussellet, M., Verneuil, V.: Improved collision-correlation power analysis on first order protected AES. In: Preneel, B., Takagi, T. (eds.) CHES 2011. LNCS, vol. 6917, pp. 49–62. Springer, Heidelberg (2011)
3. Coron, J.-S., Kizhvatov, I.: Analysis and improvement of the random delay countermeasure of CHES 2009. In: Mangard, S., Standaert, F.-X. (eds.) CHES 2010. LNCS, vol. 6225, pp. 95–109. Springer, Heidelberg (2010)
4. Dabosville, G., Doget, J., Prouff, E.: A new second-order side channel attack based on linear regression. IEEE Trans. Comput. **62**(8), 1629–1640 (2013)

5. Frigo, M., Johnson, S.G.: The design and implementation of FFTW3. Proc. IEEE **93**(2), 216–231 (2005). doi:10.1109/JPROC.2004.840301
6. Goubin, L., Patarin, J.: DES and differential power analysis. In: Koç, Ç.K., Paar, C. (eds.) CHES 1999. LNCS, vol. 1717, pp. 158–172. Springer, Heidelberg (1999)
7. Hartley., R.V.L.: A more symmetrical Fourier analysis applied to transmission problems. Proc. IRE **30**(3), 144–150 (1942)
8. Mateos, E., Gebotys, C.H.: A new correlation frequency analysis of the side channel. In: Proceedings of the 5th Workshop on Embedded Systems Security, WESS '10, pp. 4:1–4:8, ACM, New York (2010)
9. Moradi, A., Mischke, O.: On the simplicity of converting leakages from multivariate to univariate. In: Bertoni, G., Coron, J.-S. (eds.) CHES 2013. LNCS, vol. 8086, pp. 1–20. Springer, Heidelberg (2013)
10. Moradi, A., Mischke, O., Eisenbarth, T.: Correlation-enhanced power analysis collision attack. In: Mangard, S., Standaert, F.-X. (eds.) CHES 2010. LNCS, vol. 6225, pp. 125–139. Springer, Heidelberg (2010)
11. Oswald, E., Mangard, S., Herbst, C., Tillich, S.: Practical second-order DPA attacks for masked smart card implementations of block ciphers. In: Pointcheval, D. (ed.) CT-RSA 2006. LNCS, vol. 3860, pp. 192–207. Springer, Heidelberg (2006)
12. Prouff, E., Rivain, M., Bevan, R.: Statistical analysis of second order differential power analysis. IEEE Trans. Comput. **58**(6), 799–811 (2009)
13. Reparaz, O., Gierlichs, B., Verbauwhede, I.: Selecting time samples for multivariate DPA attacks. In: Prouff, E., Schaumont, P. (eds.) CHES 2012. LNCS, vol. 7428, pp. 155–174. Springer, Heidelberg (2012)
14. TELECOM ParisTech SEN Research Group. DPA Contest, 4th edn. (2013–2014). http://www.DPAcontest.org/v4/
15. Waddle, J., Wagner, D.: Towards efficient second-order power analysis. In: Joye, M., Quisquater, J.-J. (eds.) CHES 2004. LNCS, vol. 3156, pp. 1–15. Springer, Heidelberg (2004)

Software and Protocol Analysis - Session Chair: Lex Schoonen

Vulnerability Analysis of a Commercial .NET Smart Card

Behrang Fouladi[1(✉)], Konstantinos Markantonakis[2],
and Keith Mayes[2]

[1] Microsoft Security Response Center, London, UK
behrang.fouladi@microsoft.com
[2] Smart Card Centre Royal Holloway, University of London,
Egham, Surrey TW20 0EX, UK
{k.markantonakis,keith.mayes}@rhul.ac.uk

Abstract. In this paper we discuss the operating system security measures of a commercial .NET smart card for mitigating risks of malicious smart card applications. We also investigate how these security measures relate to the card resident binary by analysing its proprietary file format to develop a new vulnerability research tool for .NET card applications. This tool enables us to modify compiled card applications for creating vulnerability research test cases. We then present the details of the vulnerabilities in the target .NET virtual machine (VM) which have been discovered using this tool. The vulnerabilities relate to potential misuse of administrator privileges, therefore, we conclude with recommending countermeasures to be implemented in the card manager application and .NET VM to fix those vulnerabilities.

Keywords: .NET smart card · Embedded .NET · Smart card firewall · VM vulnerabilities · File format

1 Introduction

Modern smart cards are commonly referred to as "multi-application" cards, as they are capable of storing and running more than one application. This increases user convenience and lowers the costs of issuing and managing multiple cards for different applications. However, such a smart card system would require more complex security features in order to isolate execution and the data access context of on-card applications from each other. The card's operating system should also allow secure installation of new applications to the card without having to reissue it. There are currently three major multi-application smart card platforms in the market that allow the card issuers or content providers to securely load applications to the smart card during issuance and post-issuance. These platforms are MULTOS [1], Java Card [2] and .NET card [3].

Card applications are written in a high level programming language such as Java, Visual Basic or C# and then the applications are compiled to an intermediary format known as "bytecode". Bytecode instructions consist of a set of numeric codes, values and references that need to be translated to machine code instructions before being

A. Francillon and P. Rohatgi (Eds.): CARDIS 2013, LNCS 8419, pp. 125–139, 2014.
DOI: 10.1007/978-3-319-08302-5_9, © Springer International Publishing Switzerland 2014

executed by the smart card CPU. The VM is responsible for loading and translating the bytecode application to CPU instructions. The VM concept allows a card application to be executed on different smart card CPUs without the need to re-program it for different CPU architectures. The VM can also perform verifications and security checks on the bytecode before the translation of the bytecode to CPU instructions in order to prevent malicious code attacks. Finally, it can isolate different on-card applications from each other, only allowing controlled data exchange and sharing.

The aforementioned security principles, if implemented correctly, mitigate the risks of malicious code. However, successful attacks against smart card and desktop computer VMs have been demonstrated which exploit the implementation vulnerabilities to escape the application sandbox or bypass safe memory access controls [4, 5]. Therefore, the security of the VM and malicious bytecode threats are interesting topics for smart card vendors and security researchers. The security of the Java Card VM has been the subject for several researchers [6, 7], which demonstrated the exploitation of weaknesses in bytecode verification and translation in order to gain access to the contents of the smart card memory. However no public vulnerability research on .NET smart card VM could be found prior to this work. We aim to perform a detailed security evaluation of this platform to unveil possible vulnerabilities and provide recommendations to address those issues.

2   The .NET Smart Card

The .NET card is widely used multi-factor authentication token in Microsoft Windows based systems. A .NET card supplier will typically also supply a software development kit (SDK) which integrates with Microsoft Visual Studio and enables developers to build card applications in .NET programming languages such as C# and Visual Basic. The .NET card VM is capable of interpreting and executing Microsoft Intermediate Language (MSIL) instructions. Thus, it allows developers to write smart card applications in any .NET programming language that can be compiled into MSIL code. This gives the users similar flexibility and program portability to that provided by the Java Card VM.

A notable advantage of the .NET smart card over a typical Java Card is that the developer does not need to design and use Application Protocol Data Unit (APDU) commands that are necessary for Java Card applications to communicate with the reader terminal. The .NET smart card framework provides a proxy interface based on .NET remoting technology which allows developers to call on-card application services using TCP or HTTP as a transport protocol without having to issue and process low level APDU commands and responses. Behind the scenes, the proxy interface converts client requests and on-card application responses to the corresponding APDU commands as demonstrated in Fig. 1. This research work focused on a commercially available and widely used .NET card which from now on will simply be referred to as the target .NET card.

Since a smart card micro-chip has limited memory and processing resources, it cannot load and run the standard .NET programs compiled by Microsoft Visual Studio. These programs need to be converted to the target .NET Smart Card Framework's card resident binary format before being loaded on to the smart card.

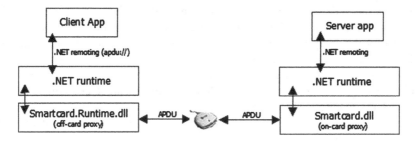

Fig. 1. Target .NET card isolates APDU layer from the application

The details of this proprietary file format and its security implications will be discussed in Sect. 3. The card resident binaries also need to be digitally signed, so that the card operating system can ensure their integrity and authenticity. The vendor supplied SDK plug-in for visual studio performs both conversion and signing operations automatically after standard Visual Studio compilation.

2.1 .NET Virtual Machine Security Model

The Microsoft .NET framework security model [8] is based on two access control mechanisms: Role Based and Evidence Based access control. The role based access control makes authorisation decisions based on the identity and roles/groups to which the user is assigned. The evidence based access control uses evidences associated with application code to make authorisation decisions. In .NET framework, executable code is maintained and managed in the form of logical units named "Assemblies". An assembly forms a container for a program's objects (classes, user-defined types, methods and fields) and data resources such as embedded fonts, graphic files, etc. An assembly can consist of multiple "EXE" and "DLL" files which are called "code modules". As a result, it forms a deployment unit which contains all required code modules for appropriate execution of the application while simplifying the application installation and update. Evidences are pieces of information that identify .NET assemblies. Some forms of evidences such as .NET Strong Names (SN) and publisher signatures are resistant to forgery and provide a stronger form of code identification compared to an application's URL or hash code. Assemblies with common or similar evidences are categorized into logical units called Code Groups. "Permission Sets", which define an access type to a protected resource or the ability to perform an operation, are then assigned to these code groups by the system administrator.

The target .NET card only supports the evidence based security mechanism with assembly SN used as identity evidence. Assembly SN is an important concept in the target .NET VM's security. It also relates to a vulnerability discussed in Sect. 4. As such, the following section describes it in more details.

2.2 Assembly Strong Name

The Microsoft .NET framework introduced the SN mechanism to generate unique assembly identities which can be used as code authentication tokens to make security decisions by the .NET runtime as well as ensuring the code integrity. The RSA public key signature algorithm, which can provide data integrity and origin authentication, is at the heart of the .NET SN mechanism. In order to bind the SN to the assembly file, an RSA digital signature for the SHA1 hash value of the file content is computed during the build process by using a private key. This key will only be known to the assembly developer. The SN and RSA digital signature are then written into the assembly file's manifest which can later be parsed by the .NET runtime to load the signer's public key. This can be used to verity the assembly's digital signature, thus ensuring code integrity and origin identification. An assembly manifest is usually embedded inside ".EXE" or ".DLL" files together with program code, but it can also be stored inside a standalone file.

The Microsoft .NET framework usually uses a 128 byte RSA key to sign an assembly which is stored inside the assembly's manifest section. The public key is not repeated again in the assembly's strong name. Instead, the .NET framework uses public key identification value called "Public Key Token" (PBKT) which is 8 bytes in size and calculated by the following algorithm:

1. Use SHA-1 hash algorithm to compute the hash value of the public key. The output is 160 bits.
2. The last 8 bytes of the generated SHA-1 hash value are used for calculating the PBKT.
3. The sequence for these bytes are reversed, providing us with the PBKT value.

The target .NET VM also uses the above SN mechanism to sign and identify on-card application assemblies. The SN and digital signature is embedded inside the card resident binary file by the .NET compiler.

The digital signature verification is performed by the card's operating system when a new application is loaded onto the smart card. We noticed that the use of a 1024 bit RSA key and the SHA-1 algorithm are no longer recommended from a security best practice viewpoint, however this is not the focus of this paper.

2.3 The Target .NET Card Code and Data Security

Each assembly file on the .NET smart card will have a PBKT derived from its RSA public key, using the algorithm mentioned in Sect. 2.2. Assembly files with the same PBKT, form code groups to which code access and file system access permissions are assigned by the card's administrator user. The PBKT also identifies on-card applications to each other, so every application can configure access lists to grant or deny access to its library files by other card applications. The target .NET card documentation describes its evidence based security model as follows: "If an on-card assembly (A1) needs to access another assembly (A2), either both assemblies must have the same public key token, or assembly A1, whose public key token is PBKT1, must be granted access to assembly A2 by adding public key token PBKT1 as an attribute on assembly A2".

The target .NET VM creates process boundary units called "Application Domains" for every on-card application, which is sometimes referred to as an

"Application Firewall", because it enforces strict data and code access controls between on-card applications. Code and data from one application domain cannot be directly accessed from within another application domain unless they are exposed via data and code sharing API.

The .NET card applications can use two types of on-card data storage: saving data as .NET objects inside assemblies and data storage on the card's file system. The application domain protects data stored inside assemblies such as remaining balance value or PIN codes from unauthorised access by other on-card applications. The developer does not need to configure any access lists for this purpose, as the application domains are managed automatically by the card's .NET VM.

In some cases, the application developers may want to store data on a card's file system instead of using application domain storage. For instance, an application that requires frequent code update can store data on the file system to separate it from the code file which may be subject to frequent change. By doing so, the application owner does not need to worry about preserving the data before a code update. File system storage can also facilitate data sharing between multiple on-card applications. Applications can directly open and read/write data files without the overhead of performing inter-domain data sharing. The file system objects are protected by evidence based security model using the PBKT that were discussed in Sect. 2. Every file or directory on the file system has two associated permissions sets: the Public and Private Permission sets. The Public permission set defines what operations (Manage, Write or Read) every on-card application is allowed to perform on the file or directory. The Private permission set defines permissions assigned to individual public key tokens. For instance, one can assign "Read" and "Write" permissions to the code group identified with PBKT of "26272048f12bffaf".

3   Analysis of the Card Resident Binary Format

The target .NET card cannot load and execute original .NET assemblies that are compiled by Microsoft Visual Studio. Those assemblies are converted to "card resident binary" format (the target format) before being loaded to the smart card. This is a proprietary and unpublished file format developed to allow loading and execution of MSIL code on resource constrained devices such as smart cards. The target .NET card vendor has developed a plug-in for Microsoft Visual Studio which parses the PE format and .NET metadata directories of the original .NET assembly compiled by the Microsoft .NET framework SDK and creates the equivalent card resident binary in the target format. The resulting file should contain .NET metadata information as well as the digital signature and SN, which were discussed in Sect. 2. Therefore, it is important to know the structure and format of the target binary file in order to perform an appropriate vulnerability analysis on the target .NET operating system and VM.

3.1   The Target .NET Converter

The converter plug-in for MS Visual Studio is developed using the Microsoft .NET framework, but its MSIL code is obfuscated to make code analysis more difficult.

To determine if it still feasible for an attacker to analyse the converter plug-in code and understand the card binary compilation process, we chose to take a hybrid approach in analysing the card binary file format via the following steps:

1. Examination of the obfuscated code of the converter plug-in in order to understand the conversion process and how it operates on the original .NET assembly metadata and code.
2. Mapping original .NET assembly metadata to the card binary file metadata by tracing and matching the relevant .NET objects in both of them.

After analysing the converter plug-in code, we located an interesting method code inside the "Converter" class. This code found and deleted two temporary files after the conversion process was completed. The MSIL code of this method was modified not to delete those temporary files, for further analysis. After compiling a simple on-card application using our modified converter plug-in, two temporary files were found in the same directory as that of the compiled application. One of the files contained the compiled card binary, however the other was a more interesting text file (which we will refer to as the map file) which listed all converted .NET namespaces, types, methods and field names from the original .NET assembly and corresponding codes. The map file contained useful information which saved lots of time during the analysis phase (Fig. 2).

3.2 Target Binary File Format

The card binary format did not have a lot in common with the Microsoft .NET assembly format, except the object reference and definition tables. An overview of the

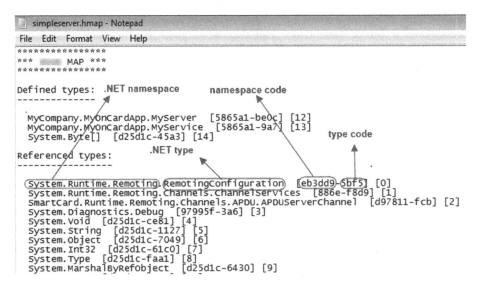

Fig. 2. Example of a map file

file structure is shown in Fig. 3. It consisted of three fixed sized headers, four object reference tables, and three object definition tables followed by program code and RSA signature. The reference tables include the identification code of referenced namespace, type, method or fields and the number of times these were referenced in the program (Fig. 4).

Finally, the target binary file ends with the RSA digital signature which has the same size as the RSA modulus (128 bytes).

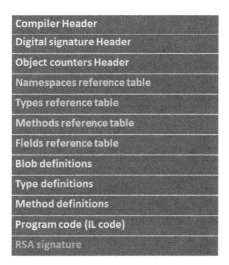

Fig. 3. Target .NET card binary structure

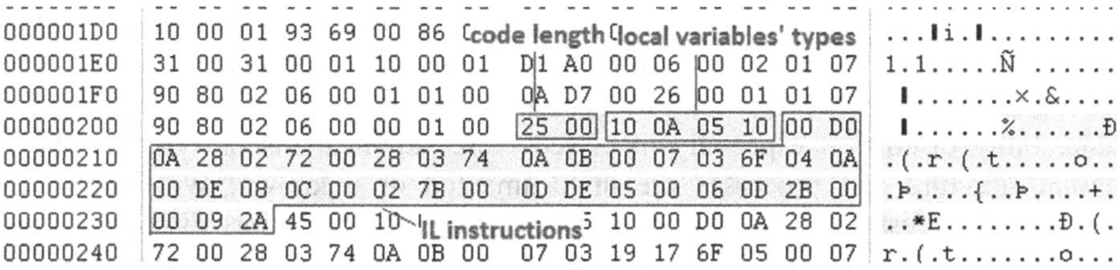

```
--------   -- -- -- -- -- -- -- --   -- -- -- -- -- -- -- --   ................
000001D0   10 00 01 93 69 00 86 ⌈code length ⌊local variables' types   ...Ii.I.........
000001E0   31 00 31 00 01 10 00 01   D|1 A0 00 06 |00 02 01 07   1.1.....Ñ ......
000001F0   90 80 02 06 00 01 01 00   0|A D7 00 26 |00 01 01 07   I.......×.&....
00000200   90 80 02 06 00 00 01 00   |25 00| |10 0A 05 10| |00 D0|   I......%......Ð
00000210   |0A 28 02 72 00 28 03 74   0A 0B 00 07 03 6F 04 0A|   .(.r.(.t.....o..
00000220   |00 DE 08 0C 00 02 7B 00   0D DE 05 00 06 0D 2B 00|   .Þ....{..Þ....+.
00000230   |00 09 2A| 45 00 10 ⌐IL instructions⌐ 10 00 D0 0A 28 02   ..*E........Ð.(.
00000240   72 00 28 03 74 0A 0B 00   07 03 19 17 6F 05 00 07   r.(.t........o...
```

Fig. 4. A method body definition in the target .NET card binary

3.3 Analysis Tool Software

Analysis of the target binary format enabled us to identify and understand key metadata information such as the digital signature header, object reference and definition tables that are used by the target .NET VM to load and prepare on-card applications for execution. Manipulating these headers and metadata tables and observing the modified assembly execution, would be an effective technique to discover possible vulnerabilities in the .NET smart card operating system or VM. However, this would require custom software capable of loading compiled card applications, allowing the user to view and modify different headers, metadata tables and code sections of the target binary and finally, re-signing the modified application with a given RSA private key so that the modified card resident binary includes a valid digital signature. We have developed such software which facilitates the visualization, manipulation and re-signing of the target .NET card applications. The software tool is written in the C# programming language and does not depend on the target .NET SDK or converter plug-in. The user interface visualizes the structure of the loaded card binary resident file and enables the user to navigate through each header, metadata table or code block and view or modify the relevant data block in the hex editor. The application automatically highlights the target binary data blocks as the user navigates though different sections. It also decodes the referenced namespace and type codes to the .NET namespace and type names, so that the user can easily make a rough idea about application functionality without reading the code section. The "Tools" menu has "Verify Signature" and "Re-Sign" options that allows the user to validate the RSA digital signature of the loaded application and sign it with a different RSA key pair.

4 .NET Smart Card Vulnerability Research

The card resident binary elements such as headers, .NET metadata tables and program code sections are directly parsed by the target .NET VM, thus they can be used as test vectors in order to trigger vulnerabilities in the target format parser engine or to provide false information such as spoofed application identities to the card's operating system. The target .NET VM and operating system is proprietary software running in a tamper resistant chip which protects the code even against invasive attack. Therefore, an attacker's strategy may be to find vulnerabilities in the card's VM by perhaps loading and executing manipulated card resident binaries and observing the VM's error codes and unexpected behaviours. This iterative testing technique of feeding random mutations of a valid input to the target program and observing the results is referred to as "Fuzz Testing" and has been used widely by security researchers for vulnerability discovery, especially in closed-source applications or systems whose internal structure and processes are undocumented or unknown. We decided to attempt "Fuzz Testing" of the target binary format for vulnerability discovery. This approach involved generating test cases by modifying a number of candidate sections in the target file instead of running a mutation engine over all sections. After building and uploading a number of test cases for both groups and observing the response from the smart card, we chose the following two sections as test candidates:

1. Digital signature header containing the application's PBKT. The PBKT is a critical value, because the evidence based security model of the .NET card is built around it.
2. Intermediate language (IL) instructions in the program code section which are used to allocate memory buffers or read and write to those buffers. Manipulating the arguments to those instructions could result in unauthorized access to the smart card RAM or EEPROM content.

The test tool software was used for modifying template target files and digitally signing the test cases. The following sections provide the details of the vulnerabilities that we have discovered by manipulating on-card application files.

4.1 Public Key Token Spoofing Vulnerability

We discussed the evidence based security model of .NET smart card in Sect. 2 and explained the concept of the PBKT which was used to identify card applications to the .NET VM and other on-card applications. The PBKT is derived from the assembly's RSA public key by applying a SHA-1 hash algorithm as explained in Sect. 2.2. The RSA public key is embedded inside the signature header of the application file and therefore the card's VM can compute the PBKT anytime by applying the SHA-1 hash algorithm (which is a fast cryptographic operation compared to asymmetric encryption algorithms). However, we noticed that the PBKT value was also stored in the target file signature header along with the RSA public key parameters, and these could be manipulated by the user before being uploaded to the smart card.

As .NET VM uses the PBKT to make security decisions such as granting or denying an application's access requests to file system objects, this could have critical security implications. For instance, an application (M) which has manipulated public key token value of $PBKT_M$, might be able to access data files owned by another application (A) whose public key token is $PBKT_A$. We prepared a vulnerability test scenario to find out if it is possible to upload card resident binaries with a modified PBKT to the .NET smart card. This would then allow the application to bypass the card's evidence-based security system and access unauthorized file system resources. This test involved the following steps:

1. The on-card application (M) was written to read a data file on the .NET smart card which it was not authorized to access. The target .NET VM threw "UnauthorizedAccessException" and denied the file read request which was the expected behaviour. Application (M) was digitally signed by the $PrivK_M$ and had a public key token value of $PBKT_M$. The data file it was trying to read, belonged to application (A) which was previously uploaded to the card and was signed with a different private key ($PrivK_A$) and having the public key token of $PBKT_A$. The access list of the target data file did not grant read access to $PBKT_M$ which prevented application (M) from accessing it.
2. Using the developed analysis tool software, we modified the PBKT value (8 bytes) at offset 0x52 of application (M) and change it to $PBKT_A$. Then it was signed by $PrivK_M$ key and saved to a new assembly file.
3. We loaded the manipulated application (M) to the .NET smart card successfully and the content manager service did not issue any errors or warnings. At this point, we successfully "spoofed" the identity of the target application (A). This allowed us to gain access to its data file.
4. Once the manipulated application (M) was deployed on the card and executed, it did not receive any security exceptions and was able to read the data file of application (A). This confirmed that the target .NET VM had trusted the PBKT

value embedded in the target binary to make security decisions. This value can, however, be modified by a malicious user in order to bypass the card's data security system.

Malicious applications could also exploit this vulnerability to bypass the code security system which defines code access permissions on PBKTs. For instance, suppose that application (A) was linked to a library assembly (.DLL file) and the code access permissions only allows code groups identified with $PBKT_A$ to execute the library's code. A malicious application (M) could exploit the aforementioned vulnerability to spoof the identity of application (A) and gain unauthorized code execution access to the target library. The root cause of this vulnerability was that the card manager service verified the RSA digital signature of the uploaded target file, but did not check if the PBKT value in the digital signature had been altered, by recalculating it on the card and comparing it with the value embedded in the uploaded target binary.

We demonstrated a PBKT spoofing attack against a "Password Wallet" application that was developed during our work to gain better knowledge about the target .NET SDK and the card application development process. The Password Wallet application demonstrates the use of the .NET smart card for secure storage of web sites' credentials. The user can only access the accounts by entering the correct PIN code which is a combination of alpha-numeric and uppercase characters. The accounts' usernames and passwords are stored on the card in a binary file called "store.dat" in the form of serialized .NET objects [9]. The malicious application "GrabtheWallet", was signed with a different private key to the one used by the Password Wallet and, attempted to access the accounts data file (store.dat). The request was denied by the .NET VM and "UnauthorizedAccessException" was thrown by the VM. We used our analysis tool software to change the PBKT of this application to the Password Wallet application PBKT, and re-signed it using the same key used for signing the GrabtheWallet.exe application. The manipulated application was successfully loaded onto the smart card. It had the exact same size and functionality, but had spoofed the PBKT of the Password Wallet application. This application was able to gain unauthorized access to the accounts data file (store.dat) of the password wallet application as demonstrated in the following Figs. 5, 6.

4.2 Virtual Machine Memory Corruption Issues

The metadata tables and program code section are parsed and processed by .NET VM to load referenced objects from other assemblies, create defined objects, allocate and initialize memory buffers and control the execution flow of the loaded program. Therefore they can expose a large attack surface to malicious application code. The IL code verifier examines those metadata tables and IL code sections for safe memory access and correct program execution flow before installing the loaded application into the card's persistent memory. Therefore, a well implemented code verifier would be able to counter malicious code threats effectively. However, implementation errors such as placing unnecessary trust on data that can be manipulated by an attacker could be exploited to cause an unsafe code to pass the verification process. We discovered

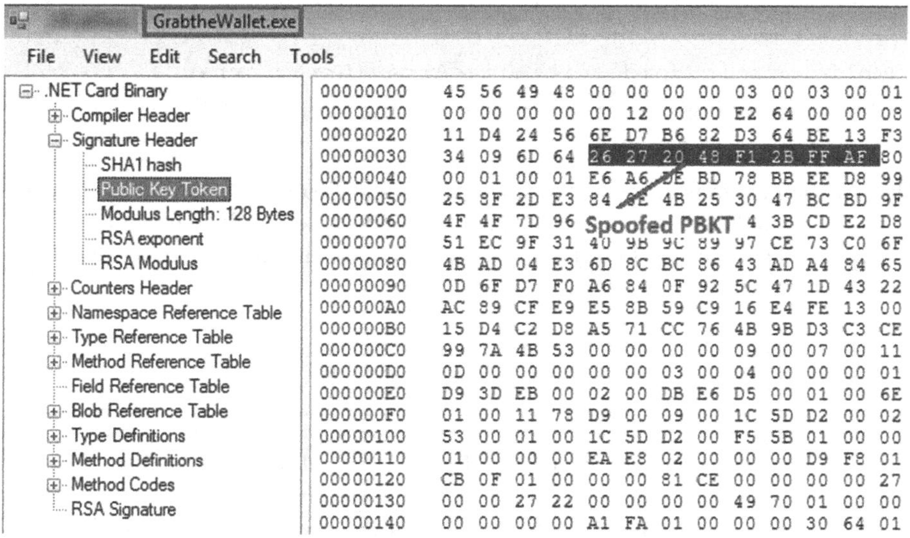

Fig. 5. Modifying the PBKT value using the analysis tool

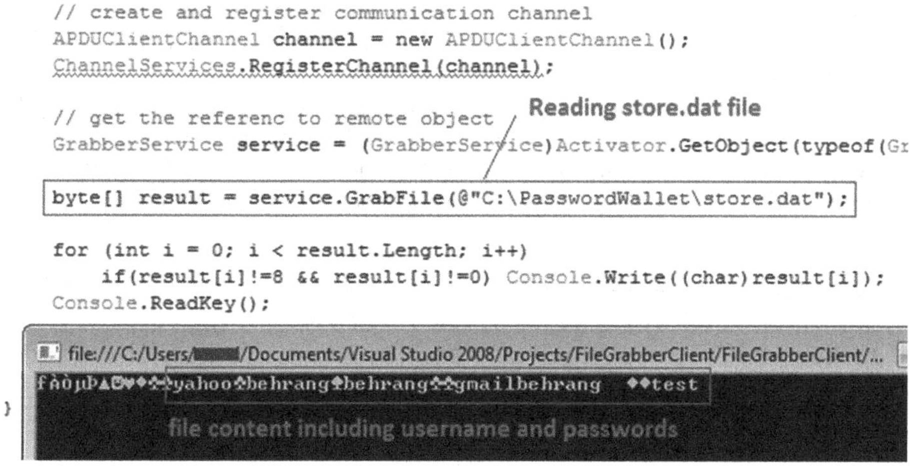

```
// create and register communication channel
APDUClientChannel channel = new APDUClientChannel();
ChannelServices.RegisterChannel(channel);

// get the referenc to remote object     Reading store.dat file
GrabberService service = (GrabberService)Activator.GetObject(typeof(Gr

byte[] result = service.GrabFile(@"C:\PasswordWallet\store.dat");

for (int i = 0; i < result.Length; i++)
    if(result[i]!=8 && result[i]!=0) Console.Write((char)result[i]);
Console.ReadKey();
```

Fig. 6. Unauthorized access to PasswordWallet data file

such vulnerability in an internal routine of the target .NET base library (mscorlib.dll) which was used for array initialization.

The RuntimeHelpers.InitializeArray method performs fast copying of static data defined in the program code to the array objects. This method had a public access modifier, and could be called by any on-card application. It had the following declaration:

```
public static void InitializeArray(Array array,
RuntimeFieldHandle fldHandle);
```

The array argument is the empty Array object which should be initialized by the data pointed to by fldHandle. This handle value represents a field defined in the FieldDefs metadata table of the target binary which was mentioned in Sect. 3.3. Each row of the FieldDefs table has the following columns:

```
[Field id][Field modifiers][TypeRefs or BlobDefs index]
```

If the field modifier contains the hasRVA (Relative Virtual Address) modifier, then the field refers to a virtual memory location. A virtual memory address is relative to the program load base address, which is the location that the program executable file is loaded to by the .NET VM into the RAM memory. For instance a field's virtual relative address could be 0x400 and the program could be loaded to the physical memory address of 0x10000000. The physical address of the field would be 0x10000400. Usually the RVA is relative to the program base load address, but it can also be relative to other sections' base load addresses in the target file. In this case, the base address was staring address of the blobs definition table. It means that the index column will point to a row in the blobs definition table that contains the data by which the array should be initialized. Runtime field handles can be obtained using the ldtoken (load token) IL instruction and providing the field index number in the field definition table. The following IL pseudo code demonstrates this instruction:

```
newarray <0x03,byte>  //create an empty byte array of
3 bytes length and push its address to the stack
ldtoken <1>   //convert the FieldDefs table token of
row number 1 and push the handle to the stack
call InitializeArray //call array initialization rou-
tine to copy data pointed by field number one to the
array
```

We found that the InitializeArray method did not check if the field handle passed in the second argument points to a field with the hasRVA modifier that refers to a relative memory address in the program's address space. As a result, it was possible to point the fldHandle to types without the hasRVA modifier set in order to copy the memory content of the VM internal structures into a user defined byte array. Some limited practical attempts to exploit this vulnerability to access smart card memory content were not successful and resulted in damage to the smart card operating system.

We also found a second potential vulnerability in the array initialization routine which could result in violation of the type safety of the .NET VM. The root cause of this vulnerability was that the InitializeArray method did not perform a security check to ensure that the provided array argument was of a primitive type (integer, byte, char and boolean types). Primitive types are data types that are commonly used by the programmers and already exist in the .NET base class library where the non-primitive types are defined by the programmer and contain memory references to the user defined objects in the memory. The target .NET VM supports both primitive and non-primitive type arrays. The elements of a non-primitive array are automatically initialized to null after allocation and the elements are later assigned with the memory references to the user-defined objects. If those object references can be manipulated by a malicious code, then it would be possible for an attacker to access arbitrary memory locations and violate the type safety of the VM.

If the array argument supplied to the InitializeArray method was of a non-primitive type such as an array of structures, then it was possible to overwrite the memory references in that array with the arbitrary data pointed to by the fldHandle argument. Unlike the pervious potential vulnerability in InitializeArray, exploiting this issue didn't result in damage to the smart card and as the code verification process was not completed successfully, the malicious application couldn't be loaded to the smart card. This limited the impact of the potential vulnerability exploitation to low.

5 Countermeasures

The public key token "spoofing" vulnerability could be mitigated by adding the required PBKT validation routine to the card manager service. This routine should recompute the PBKT from the RSA public key embedded in the uploaded target binary and compare it with the PBKT value in the digital signature header. If the values do not match, the target file has been manipulated and must be rejected. The vulnerabilities in the array initialization routine could be addressed by implementing the following two security checks:

1. The field pointed to by the fldHandle argument must have the hasRVA modifier set.
2. The array elements should not be of reference or non-primitive types.

The above security tests could be expressed using the following C pseudo-codes:

```
//Security checks before initializing the array
if (!(fldHHandle->type->modifier &
FIELD_MODIFIER_HAS_FIELD_RVA)) {
 throw new Exception("field does not have hasRVA modi-
fier!")
}
Type type= get_array_element_type(array);
if ( IS_REFERENCE_TYPE(type) || !IS_PRIMITIVE(type)) {
throw new Exception("cannot initialize array of refer-
ence or non-primitive types");
}
```

The vendor has developed a fix for the PBKT spoofing vulnerability and provided the following risk assessment: "To exploit this vulnerability, an attacker must be able to upload his malicious application on the card, and also get knowledge of the Public Key Token of the targeted application to prepare his malicious application first. To do so, he must gain administrator privilege; this is quite a strong requirement. The Administrator Key is normally set up by a Card Management System (CMS) using strong diversification algorithms based on a Master Key securely stored in a HSM or a smart card based controller. Also, the targeted application must use private file-system storage for its data to be exposed. Therefore, internal (Application Domain) storage is immune to such attack".

"The discovered memory corruption issues in Sect. 4.2 could not be exploited to gain unauthorised access to VM memory or execute arbitrary code and only resulted in denial of service through damaging the card operating system. To exploit those vulnerabilities, an attacker must be able to upload his malicious application on the card. To do so, he must gain administrator privilege; this is quite a strong requirement".

6 Conclusion

This paper records research work investigating potential security vulnerabilities in a commercial .NET smart card product. We developed and presented a .NET card binary analysis tool which was used to discover vulnerabilities in the .NET card VM. The pre-publication findings from this work were shared with the .NET card vendor so that appropriate countermeasures could be taken in a timely manner. In summary, a demonstrable vulnerability was found in the use of public key tokens that could allow malicious applications to have unauthorised access to files and library functions of legitimate applications. However, an attacker would need to have administrator privileges to exploit the vulnerability. The developed test tool can also enable the legitimate manager of a .NET smart card to detect the PBKT spoofing attack or decompile and analysis the card applications developed by third parties in order to discover possible vulnerabilities or backdoors.

References

1. Multos International. Multos Technology. http://www.multos.com/technology/
2. Sun Microsystems. Java Card Technology. http://www.oracle.com/technetwork/java/javacard/overview/index.html
3. Microsoft IT forum 2004. .NET-based Smart Cards. http://www.prnewswire.com/news-releases/hive-minded-delivers-net-based-smart-cards-75449172.html
4. Witteman, M.: Java card security. Inf. Secur. Bull. **8**, 291–298 (2003)
5. TippingPoint. Zero Day Initiative, Oracle Java IIOP Deserialization Type Confusion Remote Code Execution Vulnerability, October 2011. http://www.zerodayinitiative.com/advisories/ZDI-11-306/
6. Hogenboom, J., Mostowski, W.: Full Memory Read Attack on a Java Card. Department of Computing Science, Radboud University, Nijmegen (2009)

7. Iguchi-Cartigny, J., Lanet, J.L.: Developing trojan applets in a smart card. J. Comput. Virol. **6**(4), 343–351 (2010)
8. Microsoft. .NET Framework Security. http://msdn.microsoft.com/en-us/library/aa720329%28v=vs.71%29.aspx
9. Microsoft. Object Serialization in the .NET Framework. http://msdn.microsoft.com/en-us/library/ms973893.aspx

Manipulating the Frame Information
with an Underflow Attack

Emilie Faugeron[(✉)]

Thales Communications and Security, 18 Avenue Edouard Belin, BPI 1414
31401 Toulouse Cedex 9, France
emilie.faugeron@thalesgroup.com

Abstract. This paper presents an underflow attack performed on Java Card platforms. This underflow is based on the *dup_x* instruction that can be used in order to read and modify the current context of execution of the attacker's application. We first detail the theoretical and practical attack path by describing the method that can be used to characterize the platform and exploit the obtained information. Secondly, we show how it is possible to set up this underflow attack in a way that makes it bypass the current concept of Byte Code Verifier. Finally, we describe some countermeasures that can be implemented to prevent this kind of attack.

Keywords: Malicious application · Underflow · Java Card Open Platform

1 Introduction

Java Card technology allows loading and executing a set of applications in a secure way on a small device. This technology is widely used by smart card industry today and has been proved to reach a high level of security in the common context of use, i.e. single issuers mastering their production of Java Card platform and related applications. Nowadays, the use of those Java Card platforms is becoming more complex. In the field of telecommunication applications, for instance, the context is moving to multi-applications provided by different issuers for different Java Card platforms. Platforms refer to the combination of a secure hardware device and a secure Operating System including the Virtual Machine, the Runtime Environment and APIs. The concern is to check how multiple applets, loaded on a Java Card platform by multiple actors, can be handled in a secure way and maintain the security of the product over its whole lifecycle.

Open Java Card platforms, enabling post-issuance applet loading and induce a new actor that is responsible of application validation. Indeed, the Verification Authority is in charge of verifying the basic application against the platform guidance. It shall include at least an off-card verification of the application. If the application is invalid, it is rejected and cannot be loaded onto the targeted platform. Therefore, an attacker has two possibilities to bypass the concept of Byte Code Verification: either developing a malicious application in a way that cannot be detected by the Off-Card Verifier, or implementing a combined attack in order to perturb the application behaviour during its execution using a laser or ElectroMagnetic pulse device. In the

A. Francillon and P. Rohatgi (Eds.): CARDIS 2013, LNCS 8419, pp. 140–151, 2014.
DOI: 10.1007/978-3-319-08302-5_10, © Springer International Publishing Switzerland 2014

first case, all logical attacks using application file format manipulation are to be discarded otherwise they will be detected by the Off-Card Verifier. The attacker needs so to identify weaknesses on the Java Card platform at JCRE (Java Card Runtime Environment) level or at JCVM (Java Card Virtual Machine) level that could allow performing purely software attack. It can be a weakness in the platform implementation, or a known weakness regarding Java Card platform specification as explained in [1]. For instance, the Shareable Interface mechanism can be abused in order to perform a type confusion attack that will not be detected by the Off-Card Verifier.

The Java Card platforms are sensitive to several types of malicious applications. It can be address forging attacks by modifying specific CAP component [2, 3], type confusion attacks [1, 9] or underflow attacks [8, 10]. The first and second kinds of attacks are not relevant in that context: the first one is detected by the Off-Card Verifier, and the second one does not allow reading and modifying the context of execution of the application directly. On the other hand, the third one enables an attacker to manipulate the system information.

In this paper, we are going to focus our analysis on the underflow attack that allows manipulating the execution frame of a method associated to the current executed application. In the first part of this work we describe the theoretical and the practical attack path with a particular focus on the dup_x instruction that will be used to read and modify the frame information. In the second part, we detail the means that can be used by an attacker in order to bypass the current concept of Byte Code Verifier. Indeed, the attack described in this paper can be performed by an attacker without privilege. The attacker just needs to be able to develop an application. Finally, we present the countermeasures that can be implemented by the developer to prevent these attacks.

2 Underflow Attack: State of the Art

The underflow attack presented in this paper differs from previous works. Our hypothesis is that the malicious application is verified by Off-Card-Verifier and it uses a new type of potential vulnerability in the platform implementation.

To go back to previous work, the underflow attacks have been introduced in [8] and in [10]. The thesis [10] describes underflow attacks at a high level and is focused on countermeasures to protect a platform against such attack. The aim of an underflow attack described in [8] is to find the position of the return address onto the stack and then modify it in order to execute a code located inside an array. This underflow is performed by using non-existing local variables in order to access information located below the stack bottom. The purely software attack takes the hypothesis that there is no bytecode verification performed on the application (off-card verification or on-card verification).

Two different methods that can allow an attacker bypassing the Off-Card Verification are described in [1]. The first attack method aims abusing the transaction mechanism in order to create a type confusion. This attack is now detected by most of the platforms and cannot be applied to underflow anymore. The second attack method aims to abuse the Shareable Interface mechanism. The goal is to create type confusion using two definitions of interfaces, one for the Client and one for the Server. Actually, the attack methods described in [1] only focus on type confusion.

The aim of our paper is to describe a new way of exploiting the underflow attack despite off-card verification. Indeed, this paper describes an underflow using the instruction dup_x that is usually not checked by on card countermeasures due to the fact that the stack pointer is not decreasing at the end of the instruction processing (this kind of verification is dependent of the platform implementation). The final goal of our attack is to replace the context of the attacker's method with the JCRE context in order to gain access to out-of-context data to be able to dump and modify information link to the platform or to a sensitive application.

This attack considers that the malicious application is verified by Off-Card-Verifier. Indeed, we have extended the attack described in [1] in order to create an underflow. We have implemented two different ways of bypassing the off-card verification: (1) abusing the Shareable Interface mechanism to create an underflow, (2) abusing the library versioning to create an underflow. All steps of the attack will be further described in this paper.

3   Underflow Attack: Theoretical Attack Path

The aim of the underflow attack is to retrieve and modify the elements located before the stack of the current executed method.

All the instructions that pop elements from the stack can be used in order to perform a stack underflow attack. There are two kinds of instructions, those that lead to a modification of the stack pointer (sp) and those that pop elements from the stack without decreasing the stack pointer at the end of their processing. In the first case, if the operation is performed on an empty stack, the stack pointer will be located below the stack bottom at the end of the instruction treatment. This kind of attack can be done, for instance, with the instruction *putstatic* (Fig. 1).

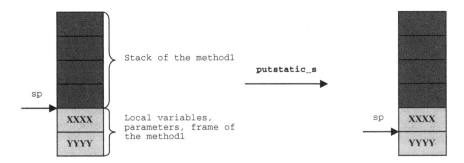

Fig. 1. *putstatic_s* instruction on empty stack

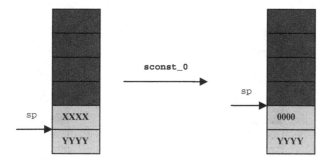

Fig. 2. Modification of the frame information thank to *sconst_0*

Once the stack pointer has been corrupted, an attacker can update any information located between the stack pointer and the stack bottom (Fig. 2):

In the second case, the stack pointer is not decreased at the end of the instruction processing but during the processing. It is for instance the case of the instruction *dup_x*. The instruction *dup_x* takes two parameters coded on 1 byte:

- m, the high nibble, that is in the range 1 to 4.
- n, the low nibble, that is in the range 0 to m + 4.

If n has a value different from 0, the top m words of the operand stack are duplicated and the copied words are inserted n words down in the operand stack. When n equals 0, the top m words are copied and placed on top of the stack [4].

Figure 3 shows the impact of a dup_x 32 on an empty stack (m is equal to 2).

This instruction can also be misused in order to update information located below the stack bottom. In this case, the attacker needs to provide a "n" different from 0 (Fig. 4).

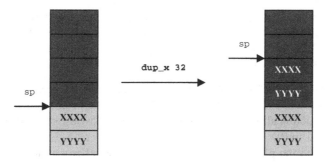

Fig. 3. *dup_x* instruction in order to read data located below the stack bottom. The two short at the top of the stack (m equal to 2) will be duplicated at the top of the stack (n equal to 0).

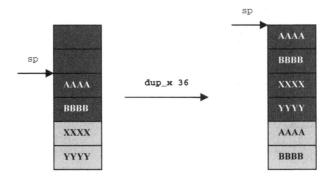

Fig. 4. *dup_x* instruction in order to modify data located below the stack bottom. The two shorts on the top of the stack (m equal to 2) will be duplicated at 4 shorts down the stack top (n equal to 4).

By using the underflow of the stack, an attacker will be able to manipulate the following information (the order of this information depends on the platform implementation):

- The local variables of the executed/caller method.
- The parameters of the executed/caller method.
- The frame information of the executed/caller method. This structure contains the context of execution of the executed or of the caller method.

In most implementation, the frame is located just before the stack. An attacker will then be able to modify the context of execution of his method.

4   Underflow Attack: Practical Attack Path

An attacker can characterize each bytecode that manipulates the stack in order to identify those that are not subject to security verification regarding underflow attacks. Each instruction can be invoked on an empty stack and then the platform behaviour is analysed for each case. In this paper, we focus our analysis on the byte code *dup_x*.

4.1   Underflow Attack Using *dup_x*

Characterisation of the Underflow Data. The first step of the attack aims reading the data located below the stack, and then to analyse and characterize each byte reading. The *dup_x* instruction allows reading 8 bytes located below the stack bottom (m equal to 4 and n equal to 0).

Depending on the platform implementation, the attacker may localize

- the frame information of the current/caller method,
- the stack number of the current/caller method,
- the stack of caller method, the number of local variables of the current/caller method,
- the local variable of the current/caller method.

The attacker needs to characterize the frame information in order to find the position of the context.

The identification of information related to the attacker's method (stack, local variable, system information) can be done by performing an underflow inside different methods of the same applet. To be efficient, these methods need to have different local variable numbers and different stack sizes. Moreover, the parameters used for each method need to be initialized with identifiable patterns:

```
public void local_method1 (short foo)
{
short var1 = (short) 0xBAB1;
short var2 = (short) 0xDED1;
short var3 = (short) 0xFEF1;
short var4 = local_method2((byte)0xDE,(byte)0xED);
return;
}
public short local_method2 (byte foo, byte bar)
{
short var1 = (short) 0xBAB2;
short var2 = (short) 0xDED2;
short var3 = local_method3();
return (short)0xDDFF;
}
public short local_method3 ()
{
//Perform the underflow attack
attr1 = (short)0x3333;
return (short)0xCDCD;
}
```

The following dump is obtained when an attacker performs an underflow using the instruction *dup_x* on an open Java Card platform:

0x01 0x0C 0x00 0x01 **0xDE 0xD2 0xBA 0xB2**

The state of the stack is the following (Fig. 5):

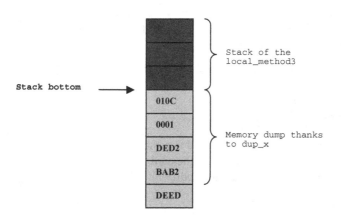

Fig. 5. State of the stack after an underflow attack using *dup_x* instruction

By analysing the dump obtained thanks to the instruction *dup_x* on an open Java Card platform, we can notice that the 3rd and the 4th words correspond to the local variables of the *local_method2*.

The identification of the context of execution of the attacker's applet can be done by loading two underflow malicious applications having different AIDs but identical code. In this case, the two applications will have the same local definition but differ on the context ID. As an example, the following data can be read when an attacker performs an underflow in an internal method of his applet:

- Underflow attack with *dup_x 64* instruction on an applet APP1 with a context APP1_context:
  0x01 0x0C 0x00 0x01 0xDE 0xD2 0xBA 0xB2
- Underflow attack with *dup_x 64* instruction on an applet APP2 with a context APP2_context:
  0x01 0x18 0x00 0x01 0xDE 0xD2 0xBA 0xB2

The first two bytes are different for the two applets: it is linked to the context of the current executed applet. The second byte needs to be fixed to 0x00 in order to take the JCRE context.

Exploitation of the Underflow. Once the frame information has been localized and in particular the context of the method of the attacker, the *dup_x* instruction can be used with n, different from zero, in order to modify the execution context (as described in the Fig. 4). Indeed, this instruction allows modifying 8 bytes located below the stack (m equal to 4 and n equal to 8).

The attacker can then update the context of his own method with the identifier of the JCRE's context (equal to 0x00) to gain access to the whole card content. Indeed, there is no firewall restriction for the JCRE [5] and as long as JCRE's context is granted to a method then it can read and modify any defined object in memory.

The instructions *baload*, *saload* or *getfield* can be used in order to read specific address in the memory. Indeed, these instructions will allow accessing different types of objects in the memory: byte array, short array and class. An address forging operation needs to be performed inside the application in order to be able to access to the targeted address (push the targeted address onto the stack).

The attacker needs then to reverse the memory access process. To perform this analysis, he can dump his application code and data in order to understand object representation into the memory:

- package/applet/instance (AIDs, CAP components,…)
- code
- standard objects (byte array, class,…)
- sensitive objects (OwnerPIN, Keys,…)

Once the characterisation has been done, the attacker is able to identify all these parts for other applications loaded onto the card. The instructions *bastore*, *sastore* and *putfield* can then be used in order to modify all objects read in memory.

By targeting the code of a sensitive application, he will be able to modify it. For instance, he can replace, directly in memory, sensitive checks by NOPs in order to avoid security/error detections. He can also modify the code of the Owner PIN object inside the memory by replacing the ciphered PIN representation of the sensitive application by the ciphered PIN representation of the attacker (if the representation of objects is not diversified by object).

4.2   Byte Code Verification

Off-Card Verifier detects classical underflow attack. Nevertheless, an attacker has several means to bypass this verification:

- Abuse the Shareable Interface mechanism as published in [1]: we have extended and adapted the attack described in [1] in order to create an underflow.
- Abuse the Library mechanism.
- Use combined attack as published in [6].

Abusing the Shareable Interface Mechanism. The Shareable Interface mechanism is used to share services between applications in different contexts. An Interface is defined and contains all methods that will be shared. A Server implements these methods and builds the Shareable Interface Object (object instance of the class that implement the Shareable Interface).

A Client uses these methods by obtaining the Shareable Interface Object thanks to the method *getAppletShareableInterfaceObject(AID serverAID, byte parameter)*.

The Shareable Interface mechanism can be abused in order to create a type confusion attack as described in [1]. Indeed, the Client is generated using one definition of the interface I1 with a function F that take, for instance, a byte array as parameter. The Server is generated using another definition of the interface I2 with a function F that takes a short array as parameter. During the application validation, the Client will be verified with I1 and the Server with I2, the verifications are done at two different times. That's why no error will be detected during the validation. Regarding application installations, only the interface I2 will be loaded onto the card. During the Client applet execution, the type confusion is created and can be exploited by the attacker (byte array read as a short array).

This principle can be applied to the underflow attack. Indeed, the method definition will be the following for the two interfaces:

- The Client is generated using the definition of the interface I1 (the Client contains the underflow attack exploitation part):

```
//creation of the Underflow onto the card
public int myShareableMethod_underflow(short S1);

//Address forging onto the card
public byte[] myShareableMethod_shortToByteArray();
public short[] myShareableMethod_shortToShortArray();
```

```
public myClass myShareableMethod_shortToMyClass();
```

- The Server is generated using another definition of the interface I2:

```
//creation of the Underflow onto the card
public void myShareableMethod_underflow(short S1);

//Address forging onto the card
public short myShareableMethod_shortToByteArray ();
public short myShareableMethod_shortToShortArray ();
public short myShareableMethod_shortToMyClass ();
```

The function *myShareableMethod_underflow* is called just before performing the underflow attack as illustrated in the following code extract:

```
sspush frame_1;
sspush frame_2;
myShareableMethod_underflow();//returns INT in I1
dup_x 36;//Underflow of 4 bytes
        //because it returns void indeed
```

The instructions *sspush* are used to push the new value of the frame on the top of the stack (*frame_1* and *frame_2*). Once the underflow is performed, the *dup_x* instruction allows assigning the new frame information.

Then the functions *myShareableMethod_shortToByteArray*, *myShareableMethod_shortToShortArray* and *myShareableMethod_shortToMyClass* are used to create address forging. The aim is to read a short as a byte array, a short array or a class object. The short used in order to forge address is the one given as parameter of *myShareableMethod_underflow*.

During the off-card verification of the Client with the Interface I1, no error will be detected. Nevertheless, during on-card execution with the Interface I2:

1. No int will be pushed onto the stack by the method *myShareableMethod_underflow*. The underflow will be created.
2. The underflow is exploited by the attacker: he is able to modify the current context by the JCRE context that is equal to 0.
3. A short will be returned by *myShareableMethod_shortToByteArray*, *myShareableMethod_shortToShortArray* and *myShareableMethod_shortToMyClass* and will be assigned as a reference to byte array, short array and class object. The address will be forged. The attacker will be able to access to the targeted address.

Abusing the Libray Mechanism. A Java Card platform can contain some libraries (applications that are not applets). A library is never instantiated; it contains only methods that can be used by other application loaded onto the card.

As for the Shareable Interface mechanism, an attacker can abuse the Library mechanism. The concept of the attack path is the same. Indeed, an attacker develops a library in two versions:

- Library L1 v1.0, this version of the library will be used for the verification of the application:
  ```
  public int myShareableMethod()
  ```
  As the method *myShareableMethod* returns an int, the underflow attack is not detected by the tool.
- Library L1 v1.1, this version of the library will be loaded onto the card:
  ```
  public void myShareableMethod()
  ```
  During the execution of the malicious application, the method *myShareableMethod* that return void is called. The underflow is activated and can be exploited by the attacker.

Creating an Underflow with Combined Attack. A combined attack [6] is a combination between a logical attack and a physical attack.

A combined attack can be used to create a mutant application. A mutant application [7] is an application that is well-formed and that becomes malicious during its execution by injecting a fault using a laser or an electromagnetic pulse in order to modify transiently a specific bytecode execution. Indeed, an attacker develops a well formed applet (successfully verified by an Off-Card Verifier) that is designed such that the modification of one byte by a NOP allows him to execute a malicious code, in our case the underflow attack. The applet of the attacker is loaded onto the card. The attacker then modifies the interpretation of specific instruction during the code execution using fault injection. The instruction is interpreted as a NOP and consequently, the instruction's parameters are not processed and are interpreted as new instructions.

A combined attack can also be performed in order to avoid on-card security checks or to bypass on-card countermeasures. An attacker can use it in order to bypass verification made during application loading. Indeed, the application of the attacker uses a library L2 that declares the following method: *public **int** myShareableMethod()*. The version of the library is 2.0. The application of the attacker is well-formed and will be verified with success. Nevertheless, the platform contains a library L1 with the following method: *public **void** myShareableMethod()*. The version of the library onto the card is 1.0. During the application loading, the platform will ensure that each imported package has the same major version than the one loaded onto the card. An attacker can perform a fault injection in order to bypass this specific security check. In this case, the application will be loaded successfully and the underflow can be exploited during the application execution.

5   Countermeasures

The underflow attack can be covered by organisational measures or by technical countermeasures.

5.1   Organisational Measures

The developer can add specific mandatory requirements in the guidance. Indeed, requirements related to versioning and imported packages can be sufficient to cover the purely software attack abusing the Shareable Interface or Library mechanism. In such case, the attack will be detected during the application verification process by the Verification Authority and the application will be rejected.

Nevertheless, this countermeasure does not cover combined attacks. Only technical measures can be used to cover that kind of attacks.

5.2   Technical Countermeasures

The developer can implement dedicated countermeasures onto the Java Card Virtual Machine in order to defend against the underflow attack. Indeed, he needs to add security checks upon the processing of each instruction that pop elements from the stack in order to ensure that the stack pointer is valid, during and after the instruction processing.

Nevertheless, an attacker could perform a combined attack to bypass this countermeasure: the attacker develops his malicious application, loads it onto the card, and finally performs a fault injection attack upon the execution of the application in order to avoid the underflow countermeasure. Therefore, in order to implement an efficient underflow countermeasure, the code must also be protected against faults injection attacks.

6   Conclusion

Open Java Card platforms, enabling post-issuance applet loading, induce a new type of attackers having privileges. These attackers are untrusted application developers or application loaders that are able to choose the application that will be loaded onto the card. In such context, the platform with its guidance needs to be protected against malicious applications.

We have presented, in this paper, an underflow attack that exploits the *dup_x* instruction in order to read and modify the current context of execution of the attacker's application. Once this modification is done, the attacker is able to acquire the context of the JCRE and so to read and modify out-of-context data. This attack can be developed in such a way that the malicious application will bypass the concept of Byte Code Verifier. Indeed, the validation of application is done in a specific time and the validation of the library or of the Shareable service is done at another time. This underflow attack can also be exploited through other instructions that pop elements from the stack. This attack has been performed with success on several Java Card platforms.

Several solutions exist to protect the platform against this kind of attacks, either organisational - if the guidance includes specific requirements -, or technical - if the platform implements dedicated security checks upon instructions processing -.

Finally, this paper shows that the current concept of Byte Code Verification is not sufficient to prevent all kinds of malicious applications. During a platform evaluation, the overall malicious application attack paths need to be taken into account. A specific care is to be applied on the platform guidance in order to ensure that it will contain all the necessary requirements to cover logical attack path.

References

1. Mostowski, W., Poll, E.: Malicious code on java card smartcards: attacks and countermeasures. In: Grimaud, G., Standaert, F.-X. (eds.) CARDIS 2008. LNCS, vol. 5189, pp. 1–16. Springer, Heidelberg (2008)
2. Lanet, J.L., Faugeron, E., Dessiatnikoff, A.: EMAN: Un cheval de Troie dans une carte à Puce. Computer & Electronics Security Applications Rendez-vous (CESAR 2008), p. 198 (2008)
3. Lanet, J.L., Iguchi-Cartigny, J.: Évaluation de l'injection de code malicieux dans une Java Card (SSTIC 09) (2009)
4. Java Card Virtual Machine Specification - Java Card Platform, Version 2.2.2, March 2006
5. Java Card Runtime Environment specification - Java Card Platform, Version 2.2.2, March 2006
6. Barbu, G., Thiebeauld, H., Guerin, V.: Attacks on java card 3.0 combining fault and logical attacks. In: Gollmann, D., Lanet, J.-L., Iguchi-Cartigny, J. (eds.) CARDIS 2010. LNCS, vol. 6035, pp. 148–163. Springer, Heidelberg (2010)
7. Vetillard, E., Ferrari, A.: Combined attacks and countermeasures. In: Gollmann, D., Lanet, J.-L., Iguchi-Cartigny, J. (eds.) CARDIS 2010. LNCS, vol. 6035, pp. 133–147. Springer, Heidelberg (2010)
8. Bouffard, G., Iguchi-Cartigny, J., Lanet, J.-L.: Combined software and hardware attacks on the java card control flow. In: Prouff, E. (ed.) CARDIS 2011. LNCS, vol. 7079, pp. 283–296. Springer, Heidelberg (2011)
9. Karsten Nohl: Rooting SIM cards. BlackHat (2013)
10. Pierre Girard thesis: Contribution à la sécurité des cartes à puce et de leur utilisation. University of Limoges (2011)

Formal Security Analysis and Improvement of a Hash-Based NFC M-Coupon Protocol

Ali Alshehri$^{(\boxtimes)}$ and Steve Schneider

Department of Computing, University of Surrey, Guildford GU2 7XH, UK
`a.a.alshehri@surrey.ac.uk`

Abstract. *Near field communication* (NFC) is a Radio Frequency (RF) technology that allows data to be exchanged between devices that are in close proximity. We formally analyse a hash based NFC mobile coupon protocol using formal methods (*Casper/FDR2*). We discover a few possible attacks which break the requirements of the protocol. We propose solutions to address these attacks based on two different threat models. In addition, we illustrate the modelling from the perspective of the underlying theory perspective, which is beyond the knowledge required for modelling using CasperFDR tool (black-box approach). Therefore, this paper is a facilitating case study for a "black-box" CasperFDR user to become a more powerful analyser.

Keywords: NFC · M-coupon · CasperFDR · Formal verification · Protocol security

1 Introduction

Near Field Communication (NFC) [1] is a radio frequency (RF) communication link, which allows data to be exchanged between devices that are normally less than 10 cm apart [2]. NFC-based mobiles are an emerging technology changing the way we communicate with objects. For instance, payments, tickets and coupons can be exchanged just by waving the NFC-based mobile at the points of sale.

NFC security is an important issue that has been emphasised in the literature [3,4]. Even though NFC has the advantage of a short communication link, security measures must be considered especially with sensitive applications to address security requirements, such as confidentiality, integrity and availability.

The NFC mobile coupon application (M-coupon) is one of the promising and popular applications [5–8]. An M-coupon is a cryptographically secured electronic message with some value. It requires secure issuing and cashing of the M-coupons, otherwise it can cause huge loss and reputation damage for a company [9].

The NFC M-coupon system has a typical scenario, see Fig. 1. All parties have NFC capability, in order to communicate with each other. Firstly, a user scans his NFC mobile against an NFC issuer (e.g., a smart poster or newspaper), and

A. Francillon and P. Rohatgi (Eds.): CARDIS 2013, LNCS 8419, pp. 152–167, 2014.
DOI: 10.1007/978-3-319-08302-5_11, © Springer International Publishing Switzerland 2014

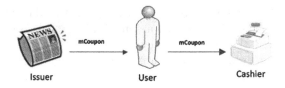

Fig. 1. General NFC mobile coupon

an M-coupon is issued and sent to his mobile. Later, the user goes to the shop to cash the M-coupon with the cashier. The cashier may authenticate the user before the cashier provides the promised bonus. Only the cashier needs to have online access, whereas the issuer and the user can both be offline. Hsiang et al. [10] have proposed a secure hash-based M-coupon protocol which allows secure issuing and cashing of M-coupons. They designed the protocol to address specific M-coupon requirements.

On the other hand, designing a security protocol is a difficult task even with strong encryption methods. Many attacks may be possible on the cryptographic protocols just by intercepting and replaying encrypted messages between entities, without decrypting any messages. Formal security analysis is a powerful approach to check the security of a protocol and whether it address its requirements [11].

In this paper we use the CasperFDR approach [12] based on *Communicating Sequential Processes* (CSP) [13], a formal method (state exploration) approach, to formally analyse the NFC M-coupon protocol proposed by Hsiang et al. [10]. Our analysis found attacks against the protocol. We then provide three solutions to address these vulnerabilities, and formally verify them with CasperFDR.

In addition, we illustrate the modelling from the underline theory angle. Modeling protocols in CasperFDR requires only an abstract description of the protocol and required security requirements to be checked. Then, CasperFDR provides the result detailing whether an attack was found or not. We call this a black-box approach as the underlying models are not shown to the user. In this paper we consider this point that we illustrate the modeling from the underlying theory perspective (CSP aspect). This is important to enable a black-box user to become more powerful in protocol analysis using CasperFDR and model the protocol and its requirements in a precise approach.

2   The Casper Approach

In our analysis we use CSP [13], with its model checker *Failures Divergence Refinement* (FDR2), which is proven to be an effective method in analysing the security of protocols [14]. However, modelling protocols in CSP is not a trivial task. Gavin Lowe developed *CasperFDR* [12], a tool that allows the user to write an abstract description of a security protocol, then the tool produces a model in the CSP language, and directly checks it with FDR2. CasperFDR has been used to analyse a huge number of protocols [15], which proves its capability of finding vulnerabilities.

CasperFDR is a formal method tool which supports symbolic protocol analysis in the Dolev-Yao model [16] which assumes that no encrypted message can be decrypted without the decryption key, thus the CasperFDR intruder model does not perform any cryptanalysis. However, the intruder does have full control of the network traffic, and tries to break the security protocol from what passes on the network.

CasperFDR performs a refinement check of the protocol against its requirements. When refinement fails, then it provides a trace which shows how the property fails, that corresponds to an attack. Moreover, CasperFDR manages the Xor operation where attacks against these algebraic properties are considered in CasperFDR.

2.1 Simple Example

Figure 2a is our demonstrating simple protocol. A two message protocol aims to authenticate Bob to Alice:

1. Alice $\rightarrow$ Bob : $\{A, N_A, K_{AB}\}PK_B$
2. Bob $\rightarrow$ Alice : $\{N_A\}K_{AB}$

Message 1 sent by Alice to Bob contains Alice identity, Nonce (number used once) and a session key K_{AB}, encrypted with Bob's public key. Then, Bob sends message 2 by encrypting the Nonce (N_A) with the session key. Alice authenticates

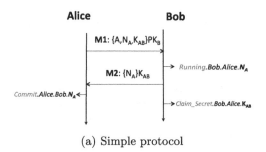

(a) Simple protocol

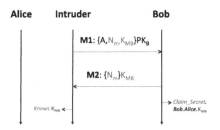

(b) Simple protocol attack

Fig. 2. Illustrating example

Bob based on the fact that since message 1 is encrypted by Bob's public key, he is the only one that can extract the session key and the nonce and send message 2. At the end of the protocol both Alice and Bob believe the session key K_{AB} is secret.

Analysing this protocol in CasperFDR is a straightforward procedure. Having modelled the exchanged messages between entities, we check the claimed authentication and secrecy using the following claims:

$$\texttt{Agreement(Bob,Alice,[N_A])}$$
$$\texttt{StrongSecret(Bob, K_{AB},[Alice])}$$

The *Agreement* specification means it will check whether Bob is authenticated to Alice and have both of them agreed on the Nonce N_A. The *StrongSecret* specification is checking whether the key K_{AB} is secret between Bob and Alice. CasperFDR will complete the remaining process for us as we explained earlier.

Nevertheless, understanding how these specifications are captured underneath CasperFDR is important if we want precise descriptions of how claimed properties are modelled in a specific application, as we will see later.

Capturing *authentication* between Alice and Bob in the protocol is done by utilising new events injected in the protocol as demonstrated in Fig. 2a. These events are *Running* and *Commit*. Initially, Alice and Bob are modelled as independent CSP processes. After message 1, Bob performs the *Running* event, which means Bob starts running the protocol apparently with Alice. Then, Alice will perform the *Commit* event at the end of her part of the protocol, which means Alice has finished a run of the protocol with Bob. Alice could make sure she was running the protocol with Bob based on the fact that if Alice reaches the *Commit* event then Bob must have reached the *Running* event before. Launching an attack relies on the possibility of the intruder, without taking Bob's role, to engineer a trace of the protocol in which Alice runs the *Commit* event without a corresponding *Running* event from Bob.

For *secrecy*, only the *Claim_Secret* event is used by Alice and Bob. Figure 2a only shows when Bob performs *Claim_Secret* event. An attack is launched if the intruder could break this claim, by finding a trace of the protocol in which the intruder knows a claimed secret, without taking Alice's or Bob's roles.

The *Running*, *Commit* and *Claim_Secret* events can also contain more information specific to the agreement required between the participants. They are constructed by:

Agent.Agent.Message

For example *Running.Bob.Alice.N_A*, which means Bob starts a run of the protocol, apparently with Alice, using nonce N_A.

The *Casper* analysis finds no attack on authentication, but there is an attack on secrecy. Figure 2b illustrates how an intruder can create a session key that Bob believes is secret with Alice. Anyone can generate message 1 since Bob's public key is publicly known. The intruder impersonates Alice by including Alice's identity. At the end of the protocol run Bob believes the session key K_{MB} is a secret shared with Alice. However, it is known by the intruder.

2.2   Hierarchy of Authentication and Secrecy

CasperFDR provides different flavours of testing authentication and secrecy. The strongest form of authentication specification is *Agreement*. If Alice and Bob meet the *Agreement* specification, then if Bob thinks he has successfully completed a run of the protocol with Alice, then Alice has previously been running the protocol, agreeing on their roles in the protocol, and there is a one-to-one relationship between Alice and Bob i.e. each run of Alice corresponds to a unique run of Bob.

A weaker authentication specification is *NonInjectiveAgreement*. The difference from *Agreement* is that the one-to-one relationship is not required. Each run of one participant matches a run of the other but they can overlap. For example, two "Commit" events may correspond to the same "Running" event.

Secrecy has two forms of specification, *Secret* and *StrongSecret*. *Secret* tests if the intruder could know the secret value at the end of the protocol. *StrongSecret* is stronger than *Secret* in that, including the *Secret* specification, it even checks whether the intruder is able to know the secret value without completing a full run of the protocol.

2.3   Channels

The CasperFDR intruder cannot open encrypted message without the decryption key, but also CasperFDR allows more restriction on the intruder's ability on any messages of the protocol. For example:

```
#Channels
1 NF NRA- NR
2 C NF NRA NR
```

The first line means that on message 1 the intruder neither can fake data *NF* (No Fake), nor honest reascribing *NRA-* (changing the sender ID except to his own ID) nor redirecting *NR* (changing the receiver ID). The second line means that on message 2 the intruder neither can eavesdrop *C*, nor fake data, nor reascribing nor redirecting.

By adjusting some of protocol's channels, we can capture assumptions made in the protocol as we will see later.

We do not restrict the ability of the intruder with respect to the wireless aspect. Even though eavesdropping is still a major threat, the intruder would not have that ability of communicating with the participants at the same time as in the normal wired network e.g. the Internet. In this paper we model the protocols in the Dolev-Yao model. If an attack occurred, we then analyse informally the feasibility in a wireless context. If no attack is found, then it means there should not be any attack in a weaker wireless model.

3   Protocol Security Requirements

The analysed protocol we consider in this paper intends to meet six security requirements, as stated by the protocol designer in [10]:

- **Confidentiality:** A third party should not be able to obtain the M-coupon by eavesdropping.
- **Data Integrity:** An attacker should not be able to modify data during the communication.
- **Forgery Protection:**
  - **No Unauthorized Generation:** An attacker should not be able to issue his own M-coupon.
  - **No Manipulation:** M-coupon should not stay valid after a manipulation.
- **Unauthorized Copying:** An attacker should not be able to produce a valid copy of an M-coupon and cash it in. This requirement can be divided into:
  - **Not Transferable:** Whatever identity is presented at issuing phase should not be changed during the protocol.
  - **User Authentication:** In addition to Not Transferable, the identity of the user is the one who it claims to be. The user who issued the M-coupon must be the one who is cashing it at the cashier. This requires the cashier to authenticate the user through some authentication methods.

  This protocol only addresses the Not Transferable requirement.
- **No Multiple Cash-in:** An attacker should not be able to use the same M-coupon multiple times.

3.1   Formal Definition

Figure 3 illustrates a formal definition in CasperFDR of these requirements and the relationship between them. The formal definitions can apply to a variety of M-coupon protocols [17].

Confidentiality requires that data representing the M-coupon in the protocol must satisfy *StrongSecret* specification between the issuer and the cashier.

NonInjectiveAgreement specification includes three requirements, and layers, of authentication between the cashier and the issuer. We are not concerned here with repeats because that is checked directly by other means, and it may be not required in some systems. For Forgery Protection, after identifying data representing the M-coupon, a *NonInjectiveAgreement* on the M-coupon between the issuer and the cashier is required. This is violated if the cashier accepts an M-coupon not been issued by the issuer. This implies either that the M-coupon has been created by an attacker (i.e. Unauthorised Generation) or else that an M-coupon generated by the issuer has been modified to another (i.e. No Manipulation). Not Transferable is a stronger specification than forgery protection that it also requires an agreement on a user identity attached to the M-coupon. The strongest *NonInjectiveAgreement* specification is Data Integrity: both the cashier and the issuer must agree on all data in the protocol.

No Multiple Cash-in requires an *Agreement* specification between the issuer and the cashier. Every time the cashier accepts an M-coupon, there must be a separate occasion where the issuer must have issued it. Hence the cashier cannot accept an M-coupon more times than it was issued.

User Authentication is an *Agreement* between the user and the cashier on some credential. Even though the M-coupon might be used many times, the user must be authenticated each time.

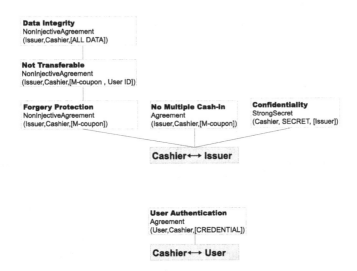

Fig. 3. Hierarchy of authentication/secrecy properties

4 Protocol Description

The M-coupon protocol of [10] uses simple hash functions, which is a computationally light cryptographic method, a suitable choice with standard RFID/NFC tags. Figure 4 shows the messages in protocol notation.

There are four messages in this protocol. Initially, the cashier C and the issuer I share a secret value, X and an offer. The cashier stores a table consisting of hashes of all issuers identities, $h[ID(i)]$.

> *1.* $U \to I$: $ID(u)$
> *2.* $I \to U$: $M = ID(u)$, V , C
> *3.* $U \to C$: $M = ID(u)$, V , C
> *4.* $C \to U$: $BONUS$

$ID(i)$	*Issuer ID*
$ID(u)$	*User ID*
Offer	*Data about the Offer*
X	*A secret key shared between the issuer and the cashier*
$\oplus$	*Exclusive or (XOR)*
$h[..]$	*Hash function*
V	$ID(u) \oplus h[ID(i)]$
C	$h[h[ID(i)] \oplus X \oplus Offer]$

Fig. 4. The hash-based M-coupon protocol

At the issuing phase, the user's mobile U sends its identity to the issuer (message 1). Then, the issuer produces a coupon, M (message 2), consisting of three parts: $ID(u)$, $V(= ID(u) \oplus h[ID(i)])$ and $C(= h[h[ID(i)] \oplus X \oplus Offer])$.

At the cashing phase, the user's mobile sends the M-coupon to the cashier (message 3). Then, the cashier obtains $h[ID(i)]$ by computing $ID(u) \oplus V$. The cashier can look up ID(i) from the hash, and then find X and *Offer*. When the cashier has $ID(u)$ and *Offer*, it can decide if the M-coupon has been used before, and reject it accordingly. Then, the cashier will check the validity of the M-coupon by computing $h[h[ID(i)] \oplus X \oplus Offer]$ and confirm it matches C. The cashier stores $ID(u)$ to prevent re-use of the coupon, and sends the Bonus to the user.

The intention is that the Confidentiality and Data Integrity requirements are ensured by use of the secret value X. By including the identity of the user's mobile and offer, Multiple Cash-in and Not Transferable can be managed. Forgery Protection is addressed by the secret value X which is known only by the cashier and the issuer.

5 Modelling

In order to capture the NFC M-coupon requirements in the protocol, we develop a model as shown in Fig. 5. The model captures the following requirements: Confidentiality, Forgery Protection, Not Transferable, Data Integrity and No Multiple Cash-in. Moreover, data representing the M-coupon in the protocol are X and *Offer*.

5.1 The Protocol's Requirements

We show in the following sections what we have to write in CasperFDR to model the protocol's requirements of Sect. 3, then how it is captured from the underneath CSP theory aspect, in terms of *Running*, *Commit* and *Claim_Secret* events. This enabling us to have formal and precise descriptions of capturing NFC mobile coupon requirements.

Confidentiality. We model confidentiality in Casper as follows:

```
StrongSecret(C, X , [I])
StrongSecret(C, Offer , [I])
```

These secrecy specifications means the cashier C claims that X and *Offer* are confidential between the cashier C and the issuer *I*. *StrongSecret* checks whether the intruder is able to break these claims without completing the protocol.

Figure 5 illustrates the first specification, secrecy of X. When the cashier C performs the *Claim_Secret.C.I.X* event, it can expect X to be a secret with the issuer I who shares the secret key X. If this is violated then the intruder can complete a run of the protocol with the cashier without taking the issuer role in the protocol, and learn the secret key X. A similar description for the *Offer* specification.

Forgery Protection. We model forgery protection in Casper as follows:

```
NonInjectiveAgreement(I,C,[X,Offer])
```

We identify the M-coupon with X and *Offer*. This states that if cashier accepts X and *Offer*, then the issuer must have issued them. *NonInjective* means that it is not concerned with repeats. I.e. the cashier can accept many times what was issued once. This is violated if the cashier accepts X and *Offer* that have not been issued by the issuer. This implies either that X and *Offer* have been created by an attacker (i.e. Unauthorised Generation) or else that an M-coupon generated by the issuer has been modified to another (i.e. No Manipulation). Hence if this property holds then we have Forgery Protection: No Unauthorised Generation and No Manipulation.

This is illustrated in Fig. 5. After the issuer completes its part of the protocol, it performs the *Running.I.C.X.Offer* event, which means the issuer I starts a running of the protocol, apparently, with the cashier C, agreeing on X and *Offer*. Later, the cashier will perform the *Commit.C.I.X.Offer* event at the end of its part of the protocol, which means the cashier C has finished the protocol with the issuer I, agreeing on the X and *Offer*.

Unauthorized Copying (Not Transferable). We model Not Transferable in Casper as follows:

```
NonInjectiveAgreement(I,C,[X,Offer,ID(u)])
```

This specification is similar to forgery protection specification, but also with an agreement on a user identity. The coupon, [X, *Offer*], must be attached to one user only *ID(u)*. Both the issuer and the cashier agree on the user to use the coupon as many times as he like, as long as the coupon has been issued by a genuine issuer, and is being used by the intended user. An example for such coupon is a frequent flyer coupon.

This is shown in Fig. 5. After the issuer completes its part of the protocol, it performs the *Running.I.C.X.Offer.ID(u)* event, which means the issuer I starts a running of the protocol, apparently with the cashier C, agreeing on X, *Offer* and *ID(u)*. Later, the cashier will perform the *Commit.C.I.X.Offer.ID(u)* event at the end of its part of the protocol, which means the cashier C has finished the protocol with the issuer I, agreeing on the X, *Offer* and *ID(u)*.

Observe that this property is stronger than Forgery Protection. If it holds then not only the m-coupon must be genuine, as for Forgery Protection, but it must also have the same user.

Data Integrity. We model Data Integrity in Casper as follows:

```
NonInjectiveAgreement(I,C,[X,Offer,ID(u),ID(i)])
```

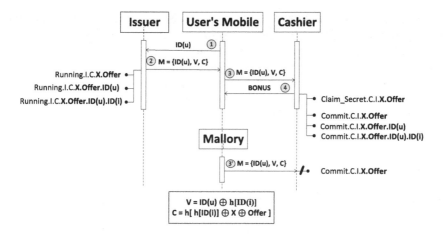

Fig. 5. Capturing hash-based NFC M-coupon requirements

This will check the integrity of the protocol. Both the cashier and the issuer must agree on all the information in the protocol.

No Multiple Cash-in. We model No Multiple Cash-in in Casper as follows:

$$\text{Agreement(I,C,[X,Offer])}$$

This specification states that every time the cashier accepts X and *Offer*, there must be a separate occasion where the issuer must have issued them. Hence cashier cannot accept X and *Offer* more times than issuer sent them.

Figure 5 illustrates a scenario where the cashier is engaging in the protocol twice, with one issuer run. The first time the cashier runs the protocol with the user's mobile, and the second, illegal, time with Mallory who might be an intruder or the user himself. The second *Commit* should not occur if there was not a separate *Running*.

5.2 Intruder Knowledge

The analysis also requires us to define the initial knowledge of the intruder. The intruder knows the following: the identities of himself, the user and the cashier, and the hash function.

5.3 Assumptions

There is an assumptions made by the protocol's designers that the client's ID is bound to the client's mobile device, and therefore the client is authenticated at issuing and cashing phases. Therefore, we analyse this protocol in two different assumptions: as no assumption made (the Dolev-Yao model) and as the user's ID is bound to the mobile.

The main goal for analysing the protocol under this assumption is that if an attack is discovered under the Dolev-Yao model, then we should examine if the attack still applies under the assumption made.

We blind message 1 from the intruder i.e. the intruder can not eavesdrop, fake, re-ascribe or redirect message 1. We model this in Casper as follows:

```
#Channels
1 C NF NRA NR
```

6   Analysis

The outcome of the analysis shows no attack on Confidentiality or Forgery Protection.

However, attacks were found on the properties of Not Transferable, Data Integrity and No Multiple Cash-in. The main vulnerability is a simple logical attack against the hashes of the M-coupon. The identity of the user attached to the M-coupon can be easily extracted and changed to any identity. If we consider the M-coupon, the identity $ID(u)$ is not attached correctly to the M-coupon. Anyone is able to compute the first two parts, $ID(u)$ and V to get $h[ID(i)]$:

$$h[ID(i)] = ID(u) \oplus V$$

By obtaining $h[ID(i)]$, the intruder is able to attach any identity, such as $ID(intruder)$ without changing the third part C, and thus produce a new coupon M':

$$V' = ID(intruder) \oplus h[ID(i)]$$
$$M' = ID(intruder) \, , \, V' \, , \, C$$

Even though this analysis was under the Dolev-Yao threat model, the properties are still broken under the assumption of a bounded user ID and in a wireless context. The attacker still could change the user identity in an eavesdropped M-coupon to his own identity, and cash it in with the cashier. The intruder could even know the user ID by pretending to be an issuer.

As far as the analysis is concerned, the *Unauthorized Copying* property can be divided into two properties: *Not Transferable* and *User Authentication*. *Not Transferable* is an agreement between the issuer and the cashier that whatever user identity presented at issuing phase, it should not be changed during the protocol. On the other hand, *User authentication* is stronger in that the identity of the user must also be the one who it is claimed to be. I.e. it is an agreement between the user and the cashier. This protocol only tries to address the requirement of Not Transferable, which may be sufficient in the case of their assumption or in a secure and trusted issuing phase.

Table 1. Hash based protocol and provided solutions against intended/addressed/failed requirements

	Hash-based	Enhanced Hash-based	Footfall	Premium
Confidentiality	$\checkmark$	$\checkmark$	$\checkmark$	$\checkmark$
Forgery protection	$\checkmark$	$\checkmark$	$\checkmark$	$\checkmark$
Data integrity	x	$\checkmark$	$\checkmark$	$\checkmark$
No multiple cash in	x	$\checkmark$	$\checkmark$	$\checkmark$
Not transferable	x	$\checkmark$		$\checkmark$
User authentication				$\checkmark$

7 Suggested Solution

We suggest three solutions to address the found vulnerability: An *enhanced hash-based protocol* which is a solution based on the assumption of the bounded ID assumption. In addition, We provide two kinds of marketing-oriented M-coupon protocols, *the footfall M-coupon protocol* and *the premium M-coupon protocol*, both of which are analysed within the Dolev-Yao model. Table 1 summarises the solutions provided against the properties they address.

7.1 Enhanced Hash-Based Protocol

In order to address the broken properties (Not Transferable, Data Integrity and No Multiple Cash-in) in the original hash-based protocol, the identity of the user must be attached correctly to the coupon. This solution must be only considered in a secure and trusted issuing phase. The change needed is to replace C in Fig. 4 to become:

$$C = h[h[ID(i)], X, \textit{Offer}, ID(u)]$$

As far as the Not Transferable property is concerned, it is only useful within a trusted issuing phase, which is not always the case. The fact that user ID can be faked by anyone makes combining the User Authentication property with Not Transferable property more useful and meaningful. So, the best choice would be to use them all: the premium protocol, or drop them all: the footfall protocol.

7.2 Marketing-Oriented Protocols Solutions

The footfall M-coupon protocol is used when the main purpose of the M-coupon is to increase the number of people visiting the shop, regardless of whom is using it. Conversely, the premium M-coupon protocol is used when the client has paid for it, and only the intended user is allowed to cash it. The premium M-coupon protocol addresses all requirements discussed in Sect. 3. The footfall M-coupon protocol addresses the same requirements, except for Not Transferable and User Authentication.

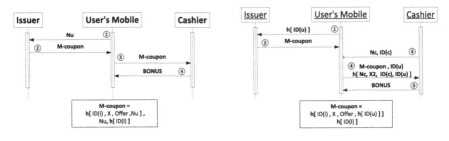

(a) the footfall M-coupon protocol   (b) the premium M-coupon protocol

Fig. 6. Suggested solution

The Footfall M-coupon Protocol. Fig. 6a shows the footfall M-coupon protocol.

Footfall/Premium protocol notations:

$ID(i)$ = Issuer ID.
$ID(u)$ = User ID.
$ID(c)$ = Cashier ID.
Offer = Data about the Offer.
X = A secret key between the issuer and the cashier.
$X2$ = A secret key between the user and the cashier.
Nu = User's nonce (random number).
Nc = Cashier's nonce.
$h[]$ = Hash function.

There are four messages in this protocol:
1. $U \rightarrow I : Nu$
2. $I \rightarrow U : M\text{-}coupon = h[ID(i), X, Offer, Nu], Nu, h[ID(i)]$
3. $U \rightarrow C: M\text{-}coupon = h[ID(i), X, Offer, Nu], Nu, h[ID(i)]$
4. $C \rightarrow U : BONUS$

After the user brings his mobile close to the issuer, his mobile sends a random number Nu (message 1). Then, the Issuer sends the M-coupon to the user (message 2). The M-coupon contains a hash of the issuer identity, the secret key X, the promised offer and user random number. In addition, a hash of the issuer identity is sent, and the user's random number. Then, the user brings his mobile near the cashier and sends the M-coupon (message 3). From the table of hashed issuer identities, the cashier uses h[ID(i)] to find the corresponding ID(i), secret X and the offer. The cashier can check the validity of the M-coupon. Through the nonce Nu the cashier can manage the M-coupon that every issued M-coupon has a unique random number. The cashier can, for example, stop using the M-coupon after five uses. Finally, if all these conditions are satisfied, then the bonus is given to the user (message 4).

Confidentiality, Data Integrity and Forgery Protection requirements are ensured by use of the secret value X and offer. Multiple Cash-in can be managed by including the nonce. However, a stronger Multiple Cash-in is provided in the premium M-coupon protocol.

```
Confidentiality-Footfall: StrongSecret(C,x,offer,[I])
Forgery Protection-Footfall: NonIAgreement(I,C,[x,offer,nu]
Data Integrity-Footfall: NonIAgreement(I,C,[x,offer,nu,I])
No Multiple Cash-in -Footfall: Agreement(I,C,[x,offer,nu])
```

The Premium M-coupon Protocol. The main enhancement in this protocol is attaching an authentic user identity to the coupon. I.e. addressing Not Transferable and User Authentication. Figure 6b illustrates the premium M-coupon protocol.

1. $U \rightarrow I : h[ID(u)]$
2. $I \rightarrow U :$ ***M-coupon***
3. $C \rightarrow U : Nc$, $ID(c)$
4. $U \rightarrow C :$ ***M-coupon*** , $ID(u)$, $h[Nc$, $X2$, $ID(c)$, $ID(u)]$
5. $C \rightarrow U : BONUS$
M-coupon $= h[ID(i)$, X , $Offer$, $h[ID(u)]]$, $h[ID(i)]$

The user's mobile sends a hash of his identity ID(u) to the issuer (message 1). Then, the issuer sends the M-coupon to the user (message 2). The M-coupon contains a hash of: the issuer identity, the secret X, the offer and the hashed user's identity. In addition, it contains a hash of the issuer identity. At the cashing phase, the cashier sends his identity and a nonce Nc (message 3). At message 4, the user sends the M-coupon and the user identity, with a new hash containing Nc, the secret value X2, the cashier identity and the user identity.

The cashier can send the bonus based on verifying the two hashes in message 4. From the table of hashed issuer identities, the cashier uses h[ID(i)] to find the corresponding ID(i), secret X and the offer, with user identity known from message 4, the cashier can check the validity of the M-coupon. The second hash authenticates the user, the cashier uses ID(u) to find the corresponding secret X2, and combines it with already known data (Nc, ID(c), ID(u)) to check the validity of the second hash. The cashier can link the M-coupon hash with the second one by checking that both of them include the same identity ID(u).

```
Confidentiality-Premium: StrongSecret(C,x,offer,x2,[I])
Forgery Protection-Premium: NonIAgreement(I,C,[x,offer]
Data Integrity-Premium: NonIAgreement(I,C,[x,offer,I,U])
No Multiple Cash-in-Premium: Agreement(I,C,[x,offer,U])
Not transfarable-Premium: NonIAgreement(I,C,[U])
User Authentecation-Premium: Agreement(U,C,[nc,x2,U])
```

We formally verify the security of these solutions: the Casper/FDR2 analysis found no attacks.

8   Conclusion

We used the formal model-checker Casper/FDR2 to examine a hash based M-coupon protocol and check whether it meets its requirements. The outcome of the analysis shows a simple logical attack in the hash combination of the M-coupon, which damages many of protocol's requirements. Solutions were provided based on two assumptions: when the issuing phase is trusted where the intruder is more restricted; and where the intruder has the power to claim any identity. This paper can be considered as a case study of how a black-box analysis can provide powerful results about NFC protocols.

Acknowledgement. This research was supported by Ministry of Higher Education in Saudi Arabia. We thank the anonymous reviewers for their constructive comments.

References

1. ISO/IEC: Information technology - telecommunications and information exchange between systems - near field communication - interface and protocol (NFCIP-1) (2004)
2. Finkenzeller, K.: RFID Handbuch: Fundamentals and Applications in Contact-less Smart Cards, Radio Frequency Identification and Near-Field Communication, 3rd edn. John Wiley and Sons, Ltd., New York (2010)
3. Haselsteiner, E., Breitfuß, K.: Security in near field communication (NFC). In: Proceedings of Workshop on RFID and Lightweight Crypto (RFIDSec06) (2006)
4. Mulliner, C.: Vulnerability analysis and attacks on NFC-enabled mobile phones. In: ARES, pp. 695–700 (2009)
5. Juniper Research: Mobile coupons – ecosystem analysis and marketing channel strategy 2011–2016. Technical report, Juniper Research (2011)
6. Clark, S.: Survey: discounts and coupons will drive adoption of mobile payments (2011). http://www.nfcworld.com/2011/06/23/38289/survey-discounts-and-coupons-will-drive-adoption-of-mobile-payments
7. Smart Card Alliance: Proximity mobile payments business scenarios: Research report on stakeholder perspective. Technical report, Smart Card Alliance (2008)
8. Brown, C.: The future is NFC says coupons.com exec (2011). http://www.nfcworld.com/2011/03/10/36399/the-future-is-nfc-says-coupons-com-exec/
9. Wolverton, T.: Disney battles coupon goof (2002). http://news.cnet.com/2100-1017-964831.html
10. Hsiang, H.C., Shih, W.K.: Secure mcoupons scheme using nfc. In: International Conference on Business and Information (2008)
11. Lowe, G.: An attack on the needham-schroeder public-key authentication protocol. Inf. Process. Lett. **56**(3), 131–133 (1995)
12. Lowe, G.: Casper: a compiler for the analysis of security protocols. J. Comput. Secur. **6**(1–2), 53–84 (1998)
13. Hoare, C.A.R.: Communicating Sequential Processes. Prentice-Hall, Upper Saddle River (1985)
14. Ryan, P.Y.A., Schneider, S.A., Goldsmith, M., Lowe, G., Roscoe, A.W.: Modelling and Analysis of Security Protocols. Addison-Wesley-Longman, New York (2001)

15. Donovan, B., Norris, P., Lowe, G.: Analyzing a library of security protocols using Casper and FDR. In: Proceedings of the Workshop on Formal Methods and Security Protocols (1999)
16. Dolev, D., Yao, A.: On the security of public-key protocols. IEEE Trans. Inf. Theory **2**(29), 198–208 (1983)
17. Alshehri, A., Schneider, S.: Formally defining NFC M-coupon requirements, with a case study. In: International Conference for Internet Technology and Secured Transactions, ICITST 2013 (2013). doi:10.1109/ICITST.2013.6750161, http://ieeexplore.ieee.org/xpl/articleDetails.jsp?arnumber=6750161&tag=1

Side Channel Countermeasures - Session Chair: Svetla Nikova

Revisiting Atomic Patterns for Scalar Multiplications on Elliptic Curves

Franck Rondepierre[(✉)]

Oberthur Technologies, Crypto Group, 420, Rue Estienne D'Orves,
92 700 Colombes, France
f.rondepierre@oberthur.com

Abstract. This paper deals with the protection of elliptic curve scalar multiplications against side-channel analysis by using the atomicity principle. Unlike other atomic patterns, we investigate new formulæ with same cost for both doubling and addition. This choice is particularly well suited to evaluate double scalar multiplications with the Straus-Shamir trick. Thus, in situations where this trick is used to evaluate single scalar multiplications our pattern allows an average improvement of 40 % when compared with the most efficient atomic scalar multiplication published so far. Surprisingly, in other cases our choice remains very efficient. Besides, we also point out a security threat when the curve parameter a is null and propose an even more efficient pattern in this case.

Keywords: Elliptic curves · Scalar multiplication · Straus-Shamir trick · Side-Channel Analysis · Atomicity

1 Introduction

The first algorithms performing public-key cryptography, such as the Rivest-Shamir-Adleman (RSA) algorithm [27], have been published in the seventies and remain widely used nowadays. However, current key lengths required with these protocols are limiting their efficiency. Elliptic Curve Cryptography (ECC) provides equivalent cryptographic primitives, but with significant improvements in terms of speed and memory, and is now recommended by governmental organizations such as the National Institute of Standards and Technology (NIST). The main resource-consuming operation in ECC is the computation of a *scalar multiplication* $[k] P$ for a secret scalar k and a public point P on an elliptic curve.

We hence consider the implementation on smart cards of scalar multiplications on standardized elliptic curves over $\mathbb{F}_p$. In this context, side-channel resistance, memory and power consumptions have to be taken into account before designing a fast implementation.

Side-Channel Analysis (SCA) is one of the main attack used to disclose secret data hidden in low-resource devices. SCA exploits the fact that a device leaks information about the processed operations and data, that can be physically measured: timing, power consumption, electromagnetic emanations, etc. Among

A. Francillon and P. Rohatgi (Eds.): CARDIS 2013, LNCS 8419, pp. 171–186, 2014.
DOI: 10.1007/978-3-319-08302-5_12, © Springer International Publishing Switzerland 2014

all kinds of SCA, the *Simple Side-Channel Analysis* (SSCA) [21] focuses on detecting on a single execution trace differences of behavior depending on a secret value. Many proposals have been made to thwart SSCA and the *atomicity principle* introduced by Chevallier-Mames et al. [3] is one of the most efficient propositions. This countermeasure has been widely studied and improved first by P. Longa [22] and then by C. Giraud and V. Verneuil [12].

In this paper, we revisit EC formulæ in a novel way and propose corresponding patterns to optimally benefit from the Straus-Shamir trick, a twice as fast method to evaluate *double scalar multiplications* $[u] P + [v] Q$. Few ECC protocols explicitly require double scalar multiplications. However as shown in [28] it can be adapted to process single scalar multiplications $[k] P$ which gives us an advantage since the best implementation known so far [12] cannot take advantage of this trick. Besides, when this method is not used (e.g. because of memory constraints) our formulæ still allow the most interesting ratio between performances and memory cost. In all cases, our implementation requires less memory than other methods. Besides, we also point out a security flaw concerning many implementations computing over Weierstrass curves with $a = 0$. Therefore, our method outperforms existing solutions in terms of security, memory and speed and is suited for low-resource devices.

The rest of the paper is organized as follows. In the next section we introduce some background on elliptic curves and detail known techniques to perform efficient scalar multiplications. Then Sect. 3 deals with the security of scalar multiplications against SSCA. In Sect. 4 we present our formulæ which allow the use of the most efficient scalar multiplication algorithms. Eventually we conclude in Sect. 5.

2   Elliptic Curve Background

2.1   Definitions

An elliptic curve $\mathcal{E}$ over $\mathbb{F}_p$, for a prime $p > 3$ is defined with the short Weierstrass equation [15]:

$$\mathcal{E} : y^2 = x^3 + ax + b, \tag{1}$$

where $x, y, a, b \in \mathbb{F}_p$ and $4a^3 + 27b^2 \neq 0$.

With the so-called *chord-and-tangent* law, the set of all points on the elliptic curve together with the point at infinity (denoted by $\mathcal{O}$) form an abelian group $\mathcal{E}(\mathbb{F}_p)$. Excepting trivial cases, the group law requires the computation of one inverse in $\mathbb{F}_p$ which is significantly more expensive than a multiplication. Therefore we use Jacobian coordinates to represent points in order to limit the number of inversions performed in a scalar multiplication. These coordinates use the following equivalence class, for non all-zero triples:

$$(X : Y : Z) = \{(\lambda^2 X, \lambda^3 Y, \lambda Z) : \lambda \in \mathbb{F}_p^*\}.$$

In this case the short Weierstrass equation (1) becomes:

$$\mathcal{E} : Y^2 = X^3 + aXZ^4 + bZ^6 \tag{2}$$

and $\mathcal{O} = (1 : 1 : 0)$. The opposite of $(X : Y : Z)$ is the point $(X : -Y : Z)$.

The sum of two points $P = (X_p : Y_p : Z_p)$ and $Q = (X_q : Y_q : Z_q)$ is the point $P + Q = (X_{p+q} : Y_{p+q} : Z_{p+q})$ such that:

$$\begin{cases} X_{p+q} = F^2 - E^3 - 2AE^2 \\ Y_{p+q} = F(AE^2 - X_{p+q}) - CE^3 \\ Z_{p+q} = Z_p Z_q E \end{cases} \text{with} \begin{array}{l} A = X_p Z_q^2 \\ B = X_q Z_p^2 \\ C = Y_p Z_q^3 \\ D = Y_q Z_p^3 \\ E = B - A \\ F = D - C \end{array} \tag{3}$$

However, the addition formula is only valid under the following assumptions: $P \neq Q$, $P \neq \mathcal{O}$ and $Q \neq \mathcal{O}$. Several operations in $\mathbb{F}_p$ are required to evaluate this formula: squarings (denoted by S), multiplications (denoted by M), additions and subtractions (both denoted by A). This formula requires $4S + 12M + 7A$.

The double of a point $P = (X : Y : Z)$ is the point $[2] P = (X_2 : Y_2 : Z_2)$ such that:

$$\begin{cases} X_2 = A^2 - 2C \\ Y_2 = A(C - X_2) - D \\ Z_2 = 2YZ \end{cases} \text{with} \begin{array}{l} A = 3X^2 + aZ^4 \\ B = 2Y \cdot Y \\ C = 2BX \\ D = 2B \cdot B \end{array} \tag{4}$$

Using this formula, the evaluation of a doubling requires $4S + 6M + 9A$.

The result of $P + P$ is naturally denoted by the point $[2] P$ and such an operation is called a *doubling* whereas the addition rather refers to the computation of $P + Q$ with $P \neq \pm Q$. More generally, the operation $P + \ldots + P$ where the point P is added k times is called a *scalar multiplication* and is denoted by $[k] P$.

2.2   Efficient Scalar Multiplication Implementation

This section presents the different known tools to optimize the implementation of an elliptic curve multiplication.

Double and Add. The scalar multiplication is efficiently computed with the so-called Double and Add algorithm [20]. Using the EC group law, this algorithm evaluates:

$$[k] P = \sum_{i=0}^{\ell-1} [k_i] [2^i] P = [k_0] P + [2] \left[\sum_{i=1}^{\ell-1} k_i 2^{i-1} \right] P$$

where digits $k_i \in \mathcal{S}$ and $\mathcal{S}$ is some set of integers containing 0 and 1, as presented in [23]. The ℓ digits of k can be evaluated in two ways, i.e. starting from least significant ones (right to left) or from most significant ones (left to right), see Algorithm 1 for the later case.

Algorithm 1. Left to Right Double and Add

Input: $k = \sum_{i=0}^{\ell-1} k_i 2^i$, $k_{\ell-1} \neq 0$, $k_i \in \mathcal{S}$, $P \in \mathcal{E}$
Output: $R = [k] P$
  Precompute $[m] P$, $\forall m \in \mathcal{S} \backslash \{0\}$
  Initialize $R = [k_{\ell-1}] P$
  for $i = \ell - 2$ **downto** 0 **do**
    $R = [2] R$
    if $k_i \neq 0$ **then**
      $R = R + [k_i] P$
    end if
  end for

Double and Add trade-off. The scalar multiplication consists in a succession of doublings and additions. Depending on the ratio between the number of evaluated additions and the number of doublings, one formula may be favored at the expense of the other in order to reduce the overall cost.

- First, the cost of the addition formula (3) can be reduced with some assumptions. Indeed, in Algorithm 1, the points $[m] P$ are constant. Hence Chudnovsky [4] proposed to compute $Z_{[m]P}^2$ and $Z_{[m]P}^3$ once for all, which saves $1S + 1M$ per point addition. Furthermore, at the cost of one inversion and few multiplications[1] during the precomputation phase, one can choose the representative of $[m] P$ with $Z_{[m]P} = 1$, which instead saves $1S + 4M$ in (3). Besides, since there is always a doubling of R before the point addition $R + [k_i] P$, we propose to move the computation of Z_r^2 and Z_r^3 in the doubling formula which also saves $1S + 1M$.
- The doubling formula (4) can be speeded up [5] with the help of one extra value W initialized with the value aZ^4. In this case, A is evaluated as $3X^2 + W$ and W_2 is equal to $2DW$, which gives a global cost of $2S + 6M + 10A$. However, in Algorithm 1, if the point R is represented as $(X_r : Y_r : Z_r : W_r)$ then the value W_r has to remain consistent when the addition $R + [k_i] P$ is performed. Therefore Formula (3) has to update this value W: $W_{r+q} = W_r (E^2 Z_{[k_i]P}^2)^2$ which costs either $1S + 2M$ if $Z_{[k_i]P} \neq 1$ or $1S + 1M$.

We will now see two techniques used to change the addition/doubling ratio.

Straus-Shamir Trick. The Straus-Shamir trick [8,30] is a simple but very efficient way of evaluating double scalar multiplications $[u] P + [v] Q$. The naive way to evaluate the double multiplication performs two multiplications and adds the results. Using two calls to Algorithm 1, this approach costs on average 2ℓ doublings and ℓ additions (for random scalars u and v). However, neither $[u] P$ nor $[v] Q$ are needed values. The trick consists then in building one sequence of intermediate results directly converging to the value $[u] P + [v] Q$ in one execution of a Double and Add algorithm. Algorithm 2 implements such a trick which only requires on average ℓ doublings and 0.75ℓ additions.

---

[1] A trick from Montgomery [24] enables to evaluate several inverses at the cost of only one inversion and few multiplications: $\frac{1}{a} = \frac{1}{ab} \cdot b$, $\frac{1}{b} = \frac{1}{ab} \cdot a$.

This trick can also be used to improve the evaluation of $[k]\,P$ if the multiplication is decomposed as:

$$[k]\,P = [k_0]\,P + [k_1]\,([\lambda]\,P).$$

Of course, the trick has an interest when k_0 and k_1 have a size $\ell/2$ and when k_0, k_1 and $Q = [\lambda]\,P$ are available with reasonable cost. As recalled in [28], one can take $\lambda = 2^{\ell/2}$ and precompute Q when the point P is reused for many scalar multiplications. One can remark that this trick – working only with left-to-right scan of digits – is generalizable for multi-multiplication.

Algorithm 2. Double Scalar Multiplication using Straus-Shamir Trick

---

Input: $u = \sum_{i=0}^{\ell-1} u_i 2^i$, $v = \sum_{i=0}^{\ell-1} v_i 2^i$, $(u_{\ell-1}, v_{\ell-1}) \neq (0,0)$, $(u_i, v_i) \in \mathcal{S}^2$, $(P,Q) \in \mathcal{E}^2$,
    $P \neq \pm Q$
Output: $R = [u]\,P + [v]\,Q$
    Precompute $W_{i,j} = [i]\,P + [j]\,Q$, $\forall (i,j) \in \mathcal{S}^2 \backslash \{(0,0)\}$
    Initialize $R = W_{u_{\ell-1}, v_{\ell-1}}$
    for $i = \ell - 2$ **downto** 0 **do**
        $R = [2]\,R$
        if $(u_i, v_i) \neq (0,0)$ **then**
            $R = R + W_{u_i, v_i}$
        end if
    end for

Scalar Recoding. The previous trick allows to cut to half the number of doublings. Independently, the number of additions can also be reduced by using windowing and signed digit representations in order to maximize the number of null digits of the scalar. The best signed digit representations to reduce the number of non-zero digits are the Non-Adjacent Form (NAF) [1] for one scalar, and the Joint Sparse Form (JSF) [28] for a couple of scalars. NAF and JSF have been generalized to larger digit set than $\{0, \pm 1\}$ [26,29] but only NAF_{w+1} (which indicates a NAF representation with window size w) fits smart card memory constraints. Tables 1 and 2 indicate, for several cases, the definition of the set $\mathcal{S}$, the number of involved points which corresponds to a certain RAM cost, and the average number of point addition performed per bit which also corresponds to the ratio between additions and doublings.

Table 1. Several scalar recoding techniques and their average number of point additions per bit of k in the context of single scalar multiplication $[k]\,P$

Recoding technique	None	NAF	$\text{NAF}_{w=3}$	$\text{NAF}_{w=4}$
Involved points	P	$\pm P$	$\pm P, \pm 3P$	$\pm P, \pm 3P, \pm 5P, \pm 7P$
$\mathcal{S}$	$\{0,1\}$	$\{-1,0,1\}$	$\{-3,-1,0,1,3\}$	$\{-7,-5,-3,-1,0,1,3,5,7\}$
Point additions/bit	$1/2$	$1/3$	$1/4$	$1/5$

Table 2. Several scalar recoding techniques and their average number of point additions per bit of k in the context of double scalar multiplication $[u]P + [v]Q$

Recoding technique	None	JSF
Involved points	$P, Q, P+Q$	$\pm P, \pm Q, \pm(P+Q), \pm(P-Q)$
S	$\{0,1\}$	$\{-1,0,1\}$
Point additions/bit	3/4	1/2

3   Secure Scalar Multiplication Implementation

As shown in Formulæ (3) and (4) the evaluation of a doubling is different from the evaluation of an addition: the number of each type of operation and the number of operations in total are not the same. These differences are easily detected via SSCA and give information on the handled scalar k. Indeed in Algorithm 1 the addition is performed only if k_i is not null, thus knowing that 2 successive doublings have been performed means that the corresponding k_i was null. If the binary representation has been used, i.e. $k_i \in S = \{0,1\}$, then the knowledge of all indexes where k_i is null is enough to retrieve the whole value k. Using other scalar representation reduces the amount of information leaked but sophisticated attacks [9] only need some bits to be successful. This section deals with the proposed countermeasures to thwart such a leakage.

3.1   State-of-the-Art

Secure Implementation. Many algorithms have been published so far to resist this SSCA with different strategies. A unified formula has been proposed [2] to evaluate the sum of two points P, Q (different from $\mathcal{O}$) without the restriction $P \neq Q$. The Double and Add Always [6] performs the addition whatever the value of the digit k_i. Other regular algorithms such as the Montgomery Ladder [2,11,18] perform a doubling and an addition for each bit but without dummy operations which is more interesting from a security point of view. Recent works [14,16] have investigated efficient Montgomery Ladder formulæ with good results, but this approach cannot benefit from scalar recoding and hence remains costly if compared with best non-secure implementations. The principle of atomicity focuses on reaching the same security level at a closer cost of non-secure implementations.

Atomicity Principle. The atomicity principle [3] can be seen as a refined unified formula. Instead of having one formula valid in both situations ($P = Q$ and $P \neq \pm Q$) this countermeasure focuses on evaluating two different formulæ using the same operations or the same flow of operations. On can notice that such an evaluation is always possible but may induce additional dummy operations. The tour-de-force of Chevallier-Mames et al. [3] was to propose such an evaluation at an almost negligible cost, which is without any dummy modular multiplication. They have split the two formulæ in a sequence of identical *atomic patterns* such

Table 3. Comparing operation cost between main atomic implementations and non-secure implementations, with $2N = A$

Algorithm	Pattern cost	Addition cost	Doubling cost
Chevallier-Mames et al. [3]	$M + 2A + N$	$16M + 40A$	$10M + 25A$
Longa L2R [22]	$2M + 3A + 2N$	$14M + 28A$	$8M + 16A$
GV R2L [12]	$2S + 6M + 10A$	$4S + 12M + 20A$	$2S + 6M + 10A$
Non-secure R2L	-	$4S + 12M + 7A$	$2S + 6M + 10A$
Non-secure L2R	-	$4S + 9M + 7A$	$2S + 6M + 10A$

that ten calls of this pattern make a doubling, while sixteen calls give an addition. Their pattern is depicted below, where the R_i's denote some intermediate values.

$$\begin{bmatrix} R_1 \leftarrow R_2 \cdot R_3 \\ R_4 \leftarrow R_5 + R_6 \\ R_7 \leftarrow -R_8 \\ R_9 \leftarrow R_{10} + R_{11} \end{bmatrix} \tag{5}$$

However, as shown in Table 3 such a pattern implies a lot of dummy additions (A) and negations (N) when evaluating Formulæ (3) and (4). If the cost of one addition or a negation is small compared to a modular multiplication it cannot be neglected yet. Another drawback of the formula lies in the loss of squares traded for multiplications, which implies a loss of efficiency when a dedicated function is available to evaluate squares faster than multiplications. Therefore, this pattern (5) has been first improved by Longa [22] and more reworked by Giraud and Verneuil (GV) [12]. In the rest of the paper, as explained in [12], we assume $a = -3$ and Chudnovsky optimization for Longa's implementation of Algorithm 1. The GV implementation optimizes doublings with the extra value W but uses a right-to-left scan of digits to limit the cost of point additions.

3.2 Scalar Evaluation

The elliptic curve formulæ are not the only part to secure when considering implementations protected with the atomicity principle. The security of the scalar treatment is also crucial to thwart SSCA similar to the following example. For instance, let us assume that the evaluation at round i of a doubling $\mathcal{D}_i$ cannot be distinguished from the evaluation of a point addition $\mathcal{A}_i$ (i.e. atomic patterns have been used), let E_i denote the scalar treatment at round i, then observing the following sequence (6) gives information on the scalar k. Indeed, patterns corresponding to a doubling and an addition are performed between E_i and E_{i-1} which means that $k_i \neq 0$ while $k_{i-1} = 0$ since only a doubling is performed between E_{i-1} and E_{i-2}.

$$\mathcal{D}_i, E_i, \mathcal{A}_i, \mathcal{D}_{i-1}, E_{i-1}, \mathcal{D}_{i-2}, E_{i-2}, \ldots \tag{6}$$

Hence, if the atomic pattern must be called x (resp. y) times to perform a point addition (resp. point doubling), then a call to the scalar treatment has to be done every gcd (x, y) pattern. Besides, this scalar treatment has to implement the atomicity principle to have the same behavior whatever the value of the digit k_i. The induced overhead required to securely evaluate the secret scalar is generally under-estimated. Actually, this consists in the main limitation of the atomic countermeasure when the scalar multiplication has to be implemented on components that cannot process the scalar treatment in parallel of the pattern evaluation. Taking $x = y$ allows to reduce the cost of this treatment.

4   New Atomic Pattern

4.1   New Fomulæ

Up to now, improvements on atomic implementations have mainly focused on optimizing the doubling formula. This strategy comes from the observation that a doubling has to be computed for each bit of the scalar, while the addition is only performed for non-zero digit. In the context of processing one scalar (e.g. Algorithm 1), there is a low addition/doubling ratio which validates this strategy (see Table 1). However this is not the case in the double scalar multiplication.

Hence, we propose hereafter to focus on improving point addition to better match double multiplication case. The new formulæ are detailed hereafter to ease the verification of the proposed atomic patterns. The sum of $P = (X : Y : Z : Z^2 : Z^3)$ and $Q = (X_q : Y_q : 1)$ is the point $P + Q = (X_3 : Y_3 : Z_3 : Z_3^2)$ such that:

$$
\begin{cases}
X_3 = F^2 - E^3 - 2AE^2 \\
Y_3 = F(AE^2 - X_3) - CE^3 \\
Z_3 = ZE \\
Z_3^2 = (Z_3)^2
\end{cases}
\text{with}
\begin{aligned}
A &= X \\
B &= X_q Z^2 \\
C &= Y \\
D &= Y_q Z^3 \\
E &= B - A \\
F &= D - C
\end{aligned}
\tag{7}
$$

The subtraction $P - Q$ is obtained by replacing F by $\bar{F} = D + 2C - C$ and then $Y_3 = \bar{F}(X_3 - AE^2) - CE^3$. The double of a point $P = (X : Y : Z : Z^2)$ is the point $[2] P = (X_2 : Y_2 : Z_2 : Z_2^2 : Z_2^3)$ such that:

$$
\begin{cases}
X_2 = A^2 - 2C \\
Y_2 = A(C - X_2) - D \\
Z_2 = 2YZ \\
Z_2^2 = (Z_2)^2 \\
Z_2^3 = (Z_2)^3
\end{cases}
\text{with}
\begin{aligned}
A &= 3(X - IZ^2)(X + IZ^2) \\
B &= 2Y \cdot Y \\
C &= 2BX \\
D &= 2B \cdot B
\end{aligned}
\tag{8}
$$

We introduce a new constant value $I = \sqrt{-a3^{-1}}$ in order to reduce the cost of doublings. For a random value a (i.e. a random curve) this constant I exists with probability 0.5. However, for most standard curves (NIST [?], Brainpool [7],

ANSSI [19]) the constant I exists and may have some particular value (e.g. $I = 1$ or $I = 0$). The case $I = 0$ has a special treatment in Sect. 4.3. A pattern working for all curves is given in Appendix A. This pattern is less efficient, trading an addition for a square, but still of interest.

Eventually we have $3S + 7M + 7A$ to evaluate the addition and $2S + 8M + 10A$ for the doubling, which means that a square has to be performed as a modular multiplication and three dummy modular additions are required in the addition formula in order to get a unified cost. Besides, in order to save some memory when using NAF or JSF recodings, we benefit from the dummy modular additions to also present a subtraction formula which avoids the storage of opposite points.

From $P = (X, Y, Z, Z^2, Z^3)$ and $Q(X_q, Y_q, 1)$, one can compute $P \leftarrow P + Q$, $P \leftarrow P - Q$ and $P \leftarrow [2]P$ with the following patterns, where each pattern requires $2S + 8M + 10A$:

Addition	Subtraction	Doubling
$R_1 \leftarrow X_q \cdot Z^2$	$R_1 \leftarrow X_q \cdot Z^2$	$R_0 \leftarrow I \cdot Z^2$
$R_1 \leftarrow R_1 - X$	$R_1 \leftarrow R_1 - X$	$R_1 \leftarrow X - R_0$
$\star \leftarrow \star + \star$	$Z^2 \leftarrow Y + Y$	$R_2 \leftarrow Y + Y$
$R_2 \leftarrow R_1 \cdot R_1$	$R_2 \leftarrow R_1 \cdot R_1$	$Z_2^2 \leftarrow Y \cdot R_2$
$\star \leftarrow \star + \star$	$\star \leftarrow \star + \star$	$Y_2 \leftarrow Z_2^2 + Z_2^2$
$R_3 \leftarrow X \cdot R_2$	$R_3 \leftarrow X \cdot R_2$	$R_3 \leftarrow R_2 \cdot Z$
$R_0 \leftarrow Y_q \cdot Z^3$	$R_0 \leftarrow Y_q \cdot Z^3$	$R_2 \leftarrow Y_2 \cdot X$
$\star \leftarrow \star + \star$	$R_0 \leftarrow Z^2 + R_0$	$X_2 \leftarrow X + R_0$
$Z^3 \leftarrow R_1 \cdot R_2$	$Z^3 \leftarrow R_1 \cdot R_2$	$R_0 \leftarrow R_1 \cdot X_2$
$R_2 \leftarrow Z \cdot R_1$	$R_2 \leftarrow Z \cdot R_1$	$R_1 \leftarrow Z_2^2 \cdot Y_2$
$X_3 \leftarrow R_3 + R_3$	$X_3 \leftarrow R_3 + R_3$	$X_2 \leftarrow R_0 + R_0$
$X_3 \leftarrow Z^3 + X_3$	$X_3 \leftarrow Z^3 + X_3$	$R_0 \leftarrow R_0 + X_2$
$Z_3^2 \leftarrow (R_2)^2$	$Z_3^2 \leftarrow (R_2)^2$	$X_2 \leftarrow (R_0)^2$
$R_0 \leftarrow R_0 - Y$	$R_0 \leftarrow R_0 - Y$	$X_2 \leftarrow X_2 - R_2$
$R_1 \leftarrow (R_0)^2$	$R_1 \leftarrow (R_0)^2$	$Z_2^2 \leftarrow (R_3)^2$
$X_3 \leftarrow R_1 - X_3$	$X_3 \leftarrow R_1 - X_3$	$X_2 \leftarrow X_2 - R_2$
$R_1 \leftarrow R_3 - X_3$	$R_1 \leftarrow X_3 - R_3$	$R_2 \leftarrow R_2 - X_2$
$R_3 \leftarrow R_1 \cdot R_0$	$R_3 \leftarrow R_1 \cdot R_0$	$Z_2^3 \leftarrow Z_2^2 \cdot R_3$
$R_0 \leftarrow Y \cdot Z^3$	$R_0 \leftarrow Y \cdot Z^3$	$Y_2 \leftarrow R_0 \cdot R_2$
$Y_3 \leftarrow R_3 - R_0$	$Y_3 \leftarrow R_3 - R_0$	$Y_2 \leftarrow Y_2 - R_1$
$Z_3 \leftarrow R_2$	$Z_3 \leftarrow R_2$	$Z_2 \leftarrow R_3$

In order to reduce the number of intermediate buffers R_i, the output buffers (e.g. X_3, X_2) have been used as intermediate buffers which allows to use 4 intermediate buffers R_i only. Besides particular attention has been paid to allow in-place EC operations (e.g. an overlap of buffers X and X_2). However, the patterns do not contain in-place modular multiplications ($R_1 \leftarrow R_1 \cdot R_2$) as discussed in [16] to limit the memory consumption.

4.2 Performances

In this section, the performances of the new pattern are compared with best known atomic patterns for both single scalar and double scalar multiplication cases. In order to evaluate the cost of an implementation we use the average per bit cost. We put aside the cost of pre-computations, or post-computations since it gives only a small advantage to the right-to-left variant. The per bit cost is obtained with the following formula:

$$\mathcal{D} + E + H \cdot (\mathcal{A} + E)$$

where $\mathcal{D}$ (resp. $\mathcal{A}$) stands for the cost of a doubling (resp. addition), E is the cost to treat the scalar and H is the average number of point additions per bit of the scalar.

Theoretical Study. We combine here the cost of point addition and doubling (see Table 3 and Sect. 4.1) with the addition/doubling ratios given in tables 1 and 2. *Remark:* As indicated in Table 3 we assume $2N = A$. Indeed the negation of a value v already reduced modulo p can be performed as the subtraction $p - v$ without the need of modular reduction.

Double Scalar Multiplication. The RAM available in the smart card context limits the ratio H to be greater than 0.5 when using Algorithm 2. As shown in Table 4, our pattern always offers the best performances when compared with Longa's pattern.

Single Scalar Multiplication. Due to smart card memory constraints, lower values for H (i.e. less than 0.5) correspond to single scalar multiplication cases. We present in Table 5 the limit of our method encountered with our practical values (Table 9). The new solution still requires less modular additions than other propositions but it requires more products. The ratios A/M and S/M will help to select the solution with the best per bit cost. The cost of exponent recoding E shall also be carefully taken into account in the case of on-the-fly scalar recoding. Indeed, protecting this heavy scalar treatment against SSCA may be costly.

Memory Cost. The smaller the ratio point additions per bit (i.e. H), the more buffers required in memory. Depending on the supported ECC bit lengths these

Table 4. Double scalar multiplication cost per bit

Algorithm	$H = 3/4$	$H = 1/2$
Longa L2R	$18.5M + 37A + 9.25E$	$15M + 30A + 7.5E$
This paper	$3.5S + 14M + 17.5A + 1.75E$	$3S + 12M + 15A + 1.5E$

Table 5. Single scalar multiplication cost per bit

Algorithm	$H = 1/4$	$H = 1/5$
Longa L2R	$11.5M + 23A + 5.75E$	$10.8M + 21.6A + 5.4E$
GV R2L	$3S + 9M + 15A + 1.5E$	$2.8S + 8.4M + 14A + 1.4E$
This paper	$2.5S + 10M + 12.5A + 1.25E$	$2.4S + 9.6M + 12A + 1.2E$

Table 6. Number of buffers required for the scalar multiplication

Operation	Recoding	H	GV R2L	Longa L2R	This paper
$[u]P + [v]Q$	None	3/4	-	22	15
	JSF	1/2	-	27	17
$[k]P$	NAF	1/3	11	12	11
	$\text{NAF}_{w=3}$	1/4	14	17	13
	$\text{NAF}_{w=4}$	1/5	20	27	17

buffers correspond to more or less RAM. Therefore the developer selects a ratio with regard to the desired memory cost. The new pattern has been optimized in order to only use four intermediate registers (see Sect. 4.1) and the same results can be obtained for the pattern of Giraud-Verneuil – and should be possible for Longa's pattern. If X denotes the number of extra points (see Tables 1 and 2), an implementation using Longa's pattern requires $12 + 5X$ buffers (assuming a subtraction pattern), $11 + 3X$ buffers are required using GV pattern and only $11 + 2X$ buffers are required with the new pattern.

Practical Values. One usually considers the chip characteristics before selecting the best matching algorithm. In Table 7 we give measured costs of elementary operations performed in the field $\mathbb{F}_p$ on our chip. We also give the relative cost of a secured on-the-fly NAF scalar recoding. Therefore, the following table 8 contains a line with $E/M = 0$ since we did not implement on-the-fly JSF recoding. This choice is greatly in favor of Longa's pattern (see Table 4) and in practice E/M may not be negligible. If we look at the 224-bit size (considered as secured in the midterm [13]) we see an improvement of at least 14.6 % for the double scalar multiplication case. In the single scalar multiplication case (Table 9), the new proposition has a performance close to the Giraud-Verneuil solution. However, a fair comparison must take into account the memory cost of each algorithm which emphasize the interest of the new pattern. Besides, the small gain/loss of the new pattern in the single scalar multiplication case may be seen as a fair cost if we consider that only one implementation is now required for both double scalar multiplication and single scalar multiplication situations. Eventually, about components with $S < M$, our propositions benefit from fast squares but to a lesser extent than GV since it relatively contains less squares (see Tables 4 and 5).

In conclusion, though the new pattern is not optimal in case of low addition/doubling ratio – i.e. when large amount of memory is available – and asymptotically not optimal – i.e. when $A/M \approx 0$ – it has revealed to be efficient in our context.

Table 7. Characteristics of our implementation on a smart card

Bit length	160	192	224	256	320	384	512	521
A/M	0.23	0.21	0.21	0.19	0.17	0.16	0.14	0.14
E/M	0.95	0.65	0.65	0.47	0.36	0.28	0.19	0.19

Table 8. Number of equivalent modular multiplications for the double scalar multiplication with $S/M = 1$

H	ECC bit size	Longa L2R	This paper	Gain (%)
$1/2$ $(E/M = 0)$	160	21.9	18.4	15.7
	224	21.2	18.1	14.6
	256	20.6	17.8	13.7
	320	20.2	17.6	12.8
	384	19.8	17.4	12.0
	521	19.1	17.1	10.8

Table 9. Number of equivalent modular multiplications for the single scalar multiplication with $S/M = 1$

H	ECC size	Longa L2R	GV R2L	This paper	Gain over GV (%)
$1/4$	160	22.2	16.9	16.5	1.8
	224	20.0	16.0	15.9	1.1
	256	18.5	15.5	15.4	0.6
	320	17.5	15.1	15.1	0.1
	384	16.8	14.8	14.8	−0.2
	521	15.7	14.3	14.4	−0.7
$1/5$	160	20.9	15.7	15.9	−0.9
	224	18.7	15.0	15.3	−1.7
	256	17.4	14.5	14.8	−2.3
	320	16.5	14.1	14.5	−2.7
	384	15.8	13.8	14.2	−3.1
	521	14.8	13.4	13.9	−3.6

4.3   The Special Case $a = 0$

If the curve parameter a is null then a multiplication with zero is performed in the doubling formula which may result in a security flaw. Indeed, such a product may have a leakage distinguishable from other products. Since the addition formula does not use this parameter a, it can hence be distinguished from a doubling. This case $a = 0$ allows to only save one multiplication in efficient doubling formulas (using an extra coordinate W or $a = -3$). Therefore, using Longa's pattern or Giraud-Verneuil pattern, one cannot benefit from this case to improve the scalar multiplication since their atomic patterns contain several multiplications. An improvement is possible with the pattern of Chevallier-Mames et al. but this pattern remains costly due to the high number of dummy additions. Hence,

Table 10. Example costs to perform a secure scalar multiplication on a 256-bit curve

Used in	Multiplication/bit	Memory cost	Algorithm
Keygen, sign	8.9	17	Algorithm 2, this paper
	10.3	27	Algorithm 2, Longa L2R
Key agreement	14.5	20	GV R2L
	14.8	17	Algorithm 1, this paper
PACE	17.8	17	Algorithm 2, this paper
	20.6	27	Algorithm 2, Longa L2R

a new formula is proposed here to thwart this attack and to benefit from the possible speed improvement.

With $a = 0$, there are no more available modular subtractions at the beginning of the doubling formula therefore the atomic pattern has to be rebuilt to match with the addition formula. The trick used here consists in saving in memory the opposite values of the coordinates of Q: $-X_q, -Y_q$. The point equivalent class is also used with $\lambda = -1$ to represent $P + Q = (X_3 : -Y_3 : -Z_3)$. However, no trick has been found to propose a subtraction formula.

The sum of $P = (X : Y : Z : Z^2 : Z^3)$ and $Q = (X_q : Y_q : 1)$ is the point $P + Q = (X_3 : Y_3 : Z_3)$. This sum is depicted in Formula (9). The double of a point $P = (X : Y : Z)$ is the point $[2]P = (X_2 : Y_2 : Z_2 : Z_2^2 : Z_2^3)$. The evaluation is performed using Formula (8) with $A = 3X^2$. The resulting pattern only contains 9 multiplications $(2S + 7M)$ and 8 additions which represents an improvement of more than 10% if compared with the case $a \neq 0$. It is depicted in Table 11 in Appendix A.

$$
\begin{cases}
X_3 = F^2 - (2A\bar{E}^2 - \bar{E}^3) \\
Y_3 = \bar{F}(A\bar{E}^2 - X_3) - C\bar{E}^3 \\
Z_3 = Z\bar{E}
\end{cases}
\quad \text{with} \quad
\begin{aligned}
A &= X \\
\bar{B} &= (-X_q)Z^2 \\
C &= Y \\
\bar{D} &= (-Y_q)Z^3 \\
\bar{E} &= \bar{B} + A \\
\bar{F} &= \bar{D} + C
\end{aligned}
\tag{9}
$$

5   Conclusion

In this paper a new atomic pattern has been proposed that outperforms the implementations of most scalar multiplications used in elliptic curve cryptography standards. Our pattern enables to securely perform double scalar multiplications on curves over $\mathbb{F}_p$ with the Straus-Shamir trick which has not been done before. The new pattern also turns out to be efficient for single scalar multiplication. We give hereafter in Table 10 the results obtained on our chip when using main standard algorithms compared with the best known implementations. The first row corresponds to the process of $[k]G$ evaluated as $[k_0]G + [k_1]2^{\ell/2}G$. The double scalar multiplication can also be used in the PACE [17] protocol to evaluate a point $\tilde{G}$. A Key Agreement requires the computation of $[k]\,P$. Longa's atomic pattern using Straus-Shamir trick is given for information only as its implementation requires too much memory to be used with our component. Hence the GV implementation was the fastest algorithm available to perform signatures and key generations and this proposal improves it by 38.6 %.

Acknowledgements. The author is grateful to Christophe Giraud and Emmanuelle Dottax for their valuable comments on preliminary versions of this article. Many thanks also go to anonymous reviewers of Cardis 2013 for their advices.

A   Atomic Patterns

The patterns for any value a allow to perform an addition or doubling at a cost of $3S + 8M + 9A$. These patterns implement Formulæ (9) and (4):

Table 11. Atomic patterns for the case $a = 0$ (left-hand side) and for any value a (right-hand side)

Addition	Doubling	Addition	Doubling
$\star \leftarrow \star + \star$	$R_0 \leftarrow Y + Y$	$R_0 \leftarrow (Z)^2$	$R_0 \leftarrow (Z)^2$
$R_0 \leftarrow (-X_q) \cdot Z^2$	$R_1 \leftarrow R_0 \cdot Y$	$\star \leftarrow \star + \star$	$R_1 \leftarrow Y + Y$
$R_1 \leftarrow X + R_0$	$Y_2 \leftarrow R_1 + R_1$	$R_1 \leftarrow (-X_q) \cdot R_0$	$R_2 \leftarrow R_1 \cdot Y$
$R_2 \leftarrow (R_1)^2$	$R_2 \leftarrow (X)^2$	$R_1 \leftarrow X + R_1$	$Y_2 \leftarrow R_2 + R_2$
$R_0 \leftarrow X \cdot R_2$	$R_3 \leftarrow R_0 \cdot Z$	$R_3 \leftarrow (-Y_q) \cdot R_0$	$R_3 \leftarrow R_1 \cdot Z$
$R_3 \leftarrow Z \cdot R_1$	$Z_2 \leftarrow Y_2 \cdot X$	$R_2 \leftarrow (R_1)^2$	$Z_2 \leftarrow (X)^2$
$X_3 \leftarrow (-Y_q) \cdot Z^3$	$R_0 \leftarrow R_1 \cdot Y_2$	$R_0 \leftarrow Z \cdot R_3$	$R_1 \leftarrow Y_2 \cdot R_2$
$Z_3 \leftarrow R_2 \cdot R_1$	$Z_2^2 \leftarrow R_3 \cdot R_3$	$R_3 \leftarrow Z \cdot R_1$	$R_2 \leftarrow Y_2 \cdot X$
$R_1 \leftarrow R_0 + R_0$	$R_1 \leftarrow R_2 + R_2$	$Z_3 \leftarrow R_1 \cdot R_2$	$X_2 \leftarrow a \cdot R_0$
$R_2 \leftarrow Y + X_3$	$R_1 \leftarrow R_1 + R_2$	$R_1 \leftarrow X \cdot R_2$	$Y_2 \leftarrow X_2 \cdot R_0$
$X_3 \leftarrow (R_2)^2$	$X_2 \leftarrow (R_1)^2$	$R_2 \leftarrow R_1 + R_1$	$R_0 \leftarrow Z_2 + Z_2$
$R_1 \leftarrow R_1 - Z_3$	$X_2 \leftarrow X_2 - Z_2$	$R_0 \leftarrow R_0 + Y$	$X_2 \leftarrow R_0 + Z_2$
$X_3 \leftarrow X_3 - R_1$	$X_2 \leftarrow X_2 - Z_2$	$\star \leftarrow \star + \star$	$R_0 \leftarrow X_2 + Y_2$
$R_0 \leftarrow R_0 - X_3$	$Z_2 \leftarrow Z_2 - X_2$	$X_3 \leftarrow (R_0)^2$	$X_2 \leftarrow (R_0)^2$
$R_1 \leftarrow Y \cdot Z_3$	$Z_2^3 \leftarrow Z_2^2 \cdot R_3$	$R_2 \leftarrow R_2 - Z_3$	$X_2 \leftarrow X_2 - R_2$
$Y_3 \leftarrow R_0 \cdot R_2$	$Y_2 \leftarrow R_1 \cdot Z_2$	$X_3 \leftarrow X_3 - R_2$	$X_2 \leftarrow X_2 - R_2$
$Y_3 \leftarrow Y_3 - R_1$	$Y_2 \leftarrow Y_2 - R_0$	$R_1 \leftarrow R_1 - X_3$	$Z_2 \leftarrow R_2 - X_2$
$Z_3 \leftarrow R_3$	$Z_2 \leftarrow R_3$	$R_2 \leftarrow Y \cdot Z_3$	$\star \leftarrow \star \cdot \star$
		$Y_3 \leftarrow R_0 \cdot R_1$	$Y_2 \leftarrow R_0 \cdot Z_2$
		$Y_3 \leftarrow Y_3 - R_2$	$Y_2 \leftarrow Y_2 - R_1$
		$Z_3 \leftarrow R_3$	$Z_2 \leftarrow R_3$

References

1. Arno, S., Wheeler, F.: Signed digit representations of minimal Hamming weight. IEEE Trans. Comput. **42**(8), 1007–1009 (1993)
2. Brier, E., Joye, M.: Weierstraß elliptic curves and side-channel attacks. In: Naccache and Paillier [25], pp. 335–345
3. Chevallier-Mames, B., Ciet, M., Joye, M.: Low-cost solutions for preventing simple side-channel analysis: side-channel atomicity. Cryptology ePrint Archive, Report 2003/237 (2003). http://eprint.iacr.org/
4. Chudnovsky, D.V., Chudnovsky, G.V.: Sequences of numbers genereated by addition in formal groups and new primality and factorization tests. Adv. Appl. Math. **7**, 385–434 (1986)
5. Cohen, H., Miyaji, A., Ono, T.: Efficient elliptic curve exponentiation using mixed coordinates. In: Ohta, K., Pei, D. (eds.) ASIACRYPT 1998. LNCS, vol. 1514, pp. 51–65. Springer, Heidelberg (1998)
6. Coron, J.-S.: Resistance against differential power analysis for elliptic curve cryptosystems. In: Koç, Ç.K., Paar, C. (eds.) CHES 1999. LNCS, vol. 1717, pp. 292–302. Springer, Heidelberg (1999)
7. ECC Brainpool: ECC brainpool standard curves and curve generation. BSI, internet Draft v. 3, (2009). http://tools.ietf.org/html/draft-lochter-pkix-brainpool-ecc-03
8. ElGamal, T.: A public-key cryptosystems and a signature scheme based on discret logarithms. IEEE Trans. Inf. Theory **31**(4), 469–472 (1985)
9. Faugère, J.-C., Goyet, C., Renault, G.: Attacking (EC)DSA given only an implicit hint. In: Knudsen, L.R., Wu, H. (eds.) SAC 2012. LNCS, vol. 7707, pp. 252–274. Springer, Heidelberg (2013)
10. FIPS PUB 186–4: Digital Signature Standard. National Institute of Standards and Technology, July 2013
11. Fischer, W., Giraud, C., Knudsen, E.W., Seifert, J.P.: Parallel scalar multiplication on general elliptic curves over $\mathbb{F}_p$ hedged against non-differential side-channel attacks. Cryptology ePrint Archive, Report 2002/007, Jan 2002. http://eprint.iacr.org/
12. Giraud, C., Verneuil, V.: Atomicity improvement for elliptic curve scalar multiplication. In: Gollmann, D., Lanet, J.-L., Iguchi-Cartigny, J. (eds.) CARDIS 2010. LNCS, vol. 6035, pp. 80–101. Springer, Heidelberg (2010)
13. Giry, D., Bulens, P.: Keylength.com - Cryptographic Key Length Recommandation, Aug 2007. http://www.keylength.com
14. Goundar, R.R., Joye, M., Miyaji, A., Rivain, M., Venelli, A.: Scalar multiplication on weierstraß elliptic curves from co- z arithmetic. J. Cryptol. **1**(2), 161–176 (2011)
15. Hankerson, D., Menezes, A., Vanstone, S.: Guide to Elliptic Curve Cryptography: Professional Computing Series. Springer, New York (2003)
16. Hutter, M., Joye, M., Sierra, Y.: Memory-constrained implementations of elliptic curve cryptography in co-Z coordinate representation. In: Nitaj, A., Pointcheval, D. (eds.) AFRICACRYPT 2011. LNCS, vol. 6737, pp. 170–187. Springer, Heidelberg (2011)
17. ISO/IEC JTC1 SC17 WG3/TF5: Supplemental Access Control for Machine Readable Travel Documents. International Civial Aviation Organization, Nov 2010
18. Izu, T., Takagi, T.: A fast parallel elliptic curve multiplication resistant against side channel attacks. In: Naccache and Paillier [25], pp. 280–296

19. JORF n: Avis relatif aux paramètres de courbes elliptiques définis par l'État français, Oct 2011
20. Knuth, D.: The Art of Computer Programming, vol. 2, 3rd edn. Addison Wesley, Reading (1988)
21. Kocher, P.C.: Timing attacks on implementations of Diffie-Hellman, RSA, DSS, and other systems. In: Koblitz, N. (ed.) CRYPTO 1996. LNCS, vol. 1109, pp. 104–113. Springer, Heidelberg (1996)
22. Longa, P.: Accelerating the scalar multiplication on elliptic curve cryptosystems over prime fields. Master's thesis, School of Information Technology and Engineering, University of Ottawa, Canada (2007)
23. Möller, B.: Improved techniques for fast exponentiation. In: Lee, P.J., Lim, C.H. (eds.) ICISC 2002. LNCS, vol. 2587, pp. 298–312. Springer, Heidelberg (2003)
24. Montgomery, P.: Modular multiplication without trial division. Math. Comp. **44**(170), 519–521 (1985)
25. Naccache, D., Paillier, P. (eds.): PKC 2002. LNCS, vol. 2274. Springer, Heidelberg (2002)
26. Okeya, K., Kato, H., Nogami, Y.: Width-3 joint sparse form. In: Kwak, J., Deng, R.H., Won, Y., Wang, G. (eds.) ISPEC 2010. LNCS, vol. 6047, pp. 67–84. Springer, Heidelberg (2010)
27. Rivest, R., Shamir, A., Adleman, L.: A method for obtaining digital signatures and public-key cryptosystems. Commun. ACM **21**(2), 120–126 (1978)
28. Solinas, J.: Low-Weight Binary Representations for Pairs of Integers. Technical report (2001). http://cacr.uwaterloo.ca/techreports/2001/corr2001-41.ps
29. Solinas, J.A.: Efficient arithmetic on koblitz curves. Des. Codes Crypt. **19**(2/3), 195–249 (2000)
30. Straus, E.G.: Addition chains of vectors (problem 5125). Am. Math. Monthly **70**, 806–808 (1964)

Efficient and First-Order DPA Resistant Implementations of Keccak

Begül Bilgin[3,4]([⊠]), Joan Daemen[1], Ventzislav Nikov[2], Svetla Nikova[3],
Vincent Rijmen[3], and Gilles Van Assche[1]

[1] STMicroelectronics, Diegem, Belgium
[2] NXP Semiconductors, Leuven, Belgium
[3] ESAT/COSIC and IMinds, KU Leuven, Leuven, Belgium
[4] DIES, University of Twente, Enschede, The Netherlands
begul.bilgin@esat.kuleuven.be

Abstract. In October 2012 NIST announced that the SHA-3 hash standard will be based on Keccak. Besides hashing, Keccak can be used in many other modes, including ones operating on a secret value. Many applications of such modes require protection against side-channel attacks, preferably at low cost. In this paper, we present threshold implementations (TI) of Keccak with three and four shares that build further on unprotected parallel and serial architectures. We improve upon earlier TI implementations of Keccak in the sense that the latter did not achieve uniformity of shares. In our proposals we do achieve uniformity at the cost of an extra share in a four-share version or at the cost of injecting a small number of fresh random bits for each computed round. The proposed implementations are efficient and provably secure against first-order side-channel attacks.

Keywords: Keccak · Side-channel attacks · Threshold implementation

1 Introduction

Keccak [6] is the best-known family of sponge functions. They can be used in a wide range of modes covering the full range of symmetric cryptographic functions [4]. These functions can take as argument a secret key (e.g., encryption, Message Authentication Code (MAC) computation, authenticated encryption, etc.) and require their internal state to remain secret for security (e.g., pseudorandom sequence generators). Such functions are subject to side-channel attacks.

A Differential Power Analysis (DPA) attack, which is a very powerful side-channel attack, exploits the dependencies between the instantaneous power consumption of a device and the intermediate results of a cryptographic algorithm. Since the security of cryptographic primitives inevitably relies on the fact that an adversary does not have access to intermediate computation results, any even partial knowledge of intermediate computation results can lead to a complete

A. Francillon and P. Rohatgi (Eds.): CARDIS 2013, LNCS 8419, pp. 187–199, 2014.
DOI: 10.1007/978-3-319-08302-5_13, © Springer International Publishing Switzerland 2014

breakdown of security, e.g., by revealing the key. Several countermeasures against DPA [12] have been proposed on different levels. For example, a circuit design approach that aims to balance the power consumption of different data values has been proposed in [19]. Another popular method is to randomize the intermediate values of an algorithm by masking, namely on algorithm level [2,9], at the gate level [10,20] or in combination with circuit design approaches [17]. Since the amount of information that is leaked by hardware is unknown, the security proofs are based on an idealized hardware model, resulting in requirements on the hardware that are very expensive to meet in practice.

In a threshold implementation [14,15], the sharing can have three properties: correctness, non-completeness and uniformity. Correctness is an obvious requirement which simply states that the sum of the output shares of a sharing for a function f equals f applied to the sum of the input shares as in boolean masking. Non-completeness states that each output share of a function is independent of at least one input share.

When the input shares are uniformly distributed, then a correct and non-complete sharing is provably immune to first-order DPA even in presence of glitches [14,15]. In a sequential computation, e.g., such in a function composed of rounds or in multi-stage implementations of S-boxes, the output shares will be used as input in another stage of the computation. Hence, it is also interesting to preserve the uniformity of the shares. As a first option, a sharing can be uniform, which means that the output shares are uniform if the input shares are uniform. As another option, uniformity of the output shares can be obtained by the use of fresh randomness. This last option is also called re-masking and has been done before, e.g., for the TI of AES in [13]. Eventhough re-masking can restore the uniformity of the input shares, and with it the provable security agasint first-order DPA, this requires fresh randomness on each round, which may become expensive in practice.

The designers of KECCAK proposed a hardware architecture that offers protection against first-order DPA [3]. They employ the threshold implementation method with three shares, but it is not uniform and hence not provably secure against first-order DPA.

Contribution. In Sect. 3 we propose an alternative way for re-masking that requires less random bits than the straightforward re-masking approach as described in [13]. In Sect. 4 we propose a sharing that uses four shares that achieves uniformity of sharing without the introduction of fresh randomness. In Sect. 5 we provide the area cost and the maximum frequency of our unprotected and threshold implementations for fully parallel and slice-based architectures. We show that the area requirement for our unprotected implementations are significantly smaller than the previous KECCAK implementations and have higher frequency. Moreover, the threshold implementations with serial architecture can be considered within the limits of a lightweight implementation. In addition, we discuss a way to reduce the area cost of the threshold implementations at the cost of extra randomness. First, we briefly recall the components of KECCAK in Sect. 2.

2   Introduction to Keccak

KECCAK is a function with variable-length input and arbitrary-length output based on the sponge construction [4]. In this construction, a b-bit permutation f is iterated. First, the input is padded and its blocks are *absorbed* sequentially into the state, with a simple XOR operation. Then, the output is *squeezed* from the state block by block. The size of the blocks is denoted by r and called the *bitrate*. The remaining number of bits $c = b - r$ is called the *capacity* and determines the security level of the function.

The simplest use case of a sponge function is to use it as a hash function. However, a MAC function can be built by taking the concatenation of a secret key and a message as input. It is also possible to use a sponge function as a stream cipher. To this purpose, it suffices to use the secret key and a nonce as input so that the resulting output can be used as a key stream. More modes of use are described in [5].

Seven permutations, denoted KECCAK-$f[b]$, are defined with width $b = 25w$ ranging from 25 to 1600 bits, with w increasing in powers of two. The state of KECCAK-$f[b]$ is organized as a set of $5 \times 5 \times w$ bits with (x, y, z) coordinates. Coordinates are taken modulo 5 for x and y and modulo w for z. A *row* is a set of 5 bits with given (y, z) coordinates, a *column* is a set of 5 bits with given (x, z) coordinates and a *lane* is a set of w bits with given (x, y) coordinates. Moreover, the set of 5×5 bits with given z coordinates is called a *slice*.

The round function of KECCAK-$f[b]$ consists of the following steps, which are only briefly summarized here. For more details, we refer to the specifications [6].

- θ is a linear mixing layer that adds a pattern depending solely on the parity of the columns of the state.
- ρ and π displace bits without altering their value.
- χ is a degree-2 non-linear mapping that processes each row independently. It can be seen as the application of a translation-invariant 5-bit quadratic S-box:

$$a_{(x,y,z)} \leftarrow a_{(x,y,z)} + (a_{(x+1,y,z)} + 1)a_{(x+2,y,z)}.$$

- ι adds a round constant.

The number of rounds in KECCAK-f is determined by the width b of the permutations. It is 12 for KECCAK-$f[25]$ and increases by two for each doubling of the size. So KECCAK-$f[1600]$ has 24 rounds.

3   Achieving Uniformity with Limited Extra Randomness

In this section, we focus on the three-share implementation proposed in [3]. A value x is shared as (A, B, C) if $x = A + B + C$ in $\mathbb{F}_2^n$. Seen as random variables over $\mathbb{F}_2^n$, shares (A, B, C) are said to be *uniform* if and only if $\Pr[A + B + C = x] = 1$ and for any fixed values $a, b \in \mathbb{F}_2^n$, $\Pr[A = a, B = b] = 2^{-2n}$. This definition is slightly more restrictive than the one in [14, 15], as we do not consider probability distributions over native values but only over their shared representation. As the computation of cryptographic primitives such as KECCAK is deterministic, this restriction does not play a role here.

3.1   The Original Three-Share TI Implementation of χ

The non-linear step of the KECCAK round function is called χ. In [7] we proposed a three-share TI implementation called χ'. We denote the three shares by A, B and C and the position of the bit within a row by i (to be taken modulo 5):

$$
\begin{aligned}
A'_i &\leftarrow \chi'_i(B,C) \triangleq B_i + (B_{i+1}+1)B_{i+2} + B_{i+1}C_{i+2} + B_{i+2}C_{i+1}, \\
B'_i &\leftarrow \chi'_i(C,A) \triangleq C_i + (C_{i+1}+1)C_{i+2} + C_{i+1}A_{i+2} + C_{i+2}A_{i+1}, \qquad (1) \\
C'_i &\leftarrow \chi'_i(A,B) \triangleq A_i + (A_{i+1}+1)A_{i+2} + A_{i+1}B_{i+2} + A_{i+2}B_{i+1}.
\end{aligned}
$$

This maps a 15-bit vector (A,B,C) to a 15-bit vector (A',B',C'). Upon inspection, we found that this mapping is not invertible and hence not uniform [14,15]. The consequence is that even if (A,B,C) is a uniform sharing of a native value x, (A',B',C') is not a uniform sharing of $\chi(x)$.

3.2   Straightforward Injection of Fresh Random Bits

KECCAK-$f[1600]$ has 320 rows. For a three-share TI implementation, this means the application of Eq. (1) 320 times per round.

To convert (A',B',C') into a uniform sharing again, we can inject random bits. Re-masking is based on the following lemma.

Lemma 1. *Let (A,B,C) be n-bit shares (not necessarily uniform) of a fixed native value and (X,Y,Z) be uniform m-bit shares. Let (D,E,F) be uniform n-bit shares statistically independent of (A,B,C) and (X,Y,Z). Then, $((A+D,X),(B+E,Y),(C+F,Z))$ are uniform $n+m$-bit shares.*

Proof. First, since $A+B+C$, $D+E+F$ and $X+Y+Z$ take a fixed value with probability one, so does $(A+B+C+D+E+F, X+Y+Z)$. Then, it suffices to verify that for each fixed value $a+d, x, b+e, y$:

$$
\begin{aligned}
&\Pr[A+D=a+d, B+E=b+e, X=x, Y=y] \\
&= \sum_{d,e} \Pr[D=d, E=e]\Pr[A=(a+d)+d, B=(b+e)+e, X=x, Y=y] \\
&= 2^{-2n} \sum_{d,e} \Pr[A=(a+d)+d, B=(b+e)+e, X=x, Y=y] \\
&= 2^{-2n} \Pr[X=x, Y=y] \\
&= 2^{-2(n+m)}.
\end{aligned}
$$

We get a realization of χ that satisfies the uniformity property at the cost of 2 uniformly distributed random bits P_i, S_i per bit of the state. The implementation of χ becomes:

$$
\begin{aligned}
A'_i &\leftarrow \chi'_i(B,C) + P_i + S_i, \\
B'_i &\leftarrow \chi'_i(C,A) + P_i, \qquad\qquad (2) \\
C'_i &\leftarrow \chi'_i(A,B) + S_i,
\end{aligned}
$$

Equation (2) can be seen as the addition of $(\chi_i'(B, C), \chi_i'(C, A), \chi_i'(A, B))$ and $(P_i + S_i, P_i, S_i)$. The result is uniform thanks to Lemma 1 as $(P_i + S_i, P_i, S_i)$ is a uniform sharing of the native value 0 obtained from independently drawn random bits.

Although from a theoretical point of view this re-masking method solves the uniformity issue raised above, the solution is not satisfactory since it requires a RNG which generates many high-quality random bits at each clock cycle.

3.3   Less Randomness per Row

In this section we reduce the number of required fresh random bits per round by using specific properties of χ'.

The function χ in KECCAK operates on 5-bit rows. It can be seen as a specific case of a convolutional mapping operating on an n-bit circular array with updating function $x_i \leftarrow x_i + (x_{i+1} + 1)x_{i+2}$. Next Lemma is a general result that holds for any value n.

Lemma 2. *If the input (A, B, C) to χ' is shared uniformly, the output truncated to any $n - 2$ consecutive bits, e.g., $(A', B', C')_{0...n-3}$, is shared uniformly.*

Proof. First, consider $(A'_{n-3}, B'_{n-3}, C'_{n-3})$. It is the result of summing $(B_{n-3}, C_{n-3}, A_{n-3})$ with bits computed from A, B and C in positions $n - 2$ and $n - 1$. As $(B_{n-3}, C_{n-3}, A_{n-3})$ is a uniform sharing of x_{n-3} independent of input bits in positions $n - 2$ and $n - 1$, Lemma 1 applies and hence $(A'_{n-3}, B'_{n-3}, C'_{n-3})$ is a uniform sharing.

Assuming $(A', B', C')_{i+1...n-3}$ is a uniform sharing, we can prove that $(A', B', C')_{i...n-3}$ is a uniform sharing. (A'_i, B'_i, C'_i) is the result of summing (B_i, C_i, A_i) with bits computed from $(A, B, C)_{i+1...i+2}$. As (B_i, C_i, A_i) is a uniform sharing of x_i and is independent of input bits in positions $i + 1$ and $i + 2$ and of $(A', B', C')_{i+1...n-3}$, Lemma 1 applies and hence $(A', B', C')_{i...n-3}$ is a uniform sharing. This can be extended till $(A', B', C')_{0...n-3}$.   □

Further (cyclic) extensions to include $(A', B', C')_{n-1}$ or $(A', B', C')_{n-2}$ is not possible as $(B_{n-2}, C_{n-2}, A_{n-2})$ is not independent of $(A', B', C')_{0...n-3}$ and Lemma 1 no longer applies.

Lemma 2 says that the truncated output with two successive bits removed is uniform. As a consequence, one can repair uniformity using only 4 fresh random bits $P_{n-2}, P_{n-1}, S_{n-2}, S_{n-1}$. In particular, we just apply Eq. (2) with $P_i = S_i = 0$ for $i \leq n - 2$.

We would like to point out that this result can also be obtained using virtual variables as proposed in [8]. Namely, let us consider each of the first two equations of χ as equations depending on one more variable Y and Z, respectively. Let (A_i, B_i, C_i) be a sharing of x_i and $(Y_1, Y_2, Y_1 + Y_2)$, $(Z_1, Z_2, Z_1 + Z_2)$ be a (therefore virtual) sharing of Y, Z then exactly the same result is obtained as in Lemma 2: 4 additional bits suffice to make the sharing uniform.

We decreased the number of fresh random bits per round from 10 to 4 bits per row. However, for KECCAK-$f[1600]$ this is $320 \times 4 = 1280$ bits, still too expensive in practice.

3.4   Jointly Satisfying Uniformity

In this section we consider the uniformity at the level of the full state rather than in the individual rows. We propose a TI implementation of χ with interaction between the rows that achieves almost uniformity at the level of the full state, greatly reducing the required number of fresh random bits per round.

Let us for convenience number the rows with index $j = y + 5z$. The idea is to make the sharing at the output of row $j + 1$ uniform by using input at row j. In straightforward way, we add $(A + B, A, B)$ at the input of row j to the output (A', B', C') of row $j + 1$. This is again a straightforward application of Lemma 1. Note that to satisfy the independence required by Lemma 1, the last row still requires injection of four fresh random bits for achieving uniformity, as in Eq. (2). The circuit complexity can be reduced greatly by combining this with Lemma 2. As a matter of fact, we have to add $(A + B, A, B)$ at the input of row j to the output (A', B', C') of row $j + 1$ in only two successive bit positions. Care must be taken in the bit positions used in each row so as to be able to rely on Lemma 2.

The above reasoning points out that each row individually can become uniform. The key point, however, is to show that the joint application on the entire state yields a uniform realization of χ. This is what the theorem below will show.

We denote the three shares of the whole state by (A, B, C), and a 5-bit row of the state as $(A^{(j)}, B^{(j)}, C^{(j)})$ with $j \in \mathbb{Z}_{5w}$. Then, the implementation of χ becomes:

$$
\begin{aligned}
A_i'^{(j)} &\leftarrow \chi_i'(B^{(j)}, C^{(j)}) + A_i^{(j-1)} + B_i^{(j-1)}, \\
B_i'^{(j)} &\leftarrow \chi_i'(C^{(j)}, A^{(j)}) + A_i^{(j-1)}, \\
C_i'^{(j)} &\leftarrow \chi_i'(A^{(j)}, B^{(j)}) + B_i^{(j-1)},
\end{aligned}
\tag{3}
$$

if $j > 0$ and $i \in \{3, 4\}$. Otherwise, Eq. (2) applies when $j = 0$, and Eq. (1) suffices for positions $i \leq 2$.

Theorem 1. *If the (whole state) input (A, B, C) to Eq. (3) if $j > 0$ and $i \in \{3, 4\}$, to Eq. (2) if $j = 0$ and $i \in \{3, 4\}$ and to Eq. (1) if $i \leq 2$, is shared uniformly, then the (whole state) output (A', B', C') is shared uniformly.*

Proof. We can apply Lemma 1 recursively, with j starting at $j = 5w - 1$ and going down to $j = 0$. Everytime, the reasoning is to show that if $(A'^{(j+1\ldots5w-1)}, B'^{(j+1\ldots5w-1)}, C'^{(j+1\ldots5w-1)})$ is uniform, then it is also uniform for rows j to $5w - 1$.

Following Eq. (3), the sharing $(A'^{(j)}, B'^{(j)}, C'^{(j)})$ is obtained by adding $(\chi'(B^{(j)}, C^{(j)}), \chi'(C^{(j)}, A^{(j)}), \chi'(A^{(j)}, B^{(j)}))$ and $(A^{(j-1)} + B^{(j-1)}, A^{(j-1)}, B^{(j-1)})$ for bit positions $i \in \{3, 4\}$. The latter expression is a uniform sharing of 0 and independent of the rows with indexes j and higher. From Lemma 2, $(\chi'(B^{(j)}, C^{(j)}), \chi'(C^{(j)}, A^{(j)}), \chi'(A^{(j)}, B^{(j)}))$ is already uniform when restricted to bit positions 0 to 2. The conditions of Lemma 1 are thus satisfied and $(A'^{(j\ldots5w-1)}, B'^{(j\ldots5w-1)}, C'^{(j\ldots5w-1)})$ is uniform.

If $j = 0$, the same reasoning applies, except that bit positions $i \in \{3, 4\}$ are obtained as in Eq (2).   □

The cost is four random bits per round, some additional XORs, registers and extra routing. As far as randomness is concerned, this amounts to 96 bits for the 24 rounds of KECCAK-f[1600], which is small compared to the 3200 random bits needed to represent the input state in three shares.

4   Achieving Uniformity with Four Shares

A uniform 3-share threshold implementation for χ or for any of its affine equivalent is not found yet. We present a uniform sharing of χ with 4 shares. For $i = 0, 1, 2, 4$, we have:

$$
\begin{aligned}
A'_i &\leftarrow B_i + B_{i+2} + ((B_{i+1} + C_{i+1} + D_{i+1})(B_{i+2} + C_{i+2} + D_{i+2})), \\
B'_i &\leftarrow C_i + C_{i+2} + (A_{i+1}(C_{i+2} + D_{i+2}) + A_{i+2}(C_{i+1} + D_{i+1}) + A_{i+1}A_{i+2}), \\
C'_i &\leftarrow D_i + D_{i+2} + (A_{i+1}B_{i+2} + A_{i+2}B_{i+1}), \\
D'_i &\leftarrow A_i + A_{i+2},
\end{aligned}
\tag{4}
$$

and for the remaining 3rd coordinate function we have:

$$
\begin{aligned}
A'_3 &\leftarrow B_3 + B_0 + C_0 + D_0 + ((B_4 + C_4 + D_4)(B_0 + C_0 + D_0)), \\
B'_3 &\leftarrow C_3 + A_0 + (A_4(C_0 + D_0) + A_0(C_4 + D_4) + A_0A_4), \\
C'_3 &\leftarrow D_3 + (A_4B_0 + A_0B_4), \\
D'_3 &\leftarrow A_3.
\end{aligned}
\tag{5}
$$

We found this sharing by using Theorem 2 of [8]. Namely, we first searched through all affine equivalent S-boxes of χ, i.e., $\chi'' = \chi(A(x))$, where $A(x)$ is an affine permutation and we found the ones that can be shared with a direct sharing. Next, we applied the corresponding inverse affine transformation to the found direct sharing to generate a uniform sharing for the function χ. We chose the one that has the smallest area over all the candidates. Therefore, this uniform sharing (although derived and close to direct) is not a direct sharing and that is why the shares can not be computed in a circular manner.

5   Hardware Implementations

There are several reports on different implementations of unprotected KECCAK-f that uses different platforms, architectures and libraries [1]. In this work, we provide unprotected (plain) and threshold implementations of KECCAK-f with a round-based (parallel, Fig. 1) and a slice-based (serial, Fig. 2) architecture. We used ModelSim to verify the correctness of our implementations and Synopsys with FARADAY, FSA0A-D and FSC0H-D libraries which are standard cell libraries tailored for UMC $0.18\,\mu\text{m}$ and UMC $0.13\,\mu\text{m}$ logic processes respectively to observe and compare the accurate area cost and maximum frequency

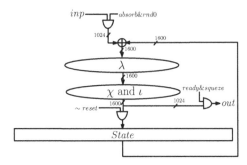

Fig. 1. Schematic of the round-based implementation of Keccak-f

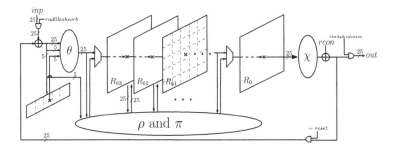

Fig. 2. Schematic of the slice-based implementation of Keccak-f

with the previous works. For all our designs, we also provide the results with NANGATE 45 nm standard cell library which is free and can be used for further comparison. The D flip-flops that take the output of a 2×1 MUX as input are implemented as scan flip-flops to reduce the area.

In the following sections, we first describe the unprotected Keccak architectures. Then, we build our threshold implementations on those architectures.

5.1 Unprotected Implementations

In our parallel implementation (Fig. 1), we fixed the rate to be at most 1024 bits. The architecture of the round function Keccak-f for this implementation is straightforward with 320 parallel instances of χ. The function θ is implemented in a slice-based manner. Namely, the 5-bit XOR of every row in each slice (i.e., the column parity) X_i, where $i \in \{0, \ldots, 63\}$ is calculated in parallel [7]. For each slice, the rotated values of X_i and X_{i-1} are XORed. This new value is concatenated five times to generate a 25-bit value which will then be XORed to its corresponding slice. With this method, the θ function can be calculated with a low cost. The rest of the linear layer, i.e., ρ and π, are executed on the whole 1600-bit state as a simple wiring and the output in each round is written to a 1600-bit register. Hence, one iteration of Keccak-f[1600] takes 24 clock cycles.

On the other hand, the serial implementation (Fig. 2) operates on the 25-bit slices. It takes 25 bits in each clock cycle starting from slice 0. The input is written to the register R_{63} after the implementation of θ, which takes as input the 5-bit XOR of every row of each input slice in the mentioned clock cycle and the previous cycle with the exception of the first slice. This is repeated for 64 cycles as the data in the registers are shifted from R_{i+1} to R_i for $i \in \{0, \ldots, 62\}$. θ for the first slice is completed in the 64th clock cycle together with the last slice. ρ and π are simple wirings executed on the same clock cycle as well. We can consider this one round of 64 cycles as the initialization round. For the following rounds, the input to θ is the output of the five χ functions executed in parallel on the slice R_0 followed by the XOR of the round constant. The output is taken from the output of the round constant injection starting from the first clock cycle of the 25th round. With this implementation, one iteration of KECCAK-$f[1600]$ takes $64 \times 25 = 1600$ clock cycles and costs around $10\,\mathrm{kGE}$ in area. We should note that it is possible to have implementations that work on 2 or 4 slices per cycle and are faster but require larger area as a trade-off. In this paper, we focus on a small implementation.

Both of these unprotected implementations are noticeably smaller than the implementations reported so far which use standard cell libraries for state storage and still provide a high frequency. On the other hand, the smallest design so far, that is proposed in CHES'13 [16] uses RAM macros and requires more clock cycles for one iteration. More detailed comparison for after synthesis results is given in Table 1.

5.2 Threshold Implementations

We propose two different types of threshold implementations. In the first type, we use as little random bits as we can. Namely, except for the initial sharing, we use at most four bits of randomness per round. In the second type, however, we relax this restriction on using minimum amount of randomness in order to reduce the area. In all these versions, we assume that the input shares are provided from an outside source, such that the sum of the shares is the unshared message.

For the first type of TI, we implement two versions as described in Sects. 3 and 4 and we use three and four shares, respectively, throughout the entire implementations. Hence, we need respectively three and four times the registers compared to the unprotected implementation. The linear layer is also tripled (and quadrupled), such that each works on one share only. During the χ operations, these shares are used together as described in (3)-(5). The round constant is inserted in one share only. In the case of the parallel three share implementation, we need 640-bit extra registers to store the re-masking masks since we need to complete the re-masking one clock cycle later as described in Sect. 3. Also, because of this re-masking, the output is ready one clock cycle after the last χ operation therefore one KECCAK-f takes 25 clock-cycles.

As expected, for the parallel implementations the cost of the combinational logic exceeds the cost of the register, since there are too many instances of θ and

Table 1. Synthesis results for different implementations of Keccak

Design	Area (kGE)						Rand. bit	Clock	Freq.
	State	θ	χ	ANDs/XORs	Other	TOTAL	per round	Cycles	MHz
UMC 0.18 µm *standard cell library*									
Parallel	9.0	9.3	7.0	8.1	0.1	33.5	-	24	572
Parallel-3sh	27.2	27.8	55.4	31.4	3.5	145.3	4	25	516
Parallel-4sh	36.3	37.1	68.8	31.9	0.1	174.2	-	24	513
Serial	10.1	0.1	0.1	0.2	0.3	10.8	-	1600	555
Serial-3sh	30.4	0.4	0.8	0.7	0.8	33.1	4	1625	553
Serial-4sh	40.5	0.6	1.0	0.7	0.3	43.1	-	1600	572
UMC 0.13 µm *standard cell library*									
Parallel	8.0	8.6	6.4	7.5	0.1	30.6	-	24	855
Parallel-3sh	24.0	25.7	52.8	29.4	3.3	135.2	4	25	746
Parallel-4sh	32.0	34.2	61.6	29.7	0.1	157.6	-	24	735
Serial	10.0	0.1	0.1	0.2	0.2	10.6	-	1600	752
Serial-3sh	30.0	0.4	0.8	0.7	0.7	32.6	4	1625	820
Serial-4sh	40.0	0.5	0.9	0.7	0.3	42.4	-	1600	775
NANGATE 45 nm *standard cell library*									
Parallel	9.0	6.4	5.6	7.0	0.1	28.1	-	24	690
Parallel-3sh	27.2	19.2	40.6	25.9	3.7	116.6	4	25	592
Parallel-4sh	36.3	25.6	48.7	28.7	0.1	139.4	-	24	588
Serial	12.2	0.1	0.1	0.2	0.2	12.8	-	1600	775
Serial-3sh	36.8	0.3	0.6	0.5	0.8	39.0	4	1625	645
Serial-4sh	49.0	0.4	0.8	0.6	0.3	51.1	-	1600	633
UMC 0.18 µm *standard cell library*									
Parallel-[18]	N/A	N/A	N/A	N/A	N/A	56.7	-	25	488
STM and UMC 0.13 µm *standard cell library*									
Parallel	N/A	N/A	N/A	N/A	N/A	48.0	-	24	526
KECCAK team									
Serial-[11]	N/A	N/A	N/A	N/A	N/A	20.0	-	1200	N/A
Serial-[16][a]	N/A	N/A	N/A	N/A	N/A	5.9	-	15427	61

[a] Uses RAM macros

χ. Even though these implementations are fast, the parallel threshold implementations are quite big and can no longer be called efficient implementations, when applied to bigger versions of KECCAK.

When the serial implementations are considered, the register cost is the dominant cost in the architecture whereas the θ and χ layers together is only 4 % of the overall implementation (Table 1). Note that for the three-share implementation, we need to keep the random bits from the previous χ function to the next (as described in Sect. 3) in every clock cycle which requires 4-bit register. Also, for proper re-masking, we need to use an extra 10-bit register to store the values after the χ operation which leads to a decrease of one clock cycle per round in speed.

The threshold implementations of the serial architecture have the same size as the unprotected parallel implementation. One can, of course, have an implementation operating on more than one slice to increase the speed with a relatively small cost.

5.3   An Architecture with 2 Shares for the Linear Part

Working on three or four shares throughout the whole implementation leads to a high area since the size of the state is big as a result of adopting the 1600-bit permutation. Furthermore, the cost of the linear θ layer is very close to the register cost as we converge to the parallel implementation (Table 1) because of multiple XORs per bit. For this second type of threshold implementation, we propose a way to reduce the area at the cost of extra random bits.

We can use two shares for the linear part λ of the KECCAK-f. Then we face the problem of increasing or decreasing the number of shares for the nonlinear layer. The re-sharing from 2 to 3 shares can be done as in Fig. 3a one clock cycle before going through the χ layer as these three new shares need to be written into registers to avoid leakage. Note, that we do not anymore need to have a uniform χ implementation as this re-sharing will also serve as re-masking in the input of the nonlinear function. Therefore, we will only consider the χ implementation with three shares and direct sharing. Moreover, reducing the number of shares from 3 to 2 can be done by only a single XOR as shown in Fig. 3b since linear layers do not require uniform input shares.

With this approach, we will need 1 more clock cycle per round for the round-based architecture and 10 extra bits of randomness for each instance of the χ function. Applying the method in a straightforward way will cost 3200 bits of extra randomness. However it is possible to use the idea of Sect. 3 and borrow randomness from the input of the previous instances of the χ function.

For a parallel implementation, this approach decreases the cost of the linear layer and the ANDs and XORs only. We need to put a register between the 2-to-3 re-sharing and the χ layer, in order to safeguard against the possibility that some of the masks do not arrive on time. Moreover, there is the extra cost of the XORs during the re-masking that compensates the area saved in the linear layer. In the end, such a parallel implementation will not save area and moreover it needs more randomness which is not preferable.

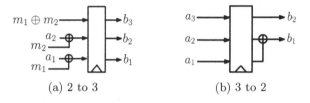

(a) 2 to 3   (b) 3 to 2

Fig. 3. Resharing

For a serial architecture, this approach is more efficient. To give an example from our slice-based implementation, we need to increase the number of shares when we shift the data in the register R_1 to the register R_0 and decrease the number of shares with the shift from R_{63} to R_{62}. Even though the θ layer is still applied on three shares, the registers from R_1 to R_{62} only requires two instances. Besides, the extra cost of re-masking is small since we only need to increase or decrease the number of shares on one slice. As a result, this implementation will require 30 % less area for the cost of four extra random bits per round and 96 extra random bits for one KECCAK-f as we need 10 bits of randomness per round.

6   Conclusions

We presented the first implementations of KECCAK that satisfy the three properties of threshold implementations. At the moment, it seems that at least four shares are required in order to be able to satisfy simultaneously correctness, non-completeness and uniformity. Implementations with three shares require extra random bits in each round. We showed how the amount of extra random bits can be brought down to as little as four per round. To illustrate our work, we made six hardware implementations and compared their merits. We have shown that even though threshold implementations increase the area significantly, by using a serial architecture instead of a parallel one, this increase can be compensated.

Acknowledgments. We would like to thank the anonymous reviewers for their constructive comments. In addition, this work has been supported in part by the Research Council of KU Leuven (OT/13/071), B. Bilgin was partially supported by the Flemish Government by the project G.0B421.13N., and V. Nikov was supported by the European Commission (FP7) within the Tamper Resistant Sensor Node (TAMPRES) project with the contract number 258754.

References

1. ATHENa: automated tool for hardware evaluation. http://cryptography.gmu.edu/athena/
2. Akkar, M.-L., Giraud, C.: An implementation of DES and AES, secure against some attacks. In: Koç, Ç.K., Naccache, D., Paar, C. (eds.) CHES 2001. LNCS, vol. 2162, pp. 309–318. Springer, Heidelberg (2001)
3. Bertoni, G., Daemen, J., Peeters, M., Van Assche, G.: Building power analysis resistant implementations of KECCAK. In: Second SHA-3 Candidate Conference, August 2010
4. Bertoni, G., Daemen, J., Peeters, M., Van Assche, G.: Cryptographic sponge functions, January 2011
5. Bertoni, G., Daemen, J., Peeters, M., Van Assche, G.: Duplexing the sponge: single-pass authenticated encryption and other applications. In: Miri, A., Vaudenay, S. (eds.) SAC 2011. LNCS, vol. 7118, pp. 320–337. Springer, Heidelberg (2012)

6. Bertoni, G., Daemen, J., Peeters, M., Van Assche, G.: The KECCAK reference, January 2011
7. Bertoni, G., Daemen, J., Peeters, M., Van Assche, G., Van Keer, R.: KECCAK implementation overview, September 2011
8. Bilgin, B., Nikova, S., Nikov, V., Rijmen, V., Stütz, G.: Threshold implementations of All 3 × 3 and 4 × 4 S-boxes. In: Prouff, E., Schaumont, P. (eds.) CHES 2012. LNCS, vol. 7428, pp. 76–91. Springer, Heidelberg (2012)
9. Chari, S., Jutla, C.S., Rao, J.R., Rohatgi, P.: Towards sound approaches to counteract power-analysis attacks. In: Wiener, M. (ed.) CRYPTO 1999. LNCS, vol. 1666, pp. 398–412. Springer, Heidelberg (1999)
10. Ishai, Y., Sahai, A., Wagner, D.: Private circuits: securing hardware against probing attacks. In: Boneh, D. (ed.) CRYPTO 2003. LNCS, vol. 2729, pp. 463–481. Springer, Heidelberg (2003)
11. Kavun, E.B., Yalcin, T.: A lightweight implementation of KECCAK hash function for radio-frequency identification applications. In: Ors Yalcin, S.B. (ed.) RFIDSec 2010. LNCS, vol. 6370, pp. 258–269. Springer, Heidelberg (2010)
12. Kocher, P.C., Jaffe, J., Jun, B.: Differential power analysis. In: Wiener, M. (ed.) CRYPTO 1999. LNCS, vol. 1666, pp. 388–397. Springer, Heidelberg (1999)
13. Moradi, A., Poschmann, A., Ling, S., Paar, C., Wang, H.: Pushing the limits: a very compact and a threshold implementation of AES. In: Paterson, K.G. (ed.) EUROCRYPT 2011. LNCS, vol. 6632, pp. 69–88. Springer, Heidelberg (2011)
14. Nikova, S., Rijmen, V., Schläffer, M.: Secure hardware implementation of nonlinear functions in the presence of glitches. In: Lee, P.J., Cheon, J.H. (eds.) ICISC 2008. LNCS, vol. 5461, pp. 218–234. Springer, Heidelberg (2009)
15. Nikova, S., Rijmen, V., Schläffer, M.: Secure hardware implementation of nonlinear functions in the presence of glitches. J. Cryptology 24(2), 292–321 (2011)
16. Pessl, P., Hutter, M.: Pushing the limits of SHA-3 hardware implementations to fit on RFID. In: Bertoni, G., Coron, J.-S. (eds.) CHES 2013. LNCS, vol. 8086, pp. 126–141. Springer, Heidelberg (2013)
17. Popp, T., Mangard, S.: Masked dual-rail pre-charge logic: DPA-resistance without routing constraints. In: Rao, J.R., Sunar, B. (eds.) CHES 2005. LNCS, vol. 3659, pp. 172–186. Springer, Heidelberg (2005)
18. Tillich, S., Feldhofer, M., Kirschbaum, M., Plos, T., Schmidt, J.-M., Szekely, A.: Uniform evaluation of hardware implementations of the round-two SHA-3 candidates. In: The Second SHA-3 Candidate Conference, Santa Barbara, USA, pp. 1–16, 23–24 August 2010
19. Tiri, K., Verbauwhede, I.: A logic level design methodology for a secure DPA resistant ASIC or FPGA implementation. In: DATE, pp. 246–251. IEEE Computer Society (2004)
20. Trichina, E., Korkishko, T., Lee, K.-H.: Small size, low power, side channel-immune AES coprocessor: design and synthesis results. In: Dobbertin, H., Rijmen, V., Sowa, A. (eds.) AES 2005. LNCS, vol. 3373, pp. 113–127. Springer, Heidelberg (2005)

Practical Analysis of RSA Countermeasures Against Side-Channel Electromagnetic Attacks

Guilherme Perin$^{(\boxtimes)}$, Laurent Imbert$^{(\boxtimes)}$, Lionel Torres$^{(\boxtimes)}$, and Philippe Maurine$^{(\boxtimes)}$

LIRMM/UM2, 161 Rue Ada, 34095 Montpellier, France
{perin,laurent.imbert,lionel.torres}@lirmm.fr,
philippe.maurine@emse.fr

Abstract. This paper analyzes the robustness of RSA countermeasures against electromagnetic analysis and collision attacks. The proposed RSA cryptosystem uses residue number systems (RNS) for fast executions of the modular calculi with large numbers. The parallel architecture is protected at arithmetic and algorithmic levels by using the Montgomery Ladder and the Leak Resistant Arithmetic countermeasures. Because the architecture can leak information through control and memory executions, the hardware RNS-RSA also relies on the randomization of RAM accesses. Experimental results, obtained with and without randomization of the RNS moduli sets, suggest that the RNS-based RSA with bases randomization and secured RAM accesses is protected.

Keywords: RSA · RNS · Montgomery exponentiation · Countermeasures · Electromagnetic analysis

1 Introduction

Side-Channel Attacks (SCA) are a serious threat for public-key cryptosystems and notably for the RSA [1]. These attacks aim at recovering a secret manipulated by cryptographic algorithms, by analyzing various sources of side-channel leakages (time, power consumption, electromagnetic (EM) radiations, etc.) during their execution on a hardware device.

Countermeasures to prevent simple (SPA) and differential (DPA) power analysis on RSA can be categorized in algorithmic and hardware countermeasures. The Square-and-Multiply Always [2] and the Montgomery Ladder [3] ensure that all operations in the binary method run in a constant sequence of operations in order to prevent SPA like attacks. To deal with DPA attacks, the idea of algorithmic countermeasures is to randomize the message or the exponent (private key) that are processed during the execution of a modular exponentiation. However, most of these countermeasures do not provide sufficient protection against high-order DPA attacks or sophisticated SPA-attacks [4,21].

A. Francillon and P. Rohatgi (Eds.): CARDIS 2013, LNCS 8419, pp. 200–215, 2014.
DOI: 10.1007/978-3-319-08302-5_14, ⓒ Springer International Publishing Switzerland 2014

Residue Number System (RNS), coupled together with SPA-protected methods, is an interesting alternative to increase the robustness at the arithmetic level. RNS provides a natural way of masking the data and the internal computations because all intermediate values can be represented in different RNS bases. However, differential, correlation and collision EM attacks [5–8] remains fully efficient if no randomization of the RNS bases are used to effectively mask sensitive computations. This idea is the foundation of the Leak Resistant Arithmetic (LRA) concept proposed in [9].

The RSA hardware approach proposed in this work implements different countermeasures. To provide protection against correlation analyses and collision attacks, the design offers protection at arithmetic level by randomizing the moduli between two sets of RNS bases, and then implies the on-the-fly calculus of the required pre-computed constants. For the modular exponentiation, the Montgomery Ladder algorithm is considered even if other algorithms can be executed by our co-processor. The successive modular multiplications are computed with the RNS Montgomery algorithm [10] that needs two sets of k moduli due to the base extension part. For this crucial operation in the Montgomery multiplication, one considers the fast approximation method [11], which is derived from the Chinese Remainder Theorem. Moreover, hardware countermeasures are adopted with randomization of the RAM addresses during the reading and writing operations.

The rest of the paper is organized as follows. Section 2 give a brief state-of-art about the use of RNS for the integration of public-key algorithms. Section 3 describes the hardware module we have designed and mapped into an FPGA. Section 4 gives experimental results about the robustness of the RNS-RSA implemented on our crypto-module. Finally, a conclusion is drawn in Sect. 5.

2 Preliminaries

2.1 Residue Number System

In the Residue Number System [12], an integer X, is represented according to a base $\mathcal{B} = (b_1, b_2, ..., b_k)$ of relatively prime integers, called moduli. The number X in base $\mathcal{B}$ is thus represented by a k-tuple of positive integers $\langle X \rangle_\mathcal{B} = (x_1, x_2, \ldots, x_k)$, where $x_i = X \bmod b_i$, i.e. the remainder of the division of X by the modulo b_i, denoted $|X|_{b_i}$ in the sequel. Arithmetic operations $(\pm, \times)$ are then performed modulo $B = \prod_{i=1}^{k} b_i$. To recover the original number X (modulo B), given the residues x_i, one may apply the Chinese Remainder Theorem (CRT):

$$|X|_B = \left| \sum_{i=1}^{k} B_i |x_i B_i^{-1}|_{b_i} \right|_B , \text{where } B_i = \frac{B}{b_i}$$

The forward conversion is a key step before starting any computation in RNS. From the radix-2^w representation of $X = \sum_{j=0}^{n-1} X_j 2^{wj}$, the residues x_i are obtained, for all $b_i \in \mathcal{B}$, by:

$$x_i = |X|_{b_i} = \left| \sum_{j=0}^{n-1} |X_j| 2^{wj}|_{b_i}|_{b_i} \right|_{b_i} , \tag{1}$$

where the constants $|2^{wj}|_{b_i}$ are pre-computed for all i, j to speed up the forward conversion in RNS hardware modules by computing all residues in parallel.

2.2   RNS Montgomery Exponentiation

The core of any RSA implementation is a modular exponentiation of x, namely $x^e \bmod N$ is computed and e is the private exponent. This is the operation to be protected! To deal with timing and SPA attacks, in this work we adopted the Montgomery Ladder exponentiation version in RNS, as given in Algorithm 1. One may observe that the computations are performed over two RNS bases $\mathcal{A}$ and $\mathcal{B}$.

The pre-computed terms for the modular exponentiation are $B \bmod N$ and $B^2 \bmod N$ in bases $\mathcal{A}$ and $\mathcal{B}$. The operation $MM(x, y, N, \mathcal{B}, \mathcal{A})$ returns the RNS Montgomery Multiplication result $xyB^{-1} \bmod N$ in the two RNS bases $\mathcal{A}$ and $\mathcal{B}$. For this crucial operation, the recent improvement proposed in [13] was adopted to accelerate the original method [11] by 18 %. This acceleration is provided by rearranging the computations within the so-called base extensions (BE). In [13], two different strategies are proposed for that operation and, in our approach, we adopted the fast approximation method, also called as Posch-Posch method [14]. Given x_i the elements of X in base $\mathcal{B}$, where $x_i = X \bmod b_i$ for $i = 1..k$, the fast approximation method ensures the existence of a certain integer $\lambda < k$, a CRT-correction coefficient, such that:

$$X = \left| \sum_{i=1}^{k} B_i |x_i B_i^{-1}|_{b_i} \right|_B = \sum_{i=1}^{k} B_i |x_i B_i^{-1}|_{b_i} - \lambda.B \tag{2}$$

and λ can be calculated by:

$$\lambda = \left\lfloor \sum_{i=1}^{k} \frac{B_i |x_i B_i^{-1}|_{b_i}}{B} \right\rfloor = \left\lfloor \sum_{i=1}^{k} \frac{|x_i B_i^{-1}|_{b_i}}{b_i} \right\rfloor = \left\lfloor \frac{1}{2^w} \sum_{i=1}^{k} |x_i B_i^{-1}|_{b_i} \right\rfloor \tag{3}$$

In Eq. 3, $|x_i B_i^{-1}|_{b_i}/b_i$ may be approximated by $|x_i B_i^{-1}|_{b_i}/2^w$ as $b_i = 2^w - c_i$, and $c_i > 0$. The resulting RNS Montgomery algorithm using the fast approximation base extension, with a cost of $2k + 7$ single multiplications at each RNS moduli, is shown in Algorithm 2.

The RNS Montgomery algorithm requires a set of precomputed terms in RNS bases $\mathcal{A}$ and $\mathcal{B}$. The term $B_{i,j}NB^{-1}$ refers to the computation $|BNB^{-1}/b_i|_{a_j}$ and $A_{i,j}$ refers to the computation $|A/a_i|_{b_j}$, for $\forall i, j$. The modular exponentiation employing the Algorithm 2 ensures that $X^e \bmod N < 2N$.

Algorithm 1. RNS Montgomery Ladder Exponentiation

Data: x in $\mathcal{A} \cup \mathcal{B}$, where $\mathcal{A} = (a_1, a_2, ..., a_k)$, $\mathcal{B} = (b_1, b_2, ..., b_k)$, $A = \prod_{i=1}^{k} a_i$,
$\quad\quad B = \prod_{i=1}^{k} b_i$, $\gcd(A, B) = 1$, $\gcd(B, N) = 1$ and $e = (e_{n-1}...e_1 e_0)_2$.

Result: $z = x^e \bmod N$ in $\mathcal{A} \cup \mathcal{B}$

1   **Pre-Computations:** $|B \bmod N|_{\mathcal{A} \cup \mathcal{B}}$ and $|B^2 \bmod N|_{\mathcal{A} \cup \mathcal{B}}$

2   $A_0 = B \bmod N$ (in $\mathcal{A} \cup \mathcal{B}$)

3   $A_1 = MM(x, B^2 \bmod N, N, \mathcal{B}, \mathcal{A})$ (in $\mathcal{A} \cup \mathcal{B}$)

4   **for** $i = n - 1$ **to** 0 **do**

5     $A_{\overline{e_i}} = MM(A_{\overline{e_i}}, A_{e_i}, N, \mathcal{B}, \mathcal{A})$ (in $\mathcal{A} \cup \mathcal{B}$)

6     $A_{e_i} = MM(A_{e_i}, A_{e_i}, N, \mathcal{B}, \mathcal{A})$ (in $\mathcal{A} \cup \mathcal{B}$)

7   **end**

8   $A_0 = MM(A_0, 1, N, \mathcal{B}, \mathcal{A})$ (in $\mathcal{A} \cup \mathcal{B}$)

Algorithm 2. RNS Montgomery Multiplication with Fast Approx. BE [13]

Data: x, y in $\mathcal{A} \cup \mathcal{B}$, where $\mathcal{A} = (a_1, a_2, ..., a_k)$, $\mathcal{B} = (b_1, b_2, ..., b_k)$, $A = \prod_{i=1}^{k} a_i$,
$\quad\quad B = \prod_{i=1}^{k} b_i$, $\gcd(B, A) = 1$, $1 \le x, y < N$, $B > 4N$ and $A > 2N$

Result: $w = xyB^{-1} \bmod N$ (in $\mathcal{A} \cup \mathcal{B}$)

1   **Pre-Computations in $\mathcal{A}$:** B^{-1}, $B_{i,j} N.B^{-1}$ for $i, j = 1..k$, $-B.N.B^{-1}$, A_j^{-1} for $j = 1..k$

2   **Pre-Computations in $\mathcal{B}$:** $-N^{-1}B_i^{-1}$ for $i = 1..k$, $A_{i,j}$ for $i, j = 1..k$, $-A$

3   $s = |x.y|_{\mathcal{B} \cup \mathcal{A}}$

4   $————————— \; Base \; extension \; 1 \; —————————$

5   $q_{b_i} = |s_i(-N^{-1}B_i^{-1})|_{b_i}$ for i=1..k

6   $f = \left\lfloor \left(\sum_{i=1}^{k} q_{b_i} \right) / 2^w \right\rfloor$

7   $w_{a_i} = |s_i B^{-1} + \sum_{j=1}^{k} q_{b_j} (B_{i,j} N B^{-1}) - f.B.N.B^{-1}|_{a_i}$ for i=1..k

8   $————————— \; Base \; extension \; 2 \; —————————$

9   $q_i = |w_{a_i}(A_i^{-1})|_{a_i}$ for i=1..k

10   $f = \left\lfloor \left(2^{w-1} + \sum_{i=1}^{k} q_{b_i} \right) / 2^w \right\rfloor$

11   $w_{b_i} = |\sum_{j=1}^{k} q_j A_{i,j} - f.A|_{b_i}$ for i=1..k

---

2.3   RNS Bases Randomization - The LRA Countermeasure

DPA attacks explore the relation between the power consumption and the internal variables to recover the bits of the private key. The leak resistant arithmetic (LRA) countermeasure [9] provides a way for completely masking the internal computations and then protect against differential or correlation power (or EM) analysis at arithmetic level.

Before each modular exponentiation, the two set of bases $\mathcal{A}$ and $\mathcal{B}$ (each of size k) are randomly selected among a set of $2k$ integers. In this way, an integer w (an intermediate result in the modular exponentiation represented in the Montgomery domain) has $C_k^{2k} \approx 2^{2k}/\sqrt{\pi k}$ different RNS representations in bases $\mathcal{A}$ or $\mathcal{B}$ and it offers a high-level of randomization. These randomly selected RNS bases are then used during the entire computation. The authors of [9] also suggested to reinforce the robustness by selecting new bases during the exponentiation, possibly before each MM. However, this second approach may become much slower; it implies two additional MM each time new RNS bases are chosen, or even four extra MM if the Montgomery Ladder is used for the

---

Algorithm 3. RNS Montgomery Powering Ladder with LRA [9]

Data: x in $\mathcal{A} \cup \mathcal{B}$, where $\mathcal{A} = (a_1, a_2, ..., a_k)$, $\mathcal{B} = (b_1, b_2, ..., b_k)$, $A = \prod_{i=1}^{k} a_i$,
$\quad\quad B = \prod_{i=1}^{k} b_i$, $\gcd(A, B) = 1$, $\gcd(B, N) = 1$ and $e = (e_{n-1}...e_1 e_0)_2$.

Result: $z = x^e \bmod N$ in $\mathcal{A} \cup \mathcal{B}$

1 **Pre-Computations:** $|AB \bmod N|_{\mathcal{A} \cup \mathcal{B}}$

2 $A_0 = MM(1, AB \bmod N, N, \mathcal{A}, \mathcal{B})$ (in $\mathcal{A} \cup \mathcal{B}$)

3 $A_1 = MM(x, AB \bmod N, N, \mathcal{A}, \mathcal{B})$ (in $\mathcal{A} \cup \mathcal{B}$)

4 **for** $i = n - 1$ **to** 0 **do**

5 $\quad\quad A_{\overline{e_i}} = MM(A_{\overline{e_i}}, A_{e_i}, N, \mathcal{B}, \mathcal{A})$ (in $\mathcal{A} \cup \mathcal{B}$)

6 $\quad\quad A_{e_i} = MM(A_{e_i}, A_{e_i}, N, \mathcal{B}, \mathcal{A})$ (in $\mathcal{A} \cup \mathcal{B}$)

7 **end**

8 $A_0 = MM(A_0, 1, N, \mathcal{B}, \mathcal{A})$ (in $\mathcal{A} \cup \mathcal{B}$)

---

exponentiation. Here, the bases randomization are performed once before each exponentiation, using Montgomery Powering Ladder as depicted in Algorithm 3. In the application of LRA countermeasure, the on-the-fly computation of Montgomery constants $B \bmod N$ and $B^2 \bmod N$ is solved by using the pre-computed term $AB \bmod N$ (in $\mathcal{A} \cup \mathcal{B}$) in the two first Montgomery multiplications. Note the order of $\mathcal{A}$ and $\mathcal{B}$ in these two first calls of MM in Algorithm 3.

The RNS Montgomery Multiplication needs pre-computed constants related to the random choice of RNS bases $\mathcal{A}$ and $\mathcal{B}$. These pre-computed constants must be obtained on-the-fly before each modular exponentiation. The LRA pre-computations necessary for the Montgomery multiplication are:

(a) $\left| B_i^{-1} \right|_{b_i} = \left| \prod_{j=1}^{k} b_j^{-1} \right|_{b_i} = \left| \left| ... \right| \left| b_0^{-1}.b_1^{-1} \right|_{b_i}.b_2^{-1} \right|_{b_i} ... b_k^{-1} \right|_{b_i} \Big|_{b_i}$

(b) $\left| A_i^{-1} \right|_{a_i} = \left| \prod_{j=1}^{k} a_j^{-1} \right|_{a_i} = \left| \left| ... \right| \left| a_0^{-1}.a_1^{-1} \right|_{a_i}.a_2^{-1} \right|_{a_i} ... a_k^{-1} \right|_{a_i} \Big|_{a_i}$

(c) $\left| B^{-1} \right|_{a_i} = \left| \prod_{j=1}^{k} b_j^{-1} \right|_{a_i} = \left| \left| ... \right| \left| b_0^{-1}.b_1^{-1} \right|_{a_i}.b_2^{-1} \right|_{a_i} ... b_k^{-1} \right|_{a_i} \Big|_{a_i}$

(d) $\left| A^{-1} \right|_{b_i} = \left| \prod_{j=1}^{k} a_j^{-1} \right|_{b_i} = \left| \left| ... \right| \left| a_0^{-1}.a_1^{-1} \right|_{b_i}.a_2^{-1} \right|_{b_i} ... a_k^{-1} \right|_{b_i} \Big|_{b_i}$

(e) $\left| B \right|_{a_i} = \left| \prod_{j=1}^{k} b_j \right|_{a_i} = \left| \left| ... \right| \left| b_0.b_1 \right|_{a_i}.b_2 \right|_{a_i} ... b_k \right|_{a_i} \Big|_{a_i}$

(f) $\left| A \right|_{b_i} = \left| \prod_{j=1}^{k} a_j \right|_{b_i} = \left| \left| ... \right| \left| a_0.a_1 \right|_{b_i}.a_2 \right|_{b_i} ... a_k \right|_{b_i} \Big|_{b_i}$

And then, we obtain:

1. $\left| -N^{-1} B_i^{-1} \right|_{b_i} = \left| -N^{-1} \right|.\left| B_i^{-1} \right|_{b_i}$ and $\left| -N^{-1} A_i^{-1} \right|_{a_i} = \left| -N^{-1} \right|.\left| A_i^{-1} \right|_{a_i}$, for $i = 1..k$

2. $\left| B_i \right|_{a_j} = \left| B \right|_{a_j}.\left| b_i^{-1} \right|_{a_j}$ and $\left| A_i \right|_{b_j} = \left| A \right|_{b_j}.\left| a_i^{-1} \right|_{b_j}$, for $j = 1..k$

3. $\left| B_i N B^{-1} \right|_{a_j} = \left| B_i \right|_{a_j}.\left| N \right|_{a_j}.\left| B^{-1} \right|_{a_j}$ and $\left| A_i N A^{-1} \right|_{b_j} = \left| A_i \right|_{b_j}.\left| N \right|_{b_j}.\left| A^{-1} \right|_{b_j}$, for $j = 1..k$

4. $\left| -B \right|_{a_i} = \left| B \right|_{a_i}.\left| -1 \right|_{a_i}$ and $\left| -A \right|_{b_i} = \left| A \right|_{b_i}.\left| -1 \right|_{b_i}$, for $i = 1..k$

5. $\left| -BNB^{-1} \right|_{a_i} = \left| -B \right|_{a_i}.\left| N \right|_{a_i}.\left| B^{-1} \right|_{a_i}$ and $\left| -ANA^{-1} \right|_{b_i} = \left| -A \right|_{b_i}.\left| N \right|_{b_i}.\left| A^{-1} \right|_{b_i}$, for $i = 1..k$

Then, all constants $|b_i^{-1}|_{b_j}$, $|a_i^{-1}|_{a_j}$, $|b_i^{-1}|_{a_j}$, $|a_i^{-1}|_{b_j}$ for all i, j, $| - N^{-1}|_{\mathcal{A} \cup \mathcal{B}}$, $|N|_{\mathcal{A} \cup \mathcal{B}}$, $| - 1|_{\mathcal{A} \cup \mathcal{B}}$ and the RNS base sets $\mathcal{A}$ and $\mathcal{B}$ should be pre-computed.

After the modular exponentiation, the result must be converted back to radix. For the LRA countermeasure, the reverse conversion using CRT-based method needs the on-the-fly computations of the values B_i and B in radix-2^w form and it represents a high level of complexity. In this case, it is adopted the Mixed-Radix System (MRS) [12] for the RNS to radix conversion. The mixed-radix system is a weighted representation of a RNS number. This method is computed in two steps: first, the MRS representation of x_i (RNS representation of X in $\mathcal{B}$) is obtained using the optimized Garner's Algorithm [17], and all the pre-computed values, the inverses $|b_i^{-1}|_{b_j}$, are obtained independently of RNS bases randomizations; second, the MRS result is converted to radix by applying the Horner's scheme, as also presented in [17]. The reverse conversion implies carry-based arithmetic. However, the time spent for these operations is negligible compared to the modular exponentiation.

3   Proposed and Developed Hardware

The proposed hardware computes the forward conversion (radix to RNS), the LRA pre-computations, the modular exponentiation and the reverse conversion (radix to RNS), using the same set of independent data-paths called RNS Units depicted in Fig. 1. The implementation follows a similar schematic than that proposed in [11] and improved in [16], called cox-rower architecture.

As described in Sect. 2, the required LRA pre-computations, which computes the pre-computed constants for the Montgomery multiplication in the RNS bases $\mathcal{A}$ and $\mathcal{B}$, needs a set of pre-computed values. To store them, the RNS Units contain dual-port RAM memories. Then, each RNS Unit contains all pre-computed elements of all moduli of $\mathcal{A}$ and $\mathcal{B}$. It causes an overhead in terms of memory, however speeds-up the on-the-fly pre-computations.

The core of each RNS Unit is the arithmetic logic unit (ALU), which computes the modular addition/subtraction, modular products and carry-based arithmetic operations in the reverse conversion (CRT or MRS). To accelerate the modular reductions, we adopted the method proposed in [15]. This solution uses pseudo-Mersenne numbers of the form $b_i = 2^w - c_i$, where $c_i < 2^{w/2}$, for the chosen set of RNS moduli. Then, to compute $x \bmod b_i$ one first performs the following step twice:

$$x \leftarrow (x \bmod 2^w) + c_i \cdot (x/2^w) \tag{4}$$

Then x will be in the range of $[0, 2^{w+1}]$ and a final conditional subtraction by b_i returns the residual value. The coefficient c_i is also an input of the ALU block. As RNS bases randomizations (LRA) makes the RNS Units operate in different moduli, all c_i (for $i = 1..2k$) are stored in a ROM memory. Each RNS Unit performs operations for one RNS channel of $\mathcal{A}$ and one of $\mathcal{B}$; the selection of these channels, and the respective coefficient c_i, is defined by the *random index* input from the control unit.

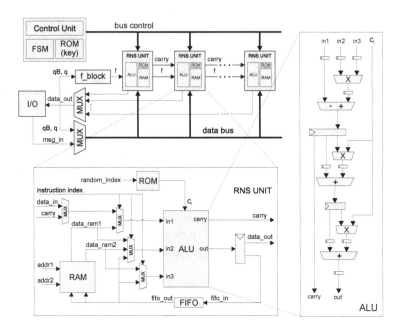

Fig. 1. RNS architecture block diagram.

The architecture also contains an adder block, called *f_block*, for computing the f values in the two base extensions. This block basically sums up all input values (q_B in the first base extension and q in the second base extension) and returns the k most significant bits of this sum, named f.

The hardware countermeasure also relies on the RAM access protection. According to the Algorithm 3 there are four registers ($A0$ in $\mathcal{A}$, $A0$ in $\mathcal{B}$, $A1$ in $\mathcal{A}$ and $A1$ in $\mathcal{B}$) for storing the intermediate values, resulting of modular multiplication or squaring executions in the binary loop of the Montgomery Ladder. So, for example, if a modular multiplication $A_0 = MM(A_0, A_1, N, \mathcal{B}, \mathcal{A})$ is executed when the exponent bit is 1, the reading and writing operations will be:

1. $read(|A0|_{\mathcal{A}}, |A0|_{\mathcal{B}}, |A1|_{\mathcal{A}}, |A1|_{\mathcal{B}})$
2. $write(|A0|_{\mathcal{A}}, |A0|_{\mathcal{B}})$

On the other hand, if a modular multiplication $A_1 = MM(A_0, A_1, N, \mathcal{B}, \mathcal{A})$ is executed when the exponent bit is 0, the reading and writing operations will be:

1. $read(|A0|_{\mathcal{A}}, |A0|_{\mathcal{B}}, |A1|_{\mathcal{A}}, |A1|_{\mathcal{B}})$
2. $write(|A1|_{\mathcal{A}}, |A1|_{\mathcal{B}})$

Note that same registers are read and different registers are written. EM analysis based on localized EM radiations [18] or on the control and RAM leakages [20] show that if the RAM accesses are unprotected, the private key bits can be recovered using sophisticated SEMA or location-based EM attacks. In order to randomize the register's position, and consequently the addresses, where the

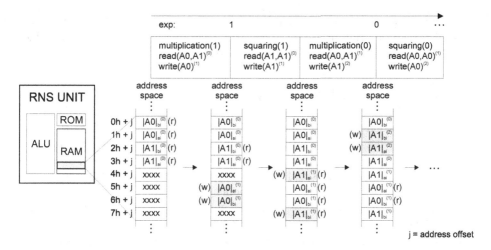

Fig. 2. RAM memory addressing randomization.

intermediate results $A0$ and $A1$ (in $\mathcal{A}$ and $\mathcal{B}$) are stored, we propose the scheme depicted in Fig. 2 in all RNS Units.

Considering the first modular multiplication $A_0 = MM(A_0, A_1, N, \mathcal{B}, \mathcal{A})$. The control reads the registers $A0$ and $A1$ (in $\mathcal{A}$ and $\mathcal{B}$) from the RAM address $0h+j$, $1h+j$, $2h+j$ and $3h+j$ (indicated by 'r') and instead of storing the modular multiplication result $A0$ (in $\mathcal{A}$ and $\mathcal{B}$) in the same positions ($0h+j$ and $1h+j$), $A0$ is stored in random positions $5h+j$, $6h+j$, indicated by 'w'. Since the exponent bit $e_i = 1$, the next operation is a modular squaring $A_1 = MM(A_1, A_1, N, \mathcal{B}, \mathcal{A})$. The control reads the registers A_1 (in $\mathcal{A}$ and $\mathcal{B}$) from addresses $2h+j$ and $3h+j$ and instead of storing the result in the same position, it is placed at random address spaces $4h+j$, $7h+j$. In the next modular multiplication, the registers $A0$ and $A1$ will be read from the previous random positions. With this hardware countermeasure, the storing position of intermediate values changes during the modular exponentiation, blurring the EM emanations. Then, the side-channel leakage due RAM memory addressing is suppressed, because the results are always stored in different addresses. Next section shows practical EM attacks on both unprotected and secured RAM.

Considering k the number of RNS moduli in each of the bases $\mathcal{A}$ and $\mathcal{B}$, the total number of clock cycles for a Montgomery multiplication is $2k + 37$. The LRA countermeasure needs an amount of $64k + 36$ clock cycles for the pre-computations. Table 1 summarizes the number of clock cycles for the 512 bits RSA, that is able to compute the CRT-RSA 1024 bits, and the synthesis results for FPGA implementation (low-cost Spartan 3E family) including the number of kilobytes that represents the pre-computed terms pre-stored before the exponentiation and the memory space needed during the exponentiation. The results are provided for the two RSA-RNS implementations. As indicated, there is a time overhead of only 1 % due to the LRA countermeasure. The memory (kilobytes) and the area overheads (LUTs and Slices) due countermeasures are 92 % and 3 %, respectively.

4   Robustness to EM Analyses

Collision or chosen-messages pair attacks, threat modular exponentiations by exploiting the existence of identical computations. Correlation electromagnetic analysis (CEMA) seeks to recover the secret information by computing the correlation between the EM traces and some guessed intermediate values manipulated or not by the device according to the exponent bits.

To evaluate the relevance of the LRA and hardware countermeasures, we first applied these attacks on an unprotected hardware design, i.e. an RNS-RSA with fixed bases to set a robustness reference level. Then, we re-applied these attacks on our protected implementation in order to quantify the robustness enhancements. To generalize the notation of the acquired EM traces, we define the following:

$$EM(T_E,x,e) = \left\{ EM(T_M,x,e_{n-1}), EM(T_S,x,e_{n-1}), ..., EM(T_M,x,e_0), EM(T_S,x,e_0) \right\}$$

where $EM(T_E,x,e)$ is the set of all multiplication and squaring intervals during a modular exponentiation with the exponent $e = \{e_{n-1}, e_{n-2}, ..., e_1, e_0\}$, input message x and:

1. $EM(T_M,x,e_i)$ = EM trace of a modular multiplication (M) done during the time window T_M with the exponent bit e_i;
2. $EM(T_S,x,e_i)$ = EM trace of a modular squaring (S) performed during the time window T_S with the exponent bit e_i;
3. T_E = time window of a full modular exponentiation.

Table 1. Cycle count and synthesis results.

	RSA without protection	RSA with LRA	Overhead
RSA-512 Clock Cycles			
LRA latency	0	1060	100 %
Radix to RNS	48	48	0 %
Mont. Expo.	78210	78210	0 %
RNS to Radix	685 (CRT)	840 (MRS)	18 %
Total	78943	80158	1 %
*Synthesis Results (*FPGA Utilization)*			
4-Input LUTs	17124 (28 %*)	17769 (29 %*)	3 %
Slices	8717 (27 %*)	9510 (30 %*)	8 %
18 × 18 Mults	104 (100 %*)	104 (100 %*)	0 %
KB (RAM)	8.5 (5 %*)	118 (66 %*)	92 %

We also define $V_{em}(t, x)$ as being the variation of the EM field at the time t of a modular exponentiation having x as input message.

The EM traces were collected with a measurement platform composed of: an oscilloscope (bandwidth: 2.5 GHz; sampling rate: 40 GS/s), an amplifier with a bandwidth of 200 MHz, a 200 μm probe, a motorized stage, an FPGA Spartan-3 XC3S1600 board and a PC to control the whole measurement setup.

4.1 EM Collision Attacks

Collision attacks are SPA like attacks based on the choice of pairs of messages. Basically, an adversary has to measure the power consumption or the EM emanations during the processing of these two chosen messages by the cryptosystem. Then, he has to apply a sliding procedure at the two collected traces to detect, by subtraction, the occurrence of an identical computation. Such collisions typically appear during the squaring operations of modular exponentiations. Several collision attacks have been proposed in the literature. The Doubling Attack (DA) [6] and Yen et al.'s Attack [7] collisions are observed in squaring operations and apply on left-to-right exponentiation algorithms. Homma et al.'s Attack [8] is a collision that also applies to right-to-left exponentiations contrarily to the DA and the Yen et al.' attack. As explained in [8], it is based on a different choice of the input messages to provoke collisions in right-to-left and left-to-right exponentiation algorithms.

Because the Montgomery powering ladder algorithm is a left-to-right algorithm, we did consider the Doubling Attack. Following the DA procedure, we truncated, re-aligned and subtracted the EM traces and we confirmed the occurrence of the same intermediate modular squaring results. Figures 3(a) and (b) show how to select and align traces related to the chosen messages in order to have a reference and a target frame.

The first experiment was done on the unprotected RNS-RSA design, when the RNS bases are always fixed. One averaged EM trace (20 trials) has been necessary for each chosen message for identifying the occurrence of collisions using our EM platform. Figure 3(c) shows the result of a collision analysis on the target RSA-RNS hardware implemented without countermeasures. Note the amplitude of the differential trace is near to zero where redundant computations are performed (depicted as 'region of interest').

To illustrate the effect of our countermeasures, Fig. 3(d) shows the differential traces when DA was applied to the RNS-RSA with randomization of RNS bases. As expected, collisions cannot be detected visually when countermeasures are activated despite the use of average mode of the oscilloscope (20 trials). To demonstrate the efficiency of the DA and quantify the effects of our countermeasures, we define a collision detection criterion by plotting the evolution of the Signal-to-Noise Ratio (SNR) with the number of trials set for the averaging. According to the DA, if the exponent presents consecutive zero bits at e_i

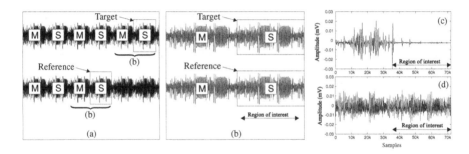

Fig. 3. (a) Electromagnetic traces. (b) Electromagnetic traces alignment for collision detecting. (c) Electromagnetic collision attack on RSA without protection and (d) with RNS bases randomizations (LRA).

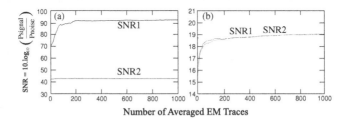

Fig. 4. SNR vs number of averaged EM traces. (a) RSA without protection. (b) RSA with RNS bases randomizations (LRA).

and e_{i-1}, the EM traces $EM(T_S,x,e_{i-1})$ and $EM(T_S,x^2,e_i)$ represent redundant squarings (collision). The SNR was computed according to:

$$SNR = 20.log_{10}\frac{P_{signal}}{P_{noise}} = 20.log_{10}\frac{\sigma^2_{(EM(T_S,x,e_{i-1}))}}{\sigma^2_{(EM(T_S,x,e_{i-1})-EM(T_S,x^2,e_i))}} \quad (5)$$

where $\sigma^2_{(EM(T_S,x,e_{i-1}))}$ is the variance of samples over the time window T_S corresponding to a squaring operation and $\sigma^2_{(EM(T_S,x,e_{i-1})-EM(T_S,x^2,e_i))}$ is the variance of the differential trace samples over the time window T_S. We defined SNR1 when $EM(T_S,x,e_{i-1}) = EM(T_S,x^2,e_i)$ (collision) and SNR2 when $EM(T_S,x,e_{i-1}) \neq EM(T_S,x^2,e_i)$ (no collision). As shown in Fig. 4a, if a collision occurs, SNR1 is significantly bigger than SNR2 because the denominator of Eq. 5 is almost 0 (suppression of the signal by the collision; only the noise remains) even with no averaging.

As shown in Fig. 4(b), collisions cannot be detected when randomization of RNS bases countermeasure is activated, even when averaging over 1000 times the two signals.

4.2 CEMA

Correlation EM Analysis (CEMA) aims at revealing the secret key K manipulated by a circuit by analyzing the correlation between its EM emanations and guesses on the secret key. The most important the correlation is, the most likely the guess is. To apply a CEMA on an RSA the adversary should have the possibility to randomly generate the input data x of the RSA implementation to be attacked or to observe cipher texts. At the same time, he has to measure the variations of the EM field $V_{em}(t, x)$ at time t. This done, he enters in the CEMA procedure that starts by choosing a selection function.

Key Guess and Selection Function: in our case, the adversary, knowing that the considered algorithm is the Montgomery Powering Ladder, may generate 8-bits guesses on the secret key, starting by the MSB. In this way, he has a manageable set of sub-key guesses. These sub-key guesses generated, the adversary computes for each guess k, the corresponding variations of the power consumption at a chosen time of the course of the algorithm, using the Hamming Weight Model $W(x, k)$. This time typically corresponds to the computation of an intermediate value by the algorithm that depends on the sub-key. For any RSA, these intermediate values could be the Montgomery multiplication results. However, for RNS-RSA, the adversary must know the set of bases $\mathcal{A}$ and $\mathcal{B}$. If this is not the case, he has first to perform a long and tedious CEMA on the forward conversion (radix to RNS conversion) to recover them. In this case, the guesses on the selection function are the values of the RNS bases itself, instead of the private key bits as used in the classic CEMA.

Assuming known these RNS bases, the latter may now predict the power consumption variations (and therefore the EM field variations) with the manipulated data x for each key guess k. As the Montgomery multiplication results are obtained in parallel, he has to choose one RNS channel to compute the Hamming weight. Assuming n is the register width, the selection function follows the linear model $d(x, k) = W(x, k) - n/2$. This is done for each guess of the 8-bits sub-key. The CEMA is expected to return an estimate $\widehat{k}$ of the key by identifying the guess leading to the highest correlation value during the course of the algorithm. The correlation is computed between $d(x, k)$ and EM trace $V_{em}(t, x)$ of single measurements as function of time t:

$$c(t, k) = \frac{\sum_i (d(x_i, k) - \overline{d(x_i, k)})(V_{em}(t, x_i) - \overline{V_{em}(x_i, t)})}{\sqrt{\sum_i (d(x_i, k) - \overline{d(x_i, k)})^2}\sqrt{\sum_i (V_{em}(t, x_i) - \overline{V_{em}(t, x_i)})^2}} \qquad (6)$$

To illustrate the effect of the RSA countermeasures against CEMA, we evaluated the relation between the number of EM traces and the peak margin observed for the correct guess of the sub-key related to incorrect ones. Figure 5(a) shows the evolution of the peak of the correlation index $c(t, k)$ with the number of EM traces when the architecture performs modular exponentiations with fixed RNS moduli. It is possible to guess the correct hypothesis after the processing of 500 EM traces when RSA presents no countermeasures. With the LRA countermeasure and secured RAM accesses, the correlation curve associated to the secret key has still drowned among the other correlation curves even after the processing of 10 k traces.

4.3 RAM Memory Randomization

The LRA countermeasure offers a high level of randomization for the internal variables. Collisions and CEMA attacks are defeated because the Hamming Weight of an internal variable can not be estimated to find the secret. Considering that an RSA hardware design is usually composed by arithmetic block (ALU), control (CPU), bus and memories (RAM, ROM), one may find some sources of leakages. The control and memories also performs executions depending on the exponent bits, mainly regarding the values of the memory addresses. The RAM leakages, in the case of Montgomery Ladder, will be generated by different addressing values for reading and writing multiplication or squaring results. Then, simple EM analysis, template attacks [22] or attacks based on a single execution (SE) of exponentiations [4,19,21], may explore the leakage caused by RAM addressing in the Montgomery Ladder and others SPA-protected exponentiation algorithms. SE attacks on exponentiation are also a threat against classical algorithmic countermeasures like message or exponent blinding, however they depend on the quality of the measured traces. If the SNR is very reduced, meaning that the trace contains a big amount of noise, the probability of recovering leaking information from a single trace is quite low. The analyses developed here illustrate the design vulnerabilities related to RAM access when the hardware countermeasure by addressing randomization is disregarded.

Initially, an adversary can do as follows: considering the exponentiation is always performed with a fixed exponent. He sends random messages x to the device and collects an averaged EM trace representing the multiplication when the exponent bit is 1 $[EM(T_M, x, 1)]$ and another representing the multiplication when the exponent bit is 0 $[EM(T_M, x, 0)]$. The adversary may then obtains the differential trace $E_{diff} = EM(T_M, x, 0) - EM(T_M, x, 1)$ which may reveals the leakages of control and RAM accesses, as illustrated in Fig. 6(a). The leakage is indicated by higher amplitudes during the RAM reading (r) and writing (w) executions. The procedure adopted by the adversary is:

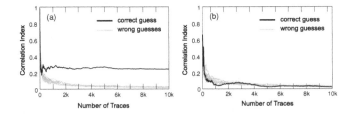

Fig. 5. Correlation electromagnetic attack on hardware RSA-RNS without countermeasures and (b) with LRA countermeasure with secured RAM accesses.

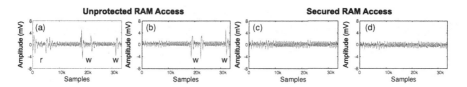

Fig. 6. (a),(c): $EM(T_M, x, 1) - EM(T_M, x, 0)$. (b),(d): $EM(T_S, x, 1) - EM(T_S, x, 0)$.

1. Consider $EM(T_E, x, e)$ the trace samples of a full modular exponentiation;
2. Consider $\{EM(T_M, x, e_i)\}$ the set of all trace samples of size T_M corresponding to the multiplications at the exponent bits e_i;
3. Set $EM(T_M, x, e_{n-1})$ as the referential trace, where $e_{n-1} = 1$ and compute the differential traces $E_{diff} = EM(T_M, x, e_{n-1}) - EM(T_M, x, e_{n-1-i})$, for $i = 0 : n - 1$.
4. Differential traces E_{diff} with higher amplitudes (higher variance) indicates the subtraction $EM(T_M, x, 1) - EM(T_M, x, 0)$.

The same procedure can be verified in Fig. 6(b) by subtracting the EM traces of modular squarings when the RAM addressing is not randomized. Following the notations of Algorithm 2, the amplitudes at the first samples of the differential traces represent the multiplications $s = x.y$ in the two RNS bases $\mathcal{A}$ and $\mathcal{B}$ and RAM memory is accessed in order to read the values x and y. The modular multiplication results w_A and w_B must also be stored in the RAM and this activity is indicated in the differential trace by higher amplitudes representing the RAM writing. Figure 6(c) and (d) show the differential EM trace obtained after randomizing the RAM addresses. As we can see, these leakages were suppressed.

Now, if the exponent is randomized ($e_r = e + r.\phi(N)$), the attack processes single traces. Template and SE attacks assumes that for each multiplication $EM(T_M, x, 0)$ or $EM(T_M, x, 1)$ there is at least one sampled point in time t_i for which the amplitude of EM emanations follows a normal distribution $N(\mu_{M0}, \sigma_{M0})$ for $EM(T_M, x, 0)$ and $N(\mu_{M1}, \sigma_{M1})$ for $EM(T_M, x, 1)$. In an advantageous scenario, the point t_i may be accurately the amplitude of the EM emanation during the RAM access. To justify this model, we acquired 10000 EM traces from the RSA design mapped on the FPGA, when the private key is known. Figure 7(a) shows the histogram of the amplitude (in mV) during a fixed point where the architecture performs memory access by writing the multiplication results in the RAM. The sample points t_i during memory accesses follow a normal distribution with different means μ_{M0}, μ_{M1} and standard deviations σ_{M0}, σ_{M1}. Yet, Fig. 7(b) illustrates the histogram during the fixed point t_i where the architecture performs a RAM writing execution after the squarings.

With RAM addressing randomization, the same points t_i for $EM(T_M, x, 0)$ and $EM(T_M, x, 1)$ present similar distributions, meaning the SNR is reduced and SE attacks are more difficult now. Figure 7(c) and (d) show the normal distribution for multiplication and squaring, respectively. Note the average and standard deviation are very close even for different exponent bits.

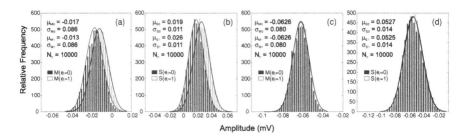

Fig. 7. Histogram and normal distribution of current measurements for (a)(b) non-randomized RAM and (c)(d) randomized RAM addressing.

5   Conclusion

In this paper, a performance and robustness evaluation of an RSA cryptocore implemented with RNS was proposed. We evaluated countermeasures at algorithmic, arithmetic and hardware levels in order to provide protection against side-channel analysis. The Montgomery Powering Ladder exponentiation is adopted in order to protect against simple side-channel analysis. We show that collision-based attacks remain efficient against an RSA-RNS. To defeat sophisticated SPA and collision attacks, we implemented countermeasures at arithmetic and hardware levels, by randomizing the RNS bases and the RAM memory addresses, respectively. The time overhead due to countermeasures is about 1 %.

References

1. Rivest, R., Shamir, A., Adleman, L.: A method for obtaining digital signatures and PKC. Commun. ACM **21**(2), 120–126 (1978)
2. Coron, J.-S.: Resistance against differential power analysis for elliptic curve cryptosystems. In: Koç, Ç.K., Paar, C. (eds.) CHES 1999. LNCS, vol. 1717, pp. 292–302. Springer, Heidelberg (1999)
3. Joye, M., Yen, S.-M.: The montgomery powering ladder. In: Kaliski Jr, B.S., Koç, Ç.K., Paar, C. (eds.) CHES 2002. LNCS, vol. 2523, pp. 291–302. Springer, Heidelberg (2003)
4. Bauer, A., Jaulmes, E., Prouff, E., Wild, J.: Horizontal and vertical side-channel attacks against secure RSA implementations. In: Dawson, E. (ed.) CT-RSA 2013. LNCS, vol. 7779, pp. 1–17. Springer, Heidelberg (2013)
5. Brier, E., Clavier, C., Olivier, F.: Correlation power analysis with a leakage model. In: Joye, M., Quisquater, J.-J. (eds.) CHES 2004. LNCS, vol. 3156, pp. 16–29. Springer, Heidelberg (2004)
6. Fouque, P.-A., Valette, F.: The doubling attack – *why upwards is better than downwards*. In: Walter, C.D., Koç, Ç.K., Paar, C. (eds.) CHES 2003. LNCS, vol. 2779, pp. 269–280. Springer, Heidelberg (2003)
7. Yen, S.-M., Lien, W.-C., Moon, S.-J., Ha, C.J.: Power analysis by exploiting chosen message and internal collisions – vulnerability of checking mechanism for RSA-decryption. In: Dawson, E., Vaudenay, S. (eds.) Mycrypt 2005. LNCS, vol. 3715, pp. 183–195. Springer, Heidelberg (2005)

8. Homma, N., Miyamoto, A., Aoki, T., Satoh, A., Shamir, A.: Comparative power analysis of modular exponentiation algorithms. IEEE Trans. Comput. **59**(6), 795–807 (2010)

9. Bajard, J.-C., Imbert, L., Liardet, P.-Y., Teglia, Y.: Leak resistant arithmetic. In: Joye, M., Quisquater, J.-J. (eds.) CHES 2004. LNCS, vol. 3156, pp. 62–75. Springer, Heidelberg (2004)

10. Bajard, J.-C., Didier, L-S., Kornerup, P.: An RNS montgomery modular multiplication algorithm. IEEE Trans. Comput. **47**(7), 766–776, 62–75 (1998)

11. Kawamura, S., Koike, M., Sano, F., Shimbo, A.: Cox-rower architecture for fast parallel montgomery multiplication. In: Preneel, B. (ed.) EUROCRYPT 2000. LNCS, vol. 1807, pp. 523–538. Springer, Heidelberg (2000)

12. Omondi, A., Prekumar, B.: Reside Number Systems: Theory and Implementation. Imperial College Press, London (2007)

13. Gandino, F., Lamberti, F., Montuschi, P., Bajard, J.-C.: A general approach for improving RNS montgomery exponentiation using pre-processing. In: ARITH20, pp. 195–204. IEEE Computer Society (2011)

14. Posch, K., Posch, R.: Modulo reduction in residue number systems. IEEE Trans. Parallel Distrib. Syst. **6**(5), 449–454 (1995)

15. Bajard, J.-C., Meloni, N., Plantard, T.: Efficient RNS bases for cryptography. In: Proceedings 17th IMACS World Congress, Scientific Computation, Applied Mathematics and Simulation, pp. 113–119 (2005)

16. Guillermin, N.: A coprocessor for secure and high speed modular arithmetic. Cryptology ePrint Archive, Report 2011/354 (2011)

17. Koc, K.: A fast algorithm for mixed-radix conversion in residue arithmetic. In: IEEE International Conference on Computer Design: VLSI in Computers and Processors, pp. 18–21, 2–4 October 1989

18. Heyszl, J., Mangard, S., Heinz, B., Stumpf, F., Sigl, G.: Localized electromagnetic analysis of cryptographic implementations. In: Dunkelman, O. (ed.) CT-RSA 2012. LNCS, vol. 7178, pp. 231–244. Springer, Heidelberg (2012)

19. Heyszl, J., Ibing, A., Mangard, S., Santis, F., Sigl, G.: Clustering algorithms for non-profiled single-execution attacks on exponentiations. IACR Cryptology ePrint Archive, vol. 2013, p. 438 (2013)

20. Perin, G., Torres, L., Benoit, P., Maurine, P.: Amplitude demodulation-based EM analysis of different RSA implementations. In: DATE, pp. 1167–1172 (2012)

21. Clavier, C., Feix, B., Gagnerot, G., Roussellet, M., Verneuil, V.: Horizontal correlation analysis on exponentiation. In: Soriano, M., Qing, S., López, J. (eds.) ICICS 2010. LNCS, vol. 6476, pp. 46–61. Springer, Heidelberg (2010)

22. Chari, S., Rao, J.R., Rohatgi, P.: Template attacks. In: Kaliski Jr, B.S., Koç, Ç.K., Paar, C. (eds.) CHES 2002. LNCS, vol. 2523, pp. 13–28. Springer, Heidelberg (2003)

Side Channel and Fault Attacks - Session Chair: Berndt Gammel

The Temperature Side Channel and Heating Fault Attacks

Michael Hutter[1]([✉]) and Jörn-Marc Schmidt[2]

[1] Institute for Applied Information Processing and Communications (IAIK),
Graz University of Technology, Inffeldgasse 16a, 8010 Graz, Austria
`Michael.Hutter@iaik.tugraz.at`
[2] Secunet Security Networks AG,
Mergenthalerallee 77, 65760 Eschborn, Germany
`joern-marc.schmidt@secunet.com`

Abstract. In this paper, we present practical results of data leakages of CMOS devices via the temperature side channel—a side channel that has been widely cited in literature but not well characterized yet. We investigate the leakage of processed data by passively measuring the dissipated heat of the devices. The temperature leakage is thereby linearly correlated with the power leakage model but is limited by the physical properties of thermal conductivity and capacitance. We further present heating faults by operating the devices beyond their specified temperature ratings. The efficiency of this kind of attack is shown by a practical attack on an RSA implementation. Finally, we introduce data remanence attacks on AVR microcontrollers that exploit the Negative Bias Temperature Instability (NBTI) property of internal SRAM cells. We show how to recover parts of the internal memory and present first results on an ATmega162. The work encourages the awareness of temperature-based attacks that are known for years now but not well described in literature. It also serves as a starting point for further research investigations.

Keywords: Temperature · Side channels · Fault injection · Negative Bias Temperature Instability · AVR · Smart cards

1 Introduction

It has been known since the late 1990s that implementations of cryptographic algorithms leak information from different side channels. The first paper that demonstrates the exploitation of a side channel was published by P. C. Kocher [24] in 1996. He highlighted that implementations might provide timing characteristics that leak information of private keys. Attacks are therefore able to extract the keys by simply measuring the runtime of the implemented algorithm. Three years later, he introduced the power-consumption side channel

---

J.-M. Schmidt – This work was done while the author was with Graz University of Technology.

A. Francillon and P. Rohatgi (Eds.): CARDIS 2013, LNCS 8419, pp. 219–235, 2014.
DOI: 10.1007/978-3-319-08302-5_15, © Springer International Publishing Switzerland 2014

together with B. Jun and J. Jaffe in [25]. They observed that key material can be also extracted from the power consumption of cryptographic devices. Since then, many researchers started to investigate the properties of these leakages on different platforms and devices. They also proposed to exploit other powerful side channels like electromagnetic (EM) emanation [1,13,16,31]. Up to now, the power and the EM side-channels have been widely established and used in academia and industry precisely because of simplicity, low-cost, and efficiency compared to other existing side channels.

Other lesser known and rather more exotic side channels (but not necessarily less powerful) are, for example, acoustic or optical emissions. Acoustic side channels have been first introduced by A. Shamir and E. Tromer [39] in 2004. They extended their work recently in 2013 [17] and provided a wide range of possible acoustic attacks, e.g., on GnuPG's RSA implementation. Heat causes mechanical stress which produces acoustic noise. This noise contains information about the power usage of CPUs and thus information about the processed data. A very related attack was also presented by D. Asonov and R. Agrawal [4] who exploited the fact that PC keyboards emanate different sounds that can be recognized at a distance. Improvements of the latter attack were reported by L. Zhuan et al. [43] in 2009. Optical emissions, in contrast, were investigated by J. Ferrigno and M. Hlaváč [15] as well as A. Schlösser et al. [35] who targeted an AES implementation. S. Skorobogatov [38] used a low-cost CCD camera to analyze the leakage of photons emitted from SRAM, EEPROM, and Flash memories.

The temperature side-channel has been often cited in literature [6,8,10,11,22, 23,30,36,42]. However, most of the publications only mention the existence and possibility to exploit this channel but without providing further investigations. In particular, H. Bar-El stated in [6] that temperature attacks on smart cards are "never documented in the open literature to the author's knowledge". The only publication that pinpoints the existence of the temperature side-channel is due to J. Brouchier et al. [10,11] from 2009. They showed that a cooling fan can carry information about the processed data indirectly through the dissipated temperature of a CPU. Within an experiment, they demonstrated how to extract bits from a secret password or possible RSA key (by assuming a low-frequency leak of the bits though, i.e., leaking a bit per three minutes). Furthermore, they emphasized that IP cores integrated in FPGAs might leak information to other IP cores in the system via the temperature side channel.

There are a few more papers on *active* temperature attacks, i.e., attacks that actively tamper the environmental temperature of a device (cooling or heating). Most of them demonstrate the efficiency of low-temperature attacks, e.g., as reported by S. Skorobogatov [40] and D. Samyde et al. [34] in 2002. They showed that by cooling down SRAM devices up to $-50\,°C$, they were able to *freeze* the data and to recover the content of the memory even after seconds after power-down (by exploiting the data retention property of SRAM cells). The same idea was used by T. Müller et al. [29] who presented a tool called FROST[1].

---

[1] FROST stands for *Forensic Recovery of Scrambled Telephones*.

The tool is able to recover the RAM content of modern Android smart phones similar to *cold boot attacks* on PCs [21]. High-temperature attacks, in contrast, have been investigated by J.-J. Quisquater and D. Samyde [32] who observed memory errors after hours of extensive heating. Similar results have been reported by S. Govindavajhala and A. Appel [19] who were able to induce errors into memories using a 50 W spotlight clip-on lamp. By heating an IBM JVM to 100 °C, they were able to inject faults with a probability of 71.4 % before their machine crashed.

In this paper, we describe a set of temperature-related attacks on common AVR and PIC 8-bit microcontrollers. There are three main contributions listed in the following:

1. We first characterize the "temperature side-channel" by presenting results of data leakages of AVR and PIC microcontrollers. We investigate the leakages and identify the linear relationship between heat radiation and circuit activity. It shows that the analyzed devices leak the Hamming weight of the processed data via the (low-frequency) temperature side channel.
2. We conduct high-temperature fault attacks on AVRs by operating the devices beyond their specified temperature ratings ($>150\,^\circ$C). A practical attack is shown on an RSA implementation where we successfully extracted the used private key.
3. Finally, we exploit the physical property of data remanence attacks on AVRs. By extensive heating, constant data like the private key gets burned in memory that can be recovered even after years. We identify permanent as well as transient NBTI degradation components and were able to fully recover 65 % of the entire memory of an ATmega162.

The rest of the paper is structured as follows. In Sect. 2, we characterize the temperature leakage of AVR microcontrollers. Section 3 presents results of heating fault attacks on RSA. In Sect. 4, we describe data remanence attacks. A discussion of the results is given in Sect. 5.

2   Temperature Leakage Characterization

In this section, we aim to characterize the temperature side channel by analyzing the leakage of an 8-bit ATmega162 AVR microcontroller [5]. This family of microcontrollers is widely used in embedded systems such as industrial automation, control, or in smart cards, e.g., integrated in the Funcard, ATmega Card, M2, KNOT, and Titanium programmable smart cards. First, we describe the setup to measure the temperature dissipation of these devices. Afterwards, we characterize the side channel in terms of its physical limits and possible exploitation efficiency.

2.1   The Setup to Measure the Temperature

Our setup is very similar to setups that are used to perform power-analysis attacks. Instead of measuring the power consumption of our target device, we

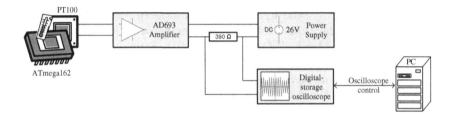

Fig. 1. Schematic view of the used setup to exploit the temperature side channel.

measure the dissipating temperature using a PT100 sensor element. The PT100 is a very common thermometer applied in various industry products. It measures the resistance of a platinum element having a resistance of 100 Ω at 0 °C. Next to the PT100, we use an AD693 amplifier (voltage to current converter) that provides a pre-calibrated Resistance Temperature Detector (RTD) interface allowing accurate measurements in the temperature range of 0 to +104 °C. In that configuration the output current span is 4 to 20 mA which was measured by calculating the voltage drop over a 390 Ω resistor in series to the power supply. We used a standard 1 GHz digital oscilloscope for that purpose and connected it to a PC that runs Matlab for controlling the measurement process. Figure 1 shows the schematic of the used setup.

In order to allow an accurate characterization of the temperature leakage, we decided to decapsulate the chip from the rear side and to measure the temperature dissipation directly on the surface of the silicon substrate. Figure 2 shows the decapsulated ATmega162 and the PT100 touching the rear side of the chip die. The PT100 has been surrounded by a thermal-conductance paste (4–10 W/(m K)) to allow a stable and accurate sensing of the temperature. Note that for the targeted device we had to remove the copper plate which is located below the chip die and the plastic package as similarly done by [36, 41]. Subsequently, we polished the substrate but we did not apply any additional thinning procedures. This can be simply done by using a skew driver.

In general, silicon substrate has a good thermal conductivity which is much higher than the conductivity of the surrounding die package. So it is advantageous to decapsulate the chip but this is not necessarily required. We also performed the experiments without decapsulating the chip and measured the temperature on the surface of the package (which corresponds to a non-invasive attack). We observed that the leakage is slightly weaker but strong enough to obtain similar results. Figure 3 shows a picture of the overall setup including a controller board that is used to communicate with the ATmega162 over a serial-communication interface.

2.2 Temperature Analysis

In order to characterize the leakage of our targeted device, we measured the temperature dissipation of various processed intermediate bytes and used a long

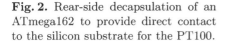

Fig. 2. Rear-side decapsulation of an ATmega162 to provide direct contact to the silicon substrate for the PT100.

Fig. 3. Side-channel measurement setup including controller board, ATmega162, and temperature-sensing circuit.

acquisition window to evaluate the impact of thermal conductivity and capacitance. As a target operation, we made use of a MOV instruction and moved all possible values of one input byte (i.e., 256) to 24 internal registers (the remaining 8 registers are used for loop indices and other temporary data). These MOV instructions were executed in a loop where the loop index and execution duration had been configurable by the PC. The temperature dissipation was then measured for a period of 20 s where in the first 10 s only zero values were moved to the registers and in the last 10 s, the current input-byte value was written to all registers[2]. For each input-byte value, we measured 100 traces and averaged them to reduce noise. Figure 4 zooms into the acquisition window showing the most interesting 10 s during the transient phase. It shows that in the first part of the traces, the temperature is equal for all inputs (the temperature is decreasing because of the fast acquisition runs and the higher temperature dissipation of previously measured traces). At the point when the actual input byte is written, the temperature increases depending on the Hamming weight of the processed value.

Figure 5 shows the temperature dissipation of all input-byte values at the time right before the end of the acquisition window, i.e., after about 18 s. It clearly shows that the temperature corresponds to the Hamming weight of the processed intermediate values ranging from 26.6 to about 26.8 °C. The temperature therefore linearly correlates with the power model of the device which was known and characterized using power analysis. If the circuit activity is high (meaning if there occur many bit transitions), the dissipated temperature increases. If the circuit activity is low due to less or no bit transitions, the temperature decreases. This, however, holds true not only for dynamic power consumption (caused by charging and discharging capacitances) but also for static power consumption

---

[2] We set all registers to zero before writing of new values to guarantee the transitions of all bits (avoiding Hamming-distance leaks).

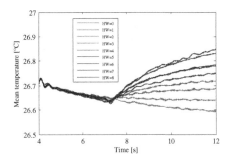

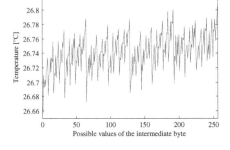

Fig. 4. Slow temperature increase of all Hamming weights that are processed by the ATmega162.

Fig. 5. The ATmega162 leaks the Hamming weight of all 256 possible intermediate values through the temperature.

(caused through sub-threshold and leakage current). Both components cause an averaged DC increase in temperature.

From Fig. 4 it is also observable that the temperature increases and decreases very slowly. While the circuit activity is constantly high or low, the temperature increases or decreases by about $0.3\,^{\circ}$C over a period of 10 s. This has its reason in the following facts. First, the temperature variation is limited by the physical property of thermal conductivity. The heat flow from the die (causing thermal power) to the sensing element can be seen as an RC network including resistance and capacitances for the junction (i.e., chip die), the package/case, heat sink, and ambient air. This RC network has the typical property that it consists of large (thermal) capacitances that causes the network to behave like a low-pass filter. The cut-off frequency is thereby very low (typically between some Hz and tens of kHz [2]). This means also that high frequency leakages (>1 MHz), which usually appear in CMOS devices, will not be easily exploitable from that side channel because the information will be largely filtered by the RC network. The measured temperature signal at the sensor element therefore contains all superimposed and integrated signal components of the power consumption. As a second reason, the used temperature sensors have a certain response time and acquisition resolution. In our experiment, we used a PT100 that has a thermal response time of 100 ms and a resolution of $0.01\,^{\circ}$C.

It shows that the temperature side-channel has a very low bandwidth limiting practical attacks. In the following, we discuss possible attack scenarios for low-frequency temperature leakages:

1. An attack exploiting the temperature side-channel is possible in case the leakage of the data is present over a period of several milliseconds or seconds. If an application repeatedly checks a password, for example in a loop, enough information is available even in limited frequency bands that allows low-bandwidth attacks [10,11].
2. Many RSA implementations involve operations that take a long time, e.g., modular exponentiations. These operations create signals in a low frequency

band that can be revealed by low-bandwidth acoustic attacks as recently shown by D. Genkin, A. Shamir, and E. Tromer [17]. These low-bandwidth signals can be also extracted from the temperature side channel.

3. A very powerful attack which is not well investigated yet is the exploitation of static power-consumption leakages. Most of side-channel based analyses are exploiting the dynamic power-consumption which is the main contributor to the total power consumption of electronic devices. With shrinking CMOS technology, static leakages become more significant. Temperature attacks exploiting the static power-consumption benefit from less strict timing constraints because the leakage is *statically* available over an infinite period of time. A. Moradi recently demonstrated successful power-analysis attacks exploiting the static leakage of FPGAs in [28]. Other works also characterized and exploited static leakages of CMOS devices, for example, in [18, 26].

3 Exploiting Heating Faults on AVRs

In this section, we intentionally operate a target device beyond its maximum temperature ratings in order to produce exploitable faults due to extensive heating. Each electronic device specifies a certain temperature range where the correct operation is guaranteed by the manufacturer. If these limits are exceeded by external influences, data might get modified that is stored in memories or processed by the CPU. Faulty cryptographic operations can then be exploited in attacks to reveal the secret key [6, 7, 23, 36].

In the following experiments, we used the same ATmega162 as used in the previous experiments. To prove the practicability of our attack, we implemented RSA, induced heating faults, and successfully extracted the private key used during encryption of data, cf. Bellcore attack [9].

Setup and RSA Implementation. We used a low-cost laboratory heating plate from Schott instruments (SLK 1) to heat-up and induce faults in an ATmega162. The microcontroller has been placed directly on top of the hot-plate surface, lying top-side down to allow a good heat transfer. The temperature of the internal IC has then been measured by calculating the mean of two PT100 sensors to be more accurate. One PT100 has been placed on the rear side of the ATmega162, the other PT100 has been placed directly on the surface of the heating plate. Both PT100 are connected to an oscilloscope similar to the setup described in the previous section. Figure 6 shows the setup.

We connected and used only six mandatory pins of the ATmega162: power supply (VCC and ground), serial communication (RX and TX), clock signal, and reset. For these connections, we used exposed wires to avoid any contact to the hot plate and the melting of solder[3] during long-time heat exposure. As a controlling device, we used an FPGA board (Spartan-3) that is connected with the measurement PC.

---

[3] The temperature melting point of Sn63/Pb37 lead solder, which is commonly used for electrical soldering, is 456 K (183 °C).

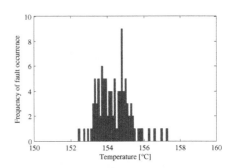

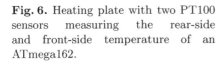

Fig. 6. Heating plate with two PT100 sensors measuring the rear-side and front-side temperature of an ATmega162.

Fig. 7. Distribution of fault occurrence between 150 and 160 °C. Mean fault-induction temperature is 154.4 °C.

We decided to target an RSA implementation that implements the Chinese Remainder Theorem (CRT). This attack is very simple and well documented in literature [6,9,36]. Only one single fault during the computation can reveal the secret RSA primes p and q. The attack and evaluation of faulty computations has been performed using Sage [33]. A description of the attack is given in Appendix A.1.

3.1   Heating-up the Target

The used heating plate provides ten heating stages that can be adjusted manually going up to 1,000 K, i.e., about 727 °C. By manual adjustment, we were able to heat up the device under test up to 150 °C within about 5 min.

In a first observation, we identified that the ATmega162 does not respond to requests anymore if the heating temperature is higher than around 160 °C. Note that this is much higher than the *operating temperature* maximum ratings given in the device specification [5], i.e., between −55 °C and +125 °C and it is approximately as high as the given maximum *storage temperature* rating of the device which is 150 °C. As a key observation, we identified that the device starts producing faults between a certain heating window of about 152 and 158 °C. During this window, the probability is high that the device outputs an incorrect result because of an induced fault during the computation of the implemented algorithm.

In order to quantify this behavior, we performed several measurements on that device taking about 70 min. We performed an RSA decryption operation every 650 ms and kept the heating temperature between 150 and 160 °C by manually adjusting the heating plate. As a result, we got 100 faults where 31 of this set have been exploitable, i.e., the attack revealed one of the used prime moduli. In the other cases, the fault was induced during I/O communication or other parts of the computation such that the difference of the faulty and a correct signature output was coprime to the RSA modulus and thus was not factorizable. In addition to these outcomes, we identified that 16 out of the 31 faulty computations, revealed the prime modulus p and 15 revealed the prime modulus q. Hence, the probability that a fault reveals p or q is expected to be about 50 %—a result that was expected since both p and q have the nearly the same size and the modular exponentiation with these primes take the same amount of time and therefore provide the same fault-induction window. Furthermore, 23 out of the 31 faulty computations have been unique and different whereas 7 faults have been repeated, i.e., the RSA decryption yielded an output that was already obtained in a previous measurement. For the latter case, we can therefore assume that either some internal memory locations or internal logic parts are more sensitive to heating than others, thus causing the same RSA outputs. Figure 7 shows the frequency of the induced faults. Most of the faults occurred between 152 and 158 °C having a mean fault-induction temperature of about 154.4 °C.

We made the same experiment also using other ATmega162 devices (new once) in order to verify our results. First, it showed that the mean fault-induction temperature for each device is slightly different and varies per device. Second, it showed that the number of faults is different per device (e.g., we got 182 faults within 30 min for another device) which is likely because the temperature has to be adjusted manually in our setup and varies per measurement. But the attack succeeded for all devices within less than 30 min.

4 Data Remanence Attacks on AVRs

In this section, we characterize the property of data remanence effects of the internal SRAM cells of an ATmega162. It is known that data which is stored in the same location after each power-up of a device (such as a secret key that is loaded from program memory/flash to RAM) leaves a permanent mark that can be recovered as, for example, detailed by P. Gutmann in [20]. He observed that data that is stored in SRAM or DRAM for a long period of time remembers the value when powered-up again even after years. This effect has been practically exploited in an attack by R. Anderson and M. Kuhn [3] who were able to recover 90–95 % of a DES master key used by an old bank security module from the late 1980s. C. Cakir et al. [12] have characterized the data remanence effect on newer 65 nm CMOS RAMs which was considered to be not that efficient because of the newer SRAM structures. However, they were able to recover about 18 % of the entire SRAM content (in fact, 82 % have been recovered correctly out of 22 % predictable bits).

The SRAM data remanence effect can be explained as follows. SRAM cells that are exposed to extensive heating are subject to accelerated aging where internal transistor parameters get changed. This effect is known under Negative Bias Temperature Instability (NBTI) and has been first observed in the late 1960s. Since then, many researchers identified that this effect decreases parameters such as speed, drive current, and noise margins. In fact, NBTI occurs when transistors are stressed with negative gate voltages at elevated temperatures, e.g., during burn-in stress. Then, the (absolute) threshold voltages of the transistors increase which change the preferred power-up state of SRAM cells. Thus, transistors get "weaker" and tend to a certain bit value after power-up. Note that NBTI has been basically observed for both PMOS and NMOS transistors while PMOS transistors are more affected [37].

The study of M. Ershov et al. [14] showed that there exist two NBTI degradation components: one component that remains after burn-in stress (permanent damage), and another component (transient damage) that recovers within a certain amount of time (seconds up to days). In the following, we identify these two degradation components in practical experiments on the ATmega162. We used the same setup as it was used in the previous section to heat up the device.

Before we started the experiments, we determined the preferred power-up values of the ATmega162 in order to evaluate the effect of burn-in stress. A small program was written that allows reading and writing of SRAM content over the serial interface. A byte array of 6,144 bits (out of the available 8,192 bits) was used for testing. After we disconnected all I/O connections from the device for some milliseconds[4], which has been accomplished with our flexible FPGA controller board, we read out the SRAM content. This has been done 100 times to average noise. It showed that 3,101 bits (50.47 %) are powered-up to the value *one* and 3,043 bits (49.53 %) are set to *zero* on average, i.e., there was almost no bias in the distributions.

4.1   Permanent Data Remanence Effects After Burn-In Stress

We programmed the internal SRAM of the ATmega162 with normally distributed random data. We set 3,072 bits to 0 and 3,072 bits to 1 at random locations[5]. A first test after a power-up reset showed that the probability of guessing the bits correctly was around 50 % as expected. After this test, we exposed the device to extensive burn-in stress to accelerate aging effects. The stress conditions were a high ambient temperature of about 100 °C and an over-voltage supply of 5.5 Volts. We applied the stress over a period of 36 h and read out the power-up SRAM content afterwards. The read out values are then compared with the initial values.

It showed that the number of bits that are one or zero got biased due to NBTI degradation. There were 3,210 bits (52.24 %) set to one and 2,934 bits (47.75 %) set to zero after the burn-in stress. Furthermore, 919 bits of the total memory changed their state (i.e., 15 %): 405 bits moved from 1 to 0 and 514 bits moved from 0 to 1. From these 405 bits there were 393 bits that moved to the correct value zero (97.04 %) and 489 from 514 bits moved to the correct value one (95.14 %).

---

[4] We disconnected not only the power supply but also the RS232 interface and the clock signal to guarantee that the device (and SRAM respectively) is completely unconnected and not powered by I/O interfaces. Note also that we used hardware relays to actually disconnect all connections.

[5] We do not assume the knowledge of "preferred power-up values" before burn-in stress to guarantee a realistic attacking scenario.

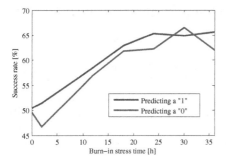

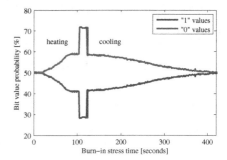

Fig. 8. Probability of predicting a SRAM bit correctly increases from 50 % to about 65 % after burn-in stress.

Fig. 9. Bit-value distribution during heating and cooling (transient data remanence effect).

Note that in our analysis, we were only able to identify half of the *unstable* SRAM cells. This is because from the set of unstable SRAM cells, statistically only half of the bits changed to the correct value while the other half already held the correct value. So, in our experiment, we can assume about 30 % of unstable SRAM cells and 70 % of cells that are *stable*, i.e., they did not change at least during our burn-in stress of 36 h. Now, by guessing 50 % of all stable cells correctly and by assuming a high probability of guessing all unstable bits correctly, we are able to successfully predict 65 % of the entire SRAM memory. This nicely corresponds to our practical results where we achieved a success rate of about 63 %, i.e., 3,842 bits have been predicted correctly as shown in Fig. 8. It shows that there is a huge increase during the first 20 h. After that, the probability keeps nearly constant. We also performed a measurement one week after the burn-in stress and identified no changes in the success rate.

4.2 Transient Data Remanence Effects During Burn-In Stress

We also characterized the transient data remanence effect during the burn-in stress process. For this experiment, we used a new ATmega162 and read out the SRAM content every 4 s while the device was heated up. Figure 9 shows the bit-value distribution during the burn-in stress and right after it. In the first 115 s, the device is heated up to 170 °C. After that, the heating plate was turned off to cool down the device. Between 105 and 125 s, the device was overheated which produced a significant jump in the probability distribution.

The experiment showed that the effect of NBTI degradation of PMOS and NMOS transistors in SRAM cells is also observable in the transient heating phase. The heating temporarily enforces the transistors to change the state. Note that this effect is only transient and the cells regenerate after cooling. The number of zero values increases during heating while the number of ones decreases accordingly. In our experiment, 820 bits changed their state to either 0 or 1. From these 820 bits, 257 bits were the same that also changed during the long-term burn-in stress, i.e., we could identify 31.3 % of all bits that are apparently unstable.

How to Exploit NBTI Degradation? Many implementations of cryptographic algorithms store the secret key in non-volatile memory and load it into SRAM when needed. This key is then loaded always at the same memory location in SRAM because the program code or hardware implementation is usually given and not changeable. Hence, the key value gets "burned" into SRAM within a period of time, e.g., some weeks or months. The key can then be extracted by the following data-remanence attacks:

1. If an attacker is in possession of several implementations that store the same secret key, the attacker can recover parts of the internal SRAM of each implementation and can then average the obtained results to reveal all bits of the memory with high probability. This attack assumes that each implementation reveals the content of different SRAM cells.
2. If an attacker is in possession of only one implementation (or several implementations using different keys), he/she can first apply a burn-in stress test over several hours in order to artificially accelerate aging. As a second step, he/she can read out the preferred SRAM content. In order to identify useful bits, the attacker can mount a transient remanence attack to reveal *unstable* SRAM cells which potentially changed their state during the burn-in stress and which contain useful information about the secret key. All other cells are then considered as stable in this attack and provide no useful information. Finally, all recovered bits are used in partial-key recovery attacks.

5   Discussion and Further Research Suggestions

In the following, we discuss further research questions arisen by this work:

- The presented attacks have been performed on microcontrollers that were fabricated in rather old process technologies. Further research has to be done to evaluate the impact of thermal attacks on ICs with newer CMOS technologies.
- The temperature side channel provides a low-bandwidth characteristic. High-frequency leakages (e.g., containing data-dependent signals in the MHz or even GHz scale) can therefore not be directly exploited due to the low-pass filter characteristics. However, there exist implementations that use long operations like exponentiations in RSA that can create low-frequency signatures that are however exploitable (as demonstrated in [17,39] using acoustic signals in the kHz range).
- In order to validate our measurement setup, we also performed the measurements using a $0\,\Omega$ resistor instead of a PT100 element. This is done because it naturally raises the question if the measured data really corresponds to the dissipated temperature or if it is caused by other side-channel sources, e.g., EM modulated signals. Using the resistor, however, we were not able to identify any data-dependent signals so that we can exclude any signal interferences or the coupling of EM signals.

- We also characterized the temperature leakage of an 8-bit PIC16F84 microcontroller from Microchip Technology. We obtained similar results and could identify temperature-dependent processing of data. Details are given in Appendix A.2.
- Heat penetrates through different materials. Thus, the thermal conductivity of CMOS devices might be exploited in attacks where the heat conducts through EM shielding countermeasures (metal plates, mesh of power lines, sensors, etc.).
- *How does the temperature affect power-analysis attacks?* This question has been answered by A. Vijaykumar [42] in her master's thesis. She evaluated temperature variation effects on Differential Power Analysis (DPA) attacks. By targeting KeeLoq and DES, she showed that the efficiency of DPA decreases with increased temperature due to decreasing power variances.
- By heating or cooling CMOS devices, the characteristics not only of memory but also of logic changes. Thermal attacks might even be used to circumvent countermeasure implementations, e.g., by increasing/decreasing the threshold voltages of watchdog implementations.
- The suitability of temperature attacks that indirectly exploit the leakage of *static* power consumption has to be investigated in future. Static power consumption is becoming more and more important as CMOS technology is shrinking. A static leak of an intermediate value of a cryptographic implementation creates a DC offset signal in the baseband that can be exploited in attacks that are provided with very low-bandwidth leakages from side channels such as the temperature or acoustic sound.

Acknowledgements. The work has been supported by the European Commission through the ICT program under contract ICT-SEC-2009-5-258754 (Tamper Resistant Sensor Node - TAMPRES), by the Austrian Science Fund (FWF) under the grant number TRP251-N23 (Realizing a Secure Internet of Things - ReSIT), and the European Cooperation in Science and Technology (COST) Action IC1204 (Trustworthy Manufacturing and Utilization of Secure Devices - TRUDEVICE).

A   Appendix

A.1   Attacking CRT-RSA Using Faults

In the following, we consider an implementation of an RSA decryption that uses the Chinese Remainder Theorem (CRT) to speed up the computation. In our scenario, an adversary is able to supply the card with an input that is encrypted using textbook RSA and receives the decrypted message from the card. Further, the adversary is able to disturb the computation of this decryption and receives the result of this faulted computation. In order to describe how an adversary can benefit from this scenario to factor the modulus and thus compute the secret decryption key, we denote $n = pq$ an RSA modulus, where p and q are two large prime numbers. Let d be the private key and $e = d^{-1} \bmod \varphi(n)$ the corresponding public exponent. Furthermore, $z = \mathrm{CRT}(x, y)$ denotes the CRT recombination of the value $z \in \mathbf{Z}_n$ from values x, y of the subgroups $\mathbf{Z}_p$ and $\mathbf{Z}_q$ where

$$\text{CRT } (x, y) = xc_p + yc_q \bmod n$$

with $c_p = q\,(q^{-1} \bmod p)$ and $c_q = p\,(p^{-1} \bmod q)$ [27].

The usage of the CRT in this scenario allows computing two exponentiations in smaller sub-groups compared to a single exponentiations modulo n:

$$S \equiv \text{CRT } ((m^d \bmod p), (m^d \bmod q)) \bmod n.$$

The first fault attack that takes advantage of injecting a random fault Δ in this scenario was presented by Boneh et al. [9]. The fault Δ causes the device to output a value $\tilde{S}$ instead of S:

$$\tilde{S} \equiv \text{CRT } ((m \bmod p)^d, (m \bmod q)^d + \Delta) \bmod n$$
$$\equiv m^d + \Delta p\,(p^{-1} \bmod q) \bmod n.$$

If an adversary gets hold of both a faulty $\tilde{S}$ and a correct signature S, the modulus n can be easily factorized by calculating $p = \gcd(\tilde{S} - S, n)$.

A.2   Temperature Leakage of a PIC16F84

We also investigated the leakage of a PIC16F84 microcontroller. We used the same measurement setup as described in Sect. 2 and measured the temperature on the decapsulated rear-side of the chip using a PT100 element. Instead of a MOV operation, we target an ADD instruction that adds either 0x00 or 0xFF to all internal registers that are previously initialized with zero. We measured 500 traces and averaged them to reduce noise.

Figure 10 shows the result where a zero value was written continuously over a period of 10 s. The value 0xFF is written afterwards for another 10 s. It shows an increase of temperature in the second half of the acquisition window. No leakage occurs in the first half of the trace. In Fig. 11, the result is shown when 0xFF is

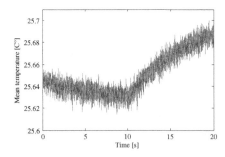

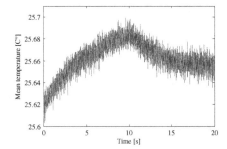

Fig. 10. Leakage of 0xFF in the second half of the acquisition window. No leakage during the first 10 s.

Fig. 11. Leakage of 0xFF in the first half of the acquisition window. The mean temperature decreases afterwards.

written during the first 10 s, and zero is written afterwards. There, it shows that the temperature slowly increases, similarly to the second half of Fig. 10. After 10 s, the temperature is decreasing again.

References

1. Agrawal, D., Archambeault, B., Rao, J.R., Rohatgi, P.: The EM side-channel(s). In: Kaliski Jr, B.S., Koç, Ç.K., Paar, C. (eds.) CHES 2002. LNCS, vol. 2523, pp. 29–45. Springer, Heidelberg (2003)
2. Altet, J., Rubio, A., Schaub, E., Dilhaire, S., Claeys, W.: Thermal coupling in integrated circuits: application to thermal testing. IEEE J. Solid-State Circ. **36**(1), 81–91 (2001)
3. Anderson, R.J., Kuhn, M.G.: Low cost attacks on tamper resistant devices. In: Christianson, B., Lomas, M., Crispo, B., Roe, M. (eds.) Security Protocols 1997. LNCS, vol. 1361, pp. 125–136. Springer, Heidelberg (1998)
4. Asonov, D., Agrawal, R.: Keyboard acoustic emanations. In: IEEE Symposium on Security and Privacy, pp. 3–11 (2004)
5. Atmel Corporation.: ATmega 162/v Datasheet (2003)
6. Bar-El, H., Choukri, H., Naccache, D., Tunstall, M., Whelan, C.: The Sorcerer's apprentice guide to fault attacks. Cryptology ePrint Archive. Report 2004/100 (2004). http://eprint.iacr.org/
7. Barenghi, A., Bertoni, G., Parrinello, E., Pelosi, G.: Low voltage fault attacks on the RSA cryptosystem. In: Workshop on Fault Diagnosis and Tolerance in Cryptography - FDTC 2009, pp. 23–31, Lausanne, Switzerland, 2009. Proceedings (2009)
8. Barenghi, A., Breveglieri, L., Koren, I., Naccache, D.: Fault injection attacks on cryptographic devices: theory, practice and countermeasures. Proc. IEEE **100**(11), 3056–3076 (2012)
9. Boneh, D., DeMillo, R.A., Lipton, R.J.: On the importance of checking cryptographic protocols for faults (extended abstract). In: Fumy, W. (ed.) EUROCRYPT 1997. LNCS, vol. 1233, pp. 37–51. Springer, Heidelberg (1997)
10. Brouchier, J., Dabbous, N., Kean, T., Marsh, C., Naccache, D.: Thermocommunication. ePrint (2009)
11. Brouchier, J., Kean, T., Marsh, C., Naccache, D.: Temperature attacks. IEEE Secur. Priv. **7**(2), 79–82 (2009)
12. Cakir, C., Bhargava, M., Mai, K.: 6 T SRAM and 3 T DRAM data retention and remanence characterization in 65 nm bulk CMOS. In: Custom Integrated Circuits Conference - CICC 2012, pp. 1–4, San Jose, USA, 9–12 Sept 2012
13. Carluccio, D., Lemke, K., Paar, C.: Electromagnetic side channel analysis of a contactless smart card: first results. In: Oswald, E. (ed.) Workshop on RFID and Lightweight Crypto (RFIDSec05), pp. 44–51, Graz, Austria, 13–15 July 2005
14. Ershov, M., Saxena, S., Karbasi, H., Winters, S., Minehane, S., Babcock, J., Lindley, R., Clifton, P., Redford, M., Shibkov, A.: Dynamic recovery of negative bias temperature instability in p-type metal-oxide-semiconductor field-effect transistors. Appl. Phys. Lett. **83**(8), 1647–1649 (2003)
15. Ferrigno, J., Hlaváč, M.: When AES blinks: introducing optical side channel. IET Inf. Secur. **2**(3), 94–98 (2008)
16. Gandolfi, K., Mourtel, C., Olivier, F.: Electromagnetic analysis: concrete results. In: Koç, Ç.K., Naccache, D., Paar, C. (eds.) CHES 2001. LNCS, vol. 2162, pp. 251–261. Springer, Heidelberg (2001)

17. Genkin, D., Shamir, A., Tromer, E.: RSA key extraction via low-bandwidth acoustic cryptanalysis. ePrint, Dec 2013
18. Giogetti, J., Scotti, G., Simonetti, A., Trifiletti, A.: Analysis of data dependence of leakage current in CMOS cryptographic hardware. In: Proceedings of the 17th ACM Great Lakes Symposium on VLSI, pp. 78–83, Stresa-Lago Maggiore, Italy. ACM, 11–13 Mar 2007
19. Govindavajhala, S., Appel, A.W.: Using memory errors to attack a virtual machine. In: Proceedings of the 2003 IEEE Symposium on Security and Privacy, pp. 154–165 (2003)
20. Gutmann, P.: Data remanence in semiconductor devices. In : USENIX 2001 - Proceedings of the 10th Conference on USENIX Security Symposium, Washington, DC, USA, Berkeley, CA, USA, 2001. USENIX Association, 13–17 Aug 2001
21. Halderman, J., Schoen, S.D., Heninger, N., Clarkson, W., Paul, W., Calandrino, J.A., Feldman, A.J., Appelbaum, J., Felten, E.W.: Lest we remember: cold boot attacks on encryption keys. In: 17th USENIX Security Symposium, pp. 45–60, San Jose, CA, July 2008
22. Hutter, M., Schmidt, J.-M., Plos, T.: RFID and its vulnerability to faults. In: Oswald, E., Rohatgi, P. (eds.) CHES 2008. LNCS, vol. 5154, pp. 363–379. Springer, Heidelberg (2008)
23. Karaklajíc, D., Schmidt, J.-M., Verbauwhede, I.: Hardware designers guide to fault attacks. In: IEEE Transactions on Very Large Scale Integration (VLSI) Systems, pp. 1–12 (2012)
24. Kocher, P.C.: Timing attacks on implementations of Diffie-Hellman, RSA, DSS, and other systems. In: Koblitz, N. (ed.) CRYPTO 1996. LNCS, vol. 1109, pp. 104–113. Springer, Heidelberg (1996)
25. Kocher, P.C., Jaffe, J., Jun, B.: Differential power analysis. In: Wiener, M. (ed.) CRYPTO 1999. LNCS, vol. 1666, pp. 388–397. Springer, Heidelberg (1999)
26. Lin, L., Burleson, W.: Leakage-based differential power analysis (LDPA) on sub-90 nm CMOS cryptosystems. In: ISCAS 2008 - IEEE International Symposium on Circuits and Systems, pp. 252–255, Seattle, USA, 18–21 May 2008
27. Menezes, A.J., van Oorschot, P.C., Vanstone, S.A.: Handbook of Applied Cryptography. Series on Discrete Mathematics and Its Applications. CRC Press, Boca Raton (1997). ISBN 0-8493-8523-7. http://www.cacr.math.uwaterloo.ca/hac/
28. Moradi, A.: Side-channel leakage through static power - should we care about in practice? ePrint, Jan 2014
29. Müller, T., Spreitzenbarth, M.: FROST. In: Jacobson, M., Locasto, M., Mohassel, P., Safavi-Naini, R. (eds.) ACNS 2013. LNCS, vol. 7954, pp. 373–388. Springer, Heidelberg (2013)
30. Otto, M.: Fault attacks and countermeasures. Ph.D. thesis, Universität Paderborn (2005)
31. Quisquater, J.-J., Samyde, D.: A new tool for non-intrusive analysis of smart cards based on electro-magnetic emissions, the SEMA and DEMA methods. Presented at the rump session of EUROCRYPT 2000 (2000)
32. Quisquater, J.-J., Samyde, D.: Eddy current for magnetic analysis with active sensor. In: Proceedings of the 3rd International Conference on Research in SmartCards (E-Smart'02), pp. 185–194, Nice, France. UCL, Sept 2002
33. SageMath.: Sage: open source mathematics software system (2013). http://sagemath.org
34. Samyde, D., Skorobogatov, S.P., Anderson, R.J., Quisquater, J.-J.: On a new way to read data from memory. In: IEEE Security in Storage Workshop (SISW02), pp. 65–69. IEEE Computer Society (2002)

35. Schlösser, A., Nedospasov, D., Krämer, J., Orlic, S., Seifert, J.-P.: Simple photonic emission analysis of AES. In: Prouff, E., Schaumont, P. (eds.) CHES 2012. LNCS, vol. 7428, pp. 41–57. Springer, Heidelberg (2012)

36. Schmidt, J.-M., Hutter, M.: Optical and EM fault-attacks on CRT-based RSA: concrete results. In: Posch, K.C., Wolkerstorfer, J. (eds.) Proceedings of Austrochip 2007, pp. 61–67, Graz, Austria. Verlag der Technischen Universität Graz, 11 Oct 2007. ISBN 978-3-902465-87-0

37. Schroder, D.K.: Negative bias temperature instability: what do we understand? J. Microelectr. Reliab. **47**(6), 841–852 (2006)

38. Skorobogatov, S.: Using optical emission analysis for estimating contribution to power consumption. In: Fault Diagnosis and Tolerance in Cryptography (FDTC) (2009)

39. Shamir, A., Tromer, E.: Acoustic cryptanalysis - on nosy people and noisy machines. http://www.wisdom.weizmann.ac.il/~tromer/acoustic/. Preliminary proof-of-concept presentation

40. Skorobogatov, S.: Low temperature data remanence in static RAM. Technical report, University of Cambridge Computer Laboratory, June 2002

41. Skorobogatov, S.P.: Semi-invasive attacks - a new approach to hardware security analysis. Ph.D. thesis, University of Cambridge - Computer Laboratory (2005). http://www.cl.cam.ac.uk/TechReports/

42. Vijaykumar, A.: DPA resistance of cryptographic circuits considering temperature and process variations. Master's thesis, University of Cincinnati, Engineering and Applied Science: Computer Engineering, July 2012

43. Zhuang, L., Zhou, F., Tyga, J.D.: Keyboard acoustic emanations revisited. ACM Trans. Inf. Syst. Secur. **13**(1), 373–382 (2009)

Glitch It If You Can: Parameter Search Strategies for Successful Fault Injection

Rafael Boix Carpi[1]([✉]), Stjepan Picek[2,3], Lejla Batina[2], Federico Menarini[1], Domagoj Jakobovic[3], and Marin Golub[3]

[1] Riscure BV, Delft, The Netherlands
{BoixCarpi,Menarini}@riscure.com
[2] Radboud University Nijmegen, Nijmegen, The Netherlands
{s.picek,lejla}@cs.ru.nl
[3] Faculty of Electrical Engineering and Computing, Zagreb, Croatia
{domagoj.jakobovic,marin.golub}@fer.hr

Abstract. Fault analysis poses a serious threat to embedded security devices, especially smart cards. In particular, modeling faults and finding effective practical approaches that are also generic is considered to be of interest for smart card industry. In this work we propose a novel methodology to deal with a difficult question of choosing multiple parameters required for effective faults. To this aim, we investigate several algorithms and find a new promising direction using evolutionary computation. Our experimental results on some of the smart cards used today show the potential of this new approach. Our best algorithm is a tailored search strategy especially developed for the purpose of finding the best choice of parameters for glitching. With this approach we found some of off-the-shelf devices, although secured against this type of attacks, still vulnerable.

Keywords: Fault analysis · Glitches · Smart cards · Self-adaptive algorithms · Evolutionary computation

1 Introduction

Since smart cards are around in our lives for the past three decades, and becoming ever more pervasive, it seems impossible that we ever lived without them. Yet, at the same time the threats to the security of those small devices are multiple and cheap and at the same time effective countermeasures against various attacks belong to the most extensively researched topics today.

In 1996 Anderson and Kuhn [1] discussed the tamper-resistance of smart cards, and in 1999 Kömmerling and Kuhn presented a set of techniques for tampering with them [2]. It became evident that the possibilities for the adversary are numerous. In general, the techniques for tampering can be classified as *passive* or *active*. In passive techniques some side-channel information is monitored and there is no interference with the normal processing of the card. An example of

A. Francillon and P. Rohatgi (Eds.): CARDIS 2013, LNCS 8419, pp. 236–252, 2014.
DOI: 10.1007/978-3-319-08302-5_16, © Springer International Publishing Switzerland 2014

these passive techniques is the analysis of power consumption, as introduced by Kocher et al. [3] or electromagnetic radiation [4]. In the case of active techniques, the device is not only monitored but also external interferences affect the normal behavior of the device. An example is Fault Injection (FI) and these interferences, the so-called *glitches*, can be of different nature: optical (laser pulses) and electrical glitches (voltage, clock), temperature changes, electromagnetic (EM) radiation, etc. are used to cause some malfunctioning, resulting in some cases in secret key recovery. Fault injection techniques by glitching are typically *non-invasive* techniques, in the sense that the smart card is not physically modified (versus other *invasive* techniques that require hardware modifications).

A fault injection attack is considered to be successful if after exposing the device under attack to a specially crafted external interference, the device shows an unexpected behavior, which can be exploited by an attacker (e.g. leaking of sensitive information, bypassing security checks, etc.). However, this external interference has to be precisely tuned for the fault injection to succeed. As an example, a complete characterization of a clock signal glitch requires from the security analyst to define more than 10 parameters (related to clock signal voltage levels, time offset of the glitch, etc.). In addition, hardware designers introduce countermeasures in their devices for preventing fault injection attacks. Hence, finding the correct parameter setting is a highly non-deterministic process, and countermeasures just add up to this non-determinism. As a consequence, security analysts usually set a value range for each parameter, and leave their fault injection setup experimenting over thousands of different parameter configurations within those given ranges to be analyzed off-line afterwards.

Finding the correct parameters for a successful FI can be considered as a search problem where one aims to find, within minimum time, the parameter configuration or ranges of parameter values which result in a successful fault injection. The search space, considering all possible combinations of the values of interest for the fault injection such as voltage, timing, offset, etc., is too large to perform an exhaustive search. For example, there are in total 8 parameters to be set for voltage (VCC) glitching even without considering multiple glitches. As a simple example, testing only 6 values yields $6^8 = 1676916$ parameter combinations! This is unfeasible to test in a reasonable amount of time as it would take over 19 days assuming a quite fast rate of one measurement per second. Here, by a measurement we mean a complete execution of the algorithm of interests on the device including the final response (which can have several different outcomes such as reset, stop, etc.) Considering this problem within the tasks of a security analyst, which often has a very limited or no knowledge about the inner design of the device (*blackbox* testing), setting an accurate range for the parameters can be quite challenging, and a bad estimation of these ranges leads to spending a lot of time in testing parameter combinations that could have been easily discarded upfront.

Due to all these issues and the unfeasibility of performing an exhaustive search due to the time constraints, there is a clear need for a methodology for parameters search that can ultimately lead to a more effective security evaluation. In this work we present several possibilities for finding and tuning the parameters keeping the assumptions on the device under attack as generic as possible. We show several effective approaches that were tested on off-the-shelf devices with different successes. We develop a search strategy that is especially tailored towards a large class of devices of today using common assumptions and defining a new model. Our best algorithm is proven to be efficient against some state-of-the-art protected (against glitching) devices. Furthermore, a new direction based on generic algorithms is also investigated and found suitable when less is known about the device under attack.

1.1 Related Work

The concept of fault analysis-based attacks is known in the research community for around twenty years. Boneh, DeMillo and Lipton published an attack on RSA about exploiting hardware faults for cryptanalysis [5,6]. The attack described, often also called the Bellcore attack, resulted in numerous contributions in, not just theoretical papers on attacks and countermeasures assuming that faults can be applied, but also in more practical works showing what is really possible in terms of inducing faults. However, the first type of papers are more common, mainly due to the lack of proper equipment at academia. All together, there are only a few works that address the practical issues that arise while applying these techniques.

Kömmerling and Kuhn [2], published a paper in 1999, which is considered to be the milestone in the context of security evaluation against fault attacks. In this work the authors present an extensive collection of techniques for fault injection and other tampering techniques and give hints on how to mitigate some of them. The paper highlights the case of VCC fault injection (referred to as *glitch attacks*) and emphasizes those as the ones most useful in practice.

Aumüller et al. published in 2002 one of the first practical works on fault analysis [7], in which they describe a real-life scenario of the impact of injecting glitches in the VCC and clock lines of an IC. They also suggest some countermeasures applicable in this specific case. Approximately at the same time, Skorobogatov and Anderson introduced optical (laser) fault injection [8], where they describe injecting faults with a laser on a decapsulated IC. This technique is still very successful nowadays for defeating the security of many protected devices, but it is out of scope for this work.

Recent paper from van Woudenberg et al. [9], describes a real attack scenario for an Optical Fault Injection attack. The practical problem of setting the parameters for fault injection is introduced in their work and the authors briefly discuss the lack of methodology to solve it as the main direction they rely on is based on heuristics. In addition, the paper gives a nice overview of all the practical issues that arise during a real execution of the FI attacks on actual hardware. Similarly, the work of Balasch et al. [10] explores the effects of glitches injected in the clock line of an IC. This work is very interesting for identifying various effects that a glitch can cause on real hardware in terms of defining all possible outcomes of a successful fault injection. However, it has to be noted that current smart cards usually run on an internal clock which makes this FI technique unfeasible.

All together, our paper continues this line of research focusing on more practical problems with fault injection but it is also unique. Namely, we first focus on the problem of finding the right set of parameters in order to optimize the glitching effects that can be explored by the adversary. Second, we derive new theoretical framework for this multi-parameters search and apply it on some actual off-the-shelf smart cards. While doing this, we evaluate several search strategies, one of which is using ideas from evolutionary computation. Our contributions are specified more precisely below.

1.2 Our Contribution

Here we summarize the contributions of this work:

– We propose a new methodology to handle the difficult problem of finding the right sets of parameters for glitching. Our methodology is based on a model that is suitable for smart cards of today. Namely, we distinguish between two phases for glitching, one focusing on voltage parameters and the other one on proper timing.
– After experimenting with several approaches, we develop a new search strategy that is time-effective and breaks some off-the-shelf devices.
– We advocate a new direction for this problem building on our first results from the approach based on genetic algorithms.

The remainder of this paper is organized as follows: in Sect. 2 we give the problem statement and the model we use for the experiments, in Sect. 3 we present several search strategies and their results. Finally, in Sect. 4 we conclude the paper and give some suggestions for future work.

2 Problem Statement

The goal is to find a search strategy for VCC FI parameters that lead to a successful fault injection. *Input of the search* consists of the parameters required by the search strategy to proceed, and an estimated initial range for every parameter. *Search space* is a set of all the possible combinations of values for every parameter required to define the VCC FI attack. Parameters that can have real values are considered as discrete-valued parameters sampled with the maximum resolution of the acquisition hardware devices, and all value ranges are bounded. The goal of the search is to get the maximum information about the behaviour of a device with the minimum number of measurements given a black-box scenario. Also, the goal is to find parameters that define a successful VCC FI attack in the case that device is vulnerable to fault attacks caused by glitching. As an *output of the search*, a report of the behavior of device is generated. Additionally, an output can include a parameter combination or a set of parameter combinations that lead to a successful VCC FI attack. Also, a parameter combination or a set of parameter combinations that trigger unexpected behavior of device can be also included although they do not lead to a successful VCC FI attack.

2.1 Model

We divide the search into two phases: in the first phase we look for the appropriate glitch shape (containing all the parameters that define the signal) and in the second phase we look for the timing instant in which we have to inject the fault. The motivation for the parameter split into two stages is obtaining a reduction in the dimensionality (thus, complexity) of the problem. The feasibility of this parameter splitting was experimentally tested to be possible and useful: all TOEs covered by this research (and also TOEs outside the scope of this research) showed a similar behavior w.r.t. glitch shape-related parameters. The second stage search consists of a time sweep with glitch shapes (glitch length, glitch voltage) output by the first stage search. The time range defined in the initial search space is discretized in n time instants[1]. In each time instant, a subset of the glitch shapes output by the first stage is tested. The verdicts of all measurements are reported as the final output of the parameter search. In this paper we give sufficient details for the first search phase only. For the second phase one should proceed similarly.

Two parameters of interest for the first phase are glitch voltage and glitch length. A verdict represents the class that, based on a response from the device, a glitch has been classified to. The assumptions that allow predicting the possible verdict of a measurement given the glitch voltage and the glitch length are as follows:

1. There exists an upper bound for the glitch voltage, VLOW[2], and if the glitch voltage is set to this value or higher, device will just ignore the glitch (it will interpret it as signal noise), and a NORMAL verdict will be obtained.
2. There exists a lower bound for the glitch voltage, VHIGH (see footnote 2), and if the glitch voltage is set to this value or lower, device interprets the glitch as a power cut or as an attempt to tamper with it, and a RESET or MUTE verdict will be obtained.

---

[1] In the time dimension, the response of the TOE could be different each time instant. However, due to the presence of internal unstable clocks in TOEs Target B and Target C, the glitch offset has been omitted in the search. The clock jitter causes a FI time instant spread bigger than the accuracy we can obtain with the testing equipment by setting a precise glitch offset in time (2 ns). Additionally, the model assumes a stable operation of the TOE, and not a drastically changing power profile over time (e.g. TOE booting) for the validity of glitch shape-related parameters in the 2nd stage of the search.

[2] Note that small glitches that are to be ignored have a length close to LLOW and voltage close to VLOW, but the glitch voltage is typically a negative value, hence the counter-intuitive naming convention for voltage boundaries.

3. There exists a lower bound for the glitch length, LLOW, and if the glitch length is set to this value or lower, device will just ignore the glitch, and a NORMAL verdict will be obtained.
4. There exists an upper bound for the glitch length, LHIGH, and if the glitch length is set to this value or higher, device interprets the glitch as a power failure or as an attempt to tamper with it, and a RESET or MUTE verdict will be obtained.
5. If the glitch voltage and the glitch length take values in the ranges of (VLOW, VHIGH) and (LLOW, LHIGH) respectively, the response of device depends also on the rest of the parameters of the glitch (both from the glitch shape and the glitch timing).

The explanations for the possible verdict classes are given below.

Verdict from the class NORMAL will be obtained if the device response was expected, verdicts RESET and MUTE are derived if the device responds accordingly while performing a measurement. If the device is vulnerable to FI, the verdicts from the class INTERESTING can be found. It points to the area defined by the decision boundary between the plane regions corresponding to the NORMAL and RESET/MUTE regions plus some threshold distance. If these two regions overlap, the class INTERESTING is to be found in the intersection of these two plane regions. (We assume here a two-dimensional space with only the glitch length and glitch voltage parameters.) The verdict CHANGING is found in the same area as the INTERESTING verdict. This verdict class is assigned when two measurements with the same parameter configuration for the glitch shape yield different verdicts. The verdict SUCCESSFUL is to be found inside the (glitch voltage, glitch length) area which produces the INTERESTING verdicts where can be more than one combination of parameters that yields a SUCCESSFUL verdict.

3   Experiments and Discussion

In this section we present different search strategies and their experimental results on several smart cards. First we give additional information about search space settings followed by the experiments. Afterwards, we present a comparison among different search strategies in terms of their effectiveness.

3.1   Search Space Settings and Experiment Definition

The initial search space parameters are given in Table 1.

The experiments are performed as follows:

For each tested device, several runs of each strategy for the first stage of the search are executed. Besides the common parameters already mentioned in Table 1, we also use the following algorithms:

Table 1. Search space parameters

Parameter name	Parameter value
Glitch voltage	$[-5, -0.05]$ V
Glitch length	$[2, 150]$ ns
VCC voltage VCC	5 V
CLK high voltage	5 V
CLK low voltage	0 V
CLK signal frequency	1 MHz
Number of glitches	Random value from $[1, 10]$[a]

[a]The number of glitches was chosen as a random value
due to not observing any statistically significant change
in the TOE response w.r.t. this parameter within the
given range

- MonteCarlo search (baseline): 2048 measurements
- FastBoxing: 2 iterations ($maxIter = 2$), $4 \cdot 4 \cdot 64 = 1024$ measurements per iteration ($n = 4$, $numMeas = 64$), 10 000 maximum iterations ($maxIter = 10\,000$)
- Adaptive zoom&bound: 10 000 maximum iterations ($maxIter = 10\,000$), $4 \cdot 4$ grid ($n = 4$), 1 and 3 measurements per iteration ($numMeas = 1$, $numMeas = 3$)
- Genetic Algorithm: maximum number of generations $= 20$, population size $= 30$, maximum number of consecutive generations without improvement $= 50$

3.2   Experimental Results

The tests are conducted on three targets. Target A is unprotected smart card and is therefore suitable for the training phase. Smart cards B and C are protected against several FI techniques, especially VCC FI. Since one of the possible outcomes of a VCC FI attack is permanent malfunction of a device, multiple samples of each card were used. For all search strategies, all samples from the same device showed the same physical behavior w.r.t. glitch shape-related parameters. In this sense, the glitch shape parameters found for a device sample are valid for all samples[3] of the same device. This behavior was not observed for the time-related parameters.

For the table listings, the following abbreviations are used:

- *TestReps*: number of repetitions of the test
- *MeasInTest*: average total number of measurements in tests, if MeasInTestT then it includes first and the second stage.

---

[3] For each device all samples were from the same batch, hardware revision and manufacturer.

- *INT(M)*: number of measurements with a INTERESTING verdict class. The figure is presented as the median value of all values in the tests. The choice of the median is for reflecting the typical performance of the search strategy.
- *INT(%)*: number of measurements with a INTERESTING verdict class per hundred (%). This value is computed from the sum of all INTERESTING measurements in all tests divided by the accumulated number of measurements in all tests, and normalized to 100 measurements.
- *SUC(M)*: same as INT(M) but for the SUCCESSFUL verdict class.
- *SUC(%)*: same as INT(%) but for the SUCCESSFUL verdict class.

3.3 Monte Carlo Strategy and Results

This search strategy consists of performing measurements with randomly selected parameter combinations within the given initial search space. The random distribution for selecting values is considered to be uniform for each parameter present in the search space. This search strategy is considered as the baseline search strategy. The short test runs with 3072 measurements had no SUCCESSFUL measurement, and only the 76800 measurement test run produced 11 SUCCESSFUL measurements.

Furthermore, due to the random nature of the parameter selection there is a significant number of repeated parameter combinations (glitch length, glitch voltage) for the glitch shape. This repetition is interesting if it is made in the plane region that yields the INTERESTING verdict class. However, it is highly undesired for measurements in which the device response is predictable.

3.4 FastBoxing Strategy and Results

FastBoxing algorithm is a simple, iterative algorithm devised for the automatic setting of the parameters in the first stage of the search. The algorithm works in the following way: search strategy assumes the boundaries for the glitch shape: VHIGH, VLOW and LLOW, LHIGH. The search algorithm will try to find these boundaries by doing two steps: a *measurements step* and a *reflection step*. For each iteration, the measurement step consists of a sampling of the search space and then it performs measurements at the sampled points. After performing the measurements, the algorithm will start the reflection step for finding out an estimate of the VHIGH, VLOW and LLOW, LHIGH boundaries. For the VLOW boundary, all points to its right should produce the NORMAL verdict, so the algorithm does the following. First column of points starting from the right is analyzed. If all the points of this column belong to the NORMAL verdict class, then the next column to its left is analyzed. If all points in the second column also belong to the NORMAL verdict class, the algorithm estimates that the VLOW boundary is not between those two columns. When the algorithm finds a column that contains some points belonging to NORMAL verdict and some points belonging to RESET or MUTE classes, it estimates that the VLOW boundary is between that column and the column to its right. Once this estimation has

Table 2. Results for the FastBoxing search strategy

Device	TestReps	MeasInTestT	INT(M)	SUC(M)	INT(%)	SUC(%)
Target A	5	3048 (2048 + 1000)	26	9	0.800	0.361
Target B	5	3048 (2048 + 1000)	0	0	0.00	0.00
Target C	1	3048 (2048 + 1000)	0	0	0.00	0.00

been done, the VLOW boundary is temporarily set to this estimation. For the rest of the boundaries, the process is analogous.

Once the algorithm stops, the last estimation for the boundary values for the glitch length and glitch voltage will be the output. The next search stage will sample points inside the box bounded by the VHIGH, VLOW, LLOW and LHIGH boundary values for its input.

In Table 2 we summarize the results of the tests for the FastBoxing strategy. The second stage of the parameter search is performed with a set of 10 (glitch length, glitch voltage) parameter combinations randomly selected from the bounded region in the OUTPUT of the FastBoxing search strategy.

In the case of the FastBoxing search for the vulnerable device Target A, the inaccurate estimation of the INTERESTING verdict class results in poor (glitch length, glitch voltage) parameter combination choices. This is especially noticeable if these parameter combinations are close to the boundary values. Because of this, the number of SUCCESSFUL measurements varies significantly depending on the random selection of parameter combinations. As an example, Run 2 of the test yielded 26 SUCCESSFUL measurements, whereas Run 3 of the test yielded only 4 SUCCESSFUL measurements.

It is worth mentioning that, to focus on the search space region in which the INTERESTING verdict class is found, the performance of the search improved significantly. All test runs of the FastBoxing search strategy yielded INTERESTING and SUCCESSFUL measurements.

3.5   Adaptive zoom&bound Strategy and Results

The Adaptive zoom&bound search strategy iteratively bounds the region that yields the INTERESTING or CHANGING verdict classes and "zooms" inside that bounded region. This is achieved by decreasing the distance between new measurements in the glitch shape search space. The region bounding is performed in an adaptive way, similar to a 2D version of a binary search. The Adaptive zoom&bound search uses the same two-step iterative process as FastBoxing algorithm, but the processing done in the reflection step is different. Reflection step works as follows: the distance between two neighbour points is set to a *pointDist* variable. The measurements are placed in a 2D plane for the glitch shape (just for ordering them). The horizontal axis is the glitch voltage parameter, and the vertical axis is the glitch length parameter. For each one of the available measurements from the last test, all neighbours of a measurement are checked for their verdict class. If all neighbour measurements in the 2D plane belong to the same

Table 3. Results for the Adaptive zoom&bound search strategy, 1 performed VCC FI attack per measurement

Device	TestReps	MeasInTestT	INT(M)	SUC(M)	INT(%)	SUC(%)
Target A	5	1198 (**198** + 1000)	47	13	**3.895**	**1.064**
Target B	5	1128 (**128** + 1000)	0	0	0.00	0.00

verdict, the decision boundary between verdict classes is not found between the point and its neighbours. If a neighbour measurement in the 2D plane belongs to a different verdict class then the boundary is estimated to be between them. A new measurement is added for the test in the next iteration and placed at a distance $pointDist/2$ between them. When all points have been analysed, a new test has been generated with a list of measurements only in the estimated region that produces the INTERESTING verdict class. The algorithm stops if all measurements in the initial measurement step belong to the same class, if no new test measurements are generated during the reflection step, or when the distance between neighbour points has reached the maximum resolution of the hardware devices. Once the algorithm stops, it outputs the set of glitch shape parameters that bound the region producing the INTERESTING verdict class.

The output of the algorithm is a set of the glitch shape parameters (glitch length, glitch voltage) of the measurements that are considered to be bounding the region that yields the INTERESTING verdict class. The output also contains the glitch shape parameters of the measurements with INTERESTING, CHANGING and SUCCESSFUL (if any) verdict classes. The decision of which glitch shapes should be the output is implemented by taking the measurements produced in the last iteration of the algorithm.

In Table 3 we summarize the results for performed tests for the Adaptive zoom&bound strategy.

The results of the Adaptive zoom&bound strategy are better than in previous search strategies. In particular, the number of measurements required for completing the first stage of the parameter search is very low, so the search speed is improved significantly. For the initial search space used throughout the experiment, the optimum performance is computed as follows:

$$N = n \cdot \lceil max(log_2(\text{rangeV}/\text{resolutionV}),$$
$$log_2(\text{rangeL}/\text{resolutionL}))\rceil = (4 \cdot 4) \cdot \lceil max(log_2(5/0.05), log_2(150/2))\rceil = 112\,\text{meas}.$$

In the case of Target A, the search strategy has more measurements due to the device behavior in the search space region that produces the INTEREST-ING verdict class. Additionally, the number of INTERESTING and SUCCESS-FUL measurements are almost four times larger than those for the FastBoxing algorithm.

Figure 1 shows the plot for the first stage of the parameter search in the case of the Adaptive zoom&bound strategy.

It can be seen that most of the measurements are performed near the decision boundary between verdict classes. Also, the distance between measurements

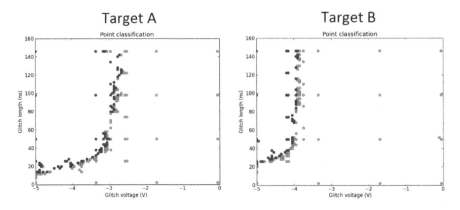

Fig. 1. First stage plot of explored measurements for different devices by the Adaptive zoom&bound search strategy. Green is NORMAL, blue is RESET (A) or MUTE (B) (Color figure online)

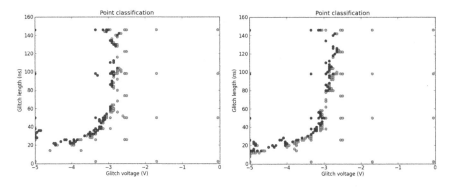

Fig. 2. First stage plot of two samples of Target A.

w.r.t. glitch shape parameters is very small. This allows to bound the region producing the INTERESTING verdict class quite accurately. The Adaptive zoom&bound search strategy also allowed to experimentally observe that the glitch shape parameters (glitch length, glitch voltage) are the same for different samples of the same device. Figure 2 shows the plot of the measurement classification for the first stage parameter search of two Target A samples. It can be experimentally verified that a (glitch length, glitch voltage) glitch shape parameter value that leads to a SUCCESSFUL verdict in one sample also does the same in other targets. It can be said then that the glitch shape parameters are exportable between samples of the devices. In contrast, time-related parameters that produce SUCCESSFUL verdicts do change between samples.

Here we also present a successful VCC FI attack on Target C. This target incorporates specific countermeasures against VCC fault injection, as indicated by the manufacturer. In addition, this card has been granted the EAL4+

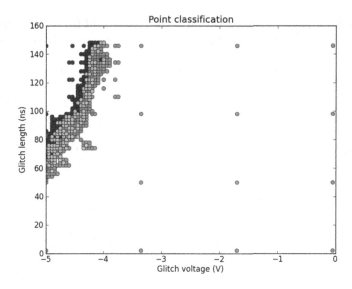

Fig. 3. Output of the measurement classification for Target C by the Adaptive zoom&bound search strategy, 3 repetitions per measurement. The orange color depicts the CHANGING verdict class (Color figure online).

Table 4. Results for the Adaptive zoom&bound search strategy with Target C, 3 VCC FI attacks performed per measurement

Device	Measurements 1st stage	Measurements 2nd stage	INT(M)	SUC(M)
Target C	812	1000	17	**19**

certification level of Common Criteria. This means that the device has been previously tested by an independent security evaluation lab against different attack techniques, including VCC fault injection. The output of the first stage of the search is depicted in Fig. 3.

We can see that due to the focus in the search space region producing the CHANGING verdict class and the multiple attempts per measurement, the jitter was mitigated and suitable (glitch length, glitch voltage) parameter settings could be found. Table 4 shows the results for the performed parameter search. As far as the authors know, this target was not known to be vulnerable to VCC FI attack before.

3.6 Genetic Algorithm Strategy and Results

Besides using deterministic algorithms as the two examples mentioned above, it is also possible to use heuristic algorithms. Since finding the correct parameter setting is a non-deterministic process that can be considered as a search problem, it is natural to try to use non-deterministic algorithms. Genetic algorithms are a subclass of evolutionary algorithms where the elements of the search space S are arrays of elementary types [11]. Since Genetic Algorithms (GAs) are typically used as function optimization algorithms, a fitness function must be defined for mapping the different verdict classes present in the device model to the fitness values. In particular, the mapping currently used is: NORMAL verdict class has value 1, RESET or MUTE verdict classes have value 2, INTERESTING verdict class has value 8, CHANGING verdict class has value 8.5 and SUCCESSFUL verdict class has value 10. Formally, the GA aims to find a (glitch length, glitch voltage) tuple such that the fitness value F is maximal. To be able to use GA on this problem, a generic GA is modified and instead of the standard operators we use custom selection and crossover operators. The GA generates an initial population of n random combinations of (glitch length, glitch voltage) parameter values. Each individual of each generation is assigned its corresponding fitness value. Each population is evolved into a new generation of the population by means of an evolution step (iteration step). The evolution step performs the following tasks: in the crossover, GA takes two individuals from different verdict classes and produces a new individual with a (glitch length, glitch voltage) parameter configuration between the values of the two parent individuals. To perform the mutation step, some individuals evolve by adding to their parameter values a random value. Finally, the algorithm preserves a certain number of individuals with the highest fitness value in the next generation.

GA performs evolution steps until a maximum number of evolution steps is reached, or until a specified number of generations without improvement is reached. A modification that has been introduced into the GA is the notion of a "good enough" fitness value. The algorithm has an internal fitness threshold value, and all generated individuals that have a fitness value equal or higher than the threshold value will be output by the algorithm as the OUTPUT of the first stage of the parameter search. With the current fitness function definition, a threshold value of 8 outputs all the measurements that had an INTERESTING, CHANGING or SUCCESSFUL verdict class. For evolutionary algorithms test suite we use the Evolutionary Computation Framework (ECF) [12]. ECF is a C++ framework intended for the application of any type of the evolutionary computation, developed at the University of Zagreb (Fig. 4).

3.7   Comparison among Different Search Strategies

In order to have an overview of the performances of the presented search strategies, Tables 5 and 6 contain the best observed metrics in tests performed with Target A (vulnerable to VCC FI) and Target C (presumably not vulnerable to VCC FI). The configuration of the second search stage is the same for all search strategies (except for the Monte Carlo search): 10 (glitch voltage, glitch length) parameter combinations, 100 time instants.

For the table listings, the following abbreviations are used:
Meas 1st *Stage*: total number of measurements in 1st stage of the parameter search;

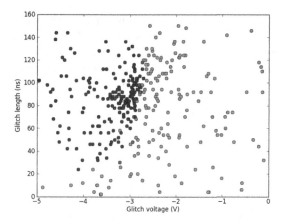

Fig. 4. First stage plot for the measurements of the GA with the Target A.

Table 5. Metrics of the different search strategies for Target A.

Strategy	Meas 1stStage	SUC(%)	Total_I	Total_S	Total_M
Monte Carlo	N/A	0.0000	19	0	3072
FastBoxing	2048	0.29526	26	9	3048
AdaptZoom	**192**	**1.17450**	**56**	**14**	**1192**
GA	1560	0.3125	21	8	2560

Table 6. Metrics of the different search strategies for Target B.

Strategy	Meas 1stStage	SUC(%)	Total_I	Total_S	Total_M
Monte Carlo	N/A	0	0	0	3072
FastBoxing	2048	0	0	0	3048
AdaptZoom	128	0	0	0	1128
GA	6868	0	0	0	7868

SUC: ratio of SUCCESSFUL measurements versus the total number of measurements (1st + 2nd stages), normalized to 1/100;
Total_I: total number of INTERESTING measurements;
Total_S: total number of SUCCESSFUL measurements;
Total_M: total number of measurements (1st + 2nd stages).

Looking at the results, the best overall strategy is the Adaptive zoom&bound search strategy. It completes the first stage of the search with the least number of measurements and it has the best ratio of SUCCESSFUL measurements, and produces the most INTERESTING and SUCCESSFUL measurements. The use of information available allows to quickly direct the parameter search towards the most promising parameter configurations.

The GA shows a promising performance, because it is able to produce a significant number of INTERESTING and SUCCESSFUL measurements. However, the performance in terms of number of measurements in the 1st stage is not very good. This is due to a large number of generations being produced without significant improvements. A parameter tuning on this approach should result in a better performance of the algorithm. This parameter tuning, in combination with the addition of new features to the algorithm, is left as future work.

Finally, it should be mentioned that the Monte Carlo search strategy has been found to be the most inefficient search strategy. However, due to its random nature, it is still a viable option if no restriction on the number of measurements is imposed.

4   Conclusions and Future Work

This work deals with the so-far unexplored topic of finding the right parameters for successful faults by glitching. We experiment with several search strategies and find some promising methodologies that are effective against some proprietary smart cards with glitching countermeasures. The best method is rather generic and shows good results against different devices. Finally, we identify another promising direction using genetic algorithms that can be further optimized as future work.

Acknowledgements. This work was supported in part by the Technology Foundation STW (project 12624 - SIDES), The Netherlands Organization for Scientific Research NWO (project ProFIL 628.001.007) and the ICT COST action IC1204 TRUDEVICE.

A   Appendix: TOE Details

A more detailed description of the TOEs described in this paper follows:

Target A: It is a smartcard based on an ATMega163+24C256 IC, CMOS technology, hardware last revision 2003. This TOE does not have any side-channel countermeasure nor fault-injection countermeasure. All processing of the card is performed in software, and the card was running on an external 4 MHz clock frequency. In particular, this target is also available from Riscure BV as the research target "Training Card 6". The code that was attacked was a vulnerable PIN (Personal Identification Number) authentication mechanism is as follows:

```
...
for (i=0;i<4;i++) {
    if (pin[i] == input[i])
        digits_ok++;
}
    if (digits_ok==4)  //BRANCH STATEMENT == CODE UNDER ATTACK
        respond_code(0x00,SW_NO_ERROR_msb,SW_NO_ERROR_lsb);
    else
        respond_code(0x00,0x69,0x85);
...
```

Target B: It is a smartcard bought in 2013 from a webshop from one of the leading manufacturers in the sector. This TOE is a protected target, and has countermeasures against SCA and FI, such as fault injection detection logic and light, temperature and clock sensors. The IC design is from late 2004. Additionally, it has dedicated logic for cryptographic operations. More in detail, this TOE implements the JavaCard OS 2.2.1 and GlobalPlatform 2.1.1 standard. It runs on an internal, unstable clock at an unknown frequency. The supplied external clock frequency was 4 MHz. The card was running exclusively on software (no crypto hardware present in the IC was used). The Java applet loaded into the card was a double nested loop with two counters and a checksum. The code was similar to the following piece of code:

```
...
for(outerLoopCounter=0;outerLoopCounter<2;outerLoopCounter++){
    checkpoint=1;
    for(innerLoopCounter=0;innerLoopCounter<1000;innerLoopCounter++){
        checkpoint=2;
        dummyOperation1();
        iterations=iterations+1;
    }
    checkpoint=3;
    dummyOperation2();
}
sendBytesToTerminal(outerLoopCounter,innerLoopCounter,iterations,
valueFlag);
...
```

Target C: It is a smartcard bought in 2013 from a webshop from one of the leading manufacturers in the sector. This TOE is a protected target, and has the same feature set as *Target B* in terms of hardware and countermeasures. This TOE implements the JavaCard OS 2.2.1 and GlobalPlatform 2.1 standard. It was also Common Criteria certified level EAL4+ in 2008. The Java applet loaded into the card was the same applet as described for *Target B*.

References

1. Anderson, R., Kuhn, M., A, E.U.S.: Tamper resistance – a cautionary note. In: Proceedings of the Second Usenix Workshop on Electronic Commerce, pp. 1–11 (1996)
2. Kömmerling, O., Kuhn, M.G.: Design principles for tamper-resistant smartcard processors. In: Proceedings of the USENIX Workshop on Smartcard Technology on USENIX Workshop on Smartcard Technology, WOST'99, Berkeley, CA, USA, p. 2. USENIX Association (1999)
3. Kocher, P.C., Jaffe, J., Jun, B.: Differential power analysis. In: Wiener, M. (ed.) CRYPTO 1999. LNCS, vol. 1666, pp. 388–397. Springer, Heidelberg (1999)
4. Quisquater, J.-J., Samyde, D.: ElectroMagnetic Analysis (EMA): measures and counter-measures for smart cards. In: Attali, S., Jensen, T. (eds.) E-smart 2001. LNCS, vol. 2140, pp. 200–210. Springer, Heidelberg (2001)

5. Boneh, D., DeMillo, R., Lipton, R.: New threat model breaks crypto codes. Bellcore 85 Press Release (1996)
6. Boneh, D., DeMillo, R.A., Lipton, R.J.: On the importance of checking cryptographic protocols for faults. In: Fumy, W. (ed.) EUROCRYPT 1997. LNCS, vol. 1233, pp. 37–51. Springer, Heidelberg (1997)
7. Aumüller, C., Bier, P., Fischer, W., Hofreiter, P., Seifert, J.-P.: Fault attacks on RSA with CRT: concrete results and practical countermeasures. In: Kaliski Jr, B.S., Koç, Ç.K., Paar, C. (eds.) CHES 2002. LNCS, vol. 2523, pp. 260–275. Springer, Heidelberg (2003)
8. Skorobogatov, S.P., Anderson, R.J.: Optical fault induction attacks. In: Kaliski Jr, B.S., Koç, Ç.K., Paar, C. (eds.) CHES 2002. LNCS, vol. 2523, pp. 2–12. Springer, Heidelberg (2003)
9. van Woudenberg, J., Witteman, M., Menarini, F.: Practical optical fault injection on secure microcontrollers. In: 2011 Workshop on Fault Diagnosis and Tolerance in Cryptography (FDTC), pp. 91–99 (2011)
10. Balasch, J., Gierlichs, B., Verbauwhede, I.: An In-depth and Black-box characterization of the effects of clock glitches on 8-bit MCUs. In: Proceedings of the 2011 Workshop on Fault Diagnosis and Tolerance in Cryptography, FDTC '11, Washington, DC, USA, pp. 105–114. IEEE Computer Society (2011)
11. Weise, T.: Global Optimization Algorithms Theory and Application (2009). http:// www.it-weise.de/
12. Jakobovic, D., et al.: Evolutionary computation framework, January 2013. http:// gp.zemris.fer.hr/ecf/

Efficient Template Attacks

Omar Choudary and Markus G. Kuhn[(⊠)]

Computer Laboratory, University of Cambridge, Cambridge, UK
{omar.choudary,markus.kuhn}@cl.cam.ac.uk

Abstract. Template attacks remain a powerful side-channel technique to eavesdrop on tamper-resistant hardware. They model the probability distribution of leaking signals and noise to guide a search for secret data values. In practice, several numerical obstacles can arise when implementing such attacks with multivariate normal distributions. We propose efficient methods to avoid these. We also demonstrate how to achieve significant performance improvements, both in terms of information extracted and computational cost, by pooling covariance estimates across all data values. We provide a detailed and systematic overview of many different options for implementing such attacks. Our experimental evaluation of all these methods based on measuring the supply current of a byte-load instruction executed in an unprotected 8-bit microcontroller leads to practical guidance for choosing an attack algorithm.

Keywords: Side-channel attacks · Template attack · Multivariate analysis

1 Introduction

Side-channel attacks are powerful tools for inferring secret algorithms or data (passwords, cryptographic keys, etc.) processed inside tamper-resistant hardware, if an attacker can monitor some channel leaking such information out of the device, most notably the power-supply current and unintended electromagnetic emissions.

One of the most powerful techniques for evaluating side-channel information is the *template attack* [4], which relies on a multivariate model of the side-channel traces. While the basic algorithm is comparatively simple (Sect. 2), there are a number of additional steps that must be performed in order to obtain a practical and efficient implementation.

In this paper we examine several problems that can arise in the implementation of template attacks (Sect. 3), especially when using a large number of voltage samples. We explain how to solve them in two steps: (*a*) using *compression techniques*, i.e. methods to reduce the number of samples involved, either by throwing away most, or by projecting them into a lower-dimensional space, using only a few linear combinations (Sect. 4); and (*b*) we contribute *efficient variants* of the template-attack algorithm, which can avoid numerical limitations of the standard approach, provide better results and execute faster (Sect. 5).

A. Francillon and P. Rohatgi (Eds.): CARDIS 2013, LNCS 8419, pp. 253–270, 2014.
DOI: 10.1007/978-3-319-08302-5_17, © Springer International Publishing Switzerland 2014

We evaluate all these methods in practice, against an unprotected 8-bit micro-controller, comparing their effectiveness using the guessing entropy (Sect. 6). We focus on gathering information about individual data values, *independent* of what algorithm these are part of. Other algorithm-specific attacks that use dependencies between different data values, e.g. to recover keys from a specific cipher, could be implemented on top of that, but are outside the scope of this paper. We show that PCA and LDA provide the best results overall, and that a previous guideline of selecting at most one point per clock cycle is not optimal in general. Based on these experiments and theoretical background, we provide practical guidance for the choice of template-attack algorithm.

2   Template Attacks

To implement a template attack, we need physical access to a pair of identical devices, which we refer to as the *profiling* and the *attacked* device. We wish to infer some secret value $k\star \in \mathcal{S}$, processed by the attacked device at some point. For an 8-bit microcontroller, $\mathcal{S} = \{0, \ldots, 255\}$ might be the set of possible byte values manipulated by a particular machine instruction.

We assume that we determined the approximate moments of time when the secret value $k\star$ is manipulated and we are able to record signal traces (e.g., supply current or electro-magnetic waveforms) around these moments. We refer to these traces as *leakage vectors*. Let $\{t_1, \ldots, t_{m^r}\}$ be the set of time *samples* and $\mathbf{x}^r \in \mathbb{R}^{m^r}$ be the random vector from which leakage traces are drawn.

During the *profiling* phase we record n_p leakage vectors $\mathbf{x}_{ki}^r \in \mathbb{R}^{m^r}$ from the profiling device for each possible value $k \in \mathcal{S}$, and combine these as row vectors $\mathbf{x}_{ki}^{r\,\prime}$ in the leakage matrix $\mathbf{X}_k^r \in \mathbb{R}^{n_p \times m^r}$.[1]

Typically, the *raw* leakage vectors $\mathbf{x}_{ki}^r$ provided by the data acquisition device contain a large number m^r of samples (random variables), due to high sampling rates used. Therefore, we might *compress* them before further processing, either by selecting only a subset of $m \ll m^r$ of those samples, or by applying some other data-dimensionality reduction method (see Sect. 4). We refer to such compressed leakage vectors as $\mathbf{x}_{ki} \in \mathbb{R}^m$ and combine all of these as rows into the compressed leakage matrix $\mathbf{X}_k \in \mathbb{R}^{n_p \times m}$. (Without any such compression step, we would have $\mathbf{X}_k = \mathbf{X}_k^r$ and $m = m^r$.)

Using $\mathbf{X}_k$ we can compute the template parameters $\bar{\mathbf{x}}_k \in \mathbb{R}^m$ and $\mathbf{S}_k \in \mathbb{R}^{m \times m}$ for each possible value $k \in \mathcal{S}$ as

$$\bar{\mathbf{x}}_k = \frac{1}{n_p} \sum_{i=1}^{n_p} \mathbf{x}_{ki}, \qquad \mathbf{S}_k = \frac{1}{n_p - 1} \sum_{i=1}^{n_p} (\mathbf{x}_{ki} - \bar{\mathbf{x}}_k)(\mathbf{x}_{ki} - \bar{\mathbf{x}}_k)', \qquad (1)$$

---

[1] Throughout this paper $\mathbf{x}'$ is the transpose of $\mathbf{x}$.

where the sample mean $\bar{\mathbf{x}}_k$ and the sample *unbiased*[2] covariance matrix $\mathbf{S}_k$ are the estimates of the true mean μ_k and true covariance Σ_k. Note that a *sum of squares and cross products* matrix such as $\sum_{i=1}^{n_p}(\mathbf{x}_{ki} - \bar{\mathbf{x}}_k)(\mathbf{x}_{ki} - \bar{\mathbf{x}}_k)'$, from (1) can also be written as

$$\sum_{i=1}^{n_p}(\mathbf{x}_{ki} - \bar{\mathbf{x}}_k)(\mathbf{x}_{ki} - \bar{\mathbf{x}}_k)' = \widetilde{\mathbf{X}}_k'\widetilde{\mathbf{X}}_k, \tag{2}$$

where $\widetilde{\mathbf{X}}_k$ is $\mathbf{X}_k$ with $\bar{\mathbf{x}}_k'$ subtracted from each row.[3]

Side-channel leakage traces can generally be modeled well by a multivariate normal distribution [4], which we also observed in our experiments. In this case, the sample mean $\bar{\mathbf{x}}_k$ and sample covariance $\mathbf{S}_k$ are *sufficient statistics*: they completely define the underlying distribution [10, Chap. 4]. Then the probability density function (pdf) of a leakage vector $\mathbf{x}$, given $\bar{\mathbf{x}}_k$ and $\mathbf{S}_k$, is

$$f(\mathbf{x} \mid \bar{\mathbf{x}}_k, \mathbf{S}_k) = \frac{1}{\sqrt{(2\pi)^m |\mathbf{S}_k|}} \exp\left(-\frac{1}{2}(\mathbf{x} - \bar{\mathbf{x}}_k)'\mathbf{S}_k^{-1}(\mathbf{x} - \bar{\mathbf{x}}_k)\right). \tag{3}$$

In the *attack* phase, we try to infer the secret value $k\star \in \mathcal{S}$ processed by the attacked device. We obtain n_a leakage vectors $\mathbf{x}_i \in \mathbb{R}^m$ from the attacked device, using the same recording technique and compression method as in the profiling phase, resulting in the leakage matrix $\mathbf{X}_{k\star} \in \mathbb{R}^{n_a \times m}$. Then, for each $k \in \mathcal{S}$, we compute a *discriminant score* $d(k \mid \mathbf{X}_{k\star})$. Finally, we try all $k \in \mathcal{S}$ on the attacked device, in order of decreasing score (optimized brute-force search, e.g. for a password or cryptographic key), until we find the correct $k\star$. Given a trace $\mathbf{x}_i$ from $\mathbf{X}_{k\star}$, a commonly used discriminant [8,11,14], derived from Bayes' rule, is

$$d(k \mid \mathbf{x}_i) = f(\mathbf{x}_i \mid \bar{\mathbf{x}}_k, \mathbf{S}_k)P(k), \tag{4}$$

where the denominator from Bayes' rule is omitted, as it is the same for each k. Assuming a uniform a-priori probability $P(k) = |\mathcal{S}|^{-1}$, applying Bayes' rule becomes equivalent to computing the likelihood

$$l(k \mid \mathbf{x}_i) = d(k \mid \mathbf{x}_i) = l(\bar{\mathbf{x}}_k, \mathbf{S}_k \mid \mathbf{x}_i) = f(\mathbf{x}_i \mid \bar{\mathbf{x}}_k, \mathbf{S}_k), \tag{5}$$

where the latter can be computed from (3). However, we do not need to compute a proper a-posteriori probability for each candidate k given a trace $\mathbf{x}_i$, but only a discriminant function that allows us to sort scores and identify the most likely candidates. Section 5 shows how the latter can be much more efficient.

---

[2] Others [8,11,14] use $1/n_p$ rather than $1/(n_p - 1)$ in $\mathbf{S}_k$, thereby computing the *maximum likelihood estimator (MLE)* of Σ_k. In theory, the correct estimator for Σ_k is the *unbiased estimator* with $1/(n_p - 1)$; the MLE merely maximises the joint likelihood from the multivariate normal distribution. In practice, we found this choice made no significant performance difference (even down to $n_p = 10, m = 6$).

[3] The matrix form allows the use of fast, vectorized linear-algebra routines.

3   Implementation Caveats

We now present several problems that can appear when implementing the template attack, especially when using a large number of samples m.

3.1   Inverse of Covariance Matrix

Several authors [14,15] noted that inverting the covariance matrix $\mathbf{S}_k$ from (1), as needed in (3), can cause numerical problems for large m. However, we consider it important to explain why $\mathbf{S}_k$ can become singular ($|\mathbf{S}_k| \approx 0$), causing these problems.

Since $\mathbf{S}_k$ is essentially the matrix product $\widetilde{\mathbf{X}}_k'\widetilde{\mathbf{X}}_k$ (2), both $\mathbf{S}_k$ and $\widetilde{\mathbf{X}}_k$ have the same rank. Therefore $\mathbf{S}_k$ is singular iff $\widetilde{\mathbf{X}}_k$ has dependent columns, which is guaranteed if $n_{\mathrm{p}} < m$. The constraint on $\widetilde{\mathbf{X}}_k$ to have zero-mean rows implies that it has dependent columns even for $n_{\mathrm{p}} = m$. Therefore, $n_{\mathrm{p}} > m$ is a *necessary* condition for $\mathbf{S}_k$ to be non-singular. See [10, Result 3.3] for a more detailed proof.

The restriction $m < n_{\mathrm{p}}$ is one main reason for reducing m through compression (see Sect. 4). However, it is not mandatory to compress m further than what is needed to keep the columns of $\widetilde{\mathbf{X}}_k$ independent. Note that in practice some samples can be highly correlated, in which case n_{p} needs to be somewhat larger than m (e.g., $n_{\mathrm{p}} \geq 3000$ for $m = 1250$ with our Sect. 6 data).

If we cannot obtain $n_{\mathrm{p}} > m$ then we can try the covariance estimator of Ledoit and Wolf [5], which gave us a non-singular $\mathbf{S}_k$ even for $n_{\mathrm{p}} < m$. However, a much better option is to use the *pooled* covariance matrix (see Sect. 5.2) when possible.

3.2   Floating-Point Limitations

One practical problem with (3) is that for large m the statistical distance

$$(\mathbf{x} - \bar{\mathbf{x}}_k)'\mathbf{S}_k^{-1}(\mathbf{x} - \bar{\mathbf{x}}_k)$$

can reach values that cause the subsequent exponentiation operation to overflow. For example, in IEEE double precision, $\exp(x)$ is only safe with $|x| < 710$, easily exceeded for large m.

Another problem is that for large m the determinant $|\mathbf{S}_k|$ can overflow. For example, considering that $|\mathbf{S}_k|$ is the product of the eigenvalues of $\mathbf{S}_k$, in some of our experiments the 100 largest eigenvalues were at least 10^6 and multiplying merely 52 such values again overflows the IEEE double precision format.

4   Compression Methods

A compression method can be used to reduce the length (dimensionality) of leakage vectors from m^{r} to m. As detailed in Sect. 3, this may be needed if we do not have enough traces for a full rank covariance matrix or to cope with computational or memory restrictions. Several approaches are described in the literature, which can be divided into two categories: (a) selecting some of the samples based on some criteria; (b) using some linear combinations of the leakage vectors, based on the principal components or Fisher's linear discriminant. All of the following techniques evaluate the differences $\bar{\mathbf{x}}_k - \bar{\mathbf{x}}$ where

$$\bar{\mathbf{x}} = \frac{1}{|\mathcal{S}|} \sum_{k \in \mathcal{S}} \bar{\mathbf{x}}_k. \tag{6}$$

4.1 Selection of Samples

In this method we first compute a signal-strength estimate $\mathbf{s}(t), t \in \{t_1, \ldots, t_{m^r}\}$, and then we select a subset of m points based on this estimate.

There are several proposals for producing $\mathbf{s}(t)$, such as *difference of means (DOM)* [4, Sect. 2.1], the *sum of squared differences (SOSD)* [9], the *Signal to Noise Ratio (SNR)* [15] and *SOST* [9]. All these are similar, with the notable difference that the first two do no take the variance of the traces into consideration, while the latter two do. We show the difference between these estimates for our experiments in Fig. 1. The methods SNR and SOST are in fact the same if we consider the variance at each sample point to be independent of the candidate k, which is expected in our setting. Under this condition SNR and SOST reduce to computing the following value used by the *F-test* in the Analysis of Variance [10]:

$$F(t) = \frac{\left(n_{\mathrm{p}} \sum_{k \in \mathcal{S}} (\bar{\mathbf{x}}_k(t) - \bar{\mathbf{x}}(t))^2 \right) / (|\mathcal{S}| - 1)}{\left(\sum_{k \in \mathcal{S}} \sum_{i=1}^{n_{\mathrm{p}}} (\mathbf{x}_{ki}(t) - \bar{\mathbf{x}}_k(t))^2 \right) / (|\mathcal{S}|(n_{\mathrm{p}} - 1))}. \tag{7}$$

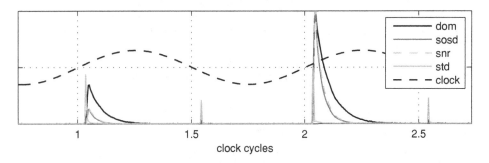

Fig. 1. Signal-strength estimates from DOM, SOSD and SNR (identical to SOST) for a LOAD instruction processing all possible 8-bit values, along with the average standard deviation (STD) of the traces and clock signal. We used 2000 traces per value. All estimates are rescaled to fit into the plot, so the vertical axis (linear) has no scale.

$F(t)$ can be used to reject, at any desired significance level, the hypothesis that the sample mean values at sample point t are equal, therefore providing a good indication of which samples contain more information about the means.

In the second step of this compression method we need to choose m samples based on the signal-strength estimate $\mathbf{s}$. The goal is to select the smallest set of samples that contains most of the information about our target. An accepted guideline, by Rechberger and Oswald [7, Sect. 3.2], is to select at most one sample per clock cycle among the samples with highest $\mathbf{s}$. In Sect. 6 we evaluate several other options, and we show that this guideline is not optimal in general.

4.2 Principal Component Analysis (PCA)

Archambeau et al. [8] proposed the following method for using PCA as a compression method for template attacks. First compute the *sample between groups* matrix $\mathbf{B}$:

$$\mathbf{B} = n_\mathrm{p} \sum_{k \in \mathcal{S}} (\bar{\mathbf{x}}_k^\mathrm{r} - \bar{\mathbf{x}}^\mathrm{r})(\bar{\mathbf{x}}_k^\mathrm{r} - \bar{\mathbf{x}}^\mathrm{r})'. \tag{8}$$

Next obtain the singular value decomposition (SVD) $\mathbf{B} = \mathbf{U}\mathbf{D}\mathbf{U}'$, where each column of $\mathbf{U} \in \mathbb{R}^{m^\mathrm{r} \times m^\mathrm{r}}$ is an eigenvector $\mathbf{u}_j$ of $\mathbf{B}$, and $\mathbf{D} \in \mathbb{R}^{m^\mathrm{r} \times m^\mathrm{r}}$ contains the corresponding eigenvalues δ_j on its diagonal.[4] The crucial point is that only the first m eigenvectors $[\mathbf{u}_1 \ldots \mathbf{u}_m] = \mathbf{U}^m$ are needed in order to preserve most of the information from the mean vectors $\bar{\mathbf{x}}_k^\mathrm{r}$. Therefore we can restrict $\mathbf{U}$ to $\mathbf{U}^m \in \mathbb{R}^{m^\mathrm{r} \times m}$. Finally, we can project the mean vectors $\bar{\mathbf{x}}_k^\mathrm{r}$ and covariance matrices $\mathbf{S}_k^\mathrm{r}$ (computed with (1) on the raw traces $\mathbf{x}_i^\mathrm{r}$) into the new coordinate system defined by $\mathbf{U}^m$ to obtain the PCA template parameters $\bar{\mathbf{x}}_k \in \mathbb{R}^m$ and $\mathbf{S}_k \in \mathbb{R}^{m \times m}$:

$$\bar{\mathbf{x}}_k = \mathbf{U}^{m\prime} \bar{\mathbf{x}}_k^\mathrm{r}, \qquad \mathbf{S}_k = \mathbf{U}^{m\prime} \mathbf{S}_k^\mathrm{r} \mathbf{U}^m. \tag{9}$$

Choice of PCA Components. Archambeau et al. [8] propose to select only those first m eigenvectors $\mathbf{u}_j$ for which the corresponding eigenvalues δ_j are a few orders of magnitude larger than the rest. This technique, also known as *elbow rule* or *Scree Graph* [6], requires manual inspection of the eigenvalues. Another technique, which does not require manual inspection of the eigenvalues, is known as the *Cumulative Percentage of Total Variation* [6]. It selects those m eigenvectors that retain at least fraction f of the total variance, by computing the score

$$\phi(m) = \frac{\sum_{1 \le j \le m} \delta_j}{\sum_{1 \le j \le m^\mathrm{r}} \delta_j}, \quad 1 \le m \le m^\mathrm{r}, \tag{10}$$

---

[4] Archambeau et al. [8] show a method for computing $\mathbf{U}$ that is more efficient when $m^\mathrm{r} \gg |\mathcal{S}|$, but in our experiments with $m^\mathrm{r} = 2500$ this direct approach worked well.

and selecting the lowest m for which $\phi(m) > f$.[5] We recommend trying both approaches, as *"there is no definitive answer [to the question of how many components to choose]"* [10, Chap. 8].

Alternative Computation of PCA Templates. Even though in [11, Sect. 4.1] the authors mention that PCA can help where computing the full covariance matrix $\mathbf{S}_k^r$ is prohibitive (due to large m^r), their approach still requires the computation of $\mathbf{S}_k^r$ (see (9)). Also, numerical artifacts during the double matrix multiplication in (9) can make $\mathbf{S}_k$ non-symmetric. One way to avoid the latter is to use the Cholesky decomposition $\mathbf{S}_k^r = \mathbf{C}'\mathbf{C}$ and compute

$$\mathbf{S}_k = \mathbf{U}^{m\prime}\mathbf{S}_k^r\mathbf{U}^m = \mathbf{U}^{m\prime}\mathbf{C}'\mathbf{C}\mathbf{U}^m = (\mathbf{C}\mathbf{U}^m)'(\mathbf{C}\mathbf{U}^m) = \mathbf{V}'\mathbf{V}. \tag{11}$$

However, to avoid both the numerical artifacts and the computation of large covariance matrices, we propose an alternative PCA method, based on the following result: given the leakage matrix $\mathbf{X}_k^r$ and the PCA projection matrix $\mathbf{U}^m$, it can be shown [10, Eq. (2-45)] that

$$\mathbf{S}_k = \mathrm{Cov}(\mathbf{X}_k^r\mathbf{U}^m) = \mathbf{U}^{m\prime}\mathrm{Cov}(\mathbf{X}_k^r)\mathbf{U}^m = \mathbf{U}^{m\prime}\mathbf{S}_k^r\mathbf{U}^m. \tag{12}$$

Therefore, instead of first computing $\mathbf{S}_k^r$ and then applying (9) or (11), we can first compute the projected leakage matrix

$$\mathbf{X}_k = \mathbf{X}_k^r\mathbf{U}^m \tag{13}$$

and then compute the PCA-based template parameters using (1). We use this method for all the results shown in Sect. 6.

4.3   Fisher's Linear Discriminant Analysis (LDA)

Given the leakage traces $\mathbf{x}_{ki}^r$ (rows of $\mathbf{X}_k^r$), Fisher's idea [2,10] was to find some coefficients $\mathbf{a}_j \in \mathbb{R}^{m^r}$ that maximise the following ratio:

$$\frac{\sum\limits_{k\in\mathcal{S}}(\bar{y}_{kj} - \bar{y}_j)^2}{\mathrm{Var}(y_j)} = \frac{\sum\limits_{k\in\mathcal{S}}(\mathbf{a}_j'(\bar{\mathbf{x}}_k^r - \bar{\mathbf{x}}^r))^2}{\mathrm{Var}(\mathbf{a}_j'\mathbf{x})} = \frac{\mathbf{a}_j'\mathbf{B}\mathbf{a}_j}{\mathbf{a}_j'\mathbf{S}_{\mathrm{pooled}}\mathbf{a}_j}, \tag{14}$$

where the linear combinations $y_j = \mathbf{a}_j'\mathbf{x}$ are known as *sample discriminants*, $\mathbf{B}$ is the treatment matrix from (8) and $\mathbf{S}_{\mathrm{pooled}} = \frac{1}{|\mathcal{S}|}\sum_{k\in\mathcal{S}}\mathbf{S}_k^r$ is the common covariance of all groups (see also Sect. 5.2). Note the similarity between the left hand side of (14) and (7) which is used by the F-test, SNR and SOST. This allows us to make an interesting observation: while in the sample selection

---

[5] In our experiments, for $f = 0.95$ and $n_p < 1000$ this method retained the $m = 4$ largest components, which correspond to the same components that we had selected using the elbow rule. However, when $n_p > 1000$ the number of components needed for $f \geq 0.95$ decreased to $m < 4$, which led to worse results of the template attack.

method we first compute (7) for each sample and then select the samples with the highest $F(t)$, Fisher's method finds the linear combinations of the trace samples that maximise (14). The coefficients $\mathbf{a}_j$ that maximise (14) are the eigenvectors $[\mathbf{u}_1 \ldots \mathbf{u}_{m^r}] = \mathbf{U}$ corresponding to the largest eigenvalues of $\mathbf{S}_{\text{pooled}}^{-1}\mathbf{B}$.[6]

As with PCA, we only need to use the first m coefficients $\mathbf{a}_1, \ldots, \mathbf{a}_m$, which can be selected using the same rules discussed in Sect. 4.2. If we let $\mathbf{A} = [\mathbf{a}_1 \ldots \mathbf{a}_m] = \mathbf{U}^m$ be the matrix of coefficients, we can project each leakage matrix as:

$$\mathbf{X}_k = \mathbf{X}_k^r \mathbf{A} = \mathbf{X}_k^r \mathbf{U}^m \tag{15}$$

and compute the LDA-based template parameters using (1).

Several authors [11,14] have used Fisher's LDA for template attacks, but without mentioning two important aspects. Firstly, the condition of equal covariances (known as *homoscedasticity*) may be important for the success of Fisher's LDA. Therefore, the PCA method (Sect. 4.2), which does not depend on this condition, might be a better choice in some settings. Secondly, the coefficients that maximise (14) can be obtained using scaled versions of $\mathbf{S}_{\text{pooled}}$[7] or different approaches [11,14], which will result in a different scale of the coefficients $\mathbf{a}_j$. This difference has a major impact on the template attack: *only* when we scale the coefficients $\mathbf{a}_j$, such that $\mathbf{a}_j'\mathbf{S}_{\text{pooled}}\mathbf{a}_j = 1$, the covariance between discriminants becomes the identity matrix [10], i.e. $\mathbf{S}_k = \mathbf{I}$. That means the sample means in (1) suffice and we can discard the covariance matrix from the discriminant scores in Sect. 5, which greatly reduces computation and storage requirements.

Continuing the steps that led to (15), we can compute the diagonal matrix $\mathbf{Q} \in \mathbb{R}^{m \times m}$, having the values $q_{jj} = (\frac{1}{\mathbf{a}_j'\mathbf{S}_{\text{pooled}}\mathbf{a}_j})^{\frac{1}{2}} = (\frac{1}{\mathbf{u}_j'\mathbf{S}_{\text{pooled}}\mathbf{u}_j})^{\frac{1}{2}}$ on its diagonal, to obtain the scaled coefficients $\mathbf{A}\mathbf{Q} = \mathbf{U}^m\mathbf{Q}$, and replace (15) by

$$\mathbf{X}_k = \mathbf{X}_k^r \mathbf{A}\mathbf{Q} = \mathbf{X}_k^r \mathbf{U}^m\mathbf{Q}. \tag{16}$$

An alternative approach is to compute the eigenvectors $\mathbf{u}_j$ of $\mathbf{S}_{\text{pooled}}^{-\frac{1}{2}}\mathbf{B}\mathbf{S}_{\text{pooled}}^{-\frac{1}{2}}$ and then obtain the coefficients $\mathbf{a}_j = \mathbf{S}_{\text{pooled}}^{-\frac{1}{2}}\mathbf{u}_j$, which leads directly to coefficients that satisfy $\mathbf{a}_j'\mathbf{S}_{\text{pooled}}\mathbf{a}_j = 1$.

5   Efficient Implementation of Template Attacks

In this section we introduce methods that avoid the problems identified in Sect. 3 and implement template attacks very efficiently.

---

[6] There are a maximum of $s = \min(m^r, |\mathcal{S}| - 1)$ non-zero eigenvectors, as that is the maximum number of independent linear combinations available in $\mathbf{B}$.

[7] Instead of $\mathbf{S}_{\text{pooled}}$ we could use $\mathbf{W} = |\mathcal{S}|(n_{\text{p}} - 1)\mathbf{S}_{\text{pooled}}$, known as a *sample within groups* matrix.

5.1   Using the Logarithm of the Multivariate Normal Distribution

Mangard et al. [15, p. 108] suggested calculating the logarithm of (3), as in

$$\log \mathrm{f}(\mathbf{x} \mid \bar{\mathbf{x}}_k, \mathbf{S}_k) = -\frac{1}{2} \left(\log \left[(2\pi)^m |\mathbf{S}_k| \right] + (\mathbf{x} - \bar{\mathbf{x}}_k)' \mathbf{S}_k^{-1} (\mathbf{x} - \bar{\mathbf{x}}_k) \right). \qquad (17)$$

They then claim that *"the template that leads to the smallest absolute value [of (17)] indicates the correct [candidate]"*.

The first problem with this approach is that (17) does not avoid the computation of $|\mathbf{S}_k|$, which we have shown to be problematic. Therefore we propose to compute the logarithm of the multivariate normal pdf as

$$\log \mathrm{f}(\mathbf{x} \mid \bar{\mathbf{x}}_k, \mathbf{S}_k) = -\frac{m}{2} \log 2\pi - \frac{1}{2} \log |\mathbf{S}_k| - \frac{1}{2} (\mathbf{x} - \bar{\mathbf{x}}_k)' \mathbf{S}_k^{-1} (\mathbf{x} - \bar{\mathbf{x}}_k), \qquad (18)$$

where we compute the logarithm of the determinant as

$$\log |\mathbf{S}_k| = 2 \sum_{c_{ii} \in \mathrm{diag}(\mathbf{C})} \log c_{ii}, \qquad (19)$$

using the Cholesky decomposition $\mathbf{S}_k = \mathbf{C}'\mathbf{C}$ of the symmetric matrix $\mathbf{S}_k$. (Since $\mathbf{C}$ is triangular, its determinant is the product of its diagonal elements.)

Secondly, it is incorrect to choose the candidate k that leads to the *"smallest absolute value"* of (17, 18), since the logarithm is a monotonic function and preserves the property that the *largest value* corresponds to the correct k.[8]

We can use (18, 19), dropping the first term which is constant across all k, to compute a discriminant score based on the log-likelihood:

$$\mathrm{d_{LOG}}(k \mid \mathbf{x}_i) = -\frac{1}{2} \log |\mathbf{S}_k| - \frac{1}{2} (\mathbf{x}_i - \bar{\mathbf{x}}_k)' \mathbf{S}_k^{-1} (\mathbf{x}_i - \bar{\mathbf{x}}_k) \qquad (20)$$

$$= \log \mathrm{f}(\mathbf{x}_i \mid \bar{\mathbf{x}}_k, \mathbf{S}_k) + \frac{m}{2} \log 2\pi = \log \mathrm{l}(k \mid \mathbf{x}_i) + \mathrm{const}.$$

5.2   Using a Pooled Covariance Matrix

When the leakages from different candidates k have different means but the same covariance $\boldsymbol{\Sigma} = \boldsymbol{\Sigma}_1 = \boldsymbol{\Sigma}_2 = \cdots = \boldsymbol{\Sigma}_k$, it is possible to *pool* the covariance estimates $\mathbf{S}_k$ into a *pooled* covariance matrix [10, Sect. 6.3]

$$\mathbf{S}_{\mathrm{pooled}} = \frac{1}{|\mathcal{S}|(n_{\mathrm{p}} - 1)} \sum_{k \in \mathcal{S}} \sum_{i=1}^{n_{\mathrm{p}}} (\mathbf{x}_{ki} - \bar{\mathbf{x}}_k)(\mathbf{x}_{ki} - \bar{\mathbf{x}}_k)', \qquad (21)$$

an average of the covariances $\mathbf{S}_k$ from (1). The great advantage of $\mathbf{S}_{\mathrm{pooled}}$ over $\mathbf{S}_k$ is that it represents a much better estimator of the real covariance $\boldsymbol{\Sigma}$, since $\mathbf{S}_{\mathrm{pooled}}$ estimates the covariance using $n_{\mathrm{p}}|\mathcal{S}|$ traces, while $\mathbf{S}_k$ uses only n_{p}. This

---

[8] Note that a pdf, such as f from (3), unlike a probability, can be both larger or smaller than 1 and therefore its logarithm can be both positive *or* negative.

in turn means that the condition for a non-singular matrix (see Sect. 3.1) relaxes to $n_p|\mathcal{S}| > m$ or $n_p > \frac{m}{|\mathcal{S}|}$. Therefore the number of traces that we must obtain for each candidate k is reduced by a factor of $|\mathcal{S}|$, a great advantage in practice. Nevertheless, the quality of the mean estimate $\bar{\mathbf{x}}_k$ still depends directly on n_p. Also note that for Fisher's LDA (Sect. 4.3) we need to compute the inverse of $\mathbf{S}_{\text{pooled}} \in \mathbb{R}^{m^r \times m^r}$, which requires $n_p|\mathcal{S}| > m^r$.

Several authors used $\mathbf{S}_{\text{pooled}}$ with template attacks [12, 16], but gave no motivation for its use. We would expect the assumption of equal covariances to hold for many side-channel applications, because $\mathbf{S}_k$ captures primarily information about how *noise*, that is variation in the recorded traces unrelated to k, is correlated across trace samples. After all, the data-dependent signal $\bar{\mathbf{x}}_k$ was already subtracted. As a result, we should not expect substantial differences between the $\mathbf{S}_k$ for different candidate values k, unless the targeted device contains a mechanism by which k can modify the correlation between samples (which we do not completely exclude).

Box's test [3] can be used to reject the hypothesis of equal covariances, although it can be misleading for large $|\mathcal{S}|$ or large m. In our experiments, with $|\mathcal{S}| = 2^8$, $m = 6$ and $n_p = 2000$, Box's variable $C \sim F_{f1,f2}(\alpha)$ had the value 2.03, which was above the rejection threshold for any realistic significance level (e.g. $F_{f1,f2}(0.99) = 1.045$). Nevertheless, we found the different $\mathbf{S}_k$ to be visually similar (viewed as bitmaps with linear colour mapping), and we consider that our hypothesis was confirmed by the superior results from using the pooled estimate (Sect. 6).

Using $\mathbf{S}_{\text{pooled}}$, we can discard the first two terms in (18) and use the generalized statistical distance

$$d_M^2(\mathbf{x} \mid \bar{\mathbf{x}}_k, \mathbf{S}_{\text{pooled}}) = (\mathbf{x} - \bar{\mathbf{x}}_k)' \mathbf{S}_{\text{pooled}}^{-1} (\mathbf{x} - \bar{\mathbf{x}}_k) \geq 0, \qquad (22)$$

also known as the *Mahalanobis distance* [1], to compare the candidates k. The inequality in (22) holds because the covariance matrix is positive semidefinite. From (18, 22) we can derive the discriminant score

$$d_{\text{MD}}(k \mid \mathbf{x}_i) = -\frac{1}{2} d_M^2(\mathbf{x}_i \mid \bar{\mathbf{x}}_k, \mathbf{S}_{\text{pooled}}) = d_{\text{LOG}}(k \mid \mathbf{x}_i) + \text{const.}, \qquad (23)$$

where the constant does not vary with k.

5.3   Linear Discriminant Score

When using the pooled covariance matrix $\mathbf{S}_{\text{pooled}}$ we can rewrite the distance from (22) as:

$$d_M^2(\mathbf{x} \mid \bar{\mathbf{x}}_k, \mathbf{S}_{\text{pooled}}) = \mathbf{x}' \mathbf{S}_{\text{pooled}}^{-1} \mathbf{x} - 2\bar{\mathbf{x}}_k' \mathbf{S}_{\text{pooled}}^{-1} \mathbf{x} + \bar{\mathbf{x}}_k' \mathbf{S}_{\text{pooled}}^{-1} \bar{\mathbf{x}}_k, \qquad (24)$$

and observe that the first term is constant for all groups k so we can discard it. That means, that we can now use the following *linear* discriminant score:

$$d_{\text{LINEAR}}(k \mid \mathbf{x}_i) = \bar{\mathbf{x}}_k' \mathbf{S}_{\text{pooled}}^{-1} \mathbf{x}_i - \frac{1}{2} \bar{\mathbf{x}}_k' \mathbf{S}_{\text{pooled}}^{-1} \bar{\mathbf{x}}_k = d_{\text{MD}}(k \mid \mathbf{x}_i) + \text{const.}, \qquad (25)$$

which depends *linearly* on $\mathbf{x}_i$ (where const. does not depend on k). Although equivalent, the linear discriminant $\mathrm{d}_{\mathrm{LINEAR}}$ can be far more efficient to compute than the quadratic d_{MD}.

5.4   Combining Multiple Attack Traces

We have to combine the n_{a} individual leakage traces $\mathbf{x}_i$ from $\mathbf{X}_{k\star}$ into the final discriminant score $\mathrm{d}(k \mid \mathbf{X}_{k\star})$. We present two sound options for doing so:

Option 1: Average all the traces in $\mathbf{X}_{k\star}$ (similar to the mean computation in (1)) in order to remove as much noise as possible and then use this single mean trace $\bar{\mathbf{x}}_{k\star}$ to compute

$$\mathrm{d}^{\mathrm{avg}}(k \mid \mathbf{X}_{k\star}) = \mathrm{d}(k \mid \bar{\mathbf{x}}_{k\star}). \tag{26}$$

This option is computationally fast, requiring $O(n_{\mathrm{a}} + m^2)$ time for any presented discriminant, but it does not use all the information from the available attack traces (in particular the noise).

Option 2: Compute the joint likelihood $\mathrm{l}(k \mid \mathbf{X}_{k\star}) = \prod_{\mathbf{x}_i \in \mathbf{X}_{k\star}} \mathrm{l}(k \mid \mathbf{x}_i)$. By applying the logarithm to both sides we have $\log \mathrm{l}(k \mid \mathbf{X}_{k\star}) = \sum_{\mathbf{x}_i \in \mathbf{X}_{k\star}} \log \mathrm{l}(k \mid \mathbf{x}_i)$ and we obtain the derived scores:

$$\mathrm{d}^{\mathrm{joint}}_{\mathrm{LOG}}(k \mid \mathbf{X}_{k\star}) = -\frac{n_{\mathrm{a}}}{2} \log |\mathbf{S}_k| - \frac{1}{2} \sum_{\mathbf{x}_i \in \mathbf{X}_{k\star}} (\mathbf{x}_i - \bar{\mathbf{x}}_k)' \mathbf{S}_k^{-1} (\mathbf{x}_i - \bar{\mathbf{x}}_k), \tag{27}$$

$$\mathrm{d}^{\mathrm{joint}}_{\mathrm{MD}}(k \mid \mathbf{X}_{k\star}) = -\frac{1}{2} \sum_{\mathbf{x}_i \in \mathbf{X}_{k\star}} (\mathbf{x}_i - \bar{\mathbf{x}}_k)' \mathbf{S}_k^{-1} (\mathbf{x}_i - \bar{\mathbf{x}}_k), \tag{28}$$

$$\mathrm{d}^{\mathrm{joint}}_{\mathrm{LINEAR}}(k \mid \mathbf{X}_{k\star}) = \bar{\mathbf{x}}_k' \mathbf{S}_{\mathrm{pooled}}^{-1} \left(\sum_{\mathbf{x}_i \in \mathbf{X}_{k\star}} \mathbf{x}_i \right) - \frac{n_{\mathrm{a}}}{2} \bar{\mathbf{x}}_k' \mathbf{S}_{\mathrm{pooled}}^{-1} \bar{\mathbf{x}}_k. \tag{29}$$

Given the n_{a} leakage traces $\mathbf{x}_i \in \mathbf{X}_{k\star}$, $\mathrm{d}_{\mathrm{LOG}}$ and d_{MD} require time $O(n_{\mathrm{a}} m^2)$ while $\mathrm{d}_{\mathrm{LINEAR}}$ only requires $O(n_{\mathrm{a}} + m^2)$, since the operations $\bar{\mathbf{x}}_k' \mathbf{S}_{\mathrm{pooled}}^{-1}$ and $\bar{\mathbf{x}}_k' \mathbf{S}_{\mathrm{pooled}}^{-1} \bar{\mathbf{x}}_k$ only need to be done once, which is a great advantage in practice. As a practical example, our evaluations of the guessing entropy (see Sect. 6) for $m = 125$ and $1 \leq n_{\mathrm{a}} \leq 1000$ took about 3.5 days with $\mathrm{d}_{\mathrm{LOG}}$ but only 30 min with $\mathrm{d}_{\mathrm{LINEAR}}$.[9] We note that for $\mathrm{d}_{\mathrm{LINEAR}}$ the computation time is the same regardless of which option we use to combine the traces, and both give the same results for the template attack.

---

[9] MATLAB, single core CPU with 3794 MIPS.

Table 1. List of compression methods evaluated in this paper.

Name	Description	m
DOM 1ppc	DOM, 1 sample per clock at most	6–10
DOM 3ppc	DOM, 3 samples per clock at most	18–30
DOM 20ppc	DOM, 20 samples per clock at most	75–79
DOM allap	DOM, all samples above 95th percentile of $F(t)$	125
PCA	Fixed selection of number of principal components	4
LDA	Fixed selection of number of coefficients	4

5.5 Unequal Prior Probabilities

In the previous descriptions we have assumed equal prior probabilities among the candidates k. When this is not the case, we only need to add the term $\log P(k)$ to the discriminant scores $d_{\text{LOG}}^{\text{avg}}$, $d_{\text{MD}}^{\text{avg}}$, $d_{\text{LINEAR}}^{\text{avg}}$, or $n_{\text{a}} \log P(k)$ to the discriminant scores $d_{\text{LOG}}^{\text{joint}}$, $d_{\text{MD}}^{\text{joint}}$, $d_{\text{LINEAR}}^{\text{joint}}$.

6 Evaluation of Methods

We evaluated the efficiency of many template-attack variants on a real hardware platform, comparing all the compression methods from Table 1[10] and all the implementation options from Sect. 5. We compare the commonly used high-compression methods, such as PCA, LDA and sample selection using the guideline [7] of 1 sample per clock at most (*1ppc*), against weak compressions providing a larger number of samples: the *3ppc*, *20ppc* and *allap* selections.[11]

6.1 Experimental Setup

Our target is the 8-bit CPU Atmel XMEGA 256 A3U, an easily available micro-controller without side-channel countermeasures, mounted on our own evaluation board to monitor the total current in all CPU ground pins via a 10 Ω resistor. We powered it from a battery via a 3.3 V regulator and supplied a 1 MHz sine clock. We used a Tektronix TDS 7054 8-bit oscilloscope with P6243 active probe, at 250 MS/s, with 500 MHz bandwidth in SAMPLE mode. We used the same device for both the profiling and the attack phase, which provides a good setting for the focus of our work.

For each candidate value $k \in \{0, \ldots, 255\}$ we recorded 3072 traces $\mathbf{x}_{ki}^{\text{r}}$ (i.e., 786 432 traces in total), which we divided into a *training* set (for the profiling phase) and an *evaluation* set (for the attack phase). Each trace contains

---

[10] We arbitrarily chose to use the DOM estimate, computed as the sum of *absolute* differences between the mean vectors. Using SNR instead of DOM as the signal strength estimate $s(t)$ has provided very similar results, omitted due to lack of space.

[11] The selections 1ppc, 3ppc and 20ppc provide a variable number of samples because of the additional restriction that the selected samples must be above the highest 95th percentile of $F(t)$, which varies with n_{p} for each clock edge.

$m^r = 2500$ samples, recorded while the target microcontroller executed the same sequence of instructions loaded from the same addresses: a MOV instruction, followed by several LOAD instructions. All the LOAD instructions require two clock cycles to transfer a value from RAM into a register, using indirect addressing. In all the experiments our goal was to determine the success of the template attacks in recovering the byte k processed by the second LOAD instruction. All the other instructions were processing the value zero, meaning that in our traces none of the variability should be caused by variable data in other nearby instructions that may be processed concurrently in various pipeline stages.[12]

6.2   Guessing Entropy

We use the *guessing entropy* as the sole figure of merit to compare all methods. It estimates the (logarithmic) cost of any optimized search following a template attack to find the correct $k\star$ among the values k with the highest discriminant scores. It gives the expected number of bits of uncertainty remaining about the target value $k\star$. The lower the guessing entropy, the more successful the attack has been and the less effort remains to search for the correct $k\star$.

To compute the guessing entropy, we compute the score $\mathrm{d}(k \mid \mathbf{X}_{k\star})$ (see Sect. 5) for each combination of candidate value k and target value $k\star$, resulting in a score matrix $\mathbf{M} \in \mathbb{R}^{|\mathcal{S}| \times |\mathcal{S}|}$ with $\mathbf{M}(k\star, k) = \mathrm{d}(k \mid \mathbf{X}_{k\star})$. Each row in $\mathbf{M}$ contains the score of each candidate value k given the traces $\mathbf{X}_{k\star}$ corresponding to a given target value $k\star$. Next we sort each row of $\mathbf{M}$, in decreasing order, to obtain a depth matrix $\mathbf{D} \in \mathbb{N}^{|\mathcal{S}| \times |\mathcal{S}|}$ with

$$\mathbf{D}(k\star, k) = \text{position of } \mathrm{d}(k \mid \mathbf{X}_{k\star}) \text{ in the sorted row of } \mathbf{M}(k\star, \cdot). \quad (30)$$

Finally, using the matrix $\mathbf{D}$ we define the guessing entropy

$$g = \log_2 \frac{1}{|\mathcal{S}|} \sum_{k \in \mathcal{S}} \mathbf{D}(k, k). \quad (31)$$

Standaert et al. [13] also used this measure, but without the logarithm.

6.3   Experimental Results and Practical Guidance

We performed each attack 10 times for each combination of n_a, k and $k\star$, using a different random selection of $\mathbf{X}_{k\star}$ for each n_a and $k\star$. We plot in Figs. 2 and 3 the averaged guessing entropy, resulting in highly reproducible graphs. The standard deviation across all experiments is around 0.1 bits.

These results, as well as the considerations discussed earlier, allow us to provide the following practical guidance regarding the choice of algorithm:

---

[12] A similar approach was used by Standaert and Archambeau [11] and Oswald and Paar [16] to report results of template attacks on (part of) the key loading stage of a block cipher.

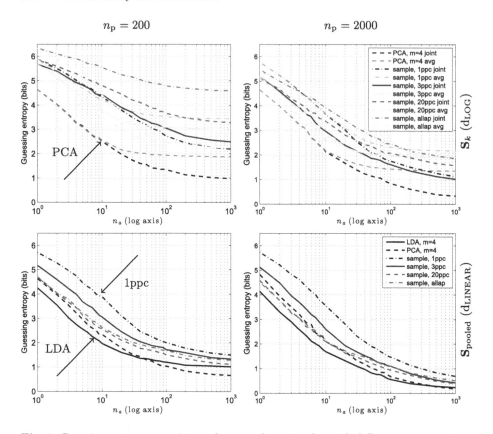

Fig. 2. Guessing entropy remaining after template attacks, with different compressions, for $n_p = 200$ (left) and $n_p = 2000$ (right) profiling traces, using individual covariances $\mathbf{S}_k$ with d_{LOG} (top) or a pooled covariance $\mathbf{S}_{\text{pooled}}$ with d_{LINEAR} (bottom).

1. *Use Option 2 (d^{joint}) in preference to Option 1 (d^{avg}) to combine the discriminant scores for $n_a > 1$ attack traces.* For $n_a = 1$ or when using $\mathbf{S}_{\text{pooled}}$, these options are equivalent. Otherwise, as the number n_a of attack traces increases and the covariance matrix is better estimated (e.g. due to a large number n_p of profiling traces or small number m of variables) d^{joint} outperforms d^{avg} for all compression methods.

2. *Try using a common covariance matrix $\mathbf{S}_{\text{pooled}}$ with d_{LINEAR}* (unless differences between individual estimates $\mathbf{S}_k$ are very evident, e.g. from visual inspection). Failing a statistical test for homoscedasticity (e.g., Box's test) alone does not imply that using individual estimates $\mathbf{S}_k$ will improve the template attack. Using individual estimates $\mathbf{S}_k$ prevents use of the significantly faster and more robust discriminant d_{LINEAR}. Then:

   (a) *If your target allows you to acquire a large number of traces ($n_a > 100$):* try the compression methods PCA, LDA and sample-selection with *large*

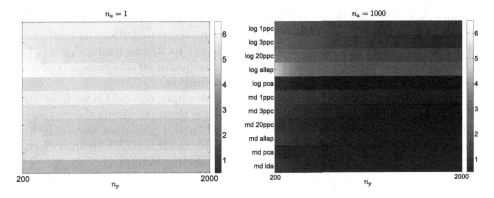

Fig. 3. Guessing entropy from the methods discussed, for $n_a = 1$ (left) and $n_a = 1000$ (right), using d^{joint} (at $n_p \in \{200, 500, 1000, 1500, 2000\}$, linearly interpolated).

m since they may perform differently based on the level of noise from the profiling traces $\mathbf{X}_k$.

(b) *If your target allows only acquisition of a limited number of attack traces ($n_a < 10$):* use LDA. Note that in this case, as the covariance estimate improves due to large $|\mathcal{S}|n_p$, performance increases with larger m (cf. *3ppc, 20ppc, allap*). In particular, for $n_a < 10$, we see in Fig. 2 (bottom) that we got more than 1 bit of data from *20ppc* and *allap* compared to *1ppc*, which contradicts the claim [7, Sect. 3.2] that "additional [samples] in the same clock cycle do not provide additional information". In this setting, *20ppc* and *allap* can outperform PCA.

3. *If you cannot use the pooled covariance $\mathbf{S}_{pooled}$, then use the individual covariances $\mathbf{S}_k$ with d_{LOG} and use PCA as the compression method.*

This guidance should work well in situations similar to our experimental conditions. Further research is needed to also consider pipelining, where other data in neighbour instructions can partially overlap in the side-channel.

7   Conclusions

In this paper, we have explored in detail the implementation of template attacks based on the multivariate normal distribution, comparing different compression methods, discriminant scores, and number of profiling and attack traces.

We explained why several numerical obstacles arise when dealing with a large number m of variables (e.g. when retaining a large part of the leakage vectors), and we presented efficient methods that can be used in this case, such as the discriminant d_{LOG}.

Based on the observation that the covariance matrices $\mathbf{S}_k$ of each candidate k are similar, we explained the use of the pooled covariance estimate $\mathbf{S}_{pooled}$ and we showed how $\mathbf{S}_{pooled}$ allows us to derive a *linear* discriminant d_{LINEAR} which is much more efficient than d_{LOG}. For $n_a = 1000$ attack traces and $m = 125$ samples, the computation of the guessing entropy remaining after the template attacks can be reduced from 3 days (using d_{LOG}) to 30 min (using d_{LINEAR}). This is a great advantage for the evaluation of template attacks, which is often a requirement to obtain Common Criteria certification.

We applied all the methods presented in this paper on real traces from an unprotected 8-bit microcontroller and we evaluated the results using the guessing entropy. Using the efficient methods presented in this paper we were able to obtain a guessing entropy close to 0, i.e. we are able to extract *all* 8 bits processed by a *single* LOAD instruction, not just their Hamming weight.

Based on these results and theoretical arguments, we proposed a practical guideline for the choice of algorithm when implementing template attacks.

Data and Code Availability: In the interest of reproducible research we make available our data and associated MATLAB scripts at:

http://www.cl.cam.ac.uk/research/security/datasets/grizzly/

Acknowledgement. Omar Choudary is a recipient of the Google Europe Fellowship in Mobile Security, and this research is supported in part by this Google Fellowship. The opinions expressed in this paper do not represent the views of Google unless otherwise explicitly stated.

A   Evaluation Board

For our experiments, we built a custom PCB for the Atmel microcontroller (see Fig. 4, left). This 4-layer PCB has inputs for the clock signal and supply voltage, a USB port to communicate with a PC, and a $10\,\Omega$ resistor in the ground line for power measurements. The PCB connects all the ground pins of the microcontroller to the same line, which leads to the measurement resistor.

 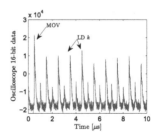

Fig. 4. Left: the device used during our experiments. Right: A single example trace $\mathbf{x}_i^r$ from our experimental setup.

B   Executed Code

During all our experiments we recorded traces with 2500 samples, covering the execution of several instructions, as shown in Fig. 4 (right). The executed instruction sequence is

```
5a5c:   00 00   nop          ; several previous NOPs ommited in this listing
5a5e:   fc 01   movw  r30, r24  ; 1 clock cycle, recorded traces start here
5a60:   81 90   ld  r8, Z+    ; 2 clock cycles per ld instruction
5a62:   91 90   ld  r9, Z+    ; this is our target instruction (2 clock cycles)
5a64:   a1 90   ld  r10, Z+   ; we want to infer the data loaded in r9
5a66:   b1 90   ld  r11, Z+
5a68:   c1 90   ld  r12, Z+   ; recorded trace ends after first clock cycle of this ld
```

The load instructions use the Z pointer (which refers to registers r31:r30) for indirect RAM addressing. The initial value of registers r8–r12 before the load operations is zero. The initial value of Z before the first load instruction is 2020.

C   Some Proofs

In Sect. 5.3 we rewrote (22) as (24). This is possible because

$$\bar{\mathbf{x}}_k' \mathbf{S}_{\text{pooled}}^{-1} \mathbf{x} = (\bar{\mathbf{x}}_k' \mathbf{S}_{\text{pooled}}^{-1} \mathbf{x})' = \mathbf{x}' \mathbf{S}_{\text{pooled}}^{-1}{}' \bar{\mathbf{x}}_k = \mathbf{x}' \mathbf{S}_{\text{pooled}}^{-1} \bar{\mathbf{x}}_k. \tag{32}$$

In Sect. 5.4 we state that d_{LINEAR} provides the same results for both options of combining the traces (from average trace and based on joint likelihood). This happens because if we let $c_k = -\frac{1}{2}\bar{\mathbf{x}}_k' \mathbf{S}_{\text{pooled}}^{-1} \bar{\mathbf{x}}_k$ for any k, then we have

$$d_{\text{LINEAR}}^{\text{joint}}(k \mid \mathbf{X}_{k\star}) = \bar{\mathbf{x}}_k' \mathbf{S}_{\text{pooled}}^{-1} \left(\sum_{\mathbf{x}_i \in \mathbf{X}_{k\star}} \mathbf{x}_i \right) + n_a c_k, \tag{33}$$

$$d_{\text{LINEAR}}^{\text{avg}}(k \mid \mathbf{X}_{k\star}) = \bar{\mathbf{x}}_k' \mathbf{S}_{\text{pooled}}^{-1} \left(\frac{1}{n_a} \sum_{\mathbf{x}_i \in \mathbf{X}_{k\star}} \mathbf{x}_i \right) + c_k, \tag{34}$$

and therefore for any $u, v \in \mathcal{S}$ it is true that

$$d_{\text{LINEAR}}^{\text{avg}}(u \mid \mathbf{X}_{k\star}) > d_{\text{LINEAR}}^{\text{avg}}(v \mid \mathbf{X}_{k\star}) \Leftrightarrow$$

$$\bar{\mathbf{x}}_u' \mathbf{S}_{\text{pooled}}^{-1} \left(\frac{1}{n_a} \sum_{\mathbf{x}_i \in \mathbf{X}_{k\star}} \mathbf{x}_i \right) + c_u > \bar{\mathbf{x}}_v' \mathbf{S}_{\text{pooled}}^{-1} \left(\frac{1}{n_a} \sum_{\mathbf{x}_i \in \mathbf{X}_{k\star}} \mathbf{x}_i \right) + c_v \Leftrightarrow$$

$$\bar{\mathbf{x}}_u' \mathbf{S}_{\text{pooled}}^{-1} \left(\sum_{\mathbf{x}_i \in \mathbf{X}_{k\star}} \mathbf{x}_i \right) + n_a c_u > \bar{\mathbf{x}}_v' \mathbf{S}_{\text{pooled}}^{-1} \left(\sum_{\mathbf{x}_i \in \mathbf{X}_{k\star}} \mathbf{x}_i \right) + n_a c_v \Leftrightarrow$$

$$d_{\text{LINEAR}}^{\text{joint}}(u \mid \mathbf{X}_{k\star}) > d_{\text{LINEAR}}^{\text{joint}}(v \mid \mathbf{X}_{k\star}).$$

References

1. Mahalanobis, P.C.: On the generalised distance in statistics. In: Proceedings National Institute of Science, India, vol. 2, pp. 49–55 (1936)
2. Fisher, R.A.: The statistical utilization of multiple measurements. Ann. Eugen. **8**, 376–386 (1938)
3. Box, G.E.P.: Problems in the analysis of growth and wear curves. Biometrics **6**, 362–389 (1950)
4. Chari, S., Rao, J., Rohatgi, P.: Template attacks. In: Kaliski Jr, B.S., Koç, Ç.K., Paar, C. (eds.) CHES 2002. LNCS, vol. 2523, pp. 51–62. Springer, Heidelberg (2003)
5. Ledoit, O., Wolf, M.: A well-conditioned estimator for large-dimensional covariance matrices. J. Multivar. Anal. **88**, 365–411 (2004)
6. Jolliffe, I.: Principal Component Analysis. Wiley, Chichester (2005)
7. Rechberger, C., Oswald, E.: Practical template attacks. In: Lim, C.H., Yung, M. (eds.) WISA 2004. LNCS, vol. 3325, pp. 440–456. Springer, Heidelberg (2005)
8. Archambeau, C., Peeters, E., Standaert, F.-X., Quisquater, J.-J.: Template attacks in principal subspaces. In: Goubin, L., Matsui, M. (eds.) CHES 2006. LNCS, vol. 4249, pp. 1–14. Springer, Heidelberg (2006)
9. Gierlichs, B., Lemke-Rust, K., Paar, C.: Templates vs. stochastic methods. In: Goubin, L., Matsui, M. (eds.) CHES 2006. LNCS, vol. 4249, pp. 15–29. Springer, Heidelberg (2006)
10. Johnson, R., Wichern, D.: Applied Multivariate Statistical Analysis, 6th edn. Pearson, Upper Saddle River (2007)
11. Standaert, F.-X., Archambeau, C.: Using subspace-based template attacks to compare and combine power and electromagnetic information leakages. In: Oswald, E., Rohatgi, P. (eds.) CHES 2008. LNCS, vol. 5154, pp. 411–425. Springer, Heidelberg (2008)
12. Batina, L., Gierlichs, B., Lemke-Rust, K.: Comparative evaluation of rank correlation based DPA on an AES prototype chip. In: Wu, T.-C., Lei, C.-L., Rijmen, V., Lee, D.-T. (eds.) ISC 2008. LNCS, vol. 5222, pp. 341–354. Springer, Heidelberg (2008)
13. Standaert, F.-X., Malkin, T.G., Yung, M.: A unified framework for the analysis of side-channel key recovery attacks. In: Joux, A. (ed.) EUROCRYPT 2009. LNCS, vol. 5479, pp. 443–461. Springer, Heidelberg (2009)
14. Eisenbarth, T., Paar, C., Weghenkel, B.: Building a side channel based disassembler. Trans. Comput. Sci. X **6340**, 78–99 (2010)
15. Mangard, S., Oswald, E., Popp, T.: Power Analysis Attacks: Revealing the Secrets of Smart Cards, 1st edn. Springer, Heidelberg (2010)
16. Oswald, D., Paar, C.: Breaking Mifare DESFire MF3ICD40: power analysis and templates in the real world. In: Preneel, B., Takagi, T. (eds.) CHES 2011. LNCS, vol. 6917, pp. 207–222. Springer, Heidelberg (2011)

Author Index

Printed in the United States
By Bookmasters